NEW TESTAMENT

Restoration Harmony

THE COMPLETE GUIDE TO
THE FOUR GOSPELS

NEW TESTAMENT
Restoration Harmony

THE COMPLETE GUIDE TO
THE FOUR GOSPELS

MONTE S. NYMAN

CFI

SPRINGVILLE, UTAH

ISBN 13: 978-1-55517-979-7
ISBN 10: 1-55517-979-7

Published by CFI, an imprint of
Cedar Fort, Inc., 2373 W. 700 S., Springville, UT, 84663
Distributed by Cedar Fort, Inc., www.cedarfort.com

LIBRARY OF CONGRESS CATALOGING-IN-PUBLICATION DATA

Nyman, Monte S.
    New Testament restoration harmony of the Four Gospels / by Monte S. Nyman.
        p. cm.
    Includes index.
    ISBN 1-55517-979-7
    1. Bible. N.T. Gospels--Harmonies. I. Title.

BS2560.N78 2006
226'.1--dc22

2006028891

Cover design by Nicole Williams
Cover design © 2006 by Lyle Mortimer

Printed in the United States of America

10   9   8   7   6   5   4   3   2   1

Printed on acid-free paper

New Testament Restoration Harmony

Table of Contents

Luke 1	JST Luke 1**	B of M	D & C

The Testimony of St. Luke*

Forasmuch as many have taken in hand to set forth in order a declaration of those things which are most surely believed among us,

2 Even as they delivered them unto us, **which** from the beginning were eye-witnesses, and ministers of the word;

3 It seemed good to me also, having had perfect understanding of all things from the very first, to write unto thee in order, most excellent Theophilus,

4 That thou mightest know the certainty of those things, wherein thou hast been instructed.

As I am a messenger of Jesus Christ, and knowing that many have taken in hand to set forth in order a declaration of those things which are most surely believed among us;

2 Even as they delivered them unto us, **who** from the beginning were eye-witnesses and ministers of the word;

1 Ne. 13:24 And the angel of the Lord said unto me: Thou hast beheld that the book proceeded forth from the mouth of a Jew; and when it proceeded forth from the mouth of a Jew it contained the fulness of the gospel of the Lord, of whom the twelve apostles bear record; and they bear record according to the truth which is in the Lamb of God.

25 Wherefore, these things go forth from the Jews in purity unto the Gentiles, according to the truth which is in God.

26 And after they go forth by the hand of the twelve apostles of the Lamb, from the Jews unto the Gentiles, thou seest the formation of that great and abominable church, which is most abominable above all other churches; for behold, they have taken away from the gospel of the Lamb many parts which are plain and most precious; and also many covenants of the Lord have they taken away.

39 And after it had come forth unto them I beheld other books, which came forth by the power of the Lamb, from the Gentiles unto them, unto the convincing of the Gentiles and the remnant of the seed of my brethren, and also the Jews who were scattered upon all the face of the earth, that the records of the prophets and of the twelve apostles of the Lamb are true.

40 And the angel spake unto me, saying: These last records, which thou hast seen among the Gentiles, shall establish the truth of the first, which are of the twelve apostles of the Lamb, and shall make known the plain and precious things which have been taken away from them; and shall make known to all kindreds, tongues, and people, that the Lamb of God is the Son of the Eternal Father, and the Savior of the world; and that all men must come unto him, or they cannot be saved.

66:2 Verily I say unto you, blessed are you for receiving mine everlasting covenant, even the fulness of my gospel, sent forth unto the children of men, that they might have life and be made partakers of the glories which are to be revealed in the last days, as it was written by the prophets and apostles in days of old.

* The Joseph Smith Translation changes all four of the titles of Matthew, Mark, Luke and John from "The Gospel According to St. Matthew" (or Mark, or Luke, or John) to "The Testimony of St. Matthew" (or Mark, or Luke, or John).

** Verses in the JST that have only spelling or tense variations between the KJV and the JST have not always been included in the JST text.

John 1	JST John	B of M	D & C

The Testimony of St. John

John 1	JST John	B of M	D & C
			93:6 And John saw and bore record of the fulness of my glory, and the fulness of John's record is hereafter to be revealed. 7 And he bore record, saying: I saw his glory, that he was in the beginning, before the world was; 8 Therefore, in the beginning the Word was, for he was the Word, even the messenger of salvation--
In the beginning was the Word, and the Word was with God, and the **Word** was God. 2 The same was in the beginning with God. 3 All things were made by him; and without him was not any thing made that was made.	In the beginning was the gospel preached through the Son. And the gospel was the word, and the word was with the Son, and the Son was with God, and the Son was of God. 3 All things were made by him; and without him was not anything made which was made.		
4 In him was **life**; and the life was the light of men. 5 And the light shineth in **darkness**; and the **darkness comprehended it not.** 6 ¶ There was a man sent from God, whose name was John. 7 The same came for a witness, to bear witness of the Light,	4 In him was the gospel, and the gospel was the life, and the life was the light of men; 5 And the light shineth in the world, and the world perceiveth it not. 7 The same came into the world for a witness, to bear witness of the light, to bear record of the gospel through the Son, unto all,		9 The light and the Redeemer of the world; the Spirit of truth, who came into the world, because the world was made by him, and in him was the life of men and the light of men. (See also D&C 34:2.)
that **all men** through him might believe. 8 He was not that Light, but was sent to bear witness of that Light. 9 **That** was the true Light, which lighteth every man that cometh into the world.	that through him **men** might believe. 8 He was not that light, but **came** to bear witness of that light, 9 **Which** was the true light, which lighteth every man **who** cometh into the world; 10 **Even the Son of God.**	3 Ne 9:15 Behold, I am Jesus Christ the Son of God. I created the heavens and the earth, and all	(See also D&C 84:46.)
10 He was in the world,	He **who** was in the world,	things that in them are.	10 The worlds were made by him; men were made by

John 1	JST John 1	B of M	D & C
and the world was made by him, and the world knew him not. 11 He came unto his own, and his own received him not. 12 But as many as received him, to them gave he power to become the sons of God, **even to them that** believe on his name: 13 **Which were** born, not of blood, nor of the will of the flesh, nor of the will of man, but of God. 14 And the Word was made flesh, and dwelt among us, (and we beheld his glory, the glory as of the only begotten of the Father,) full of grace and truth. 15 ¶ John **bare** witness of him, and cried saying, This **was he** of whom I spake, He **that** cometh after me is preferred before me: for he was before me.	and the world was made by him, and the world knew him not. 12 But as many as received him, to them gave he power to become the sons of God; **only to them who** believe on his name. 13 **He was** born, not of blood, nor of the will of the flesh, nor of the will of man, but of God. 14 And the **same word** was made flesh, and dwelt among us, and we beheld his glory, the glory as of the Only Begotten of the Father, full of grace and truth. 15 John **bear** witness of him, and cried, saying, This **is** he of whom I spake; He **who** cometh after me, is preferred before me; for he was before me. 16 **For in the beginning was the Word, even the Son, who is made flesh, and sent unto us by the will of the Father. And as many as believe on his name shall receive of his fulness.** And of his	I was with the Father from the beginning. I am in the Father, and the Father in me; and in me hath the Father glorified his name. 16 I came unto my own, and my own received me not. And the scriptures concerning my coming are fulfilled. 17 And as many as have received me, to them have I given to become the sons of God; and even so will I to as many as shall believe on my name, for behold, by me redemption cometh, and in me is the law of Moses fulfilled. 18 I am the light and the life of the world. I am Alpha and Omega, the beginning and the end.	him; all things were made by him, and through him, and of him. (See also D&C 6:21; 10:57-58; 11:28-30; 35:2; 39:2-4; 45:7-8.) 11 And I, John, bear record that I beheld his glory, as the glory of the Only Begotten of the Father, full of grace and truth, even the Spirit of truth, which came and dwelt in the flesh, and dwelt among us.
16 And of his fulness have all we received, **and grace for grace.**	fulness have all we received, **even immortality and eternal life, through his grace.**		12 And I, John, saw that he received not of the fulness at the first, but received grace for grace; 13 And he received not of the fulness at first, but continued from grace to grace, until he received a fulness; 14 And thus he was called the Son of God, because he received not of the fulness at the first. 15 And I, John, bear record, and lo, the heavens were opened, and the Holy Ghost descended upon him in the form of a dove, and sat upon him, and there

John 1	JST John 1	D & C	D & C
			came a voice out of heaven saying: This is my beloved Son. 16 And I, John, bear record that he received a fulness of the glory of the Father; 17 And he received all power, both in heaven and on earth, and the glory of the Father was with him, for he dwelt in him. 18 And it shall come to pass, that if you are faithful you shall receive the fulness of the record of John. 19 I give unto you these sayings that you may understand and know how to worship, and know what you worship, that you may come unto the Father in my name, and in due time receive of his fulness. (See also D&C 88:48-49.)
17 For the law was given by Moses, but **grace** and truth came by Jesus Christ.	17 For the law was given **through** Moses, but **life** and truth came **through** Jesus Christ. 18 **For the law was after a carnal commandment, to the administration of death; but the gospel was after the power of an endless life, through Jesus Christ, the Only Begotten Son, who is in the bosom of the Father.**	84:19 And this greater priesthood administereth the gospel and holdeth the key of the mysteries of the kingdom, even the key of the knowledge of God. 20 Therefore, in the ordinances thereof, the power of godliness is manifest. 21 And without the ordinances thereof, and authority of the priesthood, the power of godliness is not manifest unto men in the flesh;	21 And now, verily I say unto you, I was in the begining with the Father, and am the Firstborn;
18 No man hath seen God at any time; **the only begotten Son, which is in the bosom of the Father, he hath declared him.**	19 And no man hath seen God at any time, **except he hath borne record of the Son; for except it is through him no man can be saved.**	22 For without this no man can see the face of God, even the Father, and live.	67:11 For no man has seen God at any time in the flesh, except quickened by the Spirit of God.

4

Luke 1	JST Luke 1		Joseph Smith

The Birth of John the Baptist and Jesus of Nazareth

1. Jerusalem--Annunciation to Zacharias

Luke 1	JST Luke 1		Joseph Smith
5 ¶ There was in the days of Herod, the king of Judæa, a certain priest named Zacharias, of the course of Abia: and his wife **was** of the daughters of Aaron, and her name **was** Elisabeth. 6 **And they** were both righteous before God, walking in all the commandments and ordinances of the Lord blameless. 7 And they had no child, **because that** Elisabeth was barren, and they both **were now** well stricken in years. 8 And **it came to pass, that** while he executed the priest's office before God in the order of his **course,** 9 According to the **custom of the priest's office,** his lot was to burn incense when he went into the temple of the Lord. 10 **And** the whole multitude were praying without at the time of incense. 11 And there appeared unto him an angel of the Lord standing on the right side of the altar of incense. 12 And when Zacharias saw **him,** he was troubled, and fear fell upon him. 13 But the angel said unto him, Fear not, Zacharias: for thy prayer is heard; and thy wife Elisabeth shall bear thee a son, and thou shalt call his name John. 14 **And** thou shalt have joy and gladness; and many shall rejoice at his birth.	5 There was in the days of Herod, the king of Judea, a certain priest named Zacharias, of the course of Abia; and his wife **being** of the daughters of Aaron, and her name Elisabeth, 6 Were both righteous before God, walking in all the commandments and ordinances of the Lord blameless; 7 And they had no child. Elisabeth was barren, and they **were** both well stricken in years. 8 And while he executed the priest's office before God, in the order of his **priesthood,** 9 According to the **law,** (his lot was to burn incense when he went into the temple of the Lord,) 10 The whole multitude of the people were praying without at the time of incense. 12 And when Zacharias saw **the angel,** he was troubled and fear fell upon him. 14 Thou shalt have joy and gladness, and many shall rejoice at his birth;		TPJS--There is no salvation between the two lids of the Bible without a legal administrator. Jesus was then the legal administrator, and ordained His Apostles (p. 319). WJS--...Zacharias pleading with the Lord in the temple that he might have seed so that the priesthood might be preserved (p.67).

5

Luke 1	JST Luke 1	D & C	D & C
15 For he shall be great in the sight of the Lord, and shall drink neither wine nor strong drink; and he shall be filled with the Holy Ghost, even from his mother's womb. 16 And many of the children of Israel shall he turn to the Lord their God.			

TPJS--Here is a little law of which must be fulfilled. The Levitical Priesthood is forever hereditary--fixed on the head of Aaron and his sons forever, and was in active operation down to Zacharias the father of John. Zacharias would have had no child had not God given him a son. He sent his angel to declare unto Zacharias that his wife Elizabeth should bear him a son, whose name was to be called John.

The keys of the Aaronic Priesthood were committed unto him, and he was as the voice of one crying in the wilderness saying: "Prepare ye the way of the Lord and make his paths straight." (p. 319)

An angel of God also appeared unto Zacharias while in the Temple, and told him that he should have a son, whose name should be John, and he should be filled with the Holy Ghost. Zacharias was a priest of God, and officiating in the Temple, and John was a priest after his father, and held the keys of the Aaronic Priesthood, and was called of God to preach the Gospel of the kingdom of God. The Jews, as a nation, having departed from the law of God and the Gospel of the Lord, prepared the way for transferring it to the Gentiles. (pp. 272-273)

Luke 1	JST Luke 1	D & C	D & C
17 And he shall go before him in the spirit and power of Elias, to turn the hearts of the fathers to the children, and the disobedient to the wisdom of the just; to make ready a people prepared for the Lord.	17 And he shall go before **the Lord** in the spirit and power of Elias, to turn the hearts of the fathers to the children, and the disobedient to the wisdom of the just, to make ready a people prepared for the Lord.	27:6 And also with Elias, to whom I have committed the keys of bringing to pass the restoration of all things spoken by the mouth of all the holy prophets since the world began, concerning the last days;	110:12 After this, Elias appeared, and committed the dispensation of the gospel of Abraham, saying that in us and our seed all generations after us should be blessed.
18 And Zacharias said unto the angel, Whereby shall I know this? for I am an old man, and my wife well stricken in years.	18 And Zacharias said unto the angel, Whereby shall I know this? for I am an old man, and my wife is well stricken in years.	7 And also John the son of Zacharias, which Zacharias he (Elias) visited and gave promise that he should have a son, and his name should be John, and he should be filled with the spirit of Elias;	
19 And the angel answering said unto him, I am Gabriel, **that** stand in the presence of God; and am sent to speak unto thee, and to shew thee these glad tidings.	19 And the angel answering said unto him, I am Gabriel, **who** stand in the presence of God, and am sent to speak unto thee, and to show thee these glad tidings.		

TPJS-- Then to Noah, who is Gabriel: he stands next in authority to Adam in the Priesthood; he was called of God to this office, and was the father of all living in this day, and to him was given the dominion. These men held keys first on earth, and then in heaven. (p. 157)

Luke 1	JST Luke 1	D & C	D & C
20 And, behold, thou shalt be dumb, and not able to speak, until the day that these things shall be performed, because thou			

Luke 1	JST Luke 1	B of M	
believest not my words, which shall be fulfilled in their season. 21 And the people waited for Zacharias, and marvelled that he tarried so long in the temple. 22 And when he came out, he could not speak unto them: and they perceived that he had seen a vision in the temple: for he beckoned unto them, and remained speechless. 23 And **it came to pass, that,** as soon as the days of his ministration were accomplished, he departed to his own house. 24 And after those days his wife Elisabeth conceived, and hid herself five months, saying, 25 Thus hath the Lord dealt with me in the days wherein he looked on me, to take away my reproach **among** men.	23 And as soon as the days of his ministration were accomplished, he departed to his own house. 25 Thus hath the Lord dealt with me in the days wherein he looked on me, to take away my reproach **from** men.		

2. Nazareth-- Annunciation to Mary

Luke 1	JST Luke 1	B of M	
26 And in the sixth month the angel Gabriel was sent from God unto a city of Galilee, named Nazareth, 27 To a virgin espoused to a man whose name was Joseph, of the house of David; and the virgin's name was Mary. 28 And the angel came in unto her, and said, Hail, thou **that** art highly favoured, the Lord is with thee: blessed **art thou** among women. 29 And when she saw **him,** she was troubled at his saying, and **cast** in her mind what manner of salutation this should be. 30 And the angel said unto her, Fear not, Mary:	28 And the angel came in unto her and said, Hail, thou **virgin, who** art highly favored **of the Lord.** The Lord is with thee, **for thou art chosen and** blessed among women. 29 And when she saw **the angel,** she was troubled at his saying, and **pondered** in her mind what manner of salutation this should be.	Alma 7:10 And behold, he shall be born of Mary, at Jerusalem which is the land of our forefathers, she being a virgin, a precious and chosen vessel . . . Mosiah 3:8 And he shall be called Jesus Christ, the Son of God, the Father of heaven and earth, the Creator of all things from the beginning ; and his mother shall be called Mary.	

Luke 1	JST Luke 1	B of M	
for thou hast found favour with God. 31 And, behold, thou shalt conceive **in thy womb**, and bring forth a son, and shalt call his name JESUS. 32 He shall be great, and shall be called the Son of the Highest: and the Lord God shall give unto him the throne of his father David: 33 And he shall reign over the house of Jacob for ever; and of his kingdom there shall be no end. 34 Then said Mary unto the angel, How **shall this be, seeing I know not a man?** 35 And the angel answered and said unto her, The Holy Ghost **shall come upon thee**, and the power of the Highest **shall overshadow thee:** therefore also that holy **thing which** shall be born of thee shall be called the Son of God. 36 And, behold, thy cousin Elisabeth, she hath also conceived a son in her old age: and this is the sixth month with her, who **was** called barren. 37 For with God nothing **shall** be impossible. 38 And Mary said, Behold the handmaid of the Lord; be it unto me according to thy word. And the angel departed from her.	31 And behold, thou shalt conceive, and bring forth a son, and shall call his name Jesus. 34 Then said Mary unto the angel; How **can** this be? 35 And the angel answered and said unto her, **Of** the Holy Ghost, and the power of the Highest. Therefore also, that holy **child that** shall be born of thee shall be called the Son of God. 37 For with God nothing **can** be impossible.	. . . who shall be overshadowed and conceive by the power of the Holy Ghost, and bring forth a son, yea, even the Son of God. (Alma 7:10)	

3. Hill Country of Judea-- Mary Visits Elizabeth

39 And Mary **arose in those days and** went into the hill country with haste, into a city of Juda; 40 And entered into the house of Zacharias, and saluted Elisabeth. 41 And it came to pass, that, when Elisabeth heard	39 And **in those days,** Mary went into the hill country with haste, into a city of Juda,		

Luke 1	JST Luke 1	Luke 1	JST Luke 1
the salutation of Mary, the babe leaped in her womb; and Elisabeth was filled with the Holy Ghost:			
42 And she spake out with a loud voice, and said, Blessed art thou among women, and blessed is the fruit of thy womb.			
43 And **whence is this to** me, that the mother of my Lord should come to me?	43 And **why is it, that this blessing is upon** me, that the mother of my Lord should come to me? For lo, as soon as the voice of thy salutation sounded in mine ears, the babe leaped in my womb for joy.		
44 For, lo, as soon as the voice of thy salutation sounded in mine ears, the babe leaped in my womb for joy.			
45 And blessed **is she that** believed: for **there shall be a performance of** those things which were told **her from** the Lord.	44 And blessed **art thou who** believed, for those things which were told **thee by the angel of** the Lord, **shall be fulfilled.**		
46 And Mary said, My soul doth magnify the Lord,			
47 And my spirit **hath rejoiced** in God my Saviour.	46 And my spirit **rejoiceth** in God my Savior.		
48 For he hath regarded the low estate of his handmaiden: for, behold, from henceforth all generations shall call me blessed.			
49 For he **that is** mighty hath done to me great things; and holy **is his** name.	48 For he **who** is mighty hath done to me great things; and **I will magnify his** holy name,		
50 **And** his mercy is on **them that** fear him from generation to generation.	49 **For** his mercy **on those** who fear him from generation to generation.		
51 He hath shewed strength with his arm; he hath scattered the proud in the imagination of their hearts.			
52 He hath put down the mighty from their seats, and exalted them of low degree.	51 He hath put down the mighty from their **high** seats; and exalted them of low degree.	brance of **his** mercy.	remembrance of mercy,
53 He hath filled the hungry with good things; **and** the rich he hath sent empty away.	52 He hath filled the hungry with good things; **but** the rich he hath sent empty away.	55 As he spake to our fathers, to Abraham, and to his seed for ever.	
54 He hath **holpen** his servant Israel, in remem- (continued in column 3)	53 He hath **helped** his servant Israel in (continued in column 4)	56 And Mary abode with **her** about three months, and returned to her own house.	55 And Mary abode with **Elizabeth** about three months, and returned to her own house.

9

Luke 1	JST Luke 1	D & C	

4. John is Born

57 Now Elisabeth's full time came that she should be delivered; and she brought forth a son.

58 And her neighbours and her cousins heard how the Lord had shewed great mercy **upon** her; and they rejoiced with her.

59 And it came to pass, that on the eighth day they came to circumcise the child; and they called him Zacharias, after the name of his father.

60 And his mother answered and said, Not so; but he shall be called John.

61 And they said unto her, There is none of thy kindred that is called by this name.

62 And they made signs to his father, how he would have him called.

63 And he asked for a writing table, and wrote, saying, His name is John. And they marvelled **all**.

64 And his mouth was opened immediately, **and his tongue loosed**, and he spake, and praised God.

65 And fear came on all **that** dwelt round about them: and all these sayings were noised abroad throughout all the hill country of Judæa.

66 And all they that heard them laid them up in their hearts, saying, What manner of child shall this be! And the hand of the Lord was with him.

67 And his father Zacharias was filled with the Holy Ghost, and prophesied, saying,

68 Blessed be the Lord God of Israel; for he hath visited and redeemed

56 **And** now Elizabeth's full time came that she should be delivered; and she brought forth a son.

57 And her neighbors, and her cousins heard how the Lord had showed great mercy **unto** her; and they rejoiced with her.

61 And they made signs to his father, **and asked him** how he would have him called.

62 And he asked for a writing table, and wrote, saying, His name is John and they **all** marvelled.

63 And his mouth was opened immediately, and he spake **with his tongue**, and praised God.

64 And fear came on all **who** dwelt round about them. And all these sayings were noised abroad throughout all the hill country of Judea.

84:28 For he was baptized while he was yet in his childhood, and was ordained by the angel of God at the time he was eight days old unto this power, to overthrow the kingdom of the Jews, and to make straight the way of the Lord before the face of his people, to prepare them for the coming of the Lord, in whose hand is given all power.

Luke 1	JST Luke 1	Luke 1	JST Luke 1
his people,			
69 and hath raised up an horn of salvation for us in the house of his servant David;			
70 As he spake by the mouth of his holy prophets, **which have been** since the world began:	69 As he spake by the mouth of his holy prophets, **ever** since the world began,		
71 That we should be saved from our enemies, and from the hand of all **that** hate us;	70 That we should be saved from our enemies, and from the hand of all **those who** hate us;		
72 To perform the mercy promised to our fathers, and to remember his holy covenant;			
73 The oath which he sware to our father Abraham,			
74 That he would grant unto us, that we being delivered out of the hand of our enemies might serve him without fear,			
75 In holiness and righteousness before him, all the days of our **life**.	74 In holiness and righteousness before him, all the days of our **lives**.		
76 And thou, child, shalt be called the prophet of the Highest: for thou shalt go before the face of the Lord to prepare his ways;			
77 To give knowledge of salvation unto his people by the remission of their sins,	76 To give knowledge of salvation unto his people, by **baptism for** the remission of their sins,		
78 Through the tender mercy of our God; whereby the dayspring from on high hath visited us,			

TPJS—Let us come into New Testament times—so many are ever praising the Lord and His apostles. We will commence with John the Baptist. When Herod's edict went forth to destroy the young children, John was about six months older than Jesus, and came under this hellish edict, and Zacharias caused his mother to take him into the mountains, where he was raised on locusts and wild honey. When his father refused to disclose his hiding place, and being the officiating high priest at the Temple that year, was slain by Herod's order, between the porch and the altar, as Jesus said. (p. 261)

Luke 1	JST Luke 1	Luke 1	JST Luke 1
79 To give light to them **that** sit in darkness and **in the** shadow of death, to guide our feet into the way of peace. (continued in column 3)	78 To give light to them **who** sit in darkness and the shadow of death; to guide our feet into the way of peace. (continued in column 4)	80 And the child grew, and waxed strong in spirit, and was in the deserts **till** the day of his shewing unto Israel.	79 And the child grew, and waxed strong in spirit, and was in the deserts **until** the day of his showing unto Israel.

11

Matt. 1	JST Matt. 2	B of M	Isaiah

5. Nazareth-- Annunciation to Joseph

18 ¶ Now the birth of Jesus Christ was on this wise: **When as** his mother Mary was espoused to Joseph, before they came together, she was found with child of the Holy Ghost.

19 Then Joseph her husband, being a just man, and not willing to make her a publick example, was minded to put her away privily.

20 But while he thought on these things, behold, the angel of the Lord appeared unto him in a **dream**, saying, Joseph, thou son of David, fear not to take unto thee Mary thy wife: for that which is conceived in her is of the Holy Ghost.

21 And she shall bring forth a son, and thou shalt call his name JESUS: for he shall save his people from their sins.

22 Now **all** this **was done**, that **it** might be fulfilled which was spoken of the Lord by the prophet, saying,

23 Behold, a virgin shall be with child, and shall bring forth a son, and they shall call his name Emmanuel, which being interpreted is, God with us.

24 Then Joseph **being raised from sleep** did as the angel of the Lord had bidden him, and took unto him his wife:

25 And knew her not till she had brought forth her firstborn son. . .

Now, **as it is written**, the birth of Jesus Christ was on this wise. **After** his mother, Mary, was espoused to Joseph, before they came together, she was found with child of the Holy Ghost.

3 But while he thought on these things, behold, the angel of the Lord appeared unto him in a **vision**, saying, Joseph, thou son of David, fear not to take unto thee Mary thy wife; for that which is conceived in her, is of the Holy Ghost.

4 And she shall bring forth a son, and thou shalt call his name **Jesus**: for he shall save his people from their sins.

5 Now this **took place**, that **all** things might be fulfilled, which **were** spoken of the Lord, by the prophets, saying,

6 Behold, a virgin shall be with child, and shall bring forth a son, and they shall call his name Emmanuel, (which, being interpreted, is, God with us.)

7 Then Joseph, **awaking out of his vision**, did as the angel of the Lord had bidden him, and took unto him his wife;

8 And knew her not **until** she had brought forth her first-born son. . .

---

1 Ne.11:13. . . And I beheld the city of Nazareth; and in the city of Nazareth I beheld a virgin, and she was exceedingly fair and white.

14 And it came to pass that I saw the heavens open; and an angel came down and stood before me; and he said unto me: Nephi, what beholdest thou?

15 And I said unto him: A virgin, most beautiful and fair above all other virgins.

16 And he said unto me: Knowest thou the condescension of God?

17 And I said unto him: I know that he loveth his children; nevertheless, I do not know the meaning of all things.

18 And he said unto me: Behold, the virgin whom thou seest is the mother of the Son of God, after the manner of the flesh.

19 And it came to pass that I beheld that she was carried away in the Spirit; and after she had been carried away in the Spirit for the space of a time the angel spake unto me, saying: Look!

20 And I looked and beheld the virgin again, bearing a child in her arms.

21. . . And the angel said unto me: Behold the Lamb of God, yea, even the Son of the Eternal Father . . .

7:14 Therefore the Lord himself shall give you a sign; Behold, a virgin shall conceive, and bear a son, and shall call his name Immanuel.

Luke 2	JST Luke 2	B of M	Isaiah

6. Bethlehem-- Jesus is Born

Luke 2	JST Luke 2	B of M	Isaiah
And it came to pass in those days, that there went out a decree from Cæsar Augustus, that all **the world** should be taxed.	And it came to pass in those days, that there went out a decree from Caesar Augustus, that all **his empire** should be taxed.		
2 (**And** this taxing was **first made** when Cyrenius was governor of Syria.)	2 This **same** taxing was when Cyrenius was governor of Syria.		
3 And all went to be taxed, every one **into** his own city.	3 And all went to be taxed, every one in his own city.		
4 And Joseph also went up from Galilee, out of the city of Nazareth, into Judæa, unto the city of David, which is called Bethlehem; (because he was of the house and lineage of David:)			
5 To be taxed with Mary his espoused wife, being great with child.	5 To be taxed, with Mary his espoused wife, **she** being great with child.	Hel. 14:2 And behold, he said unto them: Behold, I give unto you a sign; for five years more cometh, and behold, then cometh the Son of God to redeem all those who shall believe on his name.	
6 And so it was, that, while they were there, the days were accomplished that she should be delivered.			
7 And she brought forth her firstborn son, and wrapped him in swaddling clothes, and laid him in a manger; because there was **no room** for them in the inn.	7 And she brought forth her first-born son, and wrapped him in swaddling clothes, and laid him in a manger; because there was **none to give** room for them in the inns.	3 And behold, this will I give unto you for a sign at the time of his coming; for behold, there shall be great lights in heaven, insomuch that in the night before he cometh there shall be no darkness, insomuch that it shall appear unto man as if it was day.	9:6-7 For unto us a child is born, unto us a son is given: and the government shall be upon his shoulder: and his name shall be called Wonderful, Counsellor, The mighty God, The everlasting Father, The Prince of Peace.
		4 Therefore, there shall be one day and a night and a day, as if it were one day and there were no night; and this shall be unto you for a sign; for ye shall know of the rising of the sun and also of its setting; therefore they shall know of a surety that there shall be two days and a night;	
8 And there were in the same country shepherds abiding in the field, keeping watch over their flock by night.			
9 And, lo, **the** angel of the Lord **came upon** them, and the glory of the Lord shone round about them: and they were sore afraid.	9 And lo, **an** angel of the Lord **appeared unto** them, and the glory of the Lord shone round about them; and they were sore afraid.		
10 **And** the angel said unto them, Fear not: for, behold, I bring you good tidings of great joy, which shall be to all people.	10 **But** the angel said unto them, Fear not; for behold, I bring you good tidings of great joy, which shall be to all people.	nevertheless the night shall	

Luke 2	JST Luke 2	B of M	
11 For unto you is born this day in the city of David a Saviour, **which** is Christ the Lord.	11 For unto you is born this day, in the city of David, a Savior, **who** is Christ the Lord.	not be darkened; and it shall be the night before he is born.	
12 And this **shall be a sign unto you;** Ye shall find the babe wrapped in swaddling clothes, lying in a manger.	12 And this **is the way** you shall find the babe, **he** is wrapped in swaddling clothes, **and is** lying in a manger.	3 Ne. 1:19-20 And it came to pass that there was no darkness in all that night, but it was as light as though it was mid-day. And it came to pass that the sun did rise in the morning again, according to its proper order; and they knew that it was the day that the Lord should be born, because of the sign which had been given.	
13 And suddenly there was with the angel a multitude of the heavenly host praising God, and saying,			
14 Glory to God in the highest, and on earth peace, good will **toward** men.	14 Glory to God in the highest; and on earth, peace; good will **to** men.		
15 And it came to pass, **as** the angels were gone away from them into heaven, the shepherds said one to another, Let us now go even unto Bethlehem, and see this thing which is come to pass, which the Lord has made known unto us.	15 And it came to pass, **when** the angels were gone away from them into heaven, the shepherds said one to another, Let us now go, even unto Bethlehem, and see this thing which is come to pass, which the Lord has made known unto us.	20 And it had come to pass, yea, all things, every whit, according to the words of the prophets.	
16 And they came with haste, and found Mary, and Joseph, and the babe lying in a manger.			
17 And when they had seen **it**, they made known abroad the saying which was told them concerning this child.	17 And when they had seen, they made known abroad the saying which was told them concerning this child.		
18 **And** all they **that** heard it wondered at those things which were told them by the shepherds.	18 All they **who** heard it, wondered at those things which were told them by the shepherds;		
19 But Mary kept all these things, and pondered them in her heart.			
20 And the shepherds returned, glorifying and praising God for all the things **that** they had heard and seen, as **it was told** unto them.	20 And the shepherds returned, glorifying and praising God for all the things **which** they had heard and seen, as **they were manifested** unto them.		

Matt. 1	JST Matt. 1 & 2	Luke 3	JST Luke 3

7. Jesus' Genealogy

Matt. 1	JST Matt. 1 & 2	Luke 3	JST Luke 3
25 . . . and he called his name JESUS. 1 The book of the generation of Jesus Christ, the son of David, the son of Abraham. 2 Abraham begat Isaac; and Isaac begat Jacob; and Jacob begat Judas and his brethren; 3 And Judas begat Phares and Zara of Thamar; and Phares begat Esrom; and Esrom begat Aram; 4 And Aram begat Aminadab; and Aminadab begat Naasson; and Naasson begat Salmon; 5 And Salmon begat Booz of Rachab; and Booz begat Obed of Ruth; and Obed begat Jesse; 6 And Jesse begat David the king; and David the king begat Solomon of her that had been the wife of Urias; 7 And Solomon begat Roboam; and Roboam begat Abia; and Abia begat Asa; 8 And Asa begat Josaphat; and Josaphat begat Joram; and Joram begat Ozias; 9 And Ozias begat Joatham; and Joatham begat Achaz; and Achaz begat Ezekias; 10 And Ezekias begat Manasses; and Manasses begat Amon; and Amon begat Josias; 11 And Josias begat Jechonias and his brethren, about the time they were carried away to Babylon: 12 And after they were brought to Babylon, Jechonias begat Salathiel; and Salathiel begat Zorobabel;	2:8 . . . and they called his name Jesus. 1:3 And David the king begat Solomon of her whom David had taken of Urias. . .	23 . . . being (as was supposed) the son of Joseph, which was the son of Heli, 24 Which was the son of Matthat, which was the son of Levi, which was the son of Melchi, which was the son of Janna, which was the son of Joseph, 25 Which was the son of Mattathias, which was the son of Amos, which was the son of Naum, which was the son of Esli, which was the son of Nagge, 26 Which was the son of Maath, which was the son of Mattathias, which was the son of Semei, which was the son of Joseph, which was the son of Juda, 27 Which was the son of Joanna, which was the son of Rhesa, which was the son of Zorobabel, which was the son of Salathiel, which was the son of Neri, 28 Which was the son of Melchi, which was the son of Addi, which was the son of Cosam, which was the son of Elmodam, which was the son of Er, 29 Which was the son of Jose, which was the son of Eliezer, which was the son of Jorim, which was the son of Matthat, which was the son of Levi, 30 Which was the son of Simeon, which was the son of Juda, which was the son of Joseph, which was the son of Jonan, which was the son of Eliakim,	30 . . . having lived with his father, being, as was supposed of the world, the son of Joseph, who was from the loins of Heli, 31 Who was from the loins of Matthat, who was the son of Levi, who was a descendant of Melchi, and of Janna, and of Joseph, 32 And of Mattathias, and of Amos, and of Naum, and of Esli, and of Nagge, 33 And of Maath, and of Mattathias, and of Semei, and of Joseph, and of Juda, 34 And of Joanna, and of Resa, and of Zorobabel, and of Salathiel, who was the son of Neri, 35 Who was a descendant of Melchi, and of Addi, and of Cosam, and of Elmodam, and of Er, 36 And of Jose, and of Eliezer, and of Joram, and of Matthat, and of Levi, 37 And of Simeon, and of Juda, and of Joseph, and of Jonan, and of Eliakim,

Matt. 1	JST Matt. 1	Luke 3	JST Luke 3
13 And Zorobabel begat Abiud; and Abiud begat Eliakim; and Eliakim begat Azor; 14 And Azor begat Sadoc; and Sadoc begat Achim; and Achim begat Eliud; 15 And Eliud begat Eleaz-ar; and Eleazar begat Matthan; and Matthan begat Jacob; 16 And Jacob begat Joseph the husband of Mary, of whom was born Jesus; who is called Christ.	4. . . and Jacob begat Joseph, the husband of Mary, of whom was born Jesus, **as the prophets have written,** who is called Christ.	31 **Which was the son of Melea, which was the son of Menan, which was the son of Mattatha, which was the son of Nathan,** which was the son of David, 32 **Which was the son of Jesse, which was the son of Obed, which was the son of Booz, which was the son of Salmon, which** was the son of Naasson, 33 **Which was the son of Aminadab, which was the son of Aram, which was the son of Esrom, which was the son of Phares, which was the son of Juda,** 34 **Which was the son of Jacob, which was the son of Issac, which was the son of Abraham, which was the son of Thara, which was the son of Nachor,** 35 **Which was the son of Saruch, which was the son of Ragau, which was the son of Phalec, which was the son of Heber, which was the son of Sala,** 36 **Which was the son of Cainan, which was the son of Arphaxad, which was the son of Sem, which was the son of Noe, which was the son of Lamech,** 37 **Which was the son of Mathusala, which was the son of Enoch, which was** the son of Jared, which was the son of Maleleel, **which was the son of Cainan,** 38 Which was the son of Enos, which was the son of Seth, which was the son of Adam, which was the son of God.	38 And of Melea, and of Menan, and of Mattatha, and of Nathan, and of David, 39 And of Jesse, and of Obed, and of Booz, and of Salmon, and of Naasson, 40 And of Aminadab, and of Aram, and of Esrom, and of Phares, and of Juda, 41 And of Jacob, and of Issac, and of Abraham, and of Thara, and of Nachor, 42 And of Saruch, and of Ragau, and of Phalec, and of Heber, and of Sala, 43 And of Cainan, and of Arphaxad, and of Shem, and of Noah, and of Lamech, 44 And of Mathusala, and of Enoch, and of Jared, and of Cainan, 45 And of Enos, and of Seth, and of Adam, who was formed of God, and the first man upon the earth.
17 So all the generations from Abraham to David are fourteen generations; and from David until the carrying away into Babylon **are** fourteen generations; and from the carrying away into Babylon **unto Christ are** fourteen generations.	5 So all the generations from Abraham to David, were fourteen generations; and from David until the carrying away into Babylon were fourteen generations; and from the carrying away into Babylon **until Christ, were** fourteen generations.		

16

Luke 2	JST Luke 2	B of M	B of M

8. Bethlehem and Jerusalem—Jesus is Circumcised and Blessed

Luke 2	JST Luke 2	B of M	B of M
21 And wen eight days were accomplished for the circumcising of the child, he name was called **JESUS**, which was so named of the angel before he was conceived **in the womb**. 22 And when the days of her purification according to the law of Moses were accomplished, they brought him to Jerusalem, to present him to the Lord;	21 And when eight days were accomplished for the circumcising of the child, his name was called **Jesus**; which was so named of the angel, before he was conceived.	2 Ne. 10:3 Wherefore, as I said unto you, it must needs be expedient that Christ—for in the last night the angel spake unto me that this should be his name. . .	2 Ne. 25:19 For according to the words of the prophets, the Messiah cometh in six hundred years from the time that my father left Jerusalem; and according to the words of the prophets, and also the word of the angel of God, his name shall be Jesus Christ, the Son of God.
23 (As it is written in the law of the Lord, Every male **that** openeth the womb shall be called holy to the Lord;)	23 As it is written in the law of the Lord, Every male **which** openeth the womb shall be called holy to the Lord;		
24 And to offer a sacrifice according to that which is **said** in the law of the Lord, A pair of turtledoves, or two young pigeons.	24 and to offer a sacrifice according to that which is **written** in the law of the Lord, A pair of turtledoves,, or two young pigeons.		
25 and, behold, there was a man **in** Jerusalem, whose name was Simeon; and the same man was just and devout, waiting for the consolation of Israel: and the Holy Ghost was upon him.	25 And behold, there was a man **at** Jerusalem, whose name was Simeon; and the same man was just and devout, waiting for the consolation of Israel; and the Holy Ghost was upon him.		
26 And it was revealed unto him by the Holy ghost, that he should not see death, before he had seen the Lord's Christ.			
27 And he came by the Spirit into the temple: and when the parents brought in the child Jesus, to do for him after the custom of the law,	27 And he came by the Spirit into the temple; and when the parents brought in the child, **even** Jesus, to do for him after the custom of the law,		
28 Then took he him up in his arms, and blessed god, and said,			
29 Lord, now lettest **thou** thy servant depart in peace, according to thy word:	29 Lord, now lettest thy servant depart in peace, according to thy word;		

Luke 2	JST Luke 2		
31 Which thou hast prepared before the face of all people;			
32 A light to lighten the Gentiles, and the glory of thy people Israel.			
33 And Joseph and **his mother** marvelled at those things which were spoken of **him**.	33 And Joseph, and **Mary,** marvelled at those things which were spoken **of the child.**		
34 And Simeon blessed them, and said unto Mary **his mother,** Behold, this child is set for the fall and rising again of many in Israel; and for a sign which shall be spoken against;	34 And Simeon blessed them, and said unto Mary, Behold, this child is set for the fall and rising again of many in Israel; and for a sign which shall be spoken against;		
35 (Yea, a **sword** shall pierce through **thy** own soul also,) that the thoughts of many hearts may be revealed.	35 Yea, a **spear** shall pierce through **him to the wounding of thine** own soul also; that the thoughts of many hearts may be revealed.		
36 And there was one Anna, a prophetess, the daughter of Phanuel, of the tribe of Aser: she was of **a** great age, and had lived with **an** husband seven years **from her virginity;**	36 And there was one Anna, a prophetess, the daughter of Phanuel, of the tribe of Asher. She was of great age, and had lived with a husband **only** seven years, **whom she married in her youth,**		
37 And she **was** a widow **of about** fourscore and four years, **which** departed not from the temple, but served God with fastings and prayers night and day.	37 And she **lived** a widow about fourscore and four years, **who** departed not from the temple, but served God with fastings and prayers, night and day.		
38 And she coming in that instant gave thanks likewise unto the Lord, and spake of him to all **them that** looked for redemption in Jerusalem.	38 And she, coming in that instant, gave thanks likewise unto the Lord, and spake of him, to all **those who** looked for redemption in Jerusalem.		
39 And when they had performed all things according to the law of the Lord, they returned into Galilee, to their own city Nazareth.			

Matt. 2	JST Matt. 3	Old Testament	B of M

9. The Visit of the Wise Men from the East

Matt. 2	JST Matt. 3	Old Testament	B of M
Now when Jesus was born in Bethlehem of Judæa in the days of Herod the king, behold, there came wise men from the east to Jerusalem,			
2 Saying, Where is **he** that is born **King of the Jews?** for we have seen his star in the east, and **are** come to worship him.	2 Saying, Where is **the child** that is born, **the Messiah** of the Jews? for we have seen his star in the east, and **have** come to worship him.	Num. 24:17 I shall see him, but not now: I shall behold him, but not nigh: there shall come a Star out of Jacob, and a Sceptre shall rise out of Israel, and shall smite the corners of Moab, and destroy all the children of Sheth.	3 Ne. 1:21 And it came to pass also that a new star did appear, according to the word.
3 When Herod the king had heard **these things,** he was troubled, and all Jerusalem with him.	3 When Herod the king had heard **of the child,** he was troubled, and all Jerusalem with him.		
4 And when he had gathered all the chief priests and scribes of the people together, he demanded of them where	4 And when he had gathered all the chief priests, and scribes of the people together, he demanded of them, **saying, Where is the place that is written of by the prophets, in which** Christ should be born? **For he greatly feared, yet he believed not the prophets.**		
Christ should be born.			
5 And they said unto him, In Bethlehem of Judæa: for thus **it is written by the prophet,**	5 And they said unto him, **It is written by the prophets, that he should be born** in Bethlehem of Judea: for thus **have they said,**		
	6 **The word of the Lord came unto us, saying,** And thou, Bethlehem, **which lieth in the land of Judea; in thee shall be born a prince, which art**	Micah 5:2 But thou, Bethlehem Ephratah, though thou be little among the thousands of Judah, yet out of thee shall he come forth unto me that is to be ruler in Israel; whose goings forth have been from of old, from everlasting.	
6 And thou Bethlehem, in the land of Juda,			
art not the least among the princes of Juda: for out of thee shall come a **Governor, that shall rule** my people Israel.	not the least among the princes of Judea; for out of thee shall come **the Messiah, who shall save** my people Israel.		
7 Then Herod, when he had **privily** called the wise men, enquired of them diligently what time the star appeared.	7 Then Herod, when he had called the wise men **privily,** enquired of them diligently what time the star appeared.		
8 And he sent them to Bethlehem, and said, Go	8 And he sent them to Bethlehem, and said, Go		

Matt. 2	JST Matt. 3		
and search diligently for the young child; and when ye have found **him**, bring me word again, that I may come and worship him also. 9 When they had heard the king, they departed; and, lo, the star, which they saw in the east, went before them, **till** it came and stood over where the young child was. 10 When they saw the star, they rejoiced with exceeding great joy. 11 ¶ And when they were come into the house, they saw the young child with Mary his mother, and fell down, and worshipped him: and when they had opened their treasures, they presented unto him gifts; gold, and frankincense, and myrrh. 12 And being warned of God in a dream that they should not return to Herod, they departed into their own country another way.	and search diligently for the young child; and when ye have found **the child,** bring me word again, that I may come and worship him also. 9 When they had heard the king, they departed; and lo, the star which they saw in the east, went before them, **until** it came and stood over where the young child was.		

10. Egypt-- Warned by an Angel

13 And when they were departed, behold, the angel of the Lord appeareth to Joseph in a **dream**, saying, Arise, and take the young child and his mother, and flee into Egypt, and **b e** thou there until I bring thee word: for Herod will seek the young child to destroy him. 14 **When** he arose, he took the young child and **his** mother by night, and departed into Egypt:	13 And when they were departed, behold, the angel of the Lord, **appeared to** Joseph in a **vision**, saying, Arise and take the young child and his mother, and flee into Egypt, and **tarry** thou there until I bring thee word; for Herod will seek the young child to destroy him. 14 **And then** he arose, **and** took the young child, and **the child's** mother, by night, and departed into Egypt;		

Matt. 2	JST Matt. 3	Old Testament Matt. 2	
Out of Egypt I have called my son. 16 ¶ Then Herod, when he saw that he was mocked of the wise men, was exceeding wroth, and sent forth, and slew all the children that were in Bethlehem, and in all the coasts thereof, from two years old and under, according to the time which he had diligently enquired of the wise men. 17 Then was fulfilled that which was spoken by **Jeremy** the prophet, saying, 18 In Rama **was there** a voice heard, lamentation, and weeping, and great mourning, Rachel weeping for her children, and would not be comforted, because they **are** not.		Hosea 11:1 When Israel was a child, then I loved him, and called my son out of Egypt.	
	17 Then was fulfilled that which was spoken by **Jeremiah** the prophet, saying, 18 In Ramah **there was** a voice heard, lamentation, and weeping, and great mourning; Rachael weeping for **the loss of her** children, and would not be comforted because they **were** not.	Jeremiah 31:15 ¶ Thus saith the LORD; A voice was heard in Ramah, lamentation, and bitter weeping; Rahel weeping for her children refused to be comforted for her children, because they were not.	

11. Nazareth-- Return from Egypt

Matt. 2	JST Matt. 3	Old Testament Matt. 2	
19 ¶ But when Herod was dead, behold, an angel of the Lord **appeareth** in **a dream** to Joseph in Egypt, 20 Saying, Arise, and take the young child and his mother, and go into the land of Israel: for they are dead **which** sought the young child's life. 21 And he arose, and took the young child and his mother, and came into the land of Israel. 22 But when he heard that Archelaus did reign in Judæa in the **room** of his father Herod, he was afraid to go thither: notwithstanding, being warned of God in a **dream**, he **turned aside** into the parts of Galilee: (continued in column 3)	19 But when Herod was dead, behold, an angel of the Lord **appeared** in a **vision** to Joseph in Egypt, 20 Saying, Arise, and take the young child and his mother, and go into the land of Israel; for they are dead **who** sought the young child's life. 22 But when he heard that Archelaus did reign in Judea, in the **stead** of his father Herod, he was afraid to go thither; **but,** notwithstanding, being warned of God in a vision, he **went** into the **eastern** part of Galilee;	23 And he came and dwelt in a city called Nazareth: that it might be fulfilled which was spoken by the prophets, He shall be called a Nazarene.	

21

JST Matt. 3	Luke 2	JST Luke 2	Isaiah

12. Childhood

24 And it came to pass that Jesus grew up with his brethren, and waxed strong, and waited upon the Lord for the time of his ministry to come.	40 And the child grew, and waxed strong in spirit, filled with wisdom: and the grace of God was upon him.	40 And the child grew, and waxed strong in spirit, being filled with wisdom, and the grace of God was upon him.	53:2 For he shall grow up before him as a tender plant, and as a root out of a dry ground: he hath no form nor comeliness; and when we shall see him, there is no beauty that we should desire him.

13. Age 12-30

25 And he served under his father, and he spake not as other men, neither could he be taught; for he needed not that any man should teach him.	41 Now his parents went to Jerusalem every year at the feast of the passover.		
26 And after many years, the hour of his ministry drew nigh.	42 And when he was twelve years old, they went up to Jerusalem after the custom of the feast.	42 And when he was twelve years old, they went up to Jerusalem, after the custom, to the feast.	
	43 And when they had fulfilled the days, as they returned, the child Jesus tarried behind in Jerusalem; and Joseph and his mother knew not of it.	43 And when they had fulfilled the days, as they returned, the child Jesus tarried behind, in Jerusalem; and Joseph and his mother knew not **that he tarried;**	
	44 But they, supposing him to have been in the company, went a day's journey; and they sought him among **their kinsfolk** and acquaintance.	44 But they, supposing him to have been in the company, went a day's journey; and they sought him among **his kindred** and acquaintance.	
	45 And when they found him not, they turned back again to Jerusalem, seeking him.		
	46 And it came to pass, **that** after three days they found him in the temple, sitting in the midst of the doctors, **both** hearing **them**, and asking **them** questions.	46 And it came to pass, after three days they found him in the temple, sitting in the midst of the doctors, **and they were** hearing him, and asking **him** questions.	
	47 And all **that** heard him were astonished at his understanding and answers.	47 And all **who** heard him were astonished at his understanding, and answers.	
	48 And when they saw him, they were amazed: and his mother said unto him, Son, why hast thou thus dealt with us? behold, thy father and I have	48 And when **his parents** saw him, they were amazed; and his mother said unto him, Son, why hast thou thus dealt with us? Behold, thy father and	

Luke 2	JST Luke 2	Hebrews	
sought thee sorrowing. 49 And he said unto them, **How** is it that ye sought me? **wist** ye not that I must be about my Father's business? 50 And they understood not the saying which he spake unto them. 51 And he went down with them, and came to Nazareth, and was subject unto them: **but** his mother kept all these sayings in her heart. 52 And Jesus increased in wisdom and stature, and in favour with God and man.	I have sought thee sorrowing. 49 And he said unto them, **Why** is it that ye sought me? **Knew** ye not that I must be about my Father's business? 51 And he went down with them, and came to Nazareth, and was subject unto them. **And** his mother kept all these sayings in her heart.	Jesus, the Son of God...was in all points tempted like as we are, yet without sin. (Hebrews 4:14-15).	

TPJS-- When still a boy He had all the intelligence necessary to enable Him to rule and govern the kingdom of the Jews, and could reason with the wisest and most profound doctors of law and divinity, and make their theories and practice to appear like folly compared with the wisdom He possessed; but He was a boy only, and lacked physical strength even to defend His own person; and was subject to cold, to hunger and to death. So it is with the Church of Jesus Christ of Latter-day Saints; we have the revelation of Jesus, and the knowledge within us is sufficient to organize a righteous government upon the earth, and to give universal peace to all mankind, if they would receive it, but we lack the physical strength, as did our Savior when a child, to defend our principles, and we have of necessity to be afflicted, persecuted and smitten, and to bear it patiently until Jacob is of age, then he will take care of himself. (p. 392)

Matt. 3	JST Matt. 3	Mark 1	Old Testament

The Ministry of John the Baptist

Matt. 3	JST Matt. 3	Mark 1	Old Testament
		The beginning of the gospel of Jesus Christ, the Son of God;	
In those days came John the Baptist, preaching in the wilderness of Judaea,	27 **And** in those days came John the Baptist, preaching in the wilderness of Judea,	4 John did baptize in the wilderness, and preach the baptism of repentance for the remission of sins.	
2 And saying, Repent ye: for the kingdom of heaven is at hand.		2 As it is written in the prophets, Behold, I send my messenger before thy face, which shall prepare the way before thee.	Malachi 3:1 Behold, I will send my messenger, and he shall prepare the way before me: and the Lord, whom ye seek, shall suddenly come to his temple, even the messenger of the covenant, whom ye delight in: behold, he shall come, saith the LORD of hosts.
3 For **this is** he **that** was spoken of by the prophet Esaias, saying, The voice of one crying in the wilderness, Prepare ye the way of the Lord, make his paths straight.	29 For **I am** he **who** was spoken of by the prophet Esaias, saying, The voice of one crying in the wilderness, Prepare ye the way of the Lord **and** make his paths straight.	3 The voice of one crying in the wilderness, Prepare ye the way of the Lord, make his paths straight.	Isaiah 40:3 ¶ The voice of him that crith in the wilderness, Prepare ye the way of the LORD, make straight in the desert a highway for our God.

TPJS—But, says one, the kingdom of god could not be set up in the days of John, for John said the kingdom was at hand. But I would ask if it could be any nearer to them than to be in the hands of John. The people need not wait for the days of Pentecost to find the kingdom of God, for John had it with him, and he came forth from the wilderness crying out, "Repent ye, for the kingdom of heaven is nigh at hand," as much as to say, "Out here I have got the kingdom of God, and you can get it, and I am coming after you; and if you don't receive it, you will be damned;". . . (p. 273)

Here is a little of law which must be fulfilled. The Levitical Priesthood is forever hereditary—fixed on the head of Aaron and hiss ons forever, and was in active operation down to Zacharias the father of John. Zacharias would have had no child had not God given him a son. He sent his angel to declare unto Zacharias that his wife Elizabeth should bear him a son, whose name was to be called John.
The keys of the Aaronic Priesthood were committed unto him, and he was as the voice of one crying in the wilderness saying: "Prepare ye the way of the Lord and make his paths straight."
The Kingdom of heaven suffereth violence, etc.
The Kingdom of heaven continueth in authority until John.
The authority taketh it by absolute power.
John having the power took the Kingdom by authority (p. 319).

Luke 3	JST Luke 3	JST Luke 3	D & C B of M
Now in the fifteenth year of the reign of Tiberius Caesar, Pontius Pilate being governor of Judaea, and Herod being tetrarch of Galilee, and his brother Philip tetrarch of Ituraea and the region of Trachonitis, and Lysanias the tetrarch of Abilene,			D&C 84:26 And the lesser priesthood continued, which priesthood holdeth the key of the ministering of angels and the preparatory gospel;
2 Annas and Caiaphas being the high priests, the word of God came unto John the son of Zacharias in the wilderness. 3 And he came into all the country about Jordan, preaching the baptism of repentance for the remission of sins; 4 As it is written in the book of **the words of** Esaias **the prophet**, saying,	2 **Now in this same year,** the word of God came unto John, the son of Zacharias, in the wilderness. 4 As it is written in the book of **the prophet** Esaias, **and these are the words,** saying,		27 Which gospel is the gospel of repentance and of baptism, and the remission of sins, and the law of carnal commandments, which the Lord in his wrath caused to continue with the house of Aaron among the children of Israel until John, whom God raised up, being filled with the Holy Ghost form his mother's womb.
The voice of one crying in the wilderness, Prepare ye the way of the Lord, make his paths straight.	The voice of one crying in the wilderness, Prepare ye the way of the Lord, **and** make his paths straight.		1 Ne. 10:7 And he spake also concerning a prophet who should come before the Messiah, to prepare the way of the Lord— 8 Yea, even he should go forth and cry in the wilderness: Prepare ye the way of the Lord, and make his paths straight. . .
	5 **For behold, and lo, he shall come, as it is written in the book of the prophets, to take away the sins of the world, and to bring salvation unto the heathen nations, to gather together those who are lost, who are of the sheepfold of Israel;**	**ascend up on high, to dwell on the right hand of the Father, 8 Until the fullness of time, and the law and the testimony shall be sealed, and the keys of the kingdom shall be delivered up again unto the Father;**	D&C 35:4 Thou (Sidney Rigdon) art blessed, for thou shalt do great things. Behold thou wast sent forth, even as John, to prepare the way before me, and before Elijah which should come, and thou knewest it not. (See also D&C 33:10; 34:6; 39:19-20; 42:7; 65:3.)
	6 **Yea, even the dispersed and afflicted; and also to prepare the way, and make possible the preaching of the gospel unto the Gentiles;**		
	7 **And to be a light unto all who sit in darkness, unto the uttermost parts of the earth; to bring to pass the resurrection from the dead, and to**	**9 To administer justice unto all; to come down in judgment upon all, and to convince all the ungodly of their ungodly deeds, which they have committed; and all this in the day that he shall come;**	
	(continued in column 3)		

Matt. 3	JST Matt. 3	Mark 1	JST Mark 1
4 And the same John had his raiment of camel's hair, and a leathern girdle about his loins; and his **meat** was locusts and wild honey.	30 And the same John had his raiment of camel's hair, and a leathern girdle about his loins; and his **food** was locusts and wild honey.	6 And John was clothed with camel's hair, and with a girdle of skin about his loins; and he did eat locusts and wild honey;	
5 Then went out to him Jerusalem, and all Judaea, and all the region round about Jordan,		5 And there wen tout unto him all the land of Judaea, and they of Jerusalem, and were **all** baptized of him in the river **of** Jordan, confessing their sins.	4 And there went out unto him all the land of Judea, and they of Jerusalem, and **many** were baptized of him in the river Jordan, confessing their sins.
6 And were baptized of him in Jordan, confessing their sins.	32 And **many** were baptized of him in Jordan, confessing their sins.		
7 ¶ But when he saw many of the Pharisees and Sadducees come to his baptism, he said unto them, O generation of vipers, who hath warned you to flee from the wrath to come?			
	34 **Why is it that ye receive not the preaching of him whom God hath sent? If ye receive not this in your hearts, ye receive not me; and if ye receive not me, ye receive not him of whom I am sent to bear record; and for your sins ye have no cloak.**		
8 Bring forth **therefore** fruits meet for repentance:	35 **Repent, therefore, and** bring forth fruits meet for repentance;		
9 And think not to say within yourselves, We **have** Abraham **to our father:**	36 And think not to say within yourselves, **We are the children of** Abraham, **and we only have power to bring seed unto our father Abraham;** for I say unto you that God is able of these stones to raise up children **into** Abraham.		
for I say unto you, that God is able of these stones to raise up children **unto** Abraham.			

TPJS—Of these stony Gentiles—these dogs—to raise up children unto Abraham. (p. 319)

Luke 3	JST Luke 3	D & C	
5 Every valley shall be filled, and every mountain and hill shall be brought low; **and** the crooked shall be made straight, and the rough ways **shall be** made smooth; 6 And all flesh shall see the salvation of God.	10 **For it is a day of power; yea,** every valley shall be filled, and every mountain and hill shall be brought low; the crooked shall be made straight, and the rough ways made smooth;	49:23 Wherefore, be not deceived, but continue in steadfastness, looking forth for the heavens to be shaken, and the earth to tremble and to reel to and fro as a drunken man, and for the valleys to be exalted, and for the mountains to be made low, and for the rough places to become smooth-- and all this when the angel shall sound his trumpet.	
7 Then said **he** to the multitude that came forth to be baptized of him, O generation of vipers, who hath warned you to flee from the wrath to come?	12 Then said **John** to the multitude that came forth to be baptized of him, **crying against them with a loud voice, saying,** O generation of vipers, who hath warned you to flee from the wrath to come?		
8 Bring forth therefore fruits worthy of repentance, and begin not to say within yourselves, **We have Abraham to our father:** for I say unto you, That God is able of these stones to raise up children unto Abraham.	13 Bring forth therefore fruits worthy of repentance, and begin not to say within yourselves, Abraham is our father; **we have kept the commandments of God, and none can inherit the promises but the children of Abraham;** for I say unto you, That God is able of these stones to raise up children unto Abraham.		

27

Matt. 3	JST Matt. 3	D & C	
10 And now also the axe is laid unto the root of the trees: therefore every tree which bringeth not forth good fruit is hewn down, and cast into the fire.	37 And now, also, the axe is laid unto the root of the trees; therefore every tree which bringeth not forth good fruit, **shall be hewn down, and cast into the fire.**	97:7 The ax is laid at the root of the trees; and every tree that bringeth not forth good fruit shall be hewn down and cast into the fire. I, the Lord, have spoken it.	

TPJS-- I [Joseph Smith] am the voice of one crying in the wilderness, "Repent ye of your sins and prepare the way for the coming of the Son of Man; for the kingdom of God has come unto you, and henceforth the ax is laid unto the root of the tree; and every tree that bringeth not forth good fruit, God Almighty***shall hew it down and cast it into the fire." (p. 341)

Luke 3	JST Luke 3		
9 And now also the axe is laid unto the root of the trees: every tree therefore which bringeth not forth good fruit **is** hewn down, and cast into the fire. 10 And the people asked him, saying, What shall we do then? 11 He answereth and saith unto them, He that hath two coats, let him impart to him that hath none; and he that hath meat, let him do likewise. 12 Then came also publicans to be baptized, and said unto him, Master, what shall we do? 13 And he said unto them, Exact no more than that which is appointed you.	14 And now also, the axe is laid unto the root of the trees; every tree therefore which bringeth not forth good fruit, **shall be** hewn down, and cast into the fire. 18 And he said unto them, Exact no more than that which is appointed **unto you.** 19 **For it is well known unto you, Theophilus, that after the manner of the Jews, and according to the custom of their law in receiving money into the treasury, that out of the abundance which was received, was appointed unto the poor, every man his portion;** 20 **And after this manner did the publicans also, wherefore John said unto them, Exact no more than that which is appointed you.**		
14 And the soldiers likewise demanded of him, saying, And what shall we do? And he said unto them, Do violence to no man, neither accuse any falsely; and be content with your wages. 15 And as the people were in expectation, and all men mused in their hearts of John, whether he were the Christ, or not;			

Matt. 3	JST Matt. 3	Mark 1	JST Mark 1
11 I indeed baptize you with water **unto** repent-ance: **but he that cometh after me** is mightier than I, whose shoes I am not worthy to bear: he shall baptize you with the Holy Ghost, and with fire: 12 Whose fan **is** in his hand, and he will thor-oughly purge his floor, and gather his wheat into the garner; but **he** will burn up the chaff with unquenchable fire.	38 I indeed baptize you with water, **upon your repentance; and when he of whom I bear record cometh, who is** mightier than I, whose shoes I am not worthy to bear, **(or whose place I am not able to fill,) as I said, I indeed baptize you be-fore he cometh, that when he cometh he may** baptize you with the Holy Ghost and fire. 39 **And it is he of whom I shall bear record, whose fan shall be** in his hand, and he will thoroughly purge his floor, and gather his wheat into the garner; but **in the fullness of his own time will** burn up the chaff with unquenchable fire. 40 **Thus came John, preaching and baptizing in the river of Jordan; bearing record, that he who was coming after him had power to baptize with the Holy Ghost and fire.**	7 And preached, saying, There cometh one mightier than I after me, the latchet of whose shoes I am not worthy to stoop down and unloose. 8 I indeed have baptized you with water: but he shall baptize you with the Holy Ghost.	6 I indeed have baptized you with water; but he shall **not only** baptize you with water, **but with fire, and** the Holy Ghost.

TPJS-- In the first place, suffice it to say, I went into the woods to inquire of the Lord, by prayer, His will concerning me, and I saw an angel, and he laid his hands upon my head, and ordained me to a Priest after the order of Aaron, and to hold the keys of this Priesthood, which office was to preach repentance and baptism for the remission of sins, and also to baptize. But I was informed that this office did not extend to the laying on of hands for the giving of the Holy Ghost; that that office was a greater work, and was to be given afterward; but that my ordination was a preparatory work, or a going before, which was the spirit of Elias; for the spirit of Elias was a going before to prepare the way for the greater, which was the case with John the Baptist. He came crying through the wilderness, "Prepare ye the way of the Lord, make his paths straight." And they were informed, if they could receive it, it was the spirit of Elias; and John was very particular to tell the people, he was not that Light, but was sent to bear witness of that Light.

He told the people that his mission was to preach repentance and baptize with water; but it was He that should come after him that should baptize with fire and the Holy Ghost.

If he had been an imposter, he might have gone to work beyond his bounds, and undertook to have performed ordinances which did not belong to that office and calling, under the spirit of Elias. (p. 335)

Luke 3	JST Luke 3	B of M	
16 John answered, saying unto **them** all, I indeed baptize you with water; but one mightier than I com**eth**, the latchet of whose shoes I am not worthy to unloose: he shall baptize you with the Holy Ghost and with fire: 17 Whose fan is in his hand, and he will thoroughly purge his floor, and will gather the wheat into his garner; but the chaff he will burn with fire unquenchable. 18 And many other things in his exhortation preached he unto the people.	23 John answered, saying unto all, I indeed baptize you with water, but **there cometh** one mightier than I, the latchet of whose shoes I am not worthy to unloose, he shall baptize you with the Holy Ghost, and with fire;	1 Ne. 10:8 . . . for there standeth one among you whom ye know not; and he is mightier than I, whose shoe's latchet I am not worthy to unloose . . .	

TPJS-- I will leave this subject here, and make a few remarks on the subject of baptism. The baptism of water, without the baptism of fire and the Holy Ghost attending it, is of no use; they are necessarily and inseparably connected. An individual must be born of water and the Spirit in order to get into the kingdom of God. In the German, the text bears me out the same as the revelations which I have given and taught for the last fourteen years on that subject. I have the testimony to put in their teeth. My testimony has been true all the time. You will find it in the declaration of John the Baptist. (Reads from the German.) John says, "I baptize you with water, but when Jesus comes, who has the power (or keys), he shall administer the baptism of fire and the Holy Ghost." Where is now all the sectarian world? And if this testimony is true, they are all damned as clearly as anathema can do it. I know the text is true. I call upon all you Germans who know that it is true to say, Aye. (Loud shouts of "Aye.") (p. 360)

Matt. 3	JST Matt. 3	Mark 1	JST Mark 1

14. Bethabara-- Jesus is Baptized

Matt. 3	JST Matt. 3	Mark 1	JST Mark 1
13 ¶ Then cometh Jesus from Galilee to Jordan unto John, to be baptized of him. 14 But John **forbad** him, saying, I have need to be baptized of thee, and comest thou to me? 15 And Jesus answering said unto him, Suffer **it to be so now**: for thus it becometh us to fulfil all righteousness. Then he suffered him.	41 **And** then cometh Jesus from Galilee to Jordan, unto John, to be baptized of him; 42 But John **refused** him, saying, I have need to be baptized of thee, and **why** comest thou to me? 43 And Jesus, answering, said unto him, Suffer **me to be baptized of thee**, for thus it becometh us to fulfill all righteousness. Then he suffered him. 44 **And John went down into the water and baptized him.**	9 And it came to pass in those days, that Jesus came from Nazareth Galilee,	
16 And Jesus, when he was baptized, went up straightway out of the water: and, lo, the heavens were opened unto him, and he saw the Spirit of God descending like a dove, and lighting upon **him**:	45 And Jesus when he was baptized, went up straightway out of the water; **and John saw, and** lo, the heavens were opened unto him, and he saw the Spirit of God descending like a dove and lighting upon **Jesus.**	and was baptized of John in Jordan. 10 And straightway coming up out of the water, he saw the heavens opened, and the Spirit like a dove descending upon him:	
17 And lo a voice from heaven, saying, This is my beloved Son, in whom I am well pleased.	17 And lo, **he heard a** voice from heaven, saying, This is my beloved Son, in whom I am well pleased. **Hear ye him.**	11 And there came a voice from heaven, saying, Thou art my beloved Son, in whom I am well pleased.	9 And there came a voice from heaven, saying, Thou art my beloved Son, in whom I am well pleased. **And John bare record of it.**

TPJS-- There was a legal administrator, and those that were baptized were subjects for a king; and also the laws and oracles of God were there; therefore the kingdom of God was there; for no man could have better authority to administer than John; and our Savior submitted to that authority Himself, by being baptized by John; therefore the kingdom of God was set up on the earth, even in the days of John. (p. 273)

The Savior said unto John, I must be baptized by you. Why so? To fulfil all righteousness. John refuses at first, but afterwards obeyed by administering the ordinance of baptism unto him, Jesus having no other legal administrator to apply to. (p. 319)

The sign of the dove was instituted before the creation of the world, a witness for the Holy Ghost, and the devil cannot come in the sign of a dove. The Holy Ghost is a personage, and is in the form of a personage. It does not confine itself to the *form* of the dove, but in *sign* of the dove. The Holy Ghost cannot be transformed into a dove; but the sign of a dove was given to John to signify the truth of the deed, as the dove is an emblem or token of truth and innocence. (p. 276)

. . .Jesus Christ himself . . . had no need of repentance, having no sin; according to his solemn declaration to John:-- now let me be baptized: for no man can enter the kingdom without obeying this ordinance: for thus it becometh us to fulfil ALL RIGHTEOUSNESS. Surely, then, if it became John and Jesus Christ, the Savior, to fulfil all righteousness to be baptized-- so surely, then, it will become every other person that seeks the kingdom of heaven to go and do likewise;. . .(p. 266)

Luke 3	JST Luke 3	B of M Psalms
		1 Ne. 10:9 And my father said he should baptize in Bethabara, beyond Jordan; and he also said he should baptize with water; even that he should baptize the Messiah with water. 10 And after he had baptized the Messiah with water, he should behold and bear record that he had baptized the Lamb of God, who should take away the sins of the world. (See also 1 Ne. 11: 26-27.) 2 Ne. 31:4 Wherefore, I would that ye should remember that I have spoken unto you concerning that prophet which the Lord showed unto me, that should baptize the Lamb of God, which should take away the sins of the world. 5 And now, if the Lamb of God, he being holy, should have need to be baptized by water, to fulfil all righteousness, O then, how much more need have we, being unholy, to be baptized, yea, even by water!
21 Now when all the people were baptized, it came to pass, that Jesus also being baptized, and praying, the heaven was opened, 22 And the Holy Ghost descended in a bodily shape like a dove upon him, and a voice came from heaven, which said, Thou art my beloved Son; in thee I am well pleased. 23 And Jesus himself began to be about thirty years of age. . .	28 Now when all the people were baptized, it came to pass that Jesus also came unto John; and being baptized of him, and praying, the heaven was opened; 29 And the Holy Ghost descended, in bodily shape like a dove, upon him; and a voice came from heaven, which said, Thou art my beloved Son, in thee I am well pleased.	6 And now, I would ask of you, my beloved brethren, wherein the Lamb of God did fulfil all righteousness in being baptized by water? 7 Know ye not that he was holy? But notwithstanding he being holy, he showeth unto the children of men that, according to the flesh he humbleth himself before the Father, and witnesseth unto the Father that he would be obedient unto him in keeping his commandments. 8 Wherefore, after he was baptized with water the Holy Ghost descended upon him in the form of a dove. 9 And again, it showeth unto the children of men the straitness of the path, and the narrowness of the gate, by which they should enter, he having set the example before them. (See also Morm. 7:10.) Psalm 2:7 I will declare the decree: the LORD hath said unto me, Thou art my Son; this day have I begotten thee. (See also Acts 13:33.)

Matt. 4	JST Matt. 4	Mark 1	JST Mark 1

15. Wilderness of Judea-- Jesus Communes with God-- Temptation

Then was Jesus led up of the Spirit into the wilderness to be **tempted of the devil.**	Then Jesus was led up of the Spirit, into the wilderness, to be **with God.**	12 And immediately the Spirit **driveth** him into the wilderness. 13 And he was there in the wilderness forty days, **tempted of Satan; and was with the wild beasts;**	10 And immediately the Spirit **took** him into the wilderness. 11 And he was there in the wilderness forty days, **Satan seeking to tempt him;** and was with the wild beasts;
2 And when he had fasted forty days and forty nights, he was afterward an hungred.	2 And when he had fasted forty days and forty nights, **and had communed with God,** he was afterwards an hungred, **and was left to be tempted of the devil,**		
3 And when the tempter came to him, he said, If thou be the Son of God, command that these stones be made bread.			
4 But **he** answered and said, It is written, Man shall not live by bread alone, but by every word that proceedeth out of the mouth of God.	4 But **Jesus** answered and said, It is written, Man shall not live by bread alone, but by every word that proceedeth out of the mouth of God.		

TPJS-- Thus we have no new commandment to give, but admonish elders and members to live by every word that proceedeth forth from the mouth of God, lest they come short of the glory that is reserved for the faithful. (p. 306)

5 Then **the devil taketh him** up into the holy city, and setteth him on **a** pinnacle of the temple, 6 **And saith** unto him, If thou be the Son of God, cast thyself down: for it is written, He shall give his angels charge concerning thee: and in their hands they shall bear thee up, lest at any time thou dash thy foot against a stone.	5 Then **Jesus was taken** up into the holy city, and **the Spirit** setteth him on **the** pinnacle of the temple. 6 **Then the devil came unto him and said,** If thou be the Son of God, cast thyself down, for it is written, He shall give his angels charge concerning thee, and in their hands they shall bear thee up, lest at any time thou dash thy foot against a stone.		
7 Jesus said unto him, It is written again, Thou shalt not tempt the Lord thy God.			

Luke 4	JST Luke 4	D & C	Old Testament
And Jesus being full of the Holy Ghost returned from Jordan, and was led by the Spirit into the wilderness, 2 **Being** forty days **tempted of** the devil. And in those days he did eat nothing: and when they were ended, he afterward hungered. 3 And the devil said unto him, If thou be the Son of God, command this stone that it be made bread. 4 And Jesus answered him, saying, It is written, That man shall not live by bread alone, but by every word of God.	2 **And after** forty days, the devil **came unto him, to tempt him.** And in those days, he did eat nothing; and when they were ended, he afterwards hungered.	84:43 And I now give unto you a commandment to beware concerning yourselves, to give diligent heed to the words of eternal life. 44 For ye shall live by every word that proceedeth forth from the mouth of God. 45 For the word of the Lord is truth, and whatsoever is truth is light, and whatsover is light is Spirit, even the Spirit of Jesus Christ. 98:11 And I give unto you a commandment, that ye shall forsake all evil and cleave unto all good, that ye shall live by every word which proceedeth forth out of the mouth of God.	Deut. 8:3 . . . man doth not live by bread only, but by every word that proceedeth out of the mouth of the LORD doth man live.
9 And **he** brought him to Jerusalem, and set him on a pinnacle of the temple, and said unto him, If thou be the Son of God, cast thyself down from hence: 10 For it is written, He shall give his angels charge over thee, to keep thee: 11 And **in their** hands they shall bear thee up, lest at any time thou dash thy foot against a stone. 12 And Jesus answering said unto him, It is **said**, Thou shalt not tempt the Lord thy God.	9 And **the Spirit** brought him to Jerusalem, and set him on a pinnacle of the temple. **And the devil came unto him,** and said unto him, If thou be the Son of God, cast thyself down from hence; 10 For it is written, He shall give his angels charge over thee, to keep thee; and in **his** hands they shall bear thee up, lest at any time thou dash thy foot against a stone. 11 And Jesus answering, said unto him, It is **written,** Thou shalt not tempt the Lord thy God.		Psalm 91:11 For he shall give his angels charge over thee, to keep thee in all thy ways. 12 They shall bear thee up in their hands, lest thou dash thy foot against a stone. Deut. 6:16 ¶ Ye shall not tempt the LORD your God . . .

Matt. 4	JST Matt. 4		
8 Again, **the devil** taketh him up into an exceeding high mountain, and sheweth him all the kingdoms of the world, and the glory of them:	8 **And** again, **Jesus was in the Spirit, and** it taketh him up into an exceeding high mountain, and showeth him all the kingdoms of the world and the glory of them.		
9 And **saith** unto him, All these things will I give thee,	9 And **the devil came** unto him **again, and said**, All these things will I give unto thee,		
if thou wilt fall down and worship me.	if thou wilt fall down and worship me.		
10 Then saith Jesus unto him, Get thee hence, Satan: for it is written, Thou shalt worship the Lord thy God, and him only shalt thou serve.			
11 Then the devil leaveth him,	Part of vs. 10 in the JST.		

Luke 4	JST Luke 4	Deuteronomy	
5 And the **devil, taking** him up into **an** high mountain, **shewed unto him** all the kingdoms of the world in a moment of time.	5 And the **Spirit taketh** him up into a high mountain, **and he beheld** all the kingdoms of the world, in a moment of time.		
6 And the devil said unto him, All this power will I give thee, and the glory of them: for **that is** delivered unto me; and to whomsoever I will I give **it**.	6 And the devil **came unto him, and** said unto him, All this power will I give **unto** thee, and the glory of them; for **they are** delivered unto me, and to whomsoever I will, I give **them**.		
7 If thou therefore wilt worship me, all shall be thine.			
8 **And** Jesus answered and said unto him, Get thee behind me, Satan: for it is written, Thou shalt worship the Lord thy God, and him only shalt thou serve.	8 Jesus answered and said unto him, Get thee behind me, Satan; for it is written, Thou shalt worship the Lord thy God, and him only shalt thou serve.	6:13 Thou shalt fear the LORD thy God, and serve him . . . (See also Exod. 20:3-5, Deut. 5:7-9).	
13 And when the devil had ended all temptation, he departed from him for a season.			

		John 1	JST John 1

16. Bethabara-- John Testifies of Jesus

		John 1	JST John 1
		19 ¶ And this is the record of John, when the Jews sent priests and Levites from Jerusalem to ask him, Who art thou?	
		20 And he confessed, and denied not; but confessed, I am not the Christ.	21 And he confessed, and denied not that he was Elias; but confessed, saying; I am not the Christ.
		21 And they asked him, What then? Art thou Elias? And he saith, I am not.	22 And they asked him, saying; How then art thou Elias? And he said, I am not that Elias who was to restore all things. And they asked him saying, Art thou that prophet? And he answered, No.
		Art thou that prophet? And he answered, No.	
		22 Then said they unto him, Who art thou? that we may give an answer to them that sent us. What sayest thou of thyself?	
		23 He said, I am the voice of one crying in the wilderness, Make straight the way of the Lord, as said the prophet Esaias.	
		24 And they which were sent were of the Pharisees.	25 And they who were sent were of the Pharisees.
		25 And they asked him, and said unto him, Why baptizest thou then, if thou be not that Christ, nor Elias, neither that prophet?	26 And they asked him, and said unto him; Why baptizest thou then, if thou be not the Christ, nor Elias who was to restore all things, neither that prophet?
		26 John answered them, saying, I baptize with water: but there standeth one among you, whom ye know not:	
		27 He it is, who coming after me is preferred before me, whose shoe's latchet I am not worthy to unloose.	28 He it is of whom I bear record. He is that prophet, even Elias, who, coming after me, is preferred before me, whose shoe's latchet I am not worthy to unloose, or whose place I am not able to fill; for he shall baptize, not only with

38

		John 1	JST John 1
			water, but with fire, and with the Holy Ghost. (JST Jn. 1:34)
		28 These things were done in Bethabara beyond Jordan, where John was baptizing.	
		29 ¶ The next day John seeth Jesus coming unto him, and saith, Behold the Lamb of God, **which** taketh away the sin of the world.	29 The next day John seeth Jesus coming unto him, and said; Behold the Lamb of God, **who taketh** away the sin of the world!
		30 This is he of whom I said, After me cometh a man **which** is preferred before me: for he was before me.	30 **And John bare record of him unto the people, saying,** This is he of whom I said; After me cometh a man **who** is preferred before me; for he was before me, and I knew him, **and that** he should be made manifest unto Israel; therefore am I come baptizing with water.
		31 And I knew him **not:** but that he should be made manifest unto Israel, therefore am I come baptizing with water.	
		32 And John bare record, saying, I saw the Spirit descending from heaven like a dove, and it abode upon him.	31 And John bare record, saying; **When he was baptized of me,** I saw the Spirit descending from heaven like a dove, and it abode upon him.
		33 And I knew him **not: but he that** sent me to baptize with water, the same said unto me, Upon whom thou shalt see the Spirit descending, and remaining on him, the same is he **which** baptizeth with the Holy Ghost.	32 And I knew him; **for** he **who** sent me to baptize with water, the same said unto me; Upon whom thou shalt see the Spirit descending, and remaining on him, the same is he **who** baptizeth with the Holy Ghost.
		34 And I saw, and bear record that this is the Son of God.	34 **These things were done in Bethabara, beyond Jordan, where John was baptizing.**

		John 1	JST John 1

17. Galilee-- Disciples Gathered

		John 1	JST John 1
		35 ¶ Again the next day after John stood, and two of his disciples;	
		36 And looking upon Jesus as he walked, he saith, Behold the Lamb of God!	
		37 And the two disciples heard him speak, and they followed Jesus.	
		38 Then Jesus turned, and saw them following, and saith unto them, What seek ye? They said unto him, Rabbi, (which is to say, being interpreted, Master,) where dwellest thou?	38 Then Jesus turned, and saw them following him, and said unto them, What seek ye? They say unto him, Rabbi, (which is to say, being interpreted, Master;) Where dwellest thou?
		39 He saith unto them, Come and see. They came and saw where he dwelt, and abode with him that day: for it was about the tenth hour.	39 He said unto them, Come and see. And they came and saw where he dwelt, and abode with him that day; for it was about the tenth hour.
		40 One of the two which heard John speak, and followed him, was Andrew, Simon Peter's brother.	40 One of the two who heard John, and followed Jesus, was Andrew, Simon Peter's brother.
		41 He first findeth his own brother Simon, and saith unto him, We have found the Messias, which is, being interpreted, the Christ.	
		42 And he brought him to Jesus. And when Jesus beheld him, he said, Thou art Simon the son of Jona: thou shalt be called Cephas, which is by interpretation, A stone.	42 And he brought him to Jesus. And when Jesus beheld him, he said, Thou art Simon, the son of Jona, thou shalt be called Cephas, which is, by interpretation, a seer, or a stone. And they were fishermen. And they straightway left all, and followed Jesus.
		43 ¶ The day following Jesus would go forth into Galilee, and findeth Philip, and saith unto him, Follow me.	
		44 Now Philip was of Bethsaida, the city of Andrew and Peter.	44 Now Philip was at Bethsaida, the city of Andrew and Peter.

	D & C	John 1	JST John 1
		45 Philip findeth Nathanael, and saith unto him, We have found him, of whom Moses in the law, and the prophets, did write, Jesus of Nazareth, the son of Joseph. 46 And Nathanael said unto him, Can there any good thing come out of Nazareth? Philip saith unto him, Come and see. 47 Jesus saw Nathanael coming to him, and saith of him, Behold an Israelite indeed, in whom is no guile!	
	41:11 And this because his (Edward Partridge's) heart is pure before me, for he is like unto Nathanael of old, in whom there is no guile.	48 Nathanael saith unto him, Whence knowest thou me? Jesus **answered and** said unto him, Before **that** Philip called thee, when thou wast under the fig tree, I saw thee. 49 Nathanael answered and saith unto him, Rabbi, thou art the Son of God; thou art the King of Israel. 50 Jesus answered and said unto him, Because I said unto thee, I saw thee under the fig tree, believest thou? thou shalt see greater things than these. 51 And he saith unto him, Verily, verily, I say unto you, Hereafter ye shall see heaven open, and the angels of God ascending and descending upon the Son of man.	48 Nathanael said unto him, Whence knowest thou me? Jesus **answering** said unto him, Before Philip called thee, when thou wast under the fig tree, I saw thee.

John 2	JST John 2	John 2	JST John 2

18 . Cana-- First Recorded Miracle

And the third day there was a marriage in Cana of Galilee; and the mother of Jesus was there:

2 And **both** Jesus was called, and his disciples, to the marriage.

3 And when they wanted wine, **the mother of Jesus** saith unto him, They have no wine.

4 Jesus saith unto her, Woman, what have I to do **with thee?**

mine hour is not yet come.

5 His mother saith unto the servants, Whatsoever he saith unto you, do it.

6 **And** there were set there six waterpots of stone, after the manner of the purifying of the Jews, containing two or three firkins apiece.

7 Jesus saith unto them, Fill the waterpots with water. And they filled them up to the brim.

8 And he saith **unto them,** Draw out now, and bear unto the governor of the feast. And they bear **it.**

9 When the **ruler** of the feast had tasted the water **that** was made wine, **and** knew not whence it was: (but the servants **which** drew the water knew;) the governor of the feast called the bridegroom,

10 And saith unto him, Every man at the beginning doth set forth good wine; and when men have well drunk, then that which is worse: but thou (continued in column 3)

And **on** the third day **of the week,** there was a marriage in Cana of Galilee; and the mother of Jesus was there.

2 And Jesus was called, and his disciples, to the marriage.

3 And when they wanted wine, **his** mother said unto him, They have no wine.

4 Jesus said unto her, Woman, what **wilt thou** have **me** to do **for** thee? **that will I do;** for mine hour is not yet come.

5 His mother said unto the servants, Whatsoever he saith unto you, **see that ye** do it.

6 There were set there six waterpots of stone, after the manner of the purifying of the Jews, containing two or three firkins apiece.

8 And he **said,** Draw out now, and bear unto the governor of the feast. And they bear **unto him.**

9 When the **governor** of the feast had tasted the water **which** was made wine, (he knew not whence it was, but the servants **who** drew the water knew,) the governor of the feast called the bridegroom,

(continued in column 4)

---

hast kept the good wine until now.

11 This beginning of miracles did Jesus in Cana of Galilee, and manifested forth his glory; and his disciples **believed on** him.

12 ¶ After this he went down to Capernaum, he, and his mother, and his brethren, and his disciples: and they continued there not many days.

---

11 This beginning of miracles did Jesus in Cana of Galilee, and manifested forth his glory; and **the faith of** his disciples **was strengthened in** him.

42

John 2	JST John 2	D&C	Psalms

The First Year of Jesus' Ministry -- Early Judean

John 2	JST John 2	D&C	Psalms
13 ¶ And the Jews' passover was at hand, and Jesus went up to Jerusalem,			
14 And found in the temple those **that** sold oxen and sheep and doves, and the changers of money sitting:	14 And found in the temple those **who** sold oxen, and sheep, and doves, and the changers of money sitting.	117:16 And again, verily I say unto you, let all my servants in the land of Kirtland remember the Lord their God, and mine house also, to keep and preserve it holy, and to overthrow the money-changers in mine own due time, saith the Lord. Even so Amen.	
15 And when he had made a scourge of small cords, he drove them all out of the temple, and the sheep, and the oxen; and poured out the changers' money, and overthrew the tables;			
16 And said unto them **that** sold doves, Take these things hence; make not my Father's house **an** house of merchandise.	16 And said unto them **who** sold doves, Take these things hence; make not my Father's house a house of merchandise.		
17 And his disciples remembered that it was written, The zeal of **thine** house hath eaten me up.	17 And his disciples remembered that it was written, The zeal of **thy** house hath eaten me up.	69:9 For the zeal of thine house hath eaten me up; and the reproaches of them that reproached thee are fallen upon me.	
18 ¶ Then **answered** the Jews and said unto him, What sign shewest thou unto us, seeing **that** thou doest these things?	18 Then **spake** the Jews and said unto him, What sign showest thou unto us, seeing thou doest these things?		
19 Jesus answered and said unto them, Destroy this temple, and in three days I will raise it up.			
20 Then said the Jews, Forty and six years was this temple in the building, and wilt thou rear it up in three days?			
21 But he spake of the temple of his body.			

		John 2	JST John 2

John 2	JST John 2	John 2	JST John 2
22 When therefore he was risen from the dead, his disciples remembered that he had said this unto them; and they **believed** the scripture, and the word which Jesus had said.	22 When therefore he was risen from the dead, his disciples remembered that he had said this unto them, and they **remembered** the Scripture, and the word which Jesus had said **unto them.**	23 ¶ Now when he was in Jerusalem at the passover, **in** the feast day, many believed **in** his name, when they saw the miracles which he did.	23 Now when he was in Jerusalem, at the passover, **on** the feast day, many believed **on** his name, when they saw the miracles which he did.
		24 But Jesus did not commit himself unto them, because he knew all **men,**	24 But Jesus did not commit himself unto them, because he knew all **things,**
		25 And needed not that any should testify of man: for he knew what was in man.	
(continued in column 3)	(continued in column 4)		

43

		John 3	JST John 3

19. Nicodemus the Pharisee Comes to Jesus

	John 3	JST John 3
	There was a man of the Pharisees, named Nicodemus, a ruler of the Jews:	
	2 The same came to Jesus by night, and said unto him, Rabbi, we know that thou art a teacher come from God: for no man can do these miracles **that** thou doest, except God be with him.	2 The same came to Jesus by night, and said unto him, Rabbi, we know that thou art a teacher come from God; for no man can do these miracles **which** thou doest, except God be with him.
	3 Jesus answered and said unto him, Verily, verily, I say unto thee, Except a man be born again, he cannot see the kingdom of God.	
	4 Nicodemus saith unto him, How can a man be born when he is old? can he enter the second time into his mother's womb, and be born?	
	5 Jesus answered, Verily, verily, I say unto thee, Except a man be born of water and **of** the Spirit, he cannot enter into the kingdom of God.	5 Jesus answered, Verily, verily, I say unto thee, Except a man be born of water, and the Spirit, he cannot enter into the kingdom of God.

TPJS-- But except a man be born again, he cannot see the kingdom of God. This eternal truth settles the question of all men's religion. A man may be saved, after the judgment, in the terrestrial kingdom, or in the telestial kingdom, but he can never see the celestial kingdom of God, without being born of water and the Spirit. (p. 12)

Being born again, comes by the Spirit of God through ordinances. (p. 162)

. . . I contend that baptism is a sign ordained of God, for the believer in Christ to take upon himself in order to enter into the kingdom of God, "for except ye are born of water and of the Spirit ye cannot enter into the Kingdom of God," said the Savior. It is a sign and a commandment which God has set for man to enter into His kingdom. Those who seek to enter in any other way will seek in vain; for God will not receive them, neither will the angels acknowledge their works as accepted, for they have not obeyed the ordinances, nor attended to the signs which God ordained for the salvation of man, to prepare him for, and give him a title to, a celestial glory; and God had decreed that all who will not obey His voice shall not escape the damnation of hell. What is the damnation of hell? To go with that society who have not obeyed His commands. (p. 198)

Again he says, "Except a man be born of water and of the Spirit, he cannot enter into the kingdom of God;" and, "heaven and earth shall pass away, but my words shall not pass away." If a man is born of water and of the Spirit, he can get into the kingdom of God. It is evident the kingdom of God was on the earth, and John prepared subjects for the kingdom, by preaching the Gospel to them and baptizing them, and he prepared the way before the Savior, or came as a forerunner, and prepared subjects for the preaching of Christ; and Christ preached through Jerusalem on the same ground where John had preached;. . .(p. 274)

	D & C	John 3	JST John 3

TPJS-- It is one thing to see the kingdom of God, and another thing to enter into it. We must have a change of heart to see the kingdom of God, and suscribe the articles of adoption to enter therein. (p. 328)

	D & C	John 3	JST John 3
		6 That which is born of the flesh is flesh; and that which is born of the Spirit is spirit.	
		7 Marvel not that I said unto thee, Ye must be born again.	
		8 The wind bloweth where it listeth, and thou hearest the sound thereof, but canst not tell whence it cometh, and whither it goeth: so is every one **that** is born of the Spirit.	8 The wind bloweth where it listeth, and thou hearest the sound thereof, but canst not tell whence it cometh, and whither it goeth: so is everyone **who** is born of the Spirit.
		9 Nicodemus answered and said unto him, How can these things be?	
		10 Jesus answered and said **unto him,** Art thou a master of Israel, and knowest not these things?	10 Jesus answered and said, Art thou a master of Israel, and knowest not these things?
		11 Verily, verily, I say unto thee, We speak that we do know, and testify that we have seen; and ye receive not our witness.	
		12 If I have told you earthly things, and ye believe not, how shall ye believe, if I tell you **of** heavenly things?	12 If I have told you earthly things, and ye believe not, how shall ye believe if I tell you heavenly things?
		13 **And** no man hath ascended up to heaven, but he **that** came down from heaven, **even the Son of man which** is in heaven.	13 **I tell you,** No man hath ascended up to heaven, but he **who** came down from heaven, the Son of Man **who** is in heaven.
		14 ¶ And as Moses lifted up the serpent in the wilderness, even so must the Son of man be lifted up:	
		15 That whosoever believeth **in** him should not perish, but have eternal life.	15 That whosoever believeth **on** him should not perish, but have eternal life.
	34:3 Who (Christ) so loved the world that he gave his own life, that as many as would believe might become the sons of God. Wherefore you are my son; (See also D&C 49:5.)	16 ¶ For God so loved the world, that he gave his only begotten Son, that whosoever believeth **in** him should not perish, but have everlasting life.	16 For God so loved the world, that he gave his Only Begotten Son, that whosoever believeth **on** him should not perish; but have **eternal** life.
		17 For God sent not his Son into the world to	

		John 3	JST John 3
		condemn the world; but that the world through him might be saved.	
		18 ¶ He **that** believeth on him is not condemned: but he **that** believeth not is condemned already, because he hath not believed **in** the name of the **only** begotten Son of God.	18 He **who** believeth on him is not condemned; but he **who** believeth not is condemned already, because he hath not believed **on** the name of the **Only Begotten** Son of God, **which before was preached by the mouth of the holy prophets; for they testified of me.**
		19 And this is the condemnation, that light is come into the world, and men **loved** darkness rather than light, because their deeds **were** evil.	19 And this is the condemnation, that light is come into the world, and men **love** darkness rather than light, because their deeds **are** evil.
		20 For every one **that** doeth evil hateth the light, neither cometh to the light, lest his deeds should be reproved.	20 For every one **who** doeth evil hateth the light, neither cometh to the light, lest his deeds should be reproved.
		21 But **he that doeth** truth cometh to the light, that his deeds may be manifest,	21 But he **who loveth** truth, cometh to the light, that his deeds may be manifest.
			22 And **he who obeyeth the truth, the works which he doeth** they are of God.
		that they are **wrought in** God.	

Early Judean Ministry -- Baptisms in Judea

		John 3	JST John 3
		22 ¶ After these things came Jesus and his disciples into the land of Judæa; and there he tarried with them, and baptized.	
		23 ¶ And John also was baptizing in Ænon near to Salim, because there was much water there: and they came, and were baptized.	
		24 For John was not yet cast into prison.	
		25 ¶ Then there arose a question between some of John's disciples and the Jews about purifying.	
		26 And they came unto John, and said unto him, Rabbi, he **that** was with	27 And they came unto John, and said unto him, Rabbi, he **who** was with

		John 3	JST John 3
		thee beyond Jordan, to whom thou barest witness, behold, the same baptizeth, and all men come to him.	thee beyond Jordan, to whom thou bearest witness, behold, the same baptizeth, and **he receiveth of all people who** come unto him.
		27 John answered and said, A man can receive nothing, except it be given him from heaven.	
		28 Ye yourselves bear me witness, that I said, I am not the Christ, but that I am sent before him.	
		29 He **that** hath the bride is the bridegroom: but the friend of the bridegroom, **which** standeth and heareth him, rejoiceth greatly because of the bridegroom's voice: this my joy therefore is fulfilled.	30 He **who** hath the bride, is the bridegroom; but the friend of the bridegroom, **who** standeth and heareth him, rejoiceth greatly because of the bridegroom's voice; this my joy therefore is fufilled.
		30 He must increase, but I must decrease.	
		31 He **that** cometh from above is above all: he **that** is of the earth is earthly, and speaketh of the earth: he **that** cometh from heaven is above all.	32 He **who** cometh from above is above all; he **who** is of the earth is earthly, and speaketh of the earth; he **who** cometh from heaven is above all. And
		32 And what he hath seen and heard, that he testifieth; and **no man receiveth** his testimony.	what he hath seen and heard, that he testifieth; and **but few men receive** his testimony.
		33 He **that** hath received his testimony hath set to his seal that God is true.	33 He **who** hath received his testimony, hath set to his seal that God is true.
		34 For he whom God hath sent speaketh the words of God: for God giveth not the Spirit by measure **unto him.**	34 For he whom God hath sent, speaketh the words of God; for God giveth **him** not the Spirit by measure, **for he dwelleth in him, even the fulness.**
		35 The Father loveth the Son, and hath given all things into his hand.	
		36 He **that** believeth on the Son hath everlasting life: **and he that** believeth not the Son shall not see **life; but** the wrath of God **abideth** on him.	36 And he **who** believeth on the Son hath everlasting life; **and shall receive of his fulness. But he who** believeth not the Son, shall not **receive of his fulness; for** the wrath of God **is upon him.**

Matt. 14		Mark 6	JST Mark 6

20. Jerusalem-- John is Imprisoned

Matt. 14		Mark 6	JST Mark 6
3 ¶ For Herod had laid hold on John, and bound him, and put him in prison for Herodias' sake, his brother Philip's wife.		17 For Herod himself had sent forth and laid hold upon John, and bound him in prison for Herodias' sake, his brother Philip's wife: for he had married her.	
4 For John said unto him, It is not lawful for thee to have her.		18 For John had said unto Herod, It is not lawful for thee to have thy brother's wife.	
5 And when he would have put him to death, he feared the multitude, because they counted him as a prophet.		19 Therefore Herodias had a quarrel against him, and would have killed him; but she could not:	
		20 For Herod feared John, knowing that he was a just man and an holy,	21 For Herod feared John, knowing that he was a just man, and a holy **man**, **and one who feared God** and observed to **worship** him; and when he heard him he did many things **for him**, and heard him gladly.
		and observed him; and when he heard him, he did many things, and heard him gladly.	

Matt. 4	JST Matt. 4	Mark 1	

21. Departs for Galilee

Matt. 4	JST Matt. 4	Mark 1	
11 cont. and, behold, angels came and ministered unto him.		13 cont. and the angels ministered unto him.	
12 ¶ Now **when** Jesus **had heard** that John was cast into prison,	11 **And** now Jesus **knew** that John was cast into prison, **and he sent angels, and, behold, they came and ministered unto him.**	14 Now after that John was put in prison,	
he departed into Galilee;	12 **And Jesus** departed into Galilee,	Jesus came into Galilee, preaching the gospel of the kingdom of God,	

Luke 3	JST Luke 3		

| 19 But Herod the te-trarch, being reproved by him for Herodias his brother Philip's wife, and for all the evils which Herod had done,
20 Added yet this above all, that he shut up John in prison. | 26 But Herod, the te-trarch, being reproved of him for Herodias, his brother Philip's wife, and for all the evils which Herod had done; | | |

Luke 4		John 4	JST John 4

| | | When therefore **the Lord knew how** the Pharisees had heard that Jesus made and baptized more dis-ciples than John, | When therefore the Phari-sees had heard that Jesus made and baptized more disciples than John,

2 They sought the more diligently some means that they might put him to death; for many re-ceived John as a prophet, but they believed not on Jesus.
3 Now the Lord knew this, though he himself baptized not so many as his disciples;
4 For he suffered them for an example, prefer-ring one another. |
| | | 2 (Though **Jesus** himself baptized not, but his dis-ciples,) | |

49

		John 4	JST John 4

22. Samaria--The Woman at Jacob's Well

John 4	JST John 4
4 And he must needs go through Samaria.	6 And said unto his disciples, I must needs go through Samaria.
5 Then cometh he to a city of Samaria, which is called Sychar, near the parcel of ground that Jacob gave to his son Joseph.	7 Then he cometh to the city of Samaria which is called Sychar, near to the parcel of ground which Jacob gave to his son Joseph;
6 Now Jacob's well was there. Jesus therefore, being wearied with his journey, sat thus on the well: and it was about the sixth hour.	the place where Jacob's well was. 8 Now Jesus being weary with his journey, it being about the sixth hour, sat down on the well;
7 There cometh a woman of Samaria to draw water: Jesus saith unto her, Give me to drink.	9 And there came a woman of Samaria to draw water; Jesus said unto her, Give me to drink.
8 (For his disciples were gone away unto the city to buy meat.)	10 Now his disciples were gone away into the city to buy meat.
9 Then saith the woman of Samaria unto him, How is it that thou, being a Jew, askest drink of me, which am a woman of Samaria? for the Jews have no dealings with the Samaritans.	11 Wherefore he being alone, the woman of Samaria said unto him, How is it that thou being a Jew, askest drink of me, who am a woman of Samaria? The Jews have no dealings with the Samaritans.
10 Jesus answered and said unto her, If thou knewest the gift of God, and who it is that saith to thee, Give me to drink; thou wouldest have asked of him, and he would have given thee living water.	
11 The woman saith unto him, Sir, thou hast nothing to draw with, and the well is deep: from whence then hast thou that living water?	
12 Art thou greater than our father Jacob, which gave us the well, and drank thereof himself, and his children, and his cattle?	14 Art thou greater than our father Jacob, who gave us the well, and drank therof himself, and his children, and his cattle?
13 Jesus answered and said unto her, Whosoever drinketh of this water	15 Jesus answered and said unto her, Whosoever shall drink of this well,

50

	D & C	John 4	JST John 4
		shall thirst again:	shall thirst again;
	63:23 But unto him that keepeth my commandments I will give the mysteries of my kingdom, and the same shall be in him a well of living water, springing up unto everlasting life.	14 But whosoever drinketh of the water that I shall give him shall never thirst; but the water that I shall give him shall be in him a well of water springing up into everlasting life.	
		15 The woman saith unto him, Sir, give me this water, that I thirst not, neither come hither to draw.	17 The woman said unto him, Sir, give me of this water that I thirst not, neither come hither to draw.
		16 Jesus saith unto her, Go, call thy husband, and come hither.	
		17 The woman answered and said, I have no husband. Jesus said unto her, Thou hast well said, I have no husband:	
		18 For thou hast had five husbands; and he whom thou now hast is not thy husband: in that saidst thou truly.	
		19 The woman said unto him, Sir, I perceive that thou art a prophet.	
		20 Our fathers worshipped in this mountain; and ye say, that in Jerusalem is the place where men ought to worship.	
		21 Jesus saith unto her, Woman, believe me, the hour cometh, when ye shall neither in this mountain, nor yet at Jerusalem, worship the Father.	
		22 Ye worship ye know not what: we know what we worship: for salvation is of the Jews.	24 Ye worship ye know not what; we know what we worship; and salvation is of the Jews.
		23 But the hour cometh, and now is, when the true worshippers shall worship the Father in spirit and in truth: for the Father seeketh such to worship him.	25 And the hour cometh, and now is, when the true worshippers shall worship the Father in spirit and in truth; for the Father seeketh such to worship him.
		24 God is a Spirit: and they that worship him must worship him in spirit and in truth.	26 For unto such hath God promised his Spirit. And they who worship him, must worship in spirit and in truth.

B of M	D & C	John 4	JST John 4
		25 The woman **saith** unto him, I know that Messias cometh, **which** is called Christ: when he is come, he will tell us all things.	27 The woman **said** unto him, I know that Messias cometh, **who** is called Christ; when he is come, he will tell us all things.
		26 Jesus saith unto her, I **that** speak unto thee am **he.**	28 Jesus said unto her, I **who** speak unto thee am **the Messias.**
		27 ¶ And upon this came his disciples, and marvelled that he talked with the woman: yet no man said. What seekest thou? or, Why talkest thou with her?	
		28 The woman then left her waterpot, and went her way into the city, and saith to the men,	
		29 Come, see a man, **which** told me all things that ever **I did**: is not this the Christ?	31 Come see a man **who** told me all things that **I have** ever **done**. Is not this the Christ?
Jacob 5:17-18 And it came to pass that the Lord of the vineyard looked and beheld the tree in the which the wild olive branches had been grafted; and it had sprung forth and begun to bear fruit. And he beheld that it was good; and the fruit thereof was like unto the natural fruit.		30 Then they went out of the city, and came unto him.	
18 And he said unto the servant: Behold, the branches of the wild tree have taken hold of the moisture of the root thereof, that the root thereof hath brought forth much strength; and because of the much strength of the root thereof the wild branches have brought forth tame fruit. Now, if we had not grafted in these branches, the tree thereof would have perished. And now, behold, I shall lay up much fruit, which the tree thereof hath brought forth; and the fruit thereof I shall lay up against the season, unto mine own self.		31 ¶ In the mean **while** his disciples prayed him, say-ing, Master, eat.	33 In the mean **time** his disciples prayed him, saying, Master, eat.
		32 But he said unto them, I have meat to eat that ye know not of.	
		33 Therefore said the disciples one to another, Hath any man brought him **ought** to eat?	35 Therefore said the disciples one to another, Hath any man brought him **meat** to eat?
		34 Jesus **saith** unto them, My meat is to do the will of him **that** sent me, and to finish his work	36 Jesus **said** unto them, My meat is to do the will of him **who** sent me, and to finish his work.
	6:3 Behold, the field is white already to harvest; therefore, whoso desireth to reap, let him thrust in his sickle with his might, and reap while the day lasts, that he may treasure up for his soul everlasting salvation in the kingdom of God. (See also D&C 4:3; 11:3; 12:3; 14:3; 33:3, 7.)	35 Say not ye. There are yet four months **and** then cometh the harvest? behold, I say unto you, Lift up your eyes, and look on the fields; for they are white already to harvest.	37 Say not ye there are yet four months, then cometh the harvest? Behold, I say unto you, Lift up your eyes, and look on the fields; for they are white already to harvest.
		36 And he **that** reapeth receiveth wages, and gathereth fruit unto life eternal: that both he **that** soweth and he **that** reapeth may rejoice together.	38 And he **who** reapeth, receiveth wages, and gathereth fruit unto life eternal; that both he **who** soweth, and he **who** reapeth, may rejoice together.
		37 And herein is that saying true. One soweth, and another reapeth.	

		John 4	JST John 4
		38 I sent you to reap that whereon ye bestowed no labour: **other men laboured**, and ye **are** entered into their labours.	40 I **have** sent you to reap that whereon ye bestowed no labor; **the prophets have labored**, and ye **have** entered into their labors.
		39 ¶ And many of the Samaritans of that city believed on him for the saying of the woman, **which** testified, He told me all that ever **I did**.	41 And many of the Samaritans of that city believed on him for the saying of the woman, **who** testified, saying, He told me all that **I have** ever **done**.
		40 So when the Samaritans were come unto him, they besought him that he would tarry with them: and he abode there two days.	
		41 And many more believed because of his own word.	
		42 And said unto the woman, Now we believe, not because of thy saying: **for** we have heard **him** ourselves, and know that this is indeed the Christ, the Saviour of the world.	44 And said unto the woman, Now we believe, not because of thy saying; we have heard for ourselves, and know that this is indeed the Christ, the Savior of the world.

Luke 4	JST Luke 4	John 4	JST John 4

The Great Galilean Ministry

Luke 4	JST Luke 4	John 4	JST John 4
		43 ¶ Now after two days he departed thence, and went into Galilee.	
		44 For Jesus himself testified, that a prophet hath no honour in his own country.	
		45 Then when he **was** come into Galilee, the **Galilæans** received him, having seen all the things **that** he did at Jerusalem at the feast: for they also went unto the feast.	47 Then when he **had** come into Galilee, the Galileans received him, having seen all the things **which** he did at Jerusalem at the feast; for they also went unto the feast.
15 And he taught in their synagogues, being glorified of all.	15 And he taught in their synagogues, being glorified of all **who believed on his name**.		

John 4	JST John 4	John 4	JST John 4

23. Cana--Heals Nobleman's Son

John 4	JST John 4	John 4	JST John 4
46 So Jesus came again into Cana of Galilee, where he made the water wine. And there was a certain nobleman, whose son was sick at Capernaum. 47 When he heard that Jesus was come out of Judæa into Galilee, he went unto him, and besought him that he would come down, and heal his son: for he was at the point of death. 48 Then said Jesus unto him, Except ye see signs and wonders, ye will not believe. 49 The nobleman saith unto him, Sir, come down ere my child die. 50 Jesus saith unto him, Go thy way; thy son liveth. And the man believed the word that Jesus had (continued in column 3)	51 The nobleman said unto him, Sir, come down before my child die. 52 Jesus said unto him, Go thy way, thy son liveth. And the man believed the word which Jesus had (continued in column 4)	spoken unto him, and he went his way. 51 And as he was now going down, his servants met him, and told him, saying, Thy son liveth. 52 Then enquired he of them the hour when he began to amend. And they said unto him, Yesterday at the seventh hour the fever left him. 53 So the father knew that it was at the same hour, in the which Jesus said unto him, Thy son liveth: and himself believed, and his whole house. 54 This is again the second miracle that Jesus did, when he was come out of Judæa into Galilee.	spoken unto him, and he went his way. 53 And as he was now going down to his house, his servants met him, and spake, saying, Thy son liveth. 54 Then enquired he of them the hour when he began to mend. And they said unto him, Yesterday at the seventh hour the fever left him. 55 So the father knew that his son was healed in the same hour in the which Jesus said unto him, Thy son liveth; and himself believed, and his whole house; 56 This being the second miracle which Jesus had done, when he had come out of Judea into Galilee.

Luke 4	JST Luke 4	Isaiah	TPJS

24. Nazareth--Jesus Rejected

Luke 4	JST Luke 4	Isaiah	TPJS
16 ¶ And he came to Nazareth, where he had been brought up: and, as his custom was, he went into the synagogue on the sabbath day, and stood up for to read. 17 And there was delivered unto him the book of the prophet Esaias. And when he had opened the book, he found the place where it was written, 18 The Spirit of the Lord is upon me, because he hath annointed me to preach the gospel to the poor; he hath sent me to heal the brokenhearted, to preach deliverance to the	16 And he came to Nazareth, where he had been brought up; and as his custom was he went into the synagogue on the Sabbath day, and stood up to read. 18 The Spirit of the Lord is upon me, because he hath annointed me to preach the gospel to the poor, he hath sent me to heal the broken-hearted, to preach deliverance to the	42:7 To open the blind eyes, to bring out the prisoners from the prison, and them that sit in darkness out of the prison house.	It is very evident from this that He not only went to preach to them, but to deliver, or bring them out of the prison house. (p. 219)

Luke 4	JST Luke 4	Luke 4	Isaiah
captives, and recovering of sight to the blind, to set at liberty them that are bruised,	captives, and **the** recovering of sight to the blind; to set at liberty them that are bruised;		61:1 The Spirit of the Lord GOD is upon me; because the LORD hath anointed me to teach good tidings unto the meek; he hath sent me to bind up the brokenhearted, to proclaim liberty to the captives, and the opening of the prison to them that are bound;
19 To preach the acceptable year of the Lord.			
20 And he closed the book, and he gave it again to the minister, and sat down. And the eyes of all **them that** were in the synagogue were fastened on him.	20 And he closed the book, and he gave it again to the minister, and **he** sat down. And the eyes of all **those who** were in the synagogue were fastened on him.		2 To proclaim the acceptable year of the LORD, and the day of vengeance of our God; to comfort all that mourn;
21 And he began to say unto them, This day is this scripture fulfilled in your ears.			3 To appoint unto them that mourn in Zion, to give unto them beauty for ashes, the oil of joy for mourning, the garment of praise for the spirit of heaviness; that they might be called trees of righteousness, the planting of the LORD, that he might be glorified.
22 And all bare him witness, and wondered at the gracious words which proceeded out of his mouth. And they said, Is this not Joseph's son?			
23 And he said unto them, Ye will surely say unto me this proverb, Physician, heal thyself; whatsoever we have heard done in Capernaum, do also here in thy country.	23 And he said unto them, Ye will surely say unto me this proverb, Physician, heal thyself. Whatsoever we have heard **was** done in Capernaum, do also here in thy country.		
24 And he said, Verily I say unto you, No prophet is accepted in his own country.			
25 But I tell you **of a** truth, many widows were in Israel in the days of Elias, when the heaven was shut up three years and six months, **when** great famine was throughout all the land;	25 But I tell you **the truth,** many widows were in Israel in the days of Elias, when the heaven was shut up three years and six months, **and** great famine was throughout all the land;		
26 But unto none of them was Elias sent, save unto Sarepta, **a city** of Sidon, unto a woman **that** was a widow.	26 But unto none of them was Elias sent, save unto Sarepta, of Sidon, unto a woman **who** was a widow.	28 And all they in the synagogue, when they heard these things, were filled with wrath,	
27 And many lepers were in Israel in the time of Eliseus the prophet; and none of them **was** cleansed, **saving** Naaman the Syrian.	27 And many lepers were in Israel in the time of Eliseus the prophet; and none of them **were** cleansed, **save** Naaman the Syrian.	29 And rose up, and thrust him out of the city, and led him unto the brow of the hill whereon their city was built, that they might cast him down headlong.	
(continued in column 3)		30 But he passing through the midst of them went his way,	

55

Matt. 4	JST Matt. 4	Mark 1	JST Mark 1

25. Capernaum--Jesus Dwells and Declares the Kingdom

Matt. 4	JST Matt. 4	Mark 1	JST Mark 1
13 And leaving Nazareth, he came and dwelt in Capernaum, which was upon the sea coast, in the borders of **Zabulon and Nephthalim:**	12b and leaving Nazareth, **in Zebulun,** he came and dwelt in Capernaum, which was upon the sea-coast, in the borders of Nephthalim,		
14 That it might be fulfilled which was spoken by Esaias the prophet, saying,			
15 The land of Zabulon and the land of Nephthalim, **by** the way of the sea, beyond Jordan, Galilee of the Gentiles;	14 The land of Zebulun and the land of Nephthalim, **in** the way of the sea, beyond Jordan, Galilee of the Gentiles;		
16 The people which sat in darkness saw great light; and to them **which** sat in the region and shadow of death light is sprung up.	15 The people which sat in darkness saw **a** great light; and **unto** them **that** sat in the region and shadow of death light is sprung up.		
17 From that time Jesus began to preach, and to say, Repent: for the kingdom of heaven is at hand.		15 And saying, The time is fulfilled, and the kingdom of God is at hand: repent ye, and believe the gospel.	

26. Sea of Galilee--Calls Andrew, James and John

Matt. 4	JST Matt. 4	Mark 1	JST Mark 1
18 And Jesus, walking by the sea of Galilee, saw two brethren, Simon called Peter, and Andrew his brother, casting a net into the sea: for they were fishers.		16 Now as he walked by the sea of Galilee, he saw Simon and Andrew his brother casting a net into the sea: for they were fishers.	14 **And now** as he walked by the sea of Galilee, he saw Simon and Andrew his brother casting a net into the sea: for they were fishers.

56

Luke 5	JST Luke 5	Isaiah	
		9:1 Nevertheless the dimness shall not be such as was in her vexation, when at the first he lightly afflicted the land of Zebulun and the land of Naphtali, and afterward did more grievously afflict her by the way of the sea, beyond Jordan, in Galilee of the nations. 2 The people that walked in darkness have seen a great light: they that dwell in the land of the shadow of death, upon them hath the light shined.	
And it came to pass, **that,** as the people pressed upon him to hear the word of God, he stood by the Gennesaret, 2 And saw two ships standing **by** the lake: but the fishermen were gone out of them, and were **washing** their nets. 3 And he entered into one of the ships, which was Simon's, and prayed him that he would thrust out a little from the land. And he sat down, and taught the people out of the ship.	And it came to pass, as the people pressed upon him to hear the word of God, he stood by the Gennesaret, 2 And saw two ships standing **on** the lake; but the fishermen were gone out of them, and were **wetting** their nets.		

57

Matt. 4	JST Matt. 4	Mark 1	JST Mark 1
19 And he saith unto them, Follow me, and I will make you fishers of men. 20 And they **straightway** left their nets, and followed him. 21 And going on from thence, he saw other two brethren, James **the son of Zebedee,** and John his brother, in a ship with Zebedee their father, mending their nets; and he called them. 22 And they immediately left the ship **and their father,** and followed him.	18 And he said unto them, **I am he, of whom it is written by the prophets;** follow me, and I will make you fishers of men. 19 And they, **believing on his words,** left their nets, and **straightway** followed him. 20 And going on from thence, he saw other two brethren, James, and John his brother, **the sons of Zebedee,** in a ship with Zebedee their father, mending their net; and he called them. 21 And they immediately left **their father in the** ship, and followed him.	17 And Jesus said unto them, Come ye after me, and I will make you to become fishers of men. 18 And straightway they forsook their nets, and followed him. 19 And when he had gone a little further thence, he saw James the son of Zebedee, and John his brother, who were also in the ship mending their nets. 20 And **straightway** he called them: and they left their father Zebedee in the ship with the hired servants, and went after him.	18 And he called them; and **straightway** they left their father Zebedee in the ship with the hired servants, and went after him.

Luke 5	JST Luke 5		
4 Now when he had **left** speaking, he said **unto** Simon, Launch out into the deep, and let down your nets for a draught.	4 Now, when he had **done** speaking, he said to Simon, Launch out into the deep, and let down your net for a draught.		
5 And Simon answering said unto him, Master, we have toiled all the night, and have taken nothing: nevertheless at thy word I will let down the net.			
6 And when they had **this done,** they inclosed a great multitude of fishes: and their net brake.	6 And when they had **done this,** they enclosed a great multitude of fishes; and their net brake.		
7 And they beckoned unto their partners, **which** were in the other ship, that they should come and help them. And they came, and filled both the ships, so that they began to sink.	7 And they beckoned unto their partners, **who** were in the other ship, that they should come and help them. And they came and filled both the ships, so that they began to sink.		
8 When Simon Peter saw **it,** he fell down at Jesus' knees, saying, Depart from me; for I am a sinful man, O Lord.	8 When Simon Peter saw **the multitude of fishes,** he fell down at Jesus' knees, saying, Depart from me; for I am a sinful man, O Lord.		
9 For he was astonished, and all **that** were with him, at the draught of the fishes which they had taken:	9 For he was astonished, and all **who** were with him, at the draught of the fishes which they had taken.		
10 And so **was** also James, and John, the sons of Zebedee, **which** were partners with Simon. And Jesus said unto Simon, Fear not; from henceforth thou shalt catch men.	10 And so **were** also James, and John, the sons of Zebedee, **who** were partners with Simon. And Jesus said unto Simon, Fear not from henceforth, **for** thou shalt catch men.		
11 And when they had brought their ships to land, they forsook all, and followed him.			

27. Capernaum--An Unclean Spirit Cast Out

21 And they went into Capernaum; and straightway on the sabbath day he entered into the synagogue, and taught.

22 And they were astonished at his doctrine: for he taught them as one that had authority, and not as the scribes.

23 And there was in their synagogue a man with an unclean spirit; and he cried out,

24 Saying, Let us alone; what have we to do with thee, thou Jesus of Nazareth? art thou come to destroy us? I know thee who thou art, the Holy One of God.

25 And Jesus rebuked him, saying, Hold thy peace, and come out of him.

26 And when the unclean spirit had torn him, and cried with a loud voice, he came out of him.

27 And they were all amazed, insomuch that they questioned among themselves, saying, What thing is this? what new doctrine is this? for with authority commandeth he even the unclean spirits, and they do obey him.

28 And immediately his fame spread abroad throughout all the region round about Galilee.

Luke 4	JST Luke 4		
31 And came down to Capernaum, a city of Galilee, and taught them on the sabbath days.			
32 And they were astonished at his doctrine: for his word **was with** power.	32 And they were astonished at his doctrine; for his words **were with** power.		
33 ¶ And in the synagogue there was a man, **which** had a spirit of an unclean devil, and cried out with a loud voice,	33 And in the synagogue there was a man **who** had a spirit of an unclean devil, and he cried out with a loud voice,		
34 Saying, Let us alone; what have we to do with thee, **thou** Jesus of Nazareth? art thou come to destroy us? I know thee who thou art, the Holy One of God.	34 Saying, Let us alone; what have we to do with thee, Jesus of Nazareth? Art thou come to destroy us? I know thee, who thou art, The Holy One of God.		
35 **And** Jesus rebuked him, saying, Hold thy peace, and come out of him. And when the devil had thrown him in the midst, he came out of him, and hurt him not.	35 Jesus rebuked him, saying, Hold thy peace, and come out of him. And when the devil had thrown him in the midst, he came out of him, and hurt him not.		
36 And they were all amazed, and spake among themselves, saying, What a word is this! for with authority and power he commandeth the unclean spirits, and they come out.			
37 And the fame of him went out **into** every place **of the country** round about.	37 And the fame of him went out **in** every place round about.		

Matt. 8	JST Matt. 8	Mark 1	JST Mark 1

28. Peter's Mother-in-Law Healed

Matt. 8	JST Matt. 8	Mark 1	JST Mark 1
		29 And forthwith, when they were come out of the synagogue, they entered into the house of Simon and Andrew, with James and John.	
14 ¶ And when Jesus was come into Peter's house, he saw his wife's mother laid, and sick of a fever.		30 **But** Simon's wife's mother lay sick of a fever, and **anon they tell him of** her.	27 **And** Simon's wife's mother lay sick of a fever; and they besought him for her.
15 And he touched her hand, and the fever left her: and she arose, and ministered unto them.		31 And he came and took her by the hand, and lifted her up; and immediately the fever left her, and she ministered unto them.	28 And he came and took her by the hand, and lifted her up; and immediately the fever left her, and she **came and** ministered unto them.
16 ¶ When the even was come, they brought unto him many that were possessed with devils: and he cast out the spirits with **his** word, and healed all that were sick:	16 Now when the evening was come, they brought unto him many that were possessed with devils; and he cast out the **evil** spirits with **the** word, and healed all that were sick.	32 And at even, **when the sun did set,** they brought unto him all that were diseased, and them that were possessed with devils.	29 And at evening **after** sunset, they brought unto him all that were diseased, and them that were possessed with devils;
		33 And all the city was gathered together at the door.	and all the city was gathered together at the door.
		34 And he healed many that were sick of divers diseases, and cast out many devils; and suffered not the devils to speak, because they knew him.	
17 That it might be fulfilled which was spoken by Esias the prophet, saying, Himself took our infirmities, and bare our sicknesses.			

29. Galilee--Preaches and Heals

Matt. 8	JST Matt. 8	Mark 1	JST Mark 1
		35 And in the morning, rising up a great while before day, he went out, and departed into a solitary place, and there prayed.	
		36 And Simon and they that were with him followed after him.	

Luke 4	JST Luke 4	Isaiah	
38 And he arose out of the synagogue, and entered into Simon's house. And Simon's wife's mother was taken with a great fever; and they besought him for her.	38 And he arose, **and went** out of the synagogue, and entered into Simon's house. And Simon's wife's mother was taken with a great fever; and they besought him for **to heal** her.		
39 And he stood over her, and rebuked the fever; and it left her: and immediately she arose and ministered unto them.			
40 Now when the sun was setting, all they **that** had any sick with divers diseases brought them unto him; and he laid his hands on every one of them, and healed them.	40 Now when the sun was setting, all they **who** had any sick with divers diseases brought them unto him; and he laid his hands on every one of them, and healed them.		
41 And the devils also came out of many, crying out, and saying, Thou art Christ the Son of God. And he rebuking them suffered them not to speak: for they knew that he was Christ.		53:4 Surely he hath borne our griefs, and carried our sorrows: yet we did esteem him stricken, smitten of God, and afflicted.	
42 And when it was day, he departed and went into a **desert** place: and the people sought him, and came unto him, and **stayed** him, that he should not depart from them.	42 And when it was day, he departed and went into a **solitary** place; and the people sought him, and came unto him, and **desired** him that he should not depart from them.		

63

Matt. 4	JST Matt. 4	Mark 1	
		38 And he said unto them, Let us go into the next towns, that I may preach there also: for therefore came I forth.	
23 And Jesus went about all Galilee, teaching in their synagogues, and preaching the gospel of the kingdom, and healing all manner of sickness and all manner of disease among the people.	22 And Jesus went about all Galilee teaching in their synagogues, and preaching the gospel of the kingdom; and healing all manner of sickness, and all manner of diseases among the people **which believed on his name.**	39 And he preached in their synagogues throughout all Galilee, and cast out devils.	
24 And his fame went throughout all Syria: and they brought unto him all sick people that were taken with diverse diseases and torments, and those which were possessed with devils, and those which were lunatick, and those that had the palsy; and he healed them.	23 And his fame went throughout all Syria: and they brought unto him all sick people that were taken with diverse diseases and torments, and those **who** were possessed with devils, and those who were lunatick, and those that had the palsy; and he healed them.		
25 And there followed him great multitudes of people from Galilee, and **from** Decapolis, and **from** Jerusalem, and **from** Judæa, and **from** beyond Jordan.	24 And there followed him great multitudes of people from Galilee, and Decapolis, and Jerusalem, and Judea, and beyond Jordan.		

Matt. 8	JST Matt. 8	Mark 1	JST Mark 1

30. Certain City -- Leper Cleansed

2 And, behold, there came a leper **and worshipped** him, saying, Lord, if thou wilt, thou canst make me clean.	2 And, behold, there came a leper **worshipping** him, saying, Lord, if thou wilt, thou canst make me clean.	40 And there came a leper to him, beseeching him, and kneeling down to him, **and saying unto him, If** thou wilt, thou canst make me clean.	40 And there came a leper to him, beseeching him, and kneeling down to him, **said,** If thou wilt, thou canst make me clean.
3 And Jesus put forth his hand, and touched him, saying, I will; be thou clean.		41 And Jesus, moved with compassion, put forth his hand, and touched him, and saith unto him, I will; be thou clean.	
And immediately his leprosy was cleansed.		42 And as soon as he had spoken, immediately the leprosy departed from him, and he was cleansed.	

Luke 4	JST Luke 4		
43 **And** he said unto them, I must preach the kingdom of God to other cities also: for therefore am I sent. 44 And he preached in the synagogues of Galilee.	43 **But** he said unto them, I must preach the kingdom of God to other cities also, for therefore am I sent.		

Luke 5			
12 ¶ And it came to pass, when he was in a certain city, behold a man full of leprosy: who seeing Jesus fell on his face, and besought him, saying, Lord, if thou wilt, thou canst make me clean. 13 And he put forth his hand, and touched him, saying, I will: be thou clean. And immediately the leprosy departed from him.			

Matt. 8	JST Matt. 8	Mark 1	JST Mark 1
4 And Jesus saith unto him, See thou tell no man; but go thy way, shew thyself to the priest, and offer the gift that Moses commanded, for a testimony unto them.	4 And Jesus said unto him, See thou tell no man; but go thy way **and show** thyself to the priest, and offer the gift that Moses commanded, for a testimony unto them.	43 And he straitly charged him, and forthwith sent him away; 44 And saith unto him, See thou say nothing to any man: but go thy way, shew thyself to the priest, and offer for thy cleansing those things which Moses commanded, for a testimony unto them. 45 But he went out, and began to publish it much, and to blaze abroad the matter, insomuch that Jesus could no more openly enter into the city, but was without in **desert** places: and they came to him from every quarter.	40 But he went out, and began to publish it much, and to blaze abroad the matter, insomuch that Jesus could no more openly enter into the city, but was without in **solitary** places; and they came to him from every quarter.

Matt. 9		Mark 2	JST Mark 2

31. Capernaum--Heals and Forgives Man with Palsy

Matt. 9		Mark 2	JST Mark 2
		And again he entered into Capernaum after **some** days; and it was noised that he was in the house.	And again, he entered into Capernaum after **many** days; and it was noised **abroad** that he was in the house.
		2 And straightway many were gathered together, insomuch that there was no room to receive **them**, no, not so much as about the door: and he preached the word unto them.	2 And straightway many were gathered together, insomuch that there was no room to receive **the multitude**; no, not so much as about the door; and he preached the word unto them.
2 And, behold, they brought to him a man sick of the palsy, lying on a bed:		3 And they come unto him, bringing one sick of the palsy, which was borne of four.	3 And they **came** unto him, bringing one sick of the palsy, which was borne of four **persons**.
		4 And when they could not come nigh unto him for the press, they uncovered the roof where he was: and when they had broken it up, they let down the bed wherein the sick of the palsy lay.	

66

Luke 5	JST Luke 5		
14 And he charged him to tell no man: but go, and shew thyself to the priest, and offer for thy cleansing, according as Moses commanded, for a testimony unto them. 15 But so much the more went there a fame abroad of him: and great multitudes came together to hear, and to be healed by him of their infirmities. 16 ¶ And he withdrew himself into the wilderness, and prayed.	14 And he charged him to tell no man; but **said unto him**, Go and show thyself to the priests, and offer for thy cleansing, according as Moses commanded, for a testimony unto them.		
17 And it came to pass on a certain day, as he was teaching, that there were Pharisees and doctors of the law sitting by, **which** were come out of every town of Galilee, and Judæa, and Jerusalem: and the power of the Lord was present to heal them. 18 ¶ And, behold, men brought in a bed a man **which** was taken with a palsy: and they sought **means** to bring him in, and to lay him before **him**. 19 And when they could not **find by what way they might** bring him in **because of** the multitude, they went upon the housetop, and let him down through the tiling with his couch into the midst before Jesus.	17 And it came to pass on a certain day, as he was teaching, that there were Pharisees and doctors of the law sitting by, **who** were come out of every town of Galilee, and Judea, and Jerusalem. And the power of the Lord was present to heal them. 18 And behold, men brought in a bed, a man **who** was taken with a palsy; and they sought to bring him in, and to lay him before **Jesus**. 19 And when they **found that they** could not bring him in **for** the multitude, they went upon the housetop, and let him down through the tiling, with his couch, into the midst, before Jesus.		

Matt. 9	JST Matt. 9	Mark 2	JST Mark 2
and Jesus **seeing** their faith said unto the sick of the palsy; Son, be of good cheer; thy sins be forgiven thee.	and Jesus, **knowing** their faith, said unto the sick of the palsy, Son, be of good cheer; thy sins be forgiven thee; **go thy way and sin no more.**	5 When Jesus saw their faith, he said unto the sick of the palsy, Son, thy sins be forgiven thee.	
3 And, behold, certain of the scribes said within themselves, This man blasphemeth.		6 But there were certain of the scribes sitting there, and reasoning in their hearts, 7 Why doth this man thus speak blasphemies? who can forgive sins but God only?	
4 And Jesus knowing their thoughts said, Wherefore **think** ye evil in your hearts?	4 And Jesus, knowing their thoughts, said, Wherefore **is it that ye think** evil in your hearts?	8 And immediately when Jesus perceived in his spirit that they so reasoned within themselves, he said unto them, Why reason ye these things in your hearts?	7 And immediately, when Jesus perceived in his spirit, that they so reasoned within themselves, he said unto them, Why reason ye these things in your hearts?
5 For **whether** is easier, to say, Thy sins be forgiven thee; or to say, Arise, and walk?	5 For is it **not** easier to say, Thy sins be forgiven thee, **than** to say, Arise and walk?	9 **Whether** is it easier to say to the sick of the palsy, Thy sins be forgiven thee; or to say, Arise, and take up thy bed, and walk?	Is it **not** easier to say to the sick of the palsy, Thy sins be forgiven thee; **than** to say, Arise, and take up thy bed and walk?
6 But that ye may know that the Son of man hath power on earth to forgive sins, (then saith **he** to the sick of the palsy,)	6 But **I said this** that ye may know that the Son of Man hath power on earth to forgive sins. 7 Then **Jesus** said **unto** the sick of the palsy,	10 But that ye may know that the Son of man hath power on earth to forgive sins, (he saith to the sick of the palsy,)	8 But that ye may know that the Son of Man hath power on earth to forgive sins, (he said to the sick of the palsy,)
Arise, take up thy bed, and go unto **thine** house.	Arise, take up thy bed, and go unto thy house.	11 I say unto thee, Arise, and take up thy bed, and go thy way into **thine** house.	I say unto thee, Arise, and take up thy bed, and go thy way into thy house.
7 And he arose, and departed to his house.	8 And he **immediately** arose, and departed to his house.	12 And immediately he arose, took up the bed, and went forth before them all;	9 And immediately he arose, took up the bed, and went forth before them all;
8 But when the multitudes saw it, they marvelled, and glorified God, **which** had given such power unto men.	9 But when the multitude saw it, they marvelled, and glorified God, **who** had given such power unto men.	insomuch that they were all amazed, and glorified God, saying, We never saw **it on this fashion.**	insomuch that they were all amazed, and **many** glorified God, saying, We never saw **the power of God after this manner.**
		13 And **he** went forth again by the sea side; and all the multitude resorted unto him, and he taught them.	10 And **Jesus** went forth again by the seaside, and all the multitude resorted unto him, and he taught them.

Luke 5	JST Luke 5	D&C	B of M
20 **And when** he saw their faith, **he** said unto **him**, Man, thy sins are forgiven thee.	20 **Now** he saw their faith, **and** said unto **the** man, Thy sins are forgiven thee.		
21 And the scribes and **the** Pharisees began to reason, saying, Who is this **which** speaketh blasphemies? Who can forgive sins, but God alone?	21 And the scribes and Pharisees began to reason, saying, Who is this **that** speaketh blasphemies? Who can forgive sins, but God alone?		
22 But **when** Jesus perceived their thoughts, he **answering** said unto them. What reason ye in your hearts?	22 But Jesus perceived their thoughts, **and** he said unto them, What reason ye in your hearts?	6:16 Yea, I tell thee, that thou gayest k ow that there is none else save God that knowest thy thoughts and then intents of thy heart (See also D&C 33:1).	Jacob 2:5 But behold, hearken ye unto me, and know that by the help of the all-powerful Creator of heaven and earth I can tell you concerning your thougths, how that ye are beginning to labor in sin, which sin appeareth very abominable unto me, yea, and abominable unto God (See also Alma 18:16).
23 **Whether is easier, to say, Thy sins be forgiven thee; or to say, Rise up** and walk?	23 **Does it require more power to forgive sins than to make the sick rise up** and walk?		
24 But that ye may know that the Son of man hath power upon earth to forgive sins, (he said unto the sick of the palsy,) I say unto thee, Arise, and take up thy couch, and go into **thine** house.	24 But, that ye may know that the Son of Man hath power upon earth to forgive sins, **I said it. And** he said unto the sick of the palsy, I say unto thee, Arise, and take up thy couch, and go unto **thy** house.		
25 And immediately he rose up before them, and took that whereon he lay, and departed to his own house, glorifying God.			
26 And they were all amazed, and they glorified God, and were filled with fear, saying, We have seen strange things to day.			

32. Matthew Called -- Jesus Eats with Publicans

Matt. 9	JST Matt. 9	Mark 2	JST Mark 2
9 ¶ And as Jesus passed forth from thence, he saw a man, named Matthew, sitting at the **receipt of custom:**	10 And as Jesus passed forth from thence, he saw a man named Matthew, sitting at the **place where they received tribute, as was customary in those days,** and he said unto him, Follow me. And he arose and followed him.	14 And as he passed by, he saw Levi the son of Alphæus sitting at the receipt of custom,	11 And as he passed by, he saw Levi the son of Alpheus, sitting at the **place where they receive tribute, as was customary in those days,** and he said unto him, Follow me; and he arose and followed him.
and he saith unto him, Follow me. And he arose, and followed him.		and said unto him, Follow me. And he arose and followed him.	
10 ¶ And it came to pass as Jesus sat at meat in the house, behold, many publicans and sinners came and sat down with him and his disciples.	11 And it came to pass, as Jesus sat at meat in the house, behold, many publicans and sinners came and sat down with him, and **with** his disciples.	15 And it came to pass, that, as Jesus sat at meat in his house, many publicans and sinners sat also together with **Jesus** and his disciples: for they were many, and they followed him.	12 And it came to pass, that, as Jesus sat at meat in his house, many publicans and sinners sat also together with **him** and his disciples; for there were many, and they followed him.
		16 And when the scribes and Pharisees saw him eat with publicans and sinners, they said unto his disciples, How is it that he eateth and drinketh with publicans and sinners?	
11 And when the Pharisees saw **it,** they said unto his disciples, Why eateth your Master with publicans and sinners?	12 And when the Pharisees saw **them,** they said unto his disciples, Why eateth your Master with publicans and sinners?		
12 But when Jesus heard **that,** he said unto them, They that be whole need not a physician, but they that are sick.	13 But when Jesus heard **them,** he said unto them, They that be whole need not a physician, but they that are sick.	17 When Jesus heard it, he saith unto them, They that are whole have no need of the physician, but they that are sick:	14 When Jesus heard **this,** he said unto them, They that are whole have no need of the physician, but they that are sick.
13 But go ye and learn what **that** meaneth, I will have mercy, and not sacrifice: for I am not come to call the righteous, but sinners to repentance.	14 But go ye and learn what **this** meaneth; I will have mercy and not sacrifice; for I am not come to call the righteous, but sinners to repentance.	I came not to call the righteous, but sinners to repentance.	15 I came not to call the righteous, but sinners to repentance.

TPJS-- Christ said he came to call sinners to repentance, to save them. Christ was condemned by the self-righteous Jews because He took sinners into His society; He took them upon the principle that they repented of their sins. It is the object of this society to reform persons, not to take those that are corrupt and foster them in their wickedness; but if they repent, we are bound to take them, and by kindness sanctify and cleanse them from all unrighteousness by our influence in watching over them. Nothing will have such influence over people as the fear of being disfellowshipped by so goodly a society as this.***

Nothing is so much calculated to lead people to forsake sin as to take them by the hand, and watch over them with tenderness. When persons manifest the least kindness and love to me, O what power it has over my mind, while the opposite course has a tendency to harrow up all the harsh feelings and depress the human mind. (p. 240)

Luke 5	JST Luke 5	B of M	

27 ¶ And after these things he went forth, and saw a publican, named Levi, sitting at the **receipt of** custom: and he said unto him, Follow me.

28 And he left all, rose up, and followed him.

29 And Levi made him a great feast in his own house: and there was a great company of publicans and of others that sat down with them.

27 And after these things he went forth, and saw a publican, named Levi, sitting at the **place where they received** custom; and he said unto him, Follow me.

30 But **their** scribes and Pharisees murmured against his disciples, saying, Why do ye eat and drink with publicans and sinners?

30 But **the** scribes and Pharisees murmured against his disciples, saying, Why do ye eat and drink with publicans and sinners?

31 **And** Jesus answering said unto them, They that are whole need not a physician; but they that are sick.

31 Jesus answering, said unto them, They that are whole need not a physician; but they that are sick.

Moro. 8:8 Listen to the words of Christ, your Redeemer, your Lord and your God. Behold, I came into the world not to call the righteous but sinners to repentance; the whole need no physician, but they that are sick;. . .

32 I came not to call the righteous, but sinners to repentance.

Matt. 9	JST Matt. 9	Mark 2	JST Mark 2

33. John's Disciples' Question on Fasting

Matt. 9	JST Matt. 9	Mark 2	JST Mark 2
14 ¶ **Then** came to him the disciples of John, saying, Why do we and the Pharisees fast oft, but thy disciples fast not? 15 And Jesus said unto them, Can the children of the bridechamber mourn, as long as the bridegroom is with them? but the days will come, when the bridegroom shall be taken from them, and then shall they fast.	15 **And while he was thus teaching, there came** to him the disciples of John, saying, Why do we and the Pharisees fast oft, but thy disciples fast not?	18 And the disciples of John and of the Pharisees used to fast: and **t h e y come and say unto him,** Why do the disciples of John and of the Pharisees fast, but thy disciples fast not? 19 And Jesus said unto them, Can the children of the bridechamber fast, while the bridegroom is with them? as long as they have the bridegroom with them, they cannot fast. 20 But the days will come, when the bridegroom shall be taken away from them, and then shall they fast in those days.	16 And **they came and said unto him,** The disciples of John and of the Pharisees used to fast; and why do the disciples of John and of the Pharisees fast, but thy disciples fast not?
	18 **Then said the Pharisees unto him, Why will ye not receive us with our baptism, seeing we keep the whole law?** 19 **But Jesus said unto them, Ye keep not the law. If ye had kept the law, ye would have received me, for I am he who gave the law.** 20 **I receive not you with your baptism, because it profiteth you nothing.** 21 **For when that which is new is come, the old is ready to be put away.**		
16 No man putteth a piece of new cloth **unto** an old garment, for that which is put in to fill it up taketh from the garment, and the rent is made worse. 17 Neither do men put new wine into old bottles: else the bottles break, and the wine runneth out, and the bottles perish: but they put new wine into new bottles, and both are preserved.	22 **For** no man putteth a piece of new cloth on an old garment; for that which is put in to fill it up, taketh from the garment, and the rent is made worse.	21 No man also seweth a piece of new cloth on an old garment: else the new piece that filled it up taketh away from the old, and the rent is made worse. 22 And no man putteth new wine into old bottles: else the new wine doth burst the bottles, and the wine is spilled, and the bottles will be marred: but new wine must be put into new bottles.	

Luke 5	JST Luke 5	TPJS

33 ¶ And they said unto him, Why do the disciples of John fast often, and make prayers, and likewise the disciples of the Pharisees; but thine eat and drink?

34 And he said unto them, Can ye make the children of the bridechamber fast, while the bridegroom is with them?

35 But the days will come, when the bridegroom shall be taken away from them, and then shall they fast in those days.

Luke 5	JST Luke 5
36 ¶ And he spake also a parable unto them; No man putteth a piece of **a** new **garment** upon an old; if **otherwise**, then both the new maketh a rent, and **the piece that was taken out of the new** agreeth not with the old.	36 And he spake also a parable unto them, **saying,** No man putteth a piece of new **cloth** upon an old **garment**; if **so,** then the new maketh a rent, and agreeth not with the old.
37 And no man putteth new wine into old bottles; else the new wine will burst the bottles, and be spilled, and the bottles shall perish.	
38 But new wine must be put into new bottles; and both are preserved.	
39 No man also having drunk old wine **straightway** desireth new: for he saith, The old is better.	39 No man also, having drank old wine, desireth new; for he saith, The old is better.

Many objections are urged against the Latter-day Saints for not admitting the validity of sectarian baptism, and for withholding fellowship from sectarian churches. Yet to do otherwise would be like putting new wine into old bottles, and putting old wine into new bottles. What! new revelations in the old churches? New revelations would knock out the bottom of their bottomless pit. New wine into old bottles! The bottles burst and the wine runs out! What! Sadducees in the new church! Old wine in new leathern bottles will leak through the pores and escape. So the Sadducee saints mock at authority, kick out of the traces, and run to the mountains of perdition, leaving the long echo of their braying behind them. (p. 192)

The Second Year of Jesus' Ministry --- The Second Passover

After this there was a feast of the Jews; and Jesus went up to Jerusalem.

2 Now there is at Jerusalem by the sheep market a pool, which is called in the Hebrew tongue Bethesda, having five porches.

3 In these lay a great **multitude of** impotent folk, of blind, halt, withered, waiting for the moving of the water.

4 For an angel went down at a certain season into the pool, and troubled the water: whosoever then first after the troubling of the water stepped in was made whole of whatsoever disease he had.

5 And a certain man was there, **which** had an infirmity thirty and eight years.

6 **When** Jesus saw him lie, and knew that he had been now a long time in **that case**, he saith unto him, Wilt thou be made whole?

7 The impotent man answered him, Sir, I have no man, when the water is troubled, to put me in the pool: but while I am coming, another steppeth down before me.

8 Jesus saith unto him, Rise, take up thy bed, and walk.

9 And immediately the man was made whole, and took up his bed, and walked: and on the **same** day **was the** sabbath.

10 ¶ The Jews therefore said unto him **that** was cured, It is the sabbath day: it is not lawful for thee to carry thy bed.

(continued in column 3)

---

3 In these **porches** lay a great **many** impotent folk, of blind, halt, withered, waiting for the moving of the water.

5 And a certain man was there, **who** had an infirmity thirty and eight years.

6 **And** Jesus saw him lie, and knew that he had been now a long time **afflicted; and** he said unto him, Wilt thou be made whole?

9 And immediately the man was made whole, and took up his bed, and walked; **and it was** on the Sabbath **day.**

10 The Jews therefore said unto him **who** was cured, It is the Sabbath day; it is not lawful for thee to carry thy bed.

(continued in column 4)

---

11 He answered them, He **that** made me whole, **the same** said unto me, Take up thy bed, and walk.

12 Then **asked** they him, what man is **that which** said unto thee, Take up thy bed, and walk?

13 And he that was healed **wist** not who it was: for Jesus had conveyed himself away, a multitude being in **that** place.

14 Afterward Jesus findeth him in the temple, and said unto him, Behold, thou art made whole: sin no more, lest a worse thing come unto thee.

15 The man departed, and told the Jews that it was Jesus, **which** had made him whole.

16 And therefore did the Jews persecute Jesus, and sought to slay him, because he had done these things on the sabbath day.

17 ¶ But Jesus answered them, My Father worketh hitherto, and I work.

18 Therefore the Jews sought the more to kill him, because he not only **had** broken the sabbath, but said also that God was his Father, making himself equal with God.

19 Then answered Jesus and said unto them, Verily, verily, I say unto you, The Son can do nothing of himself, but what he seeth the Father do: for what thing soever he doeth, these also doeth the Son likewise.

---

11 He answered them, He **who** made me whole, said unto me, Take up thy bed and walk.

12 Then **answered** they him, **saying,** What man is **he who** said unto thee, Take up thy bed and walk?

13 And he that was healed **knew** not who it was; for Jesus had conveyed himself away, a multitude being in **the** place.

15 The man departed, and told the Jews that it was Jesus **who** had made him whole;

18 Therefore the Jews sought the more to kill him, because he **had** not only broken the Sabbath, but said also that God was his father, making himself equal with God.

		John 5	JST John 5

TPJS-- The Son doeth what He hath seen the Father do: then the Father hath some day laid down His life and taken it again; so He has a body of His own; each one will be in His own body; and yet the sectarian world believe the body of the Son is identical with the Father's. (p. 312)

What did Jesus do? Why; I do the things I saw my Father do when worlds came rolling into existence. My Father worked out his kingdom with fear and trembling, and I must do the same; and when I get my kingdom, I shall present it to my Father, so that he may obtain kingdom upon kingdom, and it will exalt him in glory. He will then take a higher exaltation, and I will take his place, and thereby become exalted myself. So that Jesus treads in the tracks of his Father, and inherits what God did before; and God is thus glorified and exalted in the salvation and exaltation of all his children. (pp. 347-348)

	John 5	JST John 5
	20 For the Father loveth the Son, and sheweth him all things that himself doeth; and he will shew him greater works than these, that ye may marvel.	
	21 For as the Father raiseth up the dead, and quickeneth them; even so the Son quickeneth whom he will.	
	22 For the Father judgeth no man, but hath committed all judgment unto the Son:	
	23 That all **men** should honour the Son, even as they honour the Father. He **that** honoureth not the Son honoureth not the Father **which** hath sent him.	23 That all should honor the Son, even as they honor the Father. He **who** honoreth not the Son, honoreth not the Father who hath sent him.
	24 Verily, verily, I say unto you, He **that** heareth my word, and believeth on him **that** sent me, hath everlasting life, and shall not come into condemnation; but is passed from death unto life.	24 Verily, verily, I say unto you, He **who** heareth my word, and believeth on him **who** sent me, hath everlasting life, and shall not come into condemnation; but is passed from death into life.
	25 Verily, verily, I say unto you, The hour is coming, and now is, when the dead shall hear the voice of the Son of God: and they **that** hear shall live.	25 Verily, verily, I say unto you, The hour is coming, and now is, when the dead shall hear the voice of the Son of God; and they **who** hear shall live.
TPJS-- God the Father took life unto himself precisely as Jesus did. (p. 181)	26 For as the Father hath life in himself; so hath he given to the Son to have life in himself;	

75

	D & C	John 5	JST John 5
	76:15 For while we were doing the work of translation, which the Lord had appointed unto us, we came to the twenty-ninth verse of the fifth chapter of John, which was given unto us as follows--	27 And hath given him authority to execute judgment also, because he is the Son of man.	
	16 Speaking concerning the resurrection of the dead, concerning those who shall hear the voice of the Son of Man:	28 Marvel not at this: for the hour is coming, in the which all **that** are in **the** graves shall hear his voice,	28 Marvel not at this; for the hour is coming, in the which all **who** are in **their** graves shall hear his voice,
	17 And shall come forth; they who have done good, in the resurrection of the just; and they who have done evil, in the resurrection of the unjust.	29 And shall come forth; they **that** have done good, unto the resurrection of life; and they **that** have done evil, **unto** the resurrection of **damnation.**	29 And shall come forth; they **who** have done good, in the resurrection of **the just;** and they **who** have done evil, **in the** resurrection of **the unjust.**
	18 Now this caused us to marvel, for it was given unto us of the Spirit.		30 **And shall all be judged of the Son of Man. For as I hear, I judge, and my judgment is just;**
		30 I can of my own self do nothing: **as I hear, I judge: and my judgment is just;** because I seek not mine own will, but the will of the Father **which hath** sent me.	31 **For** I can of my own self do nothing; because I seek not mine own will, but the will of the Father **who** hath sent me.
		31 If I bear witness of myself, my witness is **not** true.	32 **Therefore** if I bear witness of myself, **yet my** witness is true.
		32 ¶ There is another **that** beareth witness of me; and I know that the **witness** which he **witnesseth** of me is true.	33 **For I am not alone,** there is another **who** beareth witness of me, and I know that the **testimony** which he **giveth** of me is true.
		33 Ye sent unto John, and he bear witness unto the truth.	34 Ye sent unto John, and he bear witness **also** unto the truth.
		34 But I receive not testimony **from man:**	35 **And he received not** his testimony of man, **but of God, and ye yourselves say that he is a prophet, therefore ye ought to receive his testimony.**
		but these things I say, that ye might be saved.	These things I say that ye might be saved.
		35 He was a burning and a shining light: and ye were willing for a season to rejoice in his light.	
	93:5 I was in the world and received of my Father, and the works of him were plainly manifest.	36 ¶ But I have greater witness than **that** of John: for the works which the Father hath given me to	37 But I have **a** greater witness than **the testimony** of John; for the works which the Father

		John 5	JST John 5
		finish, the same works that I do, bear witness of me, that the Father hath sent me.	hath given me to finish, the same works that I do, bear witness of me, that the Father hath sent me.
		37 And the Father himself, **which hath** sent me, hath borne witness of me.	38 And the Father himself **who** sent me, hath borne witness of me. **And verily I testify unto you, that** ye have **never** heard his voice at any time, nor seen his shape;
		Ye have **neither** heard his voice at any time, nor seen his shape.	
		38 **And** ye have not his word abiding in you: **for** whom he hath sent, **him** ye believe not.	39 **For** ye have not his word abiding in you; **and him** whom he hath sent, ye believe not.
		39 ¶ Search the scriptures; for in them ye think ye have eternal life: and they are they which testify of me.	
		40 And ye will not come to me, that ye might have life.	41 And ye will not come to me that ye might have life, **lest ye should honor me.**
		41 I receive not honour from men.	
		42 But I know you, that ye have not the love of God in you.	
		43 I am come in my Father's name, and ye receive me not: if another shall come in his own name, him ye will receive.	
		44 How can ye believe, **which receive** honour one of another, and seek not the honour **that** cometh from God only?	45 How can ye believe, **who seek** honor one of another, and seek not the honor **which** cometh from God only?
		45 Do not think that I will accuse you to the Father: there is **one that** accuseth you, **even Moses,** in whom ye trust.	46 Do not think that I will accuse you to the Father; there is **Moses who** accuseth you, in whom ye trust.
		46 For had ye believed Moses, ye would have believed me: for he wrote of me.	
		47 But if ye believe not his writings, how shall ye believe my words?	

Matt. 12	JST Matt. 12	Mark 2	JST Mark 2

34. Jesus--Lord of the Sabbath

Matt. 12	JST Matt. 12	Mark 2	JST Mark 2
At that time Jesus went on the sabbath day through the corn; and his disciples were an hungred, and began to pluck the ears of corn, and to eat.		23 And it came to pass, that he went through the corn fields on the sabbath day; and his disciples began, as they went, to pluck the ears of corn.	
2 But when the Pharisees saw it, they said unto him, Behold, thy disciples do that which is not lawful to do upon the sabbath day.	2 But when the Pharisees saw them, they said unto him, Behold, thy disciples do that which is not lawful to do upon the Sabbath day.	24 And the Pharisees said unto him, Behold, why do they on the sabbath day that which is not lawful?	22 And the Pharisees said unto him, Behold, why do thy disciples on the Sabbath day that which is not lawful?
3 But he said unto them, Have ye not read what David did, when he was an hungred, and they that were with him;		25 And he said unto them, Have ye never read what David did, when he had need, and was an hungred, he, and they that were with him?	23 And he said unto them, Have ye never read what David did, when he had need and was an hungered, he, and they who were with him?
4 How he entered into the house of God, and did eat the shewbread, which was not lawful for him to eat, neither for them which were with him, but only for the priests?		26 How he went into the house of God in the days of Abiathar the high priest, and did eat the shewbread, which is not lawful to eat but for the priests, and gave also to them which were with him?	
5 Or have ye not read in the law, how that on the sabbath days the priests in the temple profane the sabbath, and are blameless?	4 Or have ye not read in the law, how that on the Sabbath days the priests in the temple profane the Sabbath, and ye say they are blameless?		
6 But I say unto you, That in this place is one greater than the temple. 7 But if ye had known what this meaneth, I will have mercy, and not sacrifice, ye would not have condemned the guiltless.		27 And he said unto them, The sabbath was made for man, and not man for the sabbath:	26 Wherefore the Sabbath was given unto man for a day of rest; and also that man should glorify God, and not that man should not eat;
8 For the Son of man is Lord even of the sabbath day.	6. . . For the Son of Man is Lord even of the Sabbath.	28 Therefore the Son of man is Lord also of the sabbath.	27 For the Son of Man made the Sabbath day, therefore the Son of Man is Lord also of the Sabbath.

Luke 6	JST Luke 6	Old Testament	
And it came to pass on the second sabbath after **the first**, that he went through the corn fields; and his disciples plucked the ears of corn, and did eat, rubbing them in their hands.	And it came to pass on the second Sabbath after **this**, that he wen tthrough the cornfields; and his disciples plucked the ears of corn, and did eat, rubbing them in their hands.		
2 And certain of the Pharisees said unto them, Why do ye that which is not lawful to do on the sabbath days?			
3 **And** Jesus answering them said, Have ye not read so much as this, what David did, when himself was an hungered, and they **which** were with him;	3 Jesus answering them, said, Have ye not read so much as this, what David did, when **he** himself was an hungered, and they **who** were with him;	1 Sam. 21:3 Now therefore what is under thine hand? give *me* five *loaves of* bread in mine hand, or what there is present.	
4 How he went into the house of God, and did take and eat the shewbread, and gave also to them **that** were with him; which it is not lawful to eat but for the priests alone?	4 How he went into the house of God, and did take and eat the shewbread, and gave also to them **who** were with him, which it is not lawful to eat, but for the priests alone?	4 And the priest answered David, and said, *There is* no common bread under mine hand, but there is hallowed bread; if the young men have kept themselves at least from women.	
5 And he said unto them,		5 And David answered the priest, and said unto him, Of a truth women *have been* kept from us about these three days, since I came out, and the vessels of the young men are holy, and *the bread is* in a manner common, yea, though it were sanctified this day in the vessel.	
That the Son of man is Lord also of the sabbath.		6 So the priest gave him hallowed *bread*: for there was no bread there but the shewbread, that was taken from before the Lord, to put hot bread in the day when it was taken away.	

Matt. 12	JST Matt. 12	Mark 3	JST Mark 3

35. Man's Hand Healed on the Sabbath

Matt. 12	JST Matt. 12	Mark 3	JST Mark 3
9 And when he was departed thence, he went into their synagogue: 10 ¶ And, behold, there was a man which had his hand withered. And they asked him, saying, Is it lawful to heal on the sabbath days? that they might accuse him.	7 And when he was departed thence, he went into their synagogues. 8 And, behold, there was a man which had a withered hand. And they asked him, saying, Is it lawful to heal on the Sabbath days? that they might accuse him.	And he entered again into the synagogue; and there was a man there which had a withered hand. 2 And they watched him, whether he would heal him on the sabbath day; that they might accuse him. 3 And he saith unto the man which had the withered hand, Stand forth. 4 And he saith unto them, Is it lawful to do good on the sabbath days, or to do evil? to save life, or to kill? But they held their peace.	2 And they watched him to see whether he would heal him on the Sabbath day; that they might accuse him. 4 And he said unto them, Is it lawful to do good on the Sabbath days, or to do evil? To save life, or to kill? But they held their peace.
11 And he said unto them, What man shall there be among you, that shall have one sheep, and if it fall into a pit on the sabbath day, will he not lay hold on it, and lift it out? 12 How much then is a man better than a sheep? Wherefore it is lawful to do well on the sabbath days.			
13 Then saith he to the man, Stretch forth thine hand. And he stretched it forth; and it was restored whole, like as the other. 14 ¶ Then the Pharisees went out, and held a council against him, how they might destroy him.	11 Then said he to the man, Stretch forth thy hand; and he stretched it forth, and it was restored whole, like unto the other.	5 And when he had looked round about on them with anger, being grieved for the hardness of their hearts, he saith unto the man, Stretch forth thine hand. And he stretched it out: and his hand was restored whole as the other. 6 And the Pharisees went forth, and straightway took counsel with the Herodians against him, how they might destroy him.	6 And he stretched out his hand; and his hand was restored whole as the other.

Luke 6	JST Luke 6		
6 And it came to pass also on another sabbath, that he entered into the synagogue and taught: and there was a man whose right hand was withered. 7 And the scribes and Pharisees watched him, whether he would heal on the sabbath day; that they might find an accusation against him. 8 But he knew their thoughts, and said to the man **which** had the withered hand, Rise up, and stand forth in the midst. And he arose and stood forth. 9 Then said Jesus unto them, I will ask you one thing; Is it lawful on the sabbath days to do good, or to do evil? to save life, or to destroy **it**?	8 But he knew their thoughts, and said to the man **who** had the withered hand, Rise up, and stand forth in the midst. And he arose and stood forth. 9 Then said Jesus unto them, I will ask you one thing; Is it lawful on the Sabbath days to do good, or to do evil? To save life, or to destroy?		
10 And looking round about upon them all, he said unto the man, Stretch forth thy hand. And he did so: and his hand was restored whole as the other. 11 And they were filled with madness; and communed one with another what they might do to Jesus.			

Matt. 12	JST Matt. 12 Isaiah	Mark 3 D&C	JST Mark 3

36. Sea of Galilee-- Multitudes Throng

Matt. 12	JST Matt. 12 / Isaiah	Mark 3 / D&C	JST Mark 3
15 But **when Jesus knew it,** he withdrew himself from thence: and great multitudes followed him,	13 But Jesus knew **when they took counsel, and he** withdrew himself from thence; and great multitudes followed him,	7 But Jesus withdrew himself with his disciples to the sea: and a great multitude from Galilee followed him, and from Judæa, 8 And from Jerusalem, and from Idumæa, and from beyond Jordan; and they about Tyre and Sidon, a great multitude, when they **had** heard what great things he did, came unto him. 9 And he spake to his disciples, that a small ship should wait on him because of the multitude, lest they should throng him.	8 But Jesus withdrew himself, with his disciples, to the sea; and a great multitude from Galilee followed him, and from Judea, and from Jerusalem, and from Idumea and from beyond Jordan; and they about Tyre and Sidon, a great multitude, when they heard what great things he did, came unto him. 9 And he spake unto his disciples, that a small ship should wait on him because of the multitude, lest they should throng him.
and he healed **them all;**	and he healed **their sick,**	10 For he had healed many; insomuch that they pressed upon him for to touch him, as many as had plagues. 11 And unclean spirits, when they saw him, fell down before him, and cried, saying, Thou art the Son of God. 12 And he straightly charged them that they should not make him known.	
16 And charged them that they should not make him known: 17 That it might be fulfilled which was spoken by Esaias the prophet, saying. 18 Behold my servant, whom I have chosen; my beloved, in whom my soul is well pleased: I will put my spirit upon him, and he shall shew judgment to the Gentiles. 19 He shall not strive, nor cry; neither shall any man hear his voice in the streets. 20 A bruised reed shall he not break, and smoking flax shall he not quench, till he send forth judgment unto victory. 21 And in his name shall the Gentiles trust.	Isaiah 42:1 Behold my servant, whom I uphold; mine elect, in whom my soul delighteth; I have put my spirit upon him: he shall bring forth judgment to the Gentiles. 2 He shall not cry, nor lift up, nor cause his voice to be heard in the street. 3 A bruised reed shall he not break, and the smoking flax shall he not quench: he shall bring forth judgment unto truth. 4 He shall not fail nor be discouraged, till he have set judgment in the earth: and the isles shall wait for his law.	52:11 For thus saith the Lord, I will cut my work short in righteousness, for the days come that I will send forth judgment unto victory.	

Matt. 10	Mark 3	Luke 6	JST Luke 6

37. Mountain in Galilee-- Twelve Apostles Chosen

Matt. 10	Mark 3	Luke 6	JST Luke 6
	13 And he goeth up into a mountain,	12 And it came to pass in those days, that he went out into a mountain to pray, and continued all night in prayer to God.	
	and calleth **unto him** whom he would: and they came unto him.* 14 And he ordained twelve, that they should be with him, and that he might send them forth to preach, 15 And to have power to heal sicknesses, and to cast out devils:	13 And when it was day, he called **unto him** his disciples: and of them he chose twelve, whom also he named apostles;	13 And when it was day, he called his disciples: and of them he chose twelve, whom he also named apostles;
2 Now the names of the twelve apostles are these; The first, Simon, who is called Peter, and Andrew his brother; James the son of Zebedee, and John his brother;	16 And Simon he sur-named Peter; 17 And James the son of Zebedee, and John the brother of James; and he surnamed them Boanerges, which is, The sons of thunder:	14 Simon, (whom he also named Peter,) and Andrew his brother, James and John, Philip and Bartholo-mew,	
3 Philip, and Bartholo-mew; Thomas, and Mat-thew the publican; James the son of Alphæus, and Lebæus, whose surname was Thaddæus; 4 Simon the Canaanite, and Judas Iscariot, who also betrayed him.	18 And Andrew, and Philip, and Bartholomew, and Matthew, and Thomas, and James the son of Alphæus, and Thaddæus, and Simon the Canaanite, 19 And Judas Iscariot, which also betrayed him ...	15 Matthew and Thomas, James the son of Alphæus, and Simon called Zelotes, 16 And Judas the brother of James, and Judas Iscariot, **which** also was the traitor.	16 And Judas the brother of James, and Judas Iscariot, **who** also was the traitor.

---

* The JST of these verses is the same, but without the **bold** words.

3 Ne. 12	Matt. 5	JST Matt. 5

38. The Sermon on the Mount

3 Ne. 12	Matt. 5	JST Matt. 5
	And seeing the multitudes, he went up into a mountain: and when he was set, his disciples came unto him:	And Jesus, seeing the multitudes, went up into a mountain; and when he was set **down**, his disciples came unto him;
	2 And he opened his mouth, and taught them, saying,	
And it came to pass that when Jesus had spoken these words unto Nephi, and to those who had been called, (now the number of them who had been called, and received power and authority to baptize, was twelve) and behold, he stretched forth his hand unto the multitude, and cried unto them, saying: Blessed are ye if ye shall give heed unto the words of these twelve whom I have chosen from among you to minister unto you, and to be your servants; and unto them I have given power that they may baptize you with water; and after that ye are baptized with water, behold, I will baptize you with fire and with the Holy Ghost; therefore blessed are ye if ye shall believe in me and be baptized, after that ye have seen me and know that I am.		
2 And again, more blessed are they who shall believe in your words because that ye shall testify that ye have seen me, and that ye know that I am.		3 Blessed are they who shall believe on me; and again, more blessed are they who shall believe on your words, when ye shall testify that ye have seen me and that I am.
Yea, blessed are they who shall believe in your words, and come down into the depths of humility and be baptized, for they shall be visited with fire and with the Holy Ghost, and shall receive a remission of their sins.		4 Yea, blessed are they who shall believe on your words, and come down into the depth of humility, and be baptized in my name; for they shall be visited with fire and the Holy Ghost, and shall receive a remission of their sins.
3 Yea, blessed are the poor in spirit who come unto me, for theirs is the kingdom of heaven.	3 Blessed are the poor in spirit: for theirs is the kingdom of heaven.	5 Yea, blessed are the poor in spirit, who come unto me; for theirs is the kingdom of heaven.
4 And again, blessed are all they that mourn, for they shall be comforted.	4 Blessed are they that mourn: for they shall be comforted.	6 And again, blessed are they that mourn; for they shall be comforted.
5 And blessed are the meek, for they shall inherit the earth.	5 Blessed are the meek: for they shall inherit the earth.	7 And blessed are the meek; for they shall inherit the earth.

Luke 6	JST Luke 6	D & C

The Sermon on the Plain   (Some consider Luke 6 as a separate sermon. Since the basic messages are the same, it is treated herein as one sermon .)

17 And he came down with them, and stood in the plain, and the company of his disciples, and a great multitude of people out of all Judaea and Jerusalem, and from the sea coast of Tyre and Sidon, which came to hear him, and to be healed of their diseases;
18 And they that were vexed with unclean spirits; and they were healed.
19 And the whole multitude sought to touch him: for there went virtue out of him, and healed them all.

Luke 6	JST Luke 6	D & C
20 And he lifted up his eyes on his disciples, and said, Blessed **be y e** poor: for **yours** is the kingdom of God.	20 And he lifted up his eyes on his disciples, and said, Blessed **are the** poor; for **theirs** is the kingdom of God.	88:17 And the redemption of the soul is through him that quickeneth all things, in whose bosom it is decreed that the poor and the meek of the earth shall inherit it.
21. . . Blessed are **ye that** weep now: for **ye** shall laugh.	21. . . Blessed are **they who** weep now: for **they** shall laugh.	18 Therefore, it must needs be sanctified from all unrighteousness, that it may be prepared for the celestial glory;
25. . . Woe unto you **that** laugh now! for ye shall mourn and weep.	25. . . Woe unto you **who** laugh now! For ye shall mourn and weep.	

85

3 Ne. 12	Matt. 5	JST Matt. 5
6 And blessed are all they who do hunger and thirst after righteousness, for they shall be filled with the Holy Ghost.	6 Blessed are they which do hunger and thirst after righteousness: for they shall be filled.	8 And blessed are all they that do hunger and thirst after righteousness; for they shall be filled with the Holy Ghost.
7 And blessed are the merciful, for they shall obtain mercy.	7 Blessed are the merciful: for they shall obtain mercy.	9 And blessed are the merciful; for they shall obtain mercy.
8 And blessed are all the pure in heart, for they shall see God.	8 Blessed are the pure in heart: for they shall see God.	10 And blessed are all the pure in heart; for they shall see God.
9 And blessed are all the peacemakers, for they shall be called the children of God.	9 Blessed are the peacemakers: for they shall be called the children of God.	11 And blessed are all the peacemakers; for they shall be called the children of God.
10 And blessed are all they who are persecuted for my name's sake, for theirs is the kingdom of heaven.	10 Blessed are they which are persecuted for righteousness' sake: for theirs is the kingdom of heaven.	12 Blessed are all they that are persecuted for my name's sake; for theirs is the kingdom of heaven.
11 And blessed are ye when men shall revile you and persecute, and shall say all manner of evil against you falsely, for my sake;	11 Blessed are ye, when men shall revile you, and persecute you, and shall say all manner of evil against you falsely, for my sake.	13 And blessed are ye when men shall revile you, and persecute you, and shall say all manner of evil against you falsely, for my sake.
12 For ye shall have great joy and be exceedingly glad, for great shall be your reward in heaven; for so persecuted they the prophets who were before you.	12 Rejoice, and be exceeding glad: for great is your reward in heaven: for so persecuted they the prophets which were before you.	14 For ye shall have great joy, and be exceedingly glad; for great shall be your reward in heaven; for so persecuted they the prophets which were before you.

TPJS-- Now, dear brethren, if any men ever had reason to claim this promise [Matt. 5:11-12], we are the men; for we know that the world not only hate us, but they speak all manner of evil of us falsely, for no other reason than that we have been endeavoring to teach the fullness of the Gospel of Jesus Christ. (p. 124)

When all men speak evil of you falsely, blessed are ye. Shall a man be considered bad, when men speak evil of him? No. If a man stands and opposes the world of sin, he may expect to have all wicked and corrupt spirits arrayed against him. But it will be but a little season, and all these afflictions will be turned away from us, inasmuch as we are faithful, and are not overcome by these evils. (p. 259)

3 Ne. 12	Matt. 5	JST Matt. 5
13 Verily, verily, I say unto you, I give unto you to be the salt of the earth; but if the salt shall lose its savor wherewith shall the earth be salted? The salt shall be thenceforth good for nothing, but to be cast out and to be trodden under foot of men.	13 Ye are the salt of the earth: but if the salt have lost his savour, wherewith shall it be salted? it is thenceforth good for nothing, but to be cast out, and to be trodden under foot of men.	15 Verily, verily, I say unto you, I give unto you to be the salt of the earth; but if the salt shall lose its savor, wherewith shall the earth be salted? the salt shall thenceforth be good for nothing, but to be cast out, and to be trodden under foot of men.
14 Verily, verily, I say unto you, I give unto you to be the light of this people. A city that is set on a hill cannot be hid.	14 Ye are the light of the world. A city that is set on an hill cannot be hid.	16 Verily, verily, I say unto you, I give unto you to be the light of the world; a city that is set on a hill cannot be hid.
15 Behold, do men light a candle and put it under a bushel? Nay, but on a candlestick, and it giveth light to all that are in the house;	15 Neither do men light a candle, and put it under a bushel, but on a candlestick; and it giveth light unto all that are in the house.	17 Behold, do men light a candle and put it under a bushel? Nay, but on a candlestick; and it giveth light to all that are in the house.
16 Therefore let your light so shine before this people, that they may see your good works and glorify your Father who is in heaven.	16 Let your light so shine before men, that they may see your good works, and glorify your Father which is in heaven.	18 Therefore, let your light so shine before this world, that they may see your good works, and glorify your Father who is in heaven.

Luke 6 B of M	JST Luke 6 D & C	D & C B of M
21 Blessed are **ye that** hunger now: for ye shall be filled. 25a Woe unto you **that** are full! for ye shall hunger. 36 Be ye therefore merciful, as your Father also is merciful.	21 Blessed are **they who** hunger now; for **they** shall be filled. 25a Woe unto you **who** are full! For ye shall hunger.	
22 Blessed are ye, when men shall hate you, and when they shall separate you from **their company**, and shall reproach you, and cast out your name as evil, for the Son of man's sake.	22 Blessed are ye when men shall hate you, and when they shall separate you from **among them**, and shall reproach you, and cast out your name as evil, for the Son of man's sake.	
23 Rejoice ye in that day, and leap for joy: for, behold, your reward is great in heaven: for in the like manner did their fathers unto the prophets. 24 But woe unto you that are rich! for you have received your consolation. 26 Woe unto you, when all men shall speak well of you! for so did their fathers to the false prophets.	23 Rejoice ye in that day, and leap for joy; for behold your reward **shall be** great in heaven; for in the like manner did their fathers unto the prophets.	
3 Ne. 16:15 But if they will not turn unto me, and hearken unto my voice, I will suffer them, yea, I will suffer my people, O house of Israel, that they shall go through among them, and shall tread them down, and they shall be as salt that hath lost its savor, which is thenceforth good for nothing but to be cast out, and to be trodden under foot of my people, O house of Israel.	D&C 101:39 When men are called unto mine everlasting gospel, and covenant with an everlasting covenant, they are accounted as the salt of the earth and the savor of men; 40 They are called to be the savor of men; therefore, if that salt of the earth lose its savor, behold, it is thenceforth good for nothing only to be cast out and trodden under the feet of men.	103:9 For they were set to be a light unto the world, and to be the saviors of men; 10 And inasmuch as they are not the saviors of men, they are as salt that has lost its savor, and is thenceforth good for nothing but to be cast out and trodden under foot of men. 3 Ne. 18:24 Therefore, hold up your light that it may shine unto the world. Behold I am the light which ye shall hold up---that which ye have seen me do. Behold ye see that I have prayed unto the Father, and ye all have witnessed.

3 Ne. 12	Matt. 5	JST Matt. 5
17 Think not that I am come to destroy the law or the prophets. I am not come to destroy but to fulfil;	17 Think not that I am come to destroy the law, or the prophets: I am not come to destroy, but to fulfil;	
18 For verily I say unto you, one jot nor one tittle hath not passed away from the law, but in me it hath all been fulfilled.	18 For verily I say unto you, Till heaven and earth pass, one jot or one tittle shall in no wise pass from the law, till all be fulfilled.	19 For verily I say unto you, Heaven and earth **must pass away, but** one jot or one tittle shall in no wise pass from the law, **until** all be fulfilled.
	19 Whosoever therefore shall break one of these least commandments, and shall teach men so, he shall **be called the least** in the kingdom of heaven: but whosoever shall do and teach **them**, the same shall be called great in the kingdom of heaven.	21 Whosoever, therefore, shall break one of these least commandments, and shall teach men so **to do,** he shall **in no wise be saved** in the kingdom of heaven; but whosoever shall do and teach **these commandments of the law until it be fulfilled**, the same shall be called great, **and shall be saved** in the kingdom of heaven.
	20 For I say unto you, **That** except your righteousness shall exceed **the righteousness** of the scribes and the Pharisees,	20 For I say unto you, Except your righteousness shall exceed **that** of the scribes and the Pharisees,
19 And behold, I have given you the law and the commandments of my Father, that ye shall believe in me, and that ye shall repent of your sins, and come unto me with a broken heart and a contrite spirit. Behold, ye have the commandments before you, and the law is fulfilled.		
20 Therefore come unto me and be saved; for verily I say unto you, that except ye shall keep my commandments, which I have commanded you at this time, ye shall in no case enter into the kingdom of heaven.	ye shall in no case enter into the kingdom of heaven.	ye shall in no case enter into the kingdom of heaven.
21 Ye have heard that it hath been said by them of old time, and it is also written before you, that thou shalt not kill, and whosoever shall kill shall be in danger of the judgment of God;	21 Ye have heard that it **was** said by them of old time, Thou shalt not kill; and whosoever shall kill shall be in danger of the judgment:	23 Ye have heard that it **hath been** said by them of old time **that,** Thou shalt not kill; and whosoever shall kill, shall be in danger of the judgment **of God**.
22 But I say unto you, that whosoever is angry with his brother shall be in danger of his judgment. And whosoever shall say to his brother, Raca, shall be in danger of the council; and whosover shall say, Thou fool, shall be in danger of hell fire.	22 But I say unto you, That whosoever is angry with his brother **without a cause** shall be in danger of **the** judgment: and whosoever shall say to his brother, Raca, shall be in danger of the council: **but** whosoever shall say, Thou fool, shall be in danger of hell fire.	24 But I say unto you that whosoever is angry with his brother, shall be in danger of **his** judgment; and whosoever shall say to his brother, Raca, **or Rabcha,** shall be in danger of the council; **a n d** whosoever shall say **to his brother,** Thou fool, shall be in danger of hell fire.
23 Therefore, if ye shall come unto me, or shall desire to come unto me, and rememberest that thy brother hast aught against thee--	23 Therefore if thou bring thy gift to the altar, and there rememberest that thy brother hath ought against thee;	25 Therefore, **if ye shall come unto me, or shall desire to come unto me, or** if thou bring thy gift to the altar, and there rememberest that thy brother hath aught against thee;

3 Ne. 12	Matt. 5	JST Matt. 5	D & C
24 Go thy way unto thy brother, and first be reconciled to thy brother, and then come unto me with full purpose of heart, and I will receive you.	24 Leave **there** thy gift before the altar, and go thy way; first be reconciled to thy brother, and then come and offer thy gift.	26 Leave **thou** thy gift before the altar, and go thy way **unto thy brother, and** first be reconciled to thy brother, and then come and offer thy gift.	
25 Agree with thine adversary quickly while thou art in the way with him, lest at any time he shall get thee, and thou shalt be cast into prison.	25 Agree with thine adversary quickly, whiles thou art in the way with him; lest at any time **the** adversary deliver thee to the judge, and the judge deliver thee to the officer, and thou be cast into prison.	27 Agree with thine adversary quickly, while thou art in the way with him; lest at any time **thine** adversary deliver thee to the judge, and the judge deliver thee to the officer, and thou be cast into prison.	
26 Verily, verily, I say unto thee, thou shalt by no means come out thence until thou hast paid the uttermost senine. And while ye are in prison can ye pay even one senine? Verily, verily, I say unto you, Nay.	26 Verily I say unto thee, Thou shalt by no means come out thence, **till thou** hast paid the uttermost farthing.	28 Verily I say unto thee, thou shalt by no means come out thence, **until** thou hast paid the uttermost farthing.	

TPJS-- [M]any must wait myriads of years before they can receive the like blessings [resurrection]; . . .

Rejoice, O Israel! Your friends who have been murdered for the truth's sake in the persecutions shall triumph gloriously in the celestial world, while their murderers shall welter for ages in torment, even until they shall have paid the uttermost farthing. (p. 359)

3 Ne. 12	Matt. 5	JST Matt. 5	D & C
27 Behold, it is written by them of old time, that thou shalt not commit adultery;	27 ¶ **Ye have heard that it was said** by them of old time, Thou shalt not commit adultery:	29 **Behold, it is written** by them of old time, **that** thou shalt not commit adultery.	42:22 Thou shalt love thy wife with all thy heart, and shalt cleave unto her and none else.
28 But I say unto you, that whosoever looketh on a woman, to lust after her, hath committed adultery already in his heart.	28 But I say unto you, That whosoever looketh on a woman to lust after her hath committed adultery **with her** already in his heart.		23 And he that looketh upon a woman to lust after her shall deny the faith, and shall not have the Spirit; and if he repents not he shall be cast out.
29 Behold, I give unto you a commandment, that ye suffer none of these things to enter into your heart;		(The bold words are deleted in the JST.)	63:16 And verily I say unto you, as I have said before, he that looketh on a woman to lust after her, or
30 For it is better that ye should deny yourselves of these things, wherein ye will take up your cross, than that ye should be cast into hell.		31 **Behold, I give unto you a commandment, that ye suffer none of these things to enter into your heart,** **for it is better that ye should deny yourselves of these things, wherein ye will take up your cross, than that ye should be cast into hell.**	if any shall commit adultery in their hearts, they shall not have the Spirit, but shall deny the faith and shall fear.

TPJS-- Now for a man to consecrate his property, wife and children, to the Lord, is nothing more nor less than to feed the hungry, clothe the naked, visit the widow and fatherless, the sick and afflicted, and do all he can to administer to their relief in their afflictions, and for him and his house to serve the Lord. In order to do this, he and all his house must be virtuous, and must shun the very appearance of evil. (p. 127)

3 Nephi	Matt. 5	JST Matt. 5
	29 **And** if thy right eye offend thee, pluck it out, and cast if from thee: for it is profitable for thee that one of thy members should perish, and not that thy whole body should be cast into hell.	32 **Wherefore,** if thy right eye offend thee, pluck it out and cast it from thee; for it is profitable for thee that one of thy members should perish, and not that thy whole body should be cast into hell.
	30 **And** if thy right hand offend thee, cut it off, and cast it from thee: for it is profitable for thee that one of thy members should perish, and not that thy whole body should be cast into hell.	33 Or if thy right hand offend thee, cut if off and cast it from thee; for it is profitable for thee that one of thy members should perish, and not that thy whole body should be cast into hell.
		34 **And now this I speak, a parable concerning your sins; wherefore, cast them from you, that ye may not be hewn down and cast into the fire.**

TPJS—[T]hose who are innocent are compelled to suffer for the iniquities of the guilty; and I cannot account for this, only on this wise, that the saying of the Savior has not been strictly observed: [Matt. 5:29. . .]. Now the fact is, if any of the members of our body is disordered, the rest of our body will be affected with it, and then all are brought into bondage together,. . . (pp. 34-35)

3 Nephi	Matt. 5	JST Matt. 5
31 It hath been written, that whosoever shall put away his wife, let him give her a writing of divorcement.	31 It hath been **said,** Whosoever shall put away his wife, let him give her a writing of divorcement:	35 It hath been **written that,** Whosoever shall put away his wife, let him give her a writing of divorcement.
32 Verily, verily, I say unto you, that whosoever shall put away his wife, saving for the cause of fornication, causeth her to commit adultery; and whoso shall marry her who is divorced committeth adultery.	32 **But** I say unto you, That whosoever shall put away his wife, saving for the cause of fornication, causeth her to commit adultery: and whosoever shall marry her that is divorced committeth adultery.	36 **Verily, verily,** I say unto you, that whosoever shall put away his wife, saving for the cause of fornication, causeth her to commit adultery; and whosoever shall marry her that is divorced, committeth adultery.
33 And again it is written, thou shalt not forswear thyself, but shalt perform unto the Lord thine oaths;	33 ¶ Again, **ye have heard that** it hath been **said** by them of old time, Thou shalt not forswear thyself, but shalt perform unto thine Lord thy oaths:	37 Again, it hath been **written** by them of old time, Thou shalt not forswear thyself, but shalt perform unto the Lord thine oaths.
34 But verily, verily, I say unto you, swear not at all; neither by heaven, for it is God's throne;	34 But I say unto you, Swear not at all; neither by heaven; for it is God's throne:	
35 Nor by the earth, for it is his footstool;	35 Nor by the earth; for it is his footstool: neither by Jerusalem; for it is the city of the great King.	
36 Neither shalt thou swear by thy head, because thou canst not make one hair black or white;	36 Neither shalt thou swear by thy head, because thou canst not make one hair white or black	
37 But let your communication be Yea, yea; Nay, nay; for whatsoever cometh of more than these is evil.	37 But let your communication be, Yea, yea; Nay, nay: for whatsoever is more than these cometh of evil.	
38 And behold, it is written, an eye for an eye, and a tooth for a tooth;	38 ¶ Ye have heard that it hath been said, An eye for an eye, and a tooth for a tooth:	

D & C		
42:74 Behold, verily I say unto you, that whatever persons among you, having put away their companions for the cause of fornication, or in other words, if they shall testify before you in all lowliness of heart that this is the case, ye shall not cast them out from among you; 75 But if ye shall find that any persons have left their companions for the sake of adultery, and they themselves are the offenders, and their companions are living, they shall be cast out from among you.		
124:119 And again, verily I say unto you, let no man pay stock to the quorum of the Nauvoo House unless he shall be a believer in the Book of Mormon, and the revelations I have given unto you, saith the Lord God; 120 For that which is more or less than this cometh of evil, and shall be attended with cursings and not blessings, saith the Lord your God. Even so. Amen.		

3 Ne. 12	Matt. 5	JST Matt. 5
39 But I say unto you, that ye shall not resist evil, but whosoever shall smite thee on thy right cheek, turn to him the other also;	39 But I say unto you, That ye resist not evil: but whosoever shall smite thee on thy right cheek, turn to him the other also.	
40 And if any man will sue thee at the law and take away thy coat, let him have thy cloak also;	40 And if any man will sue thee at the law, and take away thy coat, let him have thy cloak also;	42 And if any man will sue thee at the law, and take away thy coat, let him have it; **and if he sue thee again, let him have** thy cloak also.
41 And whosoever shall compel thee to go a mile, go with him twain.	41 And whosoever shall compel thee to go a mile, go with him twain.	43 And whosoever shall compel thee to go a mile, go with him **a mile; and whosoever shall compel thee to go with him twain, thou shalt go with him** twain.
42 Give to him that asketh thee, and from him that would borrow of thee turn thou not away.	42 Give to him that asketh thee, and from him that would borrow of thee turn not thou away.	44 Give to him that asketh of thee; and from him that would borrow of thee, turn not thou away.
43 And behold it is written also, that thou shalt love thy neighbor and hate thine enemy;	43 ¶ Ye have heard that it hath been said, Thou shalt love thy neighbour, and hate thine enemy.	
44 But behold I say unto you, love your enemies, bless them that curse you, do good to them that hate you, and pray for them who despitefully use you and persecute you;	44 But I say unto you, Love your enemies, bless them that curse you, do good to them that hate you, and pray for them which despitefully use you, and persecute you;	
45 That ye may be the children of your Father who is in heaven; for he maketh the sun to rise on the evil and on the good.	45 That ye may be the children of your Father **which** is in heaven: for he maketh the sun to rise on the evil and on the good, and sendeth rain on the just and on the unjust.	47 That ye may be the children of your Father **who** is in heaven; for he maketh his sun to rise on the evil and on the good, and sendeth rain on the just and the unjust.

TPJS-- But while one portion of the human race is judging and condemning the other without mercy, the Great Parent of the universe looks upon the whole of the human family with a fatherly care and paternal regard; He views them as His offspring, and without any of those contracted feelings that influence the children of men, causes "His sun to rise on the evil and on the good, and sendeth rain on the just and on the unjust." (p. 218)

There is one thing under the sun which I have learned and that is that the righteousness of man is sin because it exacteth over much; nevertheless, the righteousness of God is just, because it exacteth nothing at all, but sendeth the rain on the just and the unjust, seed time and harvest, for all of which man is ungrateful. (p. 317)

3 Ne. 12	Matt. 5	JST Matt. 5
46 Therefore those things which were of old time, which were under the law, in me are all fulfilled.		
47 Old things are done away, and all things have become new.		
	46 For if ye love them which love you, what reward have ye? do not even the publicans the same?	48 For if ye love only them which love you, what reward have you? Do not even the publicans the same?
	47 And if ye salute your brethren only, what do ye more than others? do not even the publicans so?	49 And if ye salute your brethren only, what do ye more than others? Do not even the publicans **the same?**
48 Therefore I would that ye should be perfect even as I, or your Father who is in heaven is perfect.	48 **Be** ye therefore perfect, even as your Father **which** is in heaven is perfect.	50 Ye are therefore **commanded to** be perfect, even as your Father **who** is in heaven is perfect.

Luke 6	JST Luke 6	
29 And unto him **that** smiteth thee on the **one** cheek offer also the other; and him **that** taketh away thy cloak forbid not to take thy coat also.	29 And unto him **who** smiteth thee on the cheek, offer also the other; **or, in other words, it is better to offer the other, than to revile again.** And him **who** taketh away thy cloak, forbid not to take thy coat also. 30 **For it is better that thou suffer thine enemy to take these things, than to contend with him. Verily I say unto you, Your Heavenly Father who teeth in secret, shall bring that wicked one into judgement.**	
30 Give to every man **that** asketh of thee; and of him **that** taketh away thy goods ask them not again.	31 **Therefore** give to every man **who** asketh of thee; and of him **who** taketh away thy goods, ask them not again.	
27 ¶ But I say unto you **which** hear, Love your enemies, do good to them **which** hate you,	27 But I say unto you **who** hear my words Love your enemies, do good to them **who** hate you.	
28 Bless them **that** curse you, and pray for them **which** despitefully use you.	28 Bless them **who** curse you, and pray for them **who** despitefully use you **and persecute you.**	
31 And as ye would that men should do to you, do ye also to them likewise.		
32 for if ye love them **which** love you, what **thank** have **ye?** for sinners also **love those that love them.**	33 For if ye love them **only who** love you, what **reward** have **you?** for sinners also **do even the same.**	
33 And if ye do good to them which do good to you, what thank have ye? for sinners also do even the same.	(The JST omits this verse entirely.)	
34 And if ye lend to them of whom ye hope to receive, what **thank** have ye? for sinners also lend to sinners, to receive as much again.	34 And if ye lend to them of whom ye hope to receive, what **reward** have **you?** for sinners also lend to sinners, to receive as much again.	
35 But love ye your enemies, and do good, and lend, hoping for nothing again; and your reward shall be great, and ye shall be the children of the Highest: for he is kind unto the unthankful and to the evil.		
39 And he spake a parable unto them, Can the blind lead the blind? shall they not both fall into the ditch?		
40 **The** disciple is not above his master: but everyone that is perfect shall be as his master.	40 **A** disciple is not above his master; but everyone that is perfect shall be as his master.	

3 Nephi 13	Matt. 6	JST Matt. 6
Verily, verily, I say that I would that ye should do alms unto the poor; but take heed that ye do not your alms before men to be seen of them; otherwise ye have no reward of your Father who is in heaven.	Take heed that ye do not your alms before men, to be seen of them: otherwise ye have no reward of your Father **which** is in heaven.	**And it came to pass that, as Jesus taught his disciples, he said unto them,** Take heed that ye do not your alms before men, to be seen of them; otherwise ye have no reward of your Father **who** is in heaven.
2 Therefore, when ye shall do your alms do not sound a trumpet before you, as will hypocrites do in the synagogues and in the streets, that they may have glory of men. Verily I say unto you, they have their reward.	2 Therefore when thou doest **thine** alms, do not sound a trumpet before **thee**, as the hypocrites do in the synagogues and in the streets, that they may have glory of men. Verily I say unto you, **They** have their reward.	2 Therefore, when thou doest alms, do not sound a trumpet before thee, as the hypocrites do, in the synagogues and in the streets, that they may have glory of men. Verily I say unto you, they have their reward.
3 But when thou doest alms let not thy left hand know what thy right hand doeth;	3 But when thou doest alms, let **not** thy left hand **know** what thy right hand doeth:	3 But when thou doest alms, let **it be unto thee as** thy left hand **not knowing** what thy right hand doeth;
4 That thine alms may be in secret; and thy Father who seeth in secret, himself shall reward thee openly.	4 That thine alms may be in secret: and thy Father **which** seeth in secret himself shall reward thee openly.	4 That thine alms may be in secret; and thy Father **who** seeth in secret, himself shall reward thee openly.
5 And when thou prayest thou shalt not do as the hypocrites, for they love to pray, standing in the synagogues and in the corners of the streets, that they may be seen of men. Verily I say unto you, they have their reward.	5 ¶ And when thou prayest, thou shalt not be as the hypocrites **are:** for they love to pray standing in the synagogues and in the corners of the streets, that they may be seen of men. Verily I say unto you, they have their reward.	5 And when thou prayest, thou shalt not be as the hypocrites; for they love to pray standing in the synagogues and in the corners of the streets, that they may be seen of men; **for,** verily, I say unto you, they have their reward.
6 But thou, when thou prayest, enter into thy closet, and when thou hast shut thy door, pray to thy Father who is in secret; and thy Father, who seeth in secret, shall reward thee openly.	6 But thou, when thou prayest, enter into thy closet, and when thou hast shut **thy** door, pray to thy Father **which** is in secret; and thy Father **which** seeth in secret shall reward thee openly.	6 But thou, when thou prayest, enter into thy closet, and when thou hast shut **the** door, pray to thy Father **who** is in secret; and thy Father **who** seeth in secret shall reward thee openly.
7 But when ye pray, use not vain repetitions, as the heathen, for they think that they shall be heard for their much speaking.	7 But when ye pray, use not vain repetitions, as the **heathen** do: for they think that they shall be heard for their much speaking.	7 But when ye pray, use not vain repetitions, as the **hypocrites** do; for they think that they shall be heard for their much speaking.
8 Be not ye therefore like unto them, for your Father knoweth what things ye have need of before ye ask him.	8 Be **not ye therefore** like unto them: for your Father knoweth what things ye have need of, before ye ask him.	8 **Therefore** be ye **not** like unto them; for your Father knoweth what things ye have need of, before ye ask him.
9 After this manner therefore pray ye: Our Father who art in heaven, hallowed be thy name.	9 After this manner **therefore** pray ye: Our Father **which** art in heaven, Hallowed be thy name.	9 **Therefore** after this manner **shall ye pray, saying,**
		10 Our Father **who** art in heaven, Hallowed be thy name.
10 Thy will be done on earth as it is in heaven.	10 Thy kingdom come. Thy will be done **in** earth, as it is in heaven. 11 Give us this day our daily bread.	11 Thy kingdom come. Thy will be done **on** earth, as it is **done** in heaven.
11 And forgive us our debts, as we forgive our debtors.	12 And forgive us our **debts,** as we forgive **our debtors.**	13 And forgive us our **trespasses, as we forgive those who trespass against us.**

TPJS-- Joseph remarked that all was well between him and the heavens; that he had no enmity against any one; and as the prayer of Jesus, or his pattern, so prayed Joseph-- Father, forgive me my trespasses as I forgive those who trespass against me, for I freely forgive all men. If we would secure and cultivate the love of others, we must love others, even our enemies as well as friends. (pp 312-313)

3 Nephi 13	Matt. 6	JST Matt. 6	D&C B of M Luke 6
12 And lead us not into temptation, but deliver us from evil.	13 And **lead** us not into temptation, but deliver us from evil:	14 And **suffer** us not **to be led** into temptation, but deliver us from evil.	
13 For thine is the kingdom, and the power, and the glory, forever, Amen.	For thine is the kingdom, and the power, and the glory, for ever. Amen.	15 For thine is the kingdom, and the power, and the glory, forever **and ever**, Amen.	
14 For, if ye forgive men their trespasses your heavenly Father will also forgive you;	14 For if ye forgive men their trespasses, your heavenly Father will also forgive you:	16 For if ye forgive men their trespasses, **who trespass against you**, your heavenly Father will also forgive you; but if ye forgive not men their trespasses, neither will your **heavenly** Father forgive **you** your trespasses.	D&C 132:56 And again, verily I say, let mine handmaid forgive my servant Joseph his trespasses; and then shall she be forgiven her trespasses, wherein she has trespassed against me; and I, the Lord thy God, will bless her, and multiply her, and make her heart to rejoice.
15 But if ye forgive not men their trespasses neither will your Father forgive your trespasses.	15 But if ye forgive not men their trespasses, neither will your Father forgive your trespasses.		
16 Moreover, when ye fast be not as the hypocrites, of a sad countenance, for they disfigure their faces that they may appear unto men to fast. Verily I say unto you, they have their reward.	16 ¶ Moreover when ye fast, be not, as the hypocrites, of a sad countenance: for they disfigure their faces, that they may appear unto men to fast. Verily I say unto you, They have their reward.		
17 But thou, when thou fastest, anoint thy head, and wash thy face;	17 But thou, when thou fastest, anoint thine head, and wash thy face;		
18 That thou appear not unto men to fast, but unto thy Father, who is in secret: and thy Father, who teeth in secret, shall reward thee openly.	18 That thou appear not unto men to fast, but unto thy Father, **which** is in secret: and thy Father **which** teeth in secret, shall reward thee openly.	18 . . . that thou appear not unto men to fast, but unto thy Father **who** is in secret: and thy Father **who** seeth in secret, shall reward thee openly.	2 Nephi 9:30 But wo unto the rich, who are rich as to the things of the world. For because they are rich they despise the poor, and they persecute the meek, and their hearts are upon their treasures; wherefore, their treasure is their god. And behold, their treasure shall perish with them also.
19 Lay not up for yourselves treasures upon earth, where moth and rust doth corrupt, and thieves break through and steal;	19 ¶ Lay not up for yourselves treasures upon earth, where moth and rust doth corrupt, and where thieves break through and steal:		
20 But lay up for yourselves treasures in heaven, where neither moth nor rust doth corrupt, and where thieves do not break through nor steal.	20 But lay up for yourselves treasures in heaven, where neither moth nor rust doth corrupt, and where thieves do not break through nor steal:		Luke 6:45 A good man out of the good treasure of his heart bringeth forth that which is good; and an evil man out of the evil treasure of his heart bringeth forth that which is evil: for of the abundance of the heart his mouth speaketh.
21 For where your treasure is, there will your heart be also.	21 For where your treasure is, there will your heart be also.		D&C 88:67 And if your eye be single to my glory, your whole bodies shall be filled with light, and there shall be no darkness in you; and that body which is filled with light comprehendeth all things.
22 The light of the body is the eye; if, therefore, thine eye be single, thy whole body shall be full of light.	22 The light of the body is the eye: if therefore thine eye be single, thy whole body shall be full of light.	22 the light of the body is the eye; if therefore thine eye be single **to the glory of God**, thy whole body shall be full of light.	

3 Nephi 13	Matt. 6	JST Matt. 6
23 But if thine eye be evil, thy whole body shall be full of darkness. If, therefore, the light that is in thee be darkness, how great is that darkness!	23 But if thine eye be evil, thy whole body shall be full of darkness. If therefore the light that is in thee be darkness, how great is that darkness!	23 But if thine eye be evil, thy whole body shall be full of darkness. If therefore the light which is in thee be darkness, how great shall that darkness be.
24 No man can serve two masters; for either he will hate the one and love the other, or else he will hold to the one and despise the other. Ye cannot serve God and Mammon.	24 ¶ No man can serve two masters: for either he will hate the one, and love the other; or else he will hold to the one, and despise the other. Ye cannot serve God and mammon.	
25 And now it came to pass that when Jesus had spoken these words he looked upon the twelve whom he had chosen, and said unto them: Remember the words which I have spoken. For behold ye are they whom I have chosen to minister unto this people.		25 And, again, I say unto you, go ye into the world, and care not for the world; for the world will hate you, and will persecute you, and will turn you out of their synagogues.
		26 Nevertheless, ye shall go forth from house to house, teaching the people; and I will go before you.
		27 And your heavenly Father will provide for you, whatsoever things ye need for food, what ye shall eat; and for raiment, what ye shall wear or put on.
Therefore I say unto you, take no thought for your life, what ye shall eat, or what ye shall drink; nor yet for your body, what ye shall put on. Is not the life more than meat, and the body than raiment?	25 Therefore I say unto you, Take no thought for your life, what ye shall eat, or what ye shall drink; nor yet for your body, what ye shall put on. Is not the life more than meat, and the body than raiment?	28 Therefore I say unto you, take no thought for your life, what ye shall eat, or what ye shall drink; nor yet for your bodies, what ye shall put on. Is not the life more than meat, and the body than raiment?
26 Behold the fowls of the air, for they sow not, neither do they reap nor gather into barns; yet your heavenly Father feedeth them. Are ye not much better than they?	26 Behold the fowls of the air: for they sow not, neither do they reap, nor gather into barns; yet your heavenly Father feedeth them. Are ye not much better than they?	29 Behold the fowls of the air, for they sow not, neither do they reap, nor gather into barns; yet your heavenly Father feedeth them. Are ye not much better than they? How much more will he not feed you?
		30 Wherefore take no thought for these things, but keep my commandments wherewith I have commanded you.
27 Which of you by taking thought can add one cubit unto his stature?	27 Which of you by taking thought can add one cubit unto his stature?	31 For which of you by taking thought can add one cubit to his stature.

TPJS-- As concerning the resurrection, I will merely say that all men will come from the grave as they lie down, whether old or young; there will not be "added unto their stature one cubit," neither taken from it;. . .(p. 199)

28 And why take ye thought for raiment? Consider the lilies of the field how they grow; they toil not, neither do they spin;	28 And why take ye thought for raiment? Consider the lilies of the field, how they grow; they toil not, neither do they spin:	

3 Nephi 13	Matt. 6	JST Matt. 6	D&C Luke B of M
29 And yet I say unto you, that even Solomon, in all his glory, was not arrayed like one of these.	29 And yet I say unto you, That even Solomon in all his glory was not arrayed like one of these.		101:37 Therefore, care not for the body, neither the life of the body; but care for the soul, and for the life of the soul.
30 Wherefore, if god so clothe the grass of the field, which today is, and tomorrow is cast into the oven, even so will he clothe you, if ye are not of little faith.	30 **Wherefore**, if God so clothe the grass of the field, which to day is, and to morrow is cast into the oven, **shall he not** much more **clothe** you, **O** ye of little faith?	34 **Therefore**, if God so clothe the grass of the field, which today is, and tomorrow is cast into the oven, **how** much more **will he not provide for** you, **if ye are not** of little faith?	84:81 Therefore, take ye no thought for the morrow, for what ye shall eat, or what ye shall drink, or wherewithal ye shall be clothed.
31 Therefore take not thought, saying, What shall we eat? or, What shall we drink? or, Wherewithal shall we be clothed?	31 Therefore take no thought, saying, What shall we eat? or, What shall we drink? or, Wherewithal shall we be clothed?		82 For, consider the lilies of the field, how they grow, they toil not, neither do they spin; and the kingdoms of the world, in all their glory, are not arrayed like one of these.
		36 **Why is it that ye murmur among yourselves, saying, We cannot obey thy word because ye have not all these things, and seek to excuse yourselves, saying that,** After all these things do the Gentiles seek.	83 for your Father, who is in heaven, knoweth that you have need of all these things. 84 Therefore, let the morrow take thought for the things of itself.
	32 (For after all these things do the Gentiles seek:)		
32 For your heavenly Father knoweth that ye have need of all these things.	for your heavenly Father knoweth that ye have need of all these things.	37 **Behold, I say unto you, that** your heavenly Father knoweth that ye have need of all these things. 38 **Wherefore seek not the things of this world** but seek ye first **to establish** the kingdom of God, and **to establish** his righteousness, and all these things shall be added unto you.	85 Neither take ye thought beforehand what ye shall say; but treasure up in your minds continually the words of life, and it shall be given you in the very hour that portion that shall be meted unto every man.
33 But seek ye first the kingdom of God and his righteousness, and all these things shall be added unto you.	33 But seek ye first the kingdom of God, and his righteousness; and all these things shall be added unto you.		Luke 12:31 ¶ But rather seek ye the kingdom of God; and all these things shall be added unto you.
TPJS—If we seek first the kingdom of God, all good things will be added. (p. 256)			Jacob 2:18 But before ye seek for riches, seek ye for the kingdom of God.
34 Take no thought for the morrow, for the morrow shall take thought for the things of itself. Sufficient unto the day is the evil thereof.	34 Take no thought for the morrow: for the morrow shall take thought for the things of itself. Sufficient unto the day is the evil thereof.	39 Take, **therefore**, no thought for the morrow; for th morrow shall take thought for the things of itself. Sufficient unto the day **shall be** the evil thereof.	19 And after ye have obtained a hope in Christ ye shall obtain riches, if ye seek them; and ye will seek them for the intent to do good—(See rest of verse 19).

3 Ne. 14	Matt. 7	JST Matt. 7
And now it came to pass that when Jesus had spoken these words he turned again to the multitude, and did open his mouth unto them again, saying: Verily, verily, I say unto you, Judge not, that ye be not judged.	Judge not, that ye be not judged.	Now these are the words which Jesus taught his disciples that they should say unto the people. 2 Judge not unrighteously, that ye be not judged; but judge righteous judgment.
2 For with what judgment ye judge, ye shall be judged; and with what measure ye mete, it shall be measured to you again.	2 For with what judgment ye judge, ye shall be judged: and with what measure ye mete, it shall be measured to you again.	3 For with what judgment ye shall judge, ye shall be judged; and with what measure ye mete, it shall be measured to you again.
3 And why beholdest thou the mote that is in thy brother's eye, but considerest not the beam that is in thine own eye?	3 And why beholdest thou the mote that is in thy brother's eye, but considerest not the beam that is in thine own eye?	4 And again, ye shall say unto them, Why is it that thou beholdest the mote that is in thy brother's eye, but considerest not the beam that is in thine own eye?
4 Or how wilt thou say to thy brother: Let me pull the mote out of thine eye--and behold, a beam is in thine own eye?	4 Or how wilt thou say to thy brother, Let me pull out the mote out of thine eye; and, behold, a beam is in thine own eye?	5 Or how wilt thou say to thy brother, Let me pull out the mote out of thine eye; and canst not behold a beam in thine own eye?
		6 And Jesus said unto his disciples, Beholdest thou the Scribes, and the Pharisees, and the Priests, and the Levites? They teach in their synagogues, but do not observe the law, nor the commandments; and all have gone out of the way, and are under sin.
		7 Go thou and say unto them, Why teach ye men the law and the commandments, when ye yourselves are the children of corruption?
5 Thou hypocrite, first cast the beam out of thine own eye; and then shalt thou see clearly to cast the mote out of thy brother's eye.	5 Thou hypocrite, first cast out the beam out of thine own eye; and then shalt thou see clearly to cast out the mote out of thy brother's eye.	8 Say unto them, Ye hypocrites, first cast out the beam out of thine own eye; and then shalt thou see clearly to cast out the mote out of thy brother's eye.
		9 Go ye into the world, saying unto all, Repent, for the kingdom of heaven has come nigh unto you.
		10 And the mysteries of the kingdom ye shall keep within yourselves; for it is not meet to give that which is holy unto the dogs; neither cast ye your pearls unto swine, lest they trample them under their feet.
6 Give not that which is holy unto the dogs, neither cast ye your pearls before swine, lest they trample them under their feet,	6 ¶ Give not that which is holy unto the dogs, neither cast ye your pearls before swine, lest they trample them under their feet,	

Luke 6	JST Luke 6	B of M
		Moroni 7:14 Wherefore, take heed, my beloved brethren, that ye do not judge that which is evil to be of God, or that which is good and of God to be of the devil.
37 Judge not, and ye shall not be judged: condemn not, and ye shall not be condemned: forgive, and ye shall be forgiven.		15 For behold, my brethren, it is given unto you to judge, that ye may know good from evil; and the way to judge is as plain, that ye may know with a perfect knowledge, as the daylight is from the dark night.
38 Give, and it shall be given unto you; good measure, pressed down, and shaken together, and running over, shall men give into your bosom. For with the same measure that ye mete withal it shall be measured to you again.		16 For behold, the Spirit of Christ is given to every man, that he may know good form evil; wherefore, I show unto you the way to judge; for every thing which inviteth to do good, and to persuade to believe in Christ, is sent forth by the power and gift of Christ; wherefore ye may know with a perfect knowledge it is of God.
41 And why beholdest thou the mote **that** is in thy brother's eye, but perceives not the beam **that** is in thine own eye?	41 And why beholdest thou the mote **which** is in thy brother's eye, but perceives not the beam **which** is in thine own eye?	17 But whatsoever ting persuadeth men to do evil, and believe not in Christ, and deny him, and serve not God, then ye may know with a perfect knowledge it is of the devil; for after this manner doth the devil work, for he persuadeth no man to do good, no, not one; neither do his angels; neither do they who subject themselves unto him.
42 **Either** how canst thou say to thy brother, **Brother**, let me pull out the mote that is in thine eye, when thou thyself beholdest not the beam **that** is in thine own eye?	42 **Again**, how canst thou say to thy brother, Let me pull out the mote that is in thine eye, when thou thyself beholdest not the beam **which** is in thine own eye?	18 And now, my brethren, seeing that ye know the light by which ye may judge, which light is the light of Christ, see that ye do not judge wrongfully; for with that same judgment which ye judge ye shall also be judged.
Thou hypocrite, cast out first the beam out of thine own eye, and then shalt thou see clearly to pull out the mote **that** is in thy brother's eye.	Thou hypocrite, cast out first the beam out of thine own eye, and then shalt thou see clearly to pull out the mote **which** is in thy brother's eye.	19 Wherefore, I beseech of you, brethren, that ye should search diligently in the light of Christ that ye may know good from evil; and if you will lay hold upon every good thing, and condemn it not, ye certainly will be a child of Christ.

3 Ne. 14	Matt. 7	JST Matt. 7
		11 **For the world cannot receive that which ye, yourselves, are not able to bear; wherefore ye shall not give your pearls unto them, lest they turn again and rend you.**
and turn again and rend you.	**and turn again and rend you.**	

TPJS-- Strive not about the mysteries of the kingdom; cast not your pearls before swine, give not the bread of the children to dogs, lest you and the children should suffer, and you thereby offend your righteous Judge. (p. 77)

3 Ne. 14	Matt. 7	JST Matt. 7
7 Ask, and it shall be given unto you; seek, and ye shall find; knock, and it shall be opened unto you.	7 ¶ Ask, and it shall be given you; seek, and ye shall find; knock, and it shall be opened unto you:	12 **Say unto them, Ask of God;** ask, and it shall be given you; seek, and ye shall find; knock, and it shall be opened unto you.
8 For every one that asketh, receiveth; and he that seeketh, findeth; and to him that knocketh, it shall be opened.	8 For every one that asketh receiveth; and he that seeketh findeth; and to him that knocketh it shall be opened.	13 For everyone that asketh, receiveth; and he that seeketh, findeth; and **unto** him that knocketh, it shall be opened.

TPJS-- Our heavenly Father is more liberal in His views, and boundless in His mercies and blessings, than we are ready to believe or receive; and, at the same time, is more terrible to the workers of iniquity, more awful in the executions of His punishments, and more ready to detect every false way, than we are apt to suppose Him to be. He will be inquired of by His children. He says, "Ask and ye shall receive, seek and ye shall find;" but, if you will take that which is not your own, or which I have not given you, you shall be rewarded according to your deeds; but no good thing will I withhold from them who walk uprightly before me, and do my will in all things-- who will listen to my voice and to the voice of my servant whom I have sent; for I delight in those who seek diligently to know my precepts, and abide by the law of my kingdom; for all things shall be made known unto them in mine own due time, and in the end they shall have joy. (p. 257)

3 Ne. 14	Matt. 7	JST Matt. 7
		14 **And then said his disciples unto him, they will say unto us, We ourselves are righteous, and need not that any man should teach us. God, we know, heard Moses and some of the prophets; but us he will not hear.**
		15 **And they will say, We have the law for our salvation, and that is sufficient for us.**
		16 **Then Jesus answered, and said unto his disciples, thus shall ye say unto them,**
		17 **What man among you, having a son, and he shall be standing out, and shall say, Father, open thy house that I may come in and sup with thee, will not say, Come in, my son; for mine is thine, and thine is mine?**
9 Or what man is there of you, who, if his son ask bread, will give him a stone?	9 Or what man is there of you, whom if his son ask bread, will **he** give him a stone?	18 Or what man is there **among** you, who, if his son ask bread, will give him a stone?
10 Or if he ask a fish, will he give him a serpent?	10 Or if he ask a fish, will he give him a serpent?	

B of M	D & C	D & C
	41:5 He that receiveth my law and doeth it, the same is my disciple; and he that saith he receiveth it and doeth it not, the same is not my disciple, and shall be cast out from among you; 6 For it is not meet that the things which belong to the children of the kingdom should be given to them that are not worthy, or to dogs, or the pearls to be cast before swine.	
2 Ne. 32:4 Wherefore, now after I have spoken these words, if ye cannot understand them it will be because ye ask not, neither do ye knock; wherefore, ye are not brought into the light, but must perish in the dark.	75:27 Let them ask and they shall receive, knock and it shall be opened unto them, and be made known from on high, even by the Comforter, whither they shall go. (See also D&C 49: 26; 66:9; 103:31, 35.)	88:63 Draw near unto me and I will draw near unto you; seek me diligently and ye shall find me; ask, and ye shall receive; knock, and it shall be opened unto you. 64 Whatsoever ye ask the Father in my name it shall be given unto you, that is expedient for you; 65 And if ye ask anything that is not expedient for you, it shall turn unto your condemnation.

3 Ne. 14	Matt. 7	JST Matt. 7
11 If ye then, being evil, know how to give good gifts unto your children, how much more shall your Father who is in heaven give good things to them that ask him? 12 Therefore, all things whatsoever ye would that men should do to you, do ye even so to them, for this is the law and the prophets.	11 If ye then, being evil, know how to give good gifts unto your children, how much more shall your Father which is in heaven give good things to them that ask him? 12 Therefore all things whatsoever ye would that men should do to you, do ye even so to them: for this is the law and the prophets.	

TPJS-- The Messiah's kingdom on earth is of that kind of government, that there has always been numerous apostates, for the reason that it admits of no sins unrepented of without excluding the individual from its fellowship. (pp. 66-67)

3 Ne. 14	Matt. 7	JST Matt. 7
13 Enter ye in at the strait gate; for wide is the gate, and broad is the way, which leadeth to destruction, and many there be who go in thereat; 14 Because strait is the gate, and narrow is the way, which leadeth unto life, and few there be that find it.	13 ¶ Enter ye in at the strait gate: for wide is the gate, and broad is the way, that leadeth to destruction, and many there be that go in thereat: 14 Because strait is the gate, and narrow is the way, which leadeth unto life, and few there be that find it.	22 **Repent, therefore, and** enter ye in at the strait gate; for wide is the gate, and broad is the way that leadeth to destruction, and many there be that go in thereat.
15 Beware of false prophets, who come to you in sheep's clothing, but inwardly they are ravening wolves.	15 ¶ Beware of false prophets, **which** come to you in sheep's clothing, but inwardly they are ravening wolves.	24 **And, again,** beware of false prophets, **who** come to you in sheep's clothing; but inwardly they are ravening wolves.
16 Ye shall know them by their fruits. Do men gather grapes of thorns, or figs of thistles?	16 Ye shall know them by their fruits. Do men gather grapes of thorns, or figs of thistles?	25 Ye shall know them by their fruits; **for** do men gather grapes of thorns, or figs of thistles?
17 Even so every good tree bringeth forth good fruit; but a corrupt tree bringeth forth evil fruit.	17 Even so every good tree bringeth forth good fruit; but a corrupt tree bringeth forth evil fruit.	
18 A good tree cannot bring forth evil fruit, neither a corrupt tree bring forth good fruit. 19 Every tree that bringeth not forth good fruit is hewn down, and cast into the fire. 20 Wherefore, by their fruits ye shall know them.	18 A good tree cannot bring forth evil fruit, neither can a corrupt tree bring forth good fruit. 19 Every tree that bringeth not forth good fruit is hewn down, and cast into the fire. 20 Wherefore by their fruits ye shall know them.	
21 Not everyone that saith unto me, Lord, Lord, shall enter into the kingdom of heaven; but he that doeth the will of my Father who is heaven.	21 ¶ Not everyone that saith unto me, Lord, Lord, shall enter into the kingdom of heaven; but he that doeth the will of my Father **which** is heaven.	30 **Verily I say unto you, it is** not everyone that saith unto me, Lord, Lord, **that** shall enter into the kingdom of heaven; but he that doeth the will of my Father **who** is heaven.

Luke 6 B of M	B of M	B of M D & C
Lk 6:31 And as ye would that men should do to you, do ye also to them likewise.		
2 Ne 31:17 Wherefore, do the things which I have told you I have seen that your Lord and your Redeemer should do; for, for this cause have they been shown unto me, that ye might know the gate by which ye should enter. For the gate by which ye should enter is repentance and baptism by water; and then cometh a remission of your sins by fire and by the Holy Ghost.	3 Ne 27:33 And it came to pass that when Jesus had ended these sayings he said unto his disciples: Enter ye in at the strait gate; for strait is the gate, and narrow is the way that leads to life, and few there be that find it; but wide is the gate, and broad the way which leads to death, and many there be that travel therein, until the night cometh, wherein no man can work.	Jac 6:11 O then, my beloved brethren, repent ye, and enter in at the strait gate, and continue in the way which is narrow, until ye shall obtain eternal life. D&C 132:22 For strait is the gate, and narrow the way that leadeth unto the exaltation and continuation of the lives, and few there be that find it, because ye receive me not in the world neither do ye know me.
Lk 6:44 For every tree is known by his own fruit. For of thorns men do not gather figs, nor of a bramble bush gather they grapes. 45 A good man out of the good treasure of his heart bringeth forth that which is good; and an evil man out of the evil treasure of his heart bringeth forth that which is evil: for of the abundance of the heart his mouth speaketh. 43 For a good tree bringeth not forth corrupt fruit; neither doth a corrupt tree bring forth good fruit.	Moro 7:5 For I remember the word of God which saith by their works ye shall know them; for if their works be good, then they are good also. 6 For behold, God hath said a man being evil cannot do that which is good; for if he offereth a gift, or prayeth unto God, except he shall do it with real intent it profiteth him nothing. 7 For behold, it is not counted unto him for righteousness.	
46 ¶ And why call ye me, Lord, Lord, and do not the things which I say?	8 For behold, if a man being evil giveth a gift, he doeth it grudgingly; wherefore it is counted unto him the same as if he had retained the gift; wherefore he is counted evil before God.	

103

3 Ne. 14	Matt. 7	JST Matt. 7
		31 **For the day soon cometh, that men shall come before me to judgment, to be judged according to their works.**
22 Many will say to me in that day: Lord, Lord, have we not prophesied in thy name, and in thy name have cast out devils, and in thy name done many wonderful works?	22 Many will say to me in that day, Lord, Lord, have we not prophesied in thy name? and in thy name **have** cast out devils? and in thy name done many wonderful works?	32 **And** many will say **unto** me in that day, Lord, Lord, have we not prophesied in thy name; and in thy name cast out devils; and in thy name done many wonderful works?
23 And then will I profess unto them: I never knew you; depart from me, ye that work iniquity.	23 And then will I **profess unto them,** I never knew **you**: depart from me, ye that work iniquity.	33 And then will I **say, Ye** never knew **me**; depart from me ye that work iniquity.
24 Therefore, whoso heareth these sayings of mine and doeth them, I will liken him unto a wise man, who built his house upon a rock--	24 ¶ Therefore whosoever heareth these sayings of mine, and doeth them, I will liken him unto a wise man, **which** built his house upon a rock:	34 Therefore, whosoever heareth these sayings of mine and doeth them, I will liken him unto a wise man, **who** built his house upon a rock,
25 And the rain descended, and the floods came, and the winds blew, and beat upon that house; and it fell not, for it was founded upon a rock.	25 And the rain descended, and the floods came, and the winds blew, and beat upon that house; and it fell not: for it was founded upon a rock.	and the rains descended, and the floods came, and the winds blew, and beat upon that house; and it fell not: for it was founded upon a rock.
26 And every one that heareth these sayings of mine and doeth them not shall be likened unto a foolish man, who built his house upon the sand--	26 And every one that heareth these sayings of mine, and doeth them not, shall be likened unto a foolish man, **which** built his house upon the sand:	35 And every one that heareth these sayings of mine, and doeth them not, shall be likened unto a foolish man, **who** built his house upon the sand;
27 And the rain descended, and the floods came, and the winds blew, and beat upon that house; and it fell; and great was the fall of it.	27 And the rain descended, and the floods came, and the winds blew, and beat upon that house; and it fell: and great was the fall of it.	37 And the rains descended, and the floods came, and the winds blew, and beat upon that house, and it fell; and great was the fall of it.

TPJS-- It is in the order of heavenly things that God should always send a new dispensation into the world when men have apostatized from the truth and lost the priesthood, but when men come out and build upon other men's foundations, they do it on their own responsibility, without authority from God; and when the floods come and the winds blow, their foundations will be found to be sand, and their whole fabric will crumble to dust. (pp. 375-376)

	Matt. 7	JST Matt. 7
	28 And it came to pass, when Jesus had ended these sayings, the people were astonished at his doctrine:	36 And it came to pass when Jesus had ended these sayings **with his disciples**, the people were astonished at his doctrine;
	29 For he taught them as one having authority, and not as the scribes.	37 For he taught them as one having authority **from God**, and not as **having authority from** the Scribes.

Luke 6	B of M JST Luke 6	D & C B of M
	Mos 26:25 And it shall come to pass that when the second trump shall sound then shall they that never knew me come forth and shall stand before me. 26 And then shall they know that I am the Lord their God, that I am their Redeemer; but they would not be redeemed. 27 And then I will confess unto them that I never knew them; and they shall depart into everlasting fire prepared for the devil and his angels.	D&C 29:27 And the righteous shall be gathered on my right hand unto eternal life; and the wicked on my left hand will I be ashamed to own before the Father; 28 Wherefore I will say unto them --Depart from me, ye cursed, into everlasting fire, prepared for the devil and his angels. 29 And now, behold, I say unto you, never at any time have I declared from mine own mouth that they should return, for where I am they cannot come, for they have no power. (See also 6:34; 90:5.)
47 Whosoever cometh to me, and heareth my sayings, and doeth them, I will shew you to whom he is like:		3 Ne 11:39 Verily, verily, I say unto you, that this is my doctrine, and whoso buildeth upon this buildeth upon my rock, and the gates of hell shall not prevail against them.
48 He is like a man **which** built an house, and digged deep, and laid the foundation on a rock: and when the flood arose, the stream beat vehemently upon the house, and could not shake it: for it was founded upon a rock. 49 But he **that** heareth, and doeth not, is like a man that without a foundation built an house upon the earth; against which the stream did beat vehemently, and immediately it fell; and the ruin of that house was great.	JST Lk 6:48 He is like a man **who** built an house, and digged deep, and laid the foundation on a rock: and when the flood arose, the stream beat vehe-mently upon the house, and could not shake it: for it was founded upon a rock. 49 But he **who** heareth, and doeth not, is like a man that without a foundation built an house upon the earth; against which the stream did beat vehemently, and immediately it fell; and the ruin of that house was great.	40 And whoso shall declare more or less than this, and establish it for my doctrine, the same cometh of evil, and is not built upon my rock; but he buildeth upon a sandy foundation, and the gates of hell stand open to receive such when the floods come and the winds beat upon them. 41 Therefore, go forth unto this people, and declare the words which I have spoken, unto the ends of the earth. (See also 3 Ne. 18:12-13.)
	Hel. 5:12 And now, my sons, re-member, remember that it is upon the rock of our Redeemer, who is Christ, the Son of God, that ye must build your foundation; that when the devil shall send forth his mighty winds, yea, his shafts in the whirl-wind, yea, when all his hail and his mighty storm shall beat upon you, it shall have no power over you to drag you down to the gulf of misery and endless wo, because of the rock upon which ye are built, which is a sure foundation, a foundation where-on if men build they cannot fall.	

Matt. 8	JST Matt. 8	Luke 7	JST Luke

39. Capernaum-- Heals Centurion's Servant

Matt. 8	JST Matt. 8	Luke 7	JST Luke
When **he** was come down from the mountain, great multitudes followed him. 5 And when Jesus was entered into Capernaum,	**And** when **Jesus** was come down from the mountain, great multitudes followed him.	Now when he had ended all **his** sayings in the audience of the people, he entered into Capernaum. 2 And a certain centurion's servant, who was dear unto him, was sick, and ready to die.	Now when he had ended all **these** sayings in the audience of the people, he entered into Capernaum.
there came unto him a centurion, beseeching him,		3 And when he heard of Jesus, he sent unto him the elders of the Jews, beseeching him that he would come and heal his servant.	
6 And saying, Lord, my servant lieth at home sick of the palsy, grieviously tormented.		4 And when they came to Jesus, they besought him instantly, saying,	
		That he was worthy for whom he should do this: 5 For he loveth our nation, and he hath built us a synagogue.	
7 And Jesus saith unto him, I will come and heal him.		6 Then Jesus went with them. And when he was now not far from the house, the centurion sent friends to him, saying unto him, Lord, trouble not thyself: for I am not worthy that thou shouldest enter under my roof:	
8 The centurion answered and said, Lord, I am not worthy that thou shouldest come under my roof:		7 Wherefore neither thought I myself worthy to come unto thee: but say in **a** word, and my servant shall be healed.	7 Wherefore, neither thought I myself worthy to come unto thee; but say **the** word, and my servant shall be healed.
but speak the word only, and my servant shall be healed. 9 For I am a man under authority, having soldiers under me: and I say to this man, Go, and he goeth; and to another, Come, and he cometh; and to my servant, Do this, and he doeth it.		8 For I also am a man set under authority, having under me soldiers, and I say unto one, Go, and he goeth; and to another, Come, and he cometh; and to my servant, Do this, and he doeth it.	

Matt. 8	JST Matt. 8	Luke 7	JST Luke 7
10 When Jesus heard it, he **marvelled, and** said to them that followed, Verily I say unto you, I have not found so great faith, no, not in Israel.	9 **And when they that followed him, heard this, they marvelled. And** when Jesus heard **this,** he said unto them that followed,	9 When Jesus heard these things, he marvelled at him, and turned him about, and said unto the people **that** followed him, I say unto you, I have not found so great faith, no, not in Israel.	9 When Jesus heard these things, he marvelled at him, and turned him about, and said unto the people **who** followed him, I say unto you, I have not found so great faith, no, not in Israel.
11 And I say unto you, That many shall come from the east and west, and shall sit down with Abraham, and Isaac, and Jacob, in the kingdom of heaven.	11 And I say unto you, That many shall come from the east, and **the** west, and shall sit down with Abraham, and Isaac, and Jacob, in the kingdom of heaven.		
12 But the children of the **kingdom** shall be cast out into outer darkness: there shall be weeping and gnashing of teeth.	12 But the children of the **wicked one** shall be cast out into outer darkness; there shall be weeping and gnashing of teeth.		
13 And Jesus said unto the centurion, Go thy way; and as thou hast believed, so be it done unto thee. And his servant was healed in the selfsame hour.		10 And they **that** were sent, returning to the house, found the servant whole **that** had been sick.	10 And they **who** were sent, returning to the house, found the servant whole **who** had been sick.

Luke 7	JST Luke 7		

40. Nain (Galilee)-- Widow's Son Raised from the Dead

Luke 7	JST Luke 7		
11 ¶ And it came to pass the day after, that he went into a city called Nain; and many of his disciples went with him, and much people.			
12 Now when he came nigh to the gate of the city, behold, there was a dead man carried out, the only son of his mother, and she was a widow: and **much** people of the city **was** with her.	12 Now, when he came nigh to the gate of the city, behold, there was a dead man carried out, the only son of his mother, and she was a widow; and **many** people of the city **were** with her.		
13 And **when** the Lord saw her, **he** had compassion on her, and said unto her, Weep not.	13 And **now** the Lord saw her, **and** had compassion on her, and **he** said unto her, Weep not.		
14 And he came and touched the bier: and they **that** bare **him** stood still. And he said, Young man, I say unto thee, Arise.	14 And he came and touched the bier; and they **who** bare it stood still, and he said, Young man, I say unto thee, Arise.		
15 And he **that** was dead sat up, and began to speak. And he delivered him to his mother.	15 And he **who** w a s dead, sat up, and began to speak; and he delivered him to his mother.		
16 And there came a fear on all: and they glorified God, saying, That a great prophet is risen up among us; and, That God hath visited his people.			
17 And this rumour of him went forth throughout all Judæa, and throughout all the region round about.			

Matt. 11	JST Matt. 11	Luke 7	JST Luke 7

41. John Sends Messages

Matt. 11	JST Matt. 11	Luke 7	JST Luke 7
		18 And the disciples of John shewed him of all these things.	
2 Now when John had heard in the prison the works of Christ, he sent two of his disciples,		19 ¶ And John calling unto him two of his disciples sent them to Jesus, saying, Art thou he that should come? or look we for another?	19 And John calling two of his disciples, sent them to Jesus, saying, Art thou he that should come, or look we for another?
		20 When the men were come unto him, they said, John Baptist hath sent us unto thee, saying, Art thou he that should come? or look we for another?	20 When the men were come unto him, they said, John Baptist hath sent us unto thee, saying, Art thou he who should come, or look we for another?
3 And said unto him, Art thou he that should come, or do we look for another?	3 And said unto him, Art thou he of whom it is written in the prophets that he should come, or do we look for another?	21 And in that same hour he cured many of their infirmities and plagues, and of evil spirits; and unto many that were blind he gave sight.	21 And in the same hour he cured many of infirmities, and plagues, and of evil spirits, and unto many blind he gave sight.
4 Jesus answered and said unto them, Go and shew John again those things which ye do hear and see:	4 Jesus answered and said unto them, Go and tell John again of those things which ye do hear and see;	22 Then Jesus answering said unto them, Go your way, and tell John what things ye have seen and heard; how that the blind see, the lame walk, the lepers are cleansed, the deaf hear, the dead are raised, to the poor the gospel is preached.	22 Then Jesus, answering, said unto them, Go your way, and tell John what things ye have seen and heard; how that the blind see, the lame walk, the lepers are cleansed, the deaf hear, the dead are raised, and to the poor the gospel is preached.
5 The blind receive their sight, and the lame walk, the lepers are cleansed, and the deaf hear, the dead are raised up, and the poor have the gospel preached to them.	5 How the blind receive their sight, and the lame walk, and the lepers are cleansed, and the deaf hear, and the dead are raised up, and the poor have the gospel preached unto them.	(See also D&C 35:15)	
6 And blessed is he, whosoever shall not be offended in me.	6 And blessed is John, and whosoever shall not be offended in me.	23 And blessed is he, whosoever shall not be offended in me.	23 And blessed are they who shall not be offended in me.

42. Jesus Testifies of John's Greatness

Matt. 11	JST Matt. 11	Luke 7	JST Luke 7
7 ¶ And as they departed, Jesus began to say unto the multitudes concerning John, What went ye out into the wilderness to see? A reed shaken with the wind?	7 And as they departed, Jesus began to say unto the multitudes concerning John, What went ye out into the wilderness to see? Was it a reed shaken with the wind? And they answered him, No.	24 ¶ And when the messengers of John were departed, he began to speak unto the people concerning John, What went ye out into the wilderness for to see? A reed shaken with the wind?	24 And when the messengers of John were departed, he began to speak unto the people concerning John; What went ye out into the wilderness to see? A reed shaken with the wind?
8 But what went ye out for to see? A man clothed in soft raiment? behold, they that wear soft clothing are in kings' houses.	8 And he said, But what went ye out for to see? Was it a man clothed in soft raiment? Behold they that wear soft raiment are in king's houses.	25 But what went ye out for to see? A man clothed in soft raiment? Behold, they which are gorgeously apparelled, and live delicately, are in kings' courts.	Or a man clothed in soft raiment? 25 Behold, they who are gorgeously apparelled, and live delicately, are in king's courts.

Matt. 11	JST Matt. 11	Luke 7	JST Luke 7
9 But what went ye out for to see? A prophet? yea, I say unto you, and more than a prophet.		26 But what went ye out for to see? A prophet? Yea, I say unto you, and much more than a prophet.	
10 For this is **he**, of whom it is written, Behold, I send my messenger before thy face, which shall prepare thy way before thee.	10 For this is **the one** of whom it is written, Behold, I send my messenger before thy face, which shall prepare thy way before thee. (See Malachi 3:1)	27 This is **he**, of whom it is written, Behold, I send my messenger before thy face, **which** shall prepare thy way before thee.	27 This is **the one** of whom it is written, Behold I send my messenger before thy face, **who** shall prepare thy way before thee.
11 Verily I say unto you, Among them that are born of women there hath not risen a greater than John the Baptist: notwithstanding he that is least in the kingdom of heaven is greater than he.		28 For I say unto you, Among those that are born of women there is not a greater prophet than John the Baptist: but he that is least in the kingdom of God is greater than he.	

TPJS-- The question arose from the saying of Jesus-- [Matt. 11:11]. How is it that John was considered one of the greatest prophets? His miracles could not have constituted his greatness.

First. He was entrusted with a divine mission of preparing the way before the face of the Lord. Whoever had such a trust committed to him before or since? No man.

Secondly. He was entrusted with the important mission, and it was required at his hands, to baptize the Son of Man. Whoever had the honor of doing that? Whoever had so great a privilege and glory? Whoever led the Son of God into the waters of baptism, and had the privilege of beholding the Holy Ghost descend in the form of a dove, or rather in the *sign* of the dove, in witness of that administration? The sign of the dove was instituted before the creation of the world, a witness for the Holy Ghost, and the devil cannot come in the sign of a dove. The Holy Ghost is a personage, and is in the form of a personage. It does not confine itself to the *form* of the dove, but in *sign* of the dove. The Holy Ghost cannot be transformed into a dove; but the sign of a dove was given to John to signify the truth of the deed, as the dove is an emblem or token of truth and innocence.

Thirdly. John, at that time, was the only legal administrator in the affairs of the kingdom there was then on the earth, and holding the keys of power. The Jews had to obey his instructions or be damned, by their own law; and Christ Himself fulfilled all righteousness in becoming obedient to the law which he had given to Moses on the mount, and thereby magnified it and made it honorable, instead of destroying it. The son of Zacharias wrested the keys, the kingdom, the power, the glory from the Jews, by the holy anointing and decree of heaven, and these three reasons constitute him the greatest prophet born of a woman. (pp. 275-276)

Matt. 11	JST Matt. 11	Luke 7	JST Luke 7
12 And from the days of John the Baptist until now the kingdom of heaven suffereth violence, and the violent taketh it by force.			
13 For all the prophets and the law prophesied until John.	13 **But the days will come, when the violent shall have no power;** for all the prophets and the law prophesied **that it should be thus** until John. 14 **Yea, as many as have prophesied have foretold of these days.**		

TPJS-- (Cites Matt. 11:12-13.) John held the Aaronic Priesthood and was a legal administrator, and the forerunner of Christ, and came to prepare the way before him. (p. 318)

Matt. 11	JST Matt. 11	Luke 7	JST Luke 7
14 And if ye will receive it, **this is** Elias, **which** was for to come. 15 He that hath ears to hear, let him hear.	15 And if ye will receive it, **verily, he was the** Elias, **who** was for to come **and prepare all things**.		
		29 And all the people **that** heard him, and the publicans, justified God, being baptized with the baptism of John. 30 But the Pharisees and lawyers rejected the counsel of God against themselves, **being not** baptized of him. 31 And the Lord said, Whereunto then shall I liken the men of this generation? and to what are they like?	29 And all the people **who** heard him, and the publicans, justified God, being baptized with the baptism of John. 30 But the Pharisees, and lawyers, rejected the counsel of God against themselves, **not being** baptized of him.
16 ¶ But whereunto shall I liken this generation?			
It is like unto children sitting in the markets, and calling unto their fellows, 17 And saying, We have piped unto you, and ye have not danced; we have mourned **unto** you, and ye have not lamented. 18 For John came neither eating or drinking, and they say, He hath a devil.	18 It is like unto children sitting in the markets, and calling unto their fellows, and saying, We have piped unto you, and ye have not danced; we have mourned **for** you, and ye have not lamented.	32 They are like unto children sitting in the marketplace, and calling one to another, and saying, We have piped **unto** you, and ye have not danced; we have mourned **to** you, and ye have not wept. 33 For John the Baptist came neither eating bread nor drinking wine; and ye say, He hath a devil.	32 They are like unto children sitting in the marketplace, and calling one to another, and saying, We have piped **for** you, and ye have not danced; we have mourned **for** you, and ye have not wept.
19 The Son of man came eating and drinking, and they say, Behold a **man gluttnous**, and a winebibber, a friend of publicans and sinners.	20 The Son of Man came eating and drinking, and they say, Behold, a **gluttnous man** and a winebibber, a friend of publicans and sinners. 21 But **I say unto you,** Wisdom is justified of her children.	34 The Son of man is come eating and drinking; and ye say, Behold a gluttnous man, and a winebibber, a friend of publicans and sinners!	
But wisdom is justified of her children.		35 But wisdom is justified of all her children.	

<u>Luke 7</u>	<u>JST Luke 7</u>	<u>Luke 7</u>	<u>JST Luke 7</u>

43. Woman Anoints Jesus' Feet

36 ¶ And one of the Pharisees desired him that he would eat with him. And he went into the Pharisee's house, and sat down to meat.

37 And, behold, a woman in the city, **which** was a sinner, when she knew that Jesus sat at meat in the Pharisee's house, brought an alabaster box of ointment.

38 And stood at his feet **behind him** weeping, and began to wash his feet with tears, and did wipe them with the hairs of her head, and kissed his feet, and anointed them with **the** ointment.

39 Now when the Pharisee **which** had bidden him saw **it,** he spake within himself, saying, This man, if he were a prophet, would have known who **and** what manner of woman this is **that** toucheth him: for she is a sinner.

40 And Jesus answering said unto him, Simon, I have somewhat to say unto thee. And he saith, Master, say on.

41 There was a certain creditor **which** had two debtors: the one owed five hundred pence, and the other fifty.

42 And when they had nothing to pay, he frankly forgave them both. Tell me therefore, which of them will love him most?

43 Simon answered and said, I suppose **that he,** to whom he forgave most. And he said unto him, Thou hast rightly judged.
(continued in column 3)

37 And behold, a woman in the city, **who** was a sinner, when she knew that Jesus sat at meat in the Pharisee's house, brought an alabaster box of ointment.

38 And stood at his feet weeping, and began to wash his feet with tears, and did wipe them with the hairs of her head, and kissed his feet, and anointed them with ointment.

39 Now when the Pharisee **who** had bidden him saw **this,** he spake within himself, saying, This man, if he were a prophet, would have known who, **or** what manner of woman this is **who** toucheth him; for she is a sinner.

41 **And Jesus said,** There was a certain creditor, **who** had two debtors; the one owed five hundred pence, and the other fifty.

42 And when **he found** they had nothing to pay, he frankly forgave them both. Tell me therefore, which of them will love him most?

43 Simon answered and said, I suppose **the man** to whom he forgave most. And he said unto him, Thou hast rightly judged.
(continued in column 4)

44 And he turned to the woman, and said unto Simon, Seest thou this woman? I entered into **thine** house, thou gavest me no water for my feet: but she hath washed my feet with tears, and wiped them with the hairs of her head.

45 Thou gavest me no kiss: but this woman since the time I came in hath not ceased to kiss my feet.

46 My head with oil thou didst not anoint: but this woman hath anointed my feet with ointment.

47 Wherefore I say unto thee, Her sins, which are many, are forgiven; for she loved much: but
to whom little is forgiven, the same loveth little.

48 And he said unto her, Thy sins are forgiven.

49 And they that sat at meat with him began to say within themselves, Who is this that forgiveth sins also?

50 And he said to the woman, Thy faith hath saved thee; go in peace.

44 And he turned to the woman, and said unto Simon, Seest thou this woman? I entered into **thy** house, thou gavest me no water for my feet; but she hath washed my feet with tears, and wiped them with the hairs of her head.

112

Luke 8	JST Luke 8		

44. Galilee-- Tours with the Twelve and Certain Women

Luke 8	JST Luke 8		
And it came to pass afterward, that he went throughout every city and village, preaching and shewing the glad tidings of the kingdom of God: and the twelve were with him.	And it came to pass afterward, that he went throughout every city and village, preaching and showing the glad tidings of the kingdom of God; and the twelve **who were ordained of him,** were with him,		
2 And certain women, **which** had been healed of evil spirits and infirmities, Mary called Magdalene, out of whom went seven devils,	2 And certain women **who** had been healed of evil spirits and infirmities, Mary called Magdalene, out of whom went seven devils;		
3 And Joanna the wife of Chuza Herod's steward, and Susanna, and many others, **which** ministered unto him **of** their substance.	3 And Joanna the wife of Chuza, Herod's steward, and Susanna, and many others, **who** ministered unto him **with** their substance.		

Matt. 12	JST Matt. 12	Mark 3	JST Mark 3

45. Devil Cast Out-- Accused of Working with Beelzebub

Matt. 12	JST Matt. 12	Mark 3	JST Mark 3
		19. . . and they went into an house.	
		20 And the multitude cometh together again, so that they could not so much as eat bread.	
		21 And when his friends heard **of it,** they went out to lay hold on him: for they said, He is beside himself.	16 And when his friends heard **him speak,** they went out to lay hold on him; for they said, He is beside himself.
22 ¶ Then was brought unto him one possessed with a devil, blind, and dumb: and he healed him, insomuch that the blind and dumb both spake and saw.			
23 And all the people were amazed, and said, Is not this the son of David?	19 And all the people were amazed, and said, Is this the Son of David?		

113

Matt. 12	JST Matt. 12	Mark 3	JST Mark 3 B of M
24 But when the Pharisees heard **it**, they said, This **fellow** doth not cast out devils, but by Beelzebub the prince of **the** devils.	20 But when the Pharisees heard **that he had cast out the devil**, they said, This **man** doth not cast out devils, but by Beelzebub the prince of devils.	22 ¶ And the scribes which came down from Jerusalem said, He hath Beelzebub, and by the prince of the devils casteth he out devils.	
25 And Jesus knew their thoughts, and said unto them,	21 And Jesus knew their thoughts, and said unto them. . .	23 And he called them **unto him**, and said unto them in parables, How can Satan cast out Satan?	18 **Now Jesus knew this**, and he called upon them, and said unto them in parables, How can Satan cast out Satan?
Every kingdom divided against itself is brought to desolation; and every city or house divided against itself shall not stand:		24 And if a kingdom be divided against itself, that kingdom **cannot** stand. 25 And if a house be divided against itself, that house cannot stand.	And if a kingdom be divided against itself, **how can** that kingdom stand? 19 And if a house be divided against itself, that house cannot stand.
26 and if Satan cast out Satan, he is divided against himself; how **shall then** his kingdom stand?	. . . And if Satan cast out Satan, he is divided against himself; how **then shall** his kingdom stand?	26 And if Satan rise up against himself, and be divided, he cannot stand, but hath an end.	And if Satan rise up against himself and be divided, he cannot stand; but **speedily** hath an end.
27 And if I by Beelzebub cast out devils, by whom do your children cast **them out**? therefore they shall be your judges.	22 And if I by Beelzebub cast out devils, by whom do your children cast **out devils**? Therefore they shall by your judges.		
28 But if I cast out devils by the Spirit of god, then the kingdom of God is come unto you.	23 But if I cast out devils by the Spirit of God, then the kingdom of God is come unto you. **For they also cast out devils by the Spirit of God, for unto them is given power over devils, that they may cast them out.**		
29 Or else how can one enter into a strong man's house, and spoil his goods, except he first bind the strong man? and then he will spoil his house.		27 No man can enter into a strong man's house, and spoil his goods, except he will first bind the strong man; and then he will spoil his house.	2 Ne. 10:16 Wherefore, he that fighteth against Zion, both Jew and Gentile, both bond and free, both male and female, shall perish; for they are they who are the whore of all the earth; for they who are not for me are against me, saith our God.
30 He that is not with me is against me; and he that gathereth not with me scattereth abroad.			

Matt. 12	JST Matt. 12	Mark 3	JST Mark 3
			21 And then came certain men unto him, accusing him, saying, Why do ye receive sinners, seeing thou makest thyself the Son of God.
31 ¶ Wherefore I say unto you, All manner of sin and blasphemy shall be forgiven unto men:	26 Wherefore I say unto you, All manner of sin and blasphemy shall be forgiven unto men **who receive me and repent**; but the blasphemy against the Holy Ghost, it shall not be forgiven unto men.	28 Verily I say unto you, All sins shall be forgiven unto the sons of men,	22 But he answered them and said, Verily I say unto you, All sins which men have committed, when they repent, shall be forgiven them; for I came to preach repentance unto the sons of men.
but the blasphemy against the Holy Ghost shall not be forgiven unto men.			
32 And whosoever speaketh a word against the Son of man, it shall be forgiven him:		and blasphemies wherewith soever they shall blaspheme:	23 And blasphemies, wherewith soever they shall blaspheme, shall be forgiven them that come unto me, and do the works they see me do.
but whosoever speaketh against the Holy Ghost, it shall not be forgiven him, neither in this world, neither in the world to come.		29 But he that shall blaspheme against the Holy Ghost hath never forgiveness, but is in danger of eternal damnation:	24 But there is a sin which shall not be forgiven. He that shall blaspheme against the Holy Ghost, hath never forgiveness; but is in danger of being cut down out of the world. And they shall inherit eternal damnation.
		30 Because they said, He hath an unclean spirit.	25 And this he said unto them because they said, He hath an unclean spirit.

46. Blasphemy Against the Holy Ghost

TPJS-- The situation of the Christian nations after death, is a subject that has called forth all the wisdom and talent of the philosopher and the divine, and it is an opinion which is generally received, that the destiny of man is irretrievably fixed at his death, and that he is made either eternally happy, or eternally miserable; that if a man dies without a knowledge of God, he must be eternally damned, without any mitigation of his punishment, alleviation of his pain, or the most latent hope of a deliverance while endless ages shall role along. However orthodox this principle may be, we shall find that it is at variance with the testimony of Holy Writ, for our Savior says, that all manner of sin and blasphemy shall be forgiven men wherewith they shall blaspheme; but the blasphemy against the Holy Ghost shall not be forgiven, neither in this world, nor in the world to come, evidently showing that there are sins which may be forgiven in the world to come, although the sin of blasphemy [against the Holy Ghost] cannot be forgiven . (pp. 218-219)

I have a declaration to make as to the provisions which God hath made to suit the conditions of man--made from before the foundation of the world. What has Jesus said? All sins, and all blasphemies, and every transgression, except one, that man can be guilty of, may be forgiven; and there is a salvation for all men, either in this world or the world to come, who have not committed the unpardonable sin, there being a provision either in this world or the world of spirits. Hence God hath made provision that every spirit in the eternal world can be ferreted out and saved unless he has committed that unpardonable sin which cannot be remitted to him either in this world or the world of spirits. God has wrought out a salvation for all men, unless they have committed a certain sin; and every

115

Matt. 12	JST Matt. 12	TPJS

TPJS cont.-- man who has a friend in the eternal world can save him, unless he has committed the unpardonable sin. And so you can see how far you can be a savior. (pp. 356-357)

Hear it, all ye ends of the earth-- all ye priests, all ye sinners, and all men. Repent! repent! Obey the Gospel. Turn to God; for your religion won't save you, and you will be damned. I do not say how long. There have been remarks made concerning all men being redeemed from hell; but I say that those who sin against the Holy Ghost cannot be forgiven in this world or in the world to come; they shall die the second death. Those who commit the unpardonable sin are doomed to *Gnolom*-- to dwell in hell, worlds without end. As they concoct scenes of bloodshed in this world, so they shall rise to that resurrection which is as the lake of fire and brimstone. Some shall rise to the everlasting burnings of God; for God dwells in everlasting burnings, and some shall rise to the damnation of their own filthiness, which is as exquisite a torment as the lake of fire and brimstone. (p. 361)

Matt. 12	JST Matt. 12	TPJS
33 Either make the tree good, and his fruit good; or else make the tree corrupt, and his fruit corrupt: for the tree is known by his fruit.		I advise all of you to be careful what you do, or you may by-and-by find out that you have been deceived. Stay yourselves; do not give way; don't make any hasty moves, you may be saved. If a spirit of bitterness
34 O generation of vipers, how can ye, being evil, speak good things? for out of the abundance of the heart the mouth speaketh.	29 And Jesus said, O ye generation of vipers! how can ye, being evil, speak good things? For out of the abundance of the heart the mouth speaketh.	is in you, don't be in haste. You may say, that man is a sinner. Well, if he repents, he shall be forgiven. Be cautious: await. When you find a spirit that wants bloodshed---murder, the same is not of God, but is of the devil. Out of the abundance of the heart of man the mouth speaketh. (p. 358)
35 A good man out of the good treasure of the heart bringeth forth good things: and an evil man out of the evil treasure bringeth forth evil things.		
36 But I say unto you, That every idle word that men shall speak, they shall give account thereof in the day of judgment.	31 And again I say unto you, That every idle word that men shall speak, they shall give account thereof in the day of judgment.	
37 For by thy words thou shalt be justified, and by thy words thou shalt be condemned.		

47. Pharisees Seek a Sign

Matt. 12	JST Matt. 12	TPJS
38 ¶ Then certain of the scribes and of the Pharisees answered, saying, Master, we would see a sign from thee.		
39 But he answered and said unto them, An evil and adulterous generation seeketh after a sign; and there shall no sign be given to it, but the sign of the prophet Jonas:		Jesus [said] that he who seeketh a sign is an adulterous person; and that principle is eternal, undeviating, and firm as the pillars of heaven; for whenever you see a man seeking after a sign, you may set it down that he is an adulterous man. (p. 157)
40 For as Jonas was three days and three nights in		

Matt. 12	JST Matt. 12	TPJS
the whale's belly; so shall the Son of man be three days and three nights in the heart of the earth. 41 The men of Nineveh shall rise in judgment with this generation, and shall condemn it: because they repented at the preaching of Jonas; and, behold, a greater than Jonas is here. 42 The queen of the south shall rise up in the judgment with this generation, and shall condemn it: for she came from the uttermost parts of the earth to hear the wisdom of Solomon; and, behold, a greater than Solomon is here.	35 The men of Nineveh shall rise **up** in judgment with this generation, and shall condemn it, because they repented at the preaching of Jonas; and, ye behold, a greater than Jonas is here. 36 The queen of the south shall rise up in the **day of** judgment with this generation, and shall condemn it; for she came from the uttermost parts of the earth to hear the wisdom of Solomon; and, ye behold, a greater than Solomon is here. 37 **Then came some of the Scribes and said unto him, Master, it is written that, Every sin shall be forgiven; but ye say, Whosoever speaketh a-gainst the Holy Ghost shall not be forgiven And they asked him, saying, How can these things be?** 43 **And he said unto them,** When the unclean spirit is gone out of a man, he walketh through dry places, seeking rest, and findeth none; **but when a man speaketh against the Holy Ghost, then he saith,**	A man cannot commit the unpardonable sin after the dissolution of the body, and there is a way possible for escape. Knowledge saves a man; and in the world of spirits no man can be exalted but by knowledge. So long as a man will not give heed to the commandments, he must abide without salvation. If a man has knowledge, he can be saved; although, if he has been guilty of great sins, he will be punished for them. But when he consents to obey the Gospel, whether here or in the world of spirits, he is saved. A man is his own tormenter and his own condemner. Hence the saying, They shall go into the lake that burns with fire and brimstone. The torment of disappointment in the mind of man is as exquisite as a lake burning with fire and brimstone. I say, so is the torment of man. I know the Scriptures and understand them. I said, no man can commit the unpardonable sin after the dissolution of the body, nor in this life, until he receives the Holy Ghost; but they must do it in this world. Hence the salvation of Jesus Christ was wrought out for all men, in order to triumph over the devil; for if it did not catch him in one place, it would in another; for he stood up as a Savior. All will suffer until they obey Christ himself. (p. 357)
43 When the unclean spirit is gone out of a man, he walketh through dry places, seeking rest, and findeth none. 44 Then he saith, I will return into my house from whence I came out; and when he is come, he findeth it empty, swept, and garnished.	I will return into my house from whence I came out; and when he is come, he findeth **him** empty, swept and garnished; **for the good spirit leaveth him unto himself.** 39 Then goeth **the evil spirit,** and taketh with himself seven other spirits more wicked than himself;	
45 Then goeth **he,** and taketh with himself seven other spirits more wicked than himself, and they enter in and dwell there: and the last **state** of that man is worse than the first. Even so shall it be also unto this wicked generation.	and they enter in and dwell there; and the last **end** of that man is worse than the first. Even so shall it be also unto this wicked generation.	All sins shall be forgiven, except the sin against the Holy Ghost; for Jesus will save all except the sons of perdition. What must a man do to commit the unpardonable sin? He must receive the Holy Ghost, have the heavens opened unto him, and know God, and then sin against Him. After a man has sinned against the Holy Ghost, there is no repentance for him. He has got to say that the sun does not shine while he sees it; he has got to deny Jesus Christ when the heavens have been opened unto him, and to deny the plan of salvation with his eyes open to the truth of it; and from that time he begins to be an enemy. This is the case with many apostates of the Church of Jesus Christ of Latter-day Saints. When a man begins to be an enemy to this work, he hunts me, he seeks to kill me, and never ceases to thirst for my blood. He gets the spirit of the devil---the same spirit that they had who crucified the Lord of Life-- the same spirit that sins against the Holy Ghost. You cannot save such persons; you cannot bring them to repentance; they make open war, like the devil, and awful is the consequence. (p. 358)

Matt. 12	JST Matt. 12	Mark 3	JST Mark 3

48. Jesus' Mother and Brethren

Matt. 12	JST Matt. 12	Mark 3	JST Mark 3
			26 **While he was yet with them, and while he was yet speaking, there came** then some of his brethren, and his mother; and standing without, sent unto him, **calling** unto him.
46 ¶ While he yet talked to the people, behold, his mother and his brethren stood without, desiring to speak with him.	40 **And while he yet talked to the people, behold, his mother and his brethren stood without, desiring to speak with him.**	31 ¶ There came then his brethren and his mother, and, standing without, sent unto him, calling him.	
47 Then one said unto him, Behold, thy mother and thy brethren stand without, desiring to speak with thee.		32 And the multitude sat about him, and they said unto him, Behold, thy mother and thy brethren without seek for thee.	
48 But he answered and said unto **him** that told him, Who is my mother? and who are my brethren?	42 **But he answered and said unto the man that told him, Who is my mother? and who are my brethren?**	33 And he answered them, saying, Who is my mother, or my brethren?	28 And he answered them, saying, Who is my mother, or **who are my brethren?**
49 And he stretched forth his hand toward his disciples, and said, Behold my mother and my brethren!		34 And he looked round about on them which sat about him, and said, Behold my mother and my brethren!	
	44 **And he gave them charge concerning her, saying, I go my way, for my Father hath sent me.**		
50 For whosoever shall do the will of my Father which is in heaven, the same is my brother, and sister, and mother.	**And** whosoever shall do the will of my Father which is in heaven, the same is my brother, and sister, and mother.	35 For whosoever shall do the will of God, the same is my brother, and my sister, and mother.	

Matt. 13	JST Matt. 13	Mark 4	JST Mark 4

49. Parable of the Sower

Matt. 13	JST Matt. 13	Mark 4	JST Mark 4
The same day **went Jesus** out of the house, and sat by the sea side.	**And it came to pass the same day, Jesus went out** of the house, and sat by the sea side.	And he began again to teach by the sea side: and there was gathered unto him a great multitude, so that he entered into a ship, and sat in the sea; and the whole multitude was by the sea on the land.	
2 And great multitudes were gathered together unto him, so that he went into a ship, and sat; and the whole multitude stood on the shore.			
3 And he spake many things unto them in parables, saying,		2 And he taught them many things by parables, and said unto them in his doctrine,	3 And **he** said unto them in his doctrine,

Luke 8	JST Luke 8		

19 ¶ Then came to him his mother and his brethren, and could not **come at** him for the **press.** 20 And **it was told him by certain which** said, Thy mother and thy brethren stand without, desiring to see thee.	19 Then came to him his mother and his brethren, and could not **speak to** him for the **multitude.** 20 And **some who stood by,** said **unto him,** Thy mother and thy brethren stand without, desiring to see thee.		
21 And he answered and said unto them, My mother and my brethren are **these which** hear the word of God, and do it.	21 And he answered and said unto them, My mother and my brethren are **those who** hear the word of God, and do it.		

TPJS-- [T]he 13th chapter of His Gospel according to St. Matthew, which, in my mind, afford[s] us as clear an understanding upon the important subject of the gathering, as anything recorded in the Bible. (p. 94)

4 ¶ And when much people were gathered together, and were come to him out of every city, he spake by a parable:	4 And when much people were gathered together, and were come to him out of every city, he spake by a parable, **saying,**		

Matt. 13	JST Matt. 13	Mark 4	JST Mark 4
Behold, a sower went forth to sow; 4 And when he sowed, some seeds fell by the way side, and the fowls came and devoured them up:		3 Hearken; Behold, there went out a sower to sow: 4 And it came to pass, as he sowed, some fell by the way side, and the fowls of the air came and devoured it up.	Hearken; Behold, there went out a sower to sow;
5 Some fell upon stony places, where they had not much earth: and forthwith they sprung up, **because they had no deepness of earth:**	5 Some fell upon stony places, where they had not much earth: and forthwith they sprung up:	5 And some fell on stony ground, where it had not much earth; and immediately it sprang up, because it had no depth of earth:	
6 And when the sun was up, they were scorched; and because they had no root, they withered away.	and when the sun was up, they were scorched; **because they had no deepness of earth; and because they had no root, they withered away.**	6 But when the sun was up, it was scorched; and because it had no root, it withered away.	
7 And some fell among thorns; and the thorns sprung up, and choked them:		7 And some fell among thorns, and the thorns grew up, and choked it, and it yielded no fruit.	
8 But other fell into good ground, and brought forth fruit, some an hundred-fold, some sixtyfold, some thirtyfold.	7 But others fell into good ground, and brought forth fruit; some an hundred-fold, some sixty-fold, **and** some thirty-fold.	8 And other fell on good ground, and did yield fruit that sprang up and in-creased; and brought forth, some thirty, and some six-ty, and some an hundred.	7 And other **seed** fell on good ground, and did yield fruit, that sprang up and increased, and brought forth, some thirty-**fold,** and some sixty and some an hundred.
9 Who hath ears to hear, let him hear.	Who hath ears to hear, let him hear.	9 And he said unto them, He that hath ears to hear, let him hear.	
10 **And** the disciples came, and said unto him, Why speakest thou unto them in parables?	8 **Then** the disciples came and said unto him, Why speakest thou unto them in parables?	10 And when he was alone,	9 And when he was alone **with the twelve, and they that believed in him,** they that were about him with the twelve, asked of him the parable.
		they that were about him with the twelve asked of him the parable.	
11 He answered and said unto them, Because it is given unto you to know the mysteries of the king-dom of heaven, but to them it is not given.		11 And he said unto them, Unto you it is given to know the mystery of the kingdom of God: but unto them that are without, all **these** things are done in parables:	10 And he said unto them, Unto you it is given to know the mystery of the kingdom of God; but unto them that are without, all things are done in para-bles;
12 For whosoever **hath,** to him shall be given, and he shall have more abun-dance: but whosoever **hath not,** from him shall be taken away even that he hath.	10 For whosoever **receiv-eth,** to him shall be given, and he shall have more abundance;		
13 Therefore speak I to them in parables: because they seeing see not; and hearing they hear not, nei-ther do they understand.	11 But whosoever **contin-ueth not to receive,** from him shall be taken away even that he hath.	12 That seeing they may see, and not perceive; and hearing they may hear, and not understand;	

Luke 8	JST Luke 8	TPJS
5 A sower went out to sow his seed: and as he sowed, some fell by the way side; and it was trodden down, and the fowls of the air devoured it. 6 And some fell upon a rock; and as soon as it was sprung up, it withered away, because it lacked moisture.		
7 And some fell among thorns; and the thorns sprang up with it, and choked it. 8 And other fell on good ground, and sprang up, and bare fruit an hundredfold.	8 And others fell on good ground, and sprang up, and bare fruit an hundredfold.	
And when he had said these things, he cried, He that hath ears to hear, let him hear.	9 And when he had said these things, he cried, He who hath ears to hear, let him hear.	
9 And his disciples asked him, saying, What might this parable be?		(Cites Matt. 13:10.) [I would here remark, that the 'them' made use of in this interrogation, is a personal pronoun, and refers to the multitude] (pp. 94-95)
10 And he said, Unto you it is given to know the mysteries of the kingdom of God: but to others in parables;		He answered and said unto them, [that is unto the disciples] because it is given unto you, to know the mysteries of the Kingdom of Heaven, but to them, [that is, unbelievers] it is not given; (Cites Matt. 13:11-12.) We understand from this saying, that those who had been previously looking for a Messiah to come, according to the testimony of the prophets, and were then, at that time looking for a Messiah, but had not sufficient light, on account of their unbelief, to discern Him to be their Savior; and He being the true Messiah, consequently they must be disappointed, and lose even all the knowledge, or have taken away from them all the light, understanding, and faith which they had upon this subject; therefore he that will not receive the greater light, must have taken away from him all the light which he hath; and if the light which is in you become darkness, behold, how great is that darkness! (p. 95)
that seeing they might not see, and hearing they might not understand.		

121

Matt. 13	JST Matt. 13	Mark 4	Isaiah JST Mark 4
14 And in them is ful-filled the prophecy of Esaias, which saith, By hearing ye shall hear, and shall not understand; and seeing ye shall see, and shall not perceive:	13 And in them is fulfilled the prophecy of Esaias **concerning them**, which saith, By hearing, ye shall hear and shall not under-stand; and seeing, ye shall see and shall not perceive.		Isaiah 6:9 ¶ And he said, Go, and tell this people, Hear ye indeed, but understand not; and see ye indeed, but perceive not.
15 For this people's heart is waxed gross, and their ears are dull of hearing, and their eyes they have closed; lest at any time they should see with their eyes, and hear with their ears, and should under-stand with their heart, and should be converted, and I should heal them.	14 For this people's heart is waxed gross, and their ears are dull of hearing, and their eyes they have closed; lest at any time they should see with their eyes, and hear with their ears, and should under-stand with their hearts, and should be converted, and I should heal them.	lest at any time they should be converted, and their sins should be forgiv-en them.	10 Make the heart of this people fat, and make their ears heavy, and shut their eyes; lest they see with their eyes, and hear with their ears, and understand with their heart, and convert, and be healed.
16 But blessed are your eyes, for they see: and your ears, for they hear.	15 But blessed are your eyes, for they see; and your ears, for they hear. **And blessed are you be-cause these things are come unto you, that you might understand them.**		
17 For verily I say unto you, **That** many prophets **and righteous men** have desired to see **those things** which ye see, and have not seen them; and to hear **those things** which y e hear, and have not heard **them.**	16 **And** verily, I say unto you, many **righteous** pro-phets have desired to see **these days** which you see, and have not seen them; and to hear **that which you** hear, and have not heard.		
		13 And he said unto them, Know ye not this parable? and how then will ye know all parables?	
18 ¶ Hear ye therefore the parable of the sower.		14 ¶ The sower soweth the word.	
19 When any one heareth the word of the kingdom, and understandeth it not, then cometh the wicked one, and catcheth away that which was sown in his heart. This is he which re-ceived seed by the way side.	18 When any one heareth the word of the kingdom, and understandeth not, then cometh the wicked one, and catcheth away that which was sown in his heart; this is he who received seed by the way-side.	15 And these are they by the way side, where the word is sown; but when they have heard, Satan cometh immediately, and taketh away the word that was sown in their hearts.	
20 But he that received the seed into stony places, the same is he that heareth the word, and **anon** with joy receiveth it;	19 But he that received the seed into stony places, the same is he that heareth the word and **readily** with joy receiveth it,	16 And these are they likewise which **are sown** on stony ground; who, when they have heard the word, immediately receive it with gladness;	JST Mark 4:15 And these are they likewise which **receive the word** on stony ground; who, when they have heard the word, immediately receive it with gladness,

Luke 8	JST Luke 8	TPJS B of M
		2 Nephi 9:31 And wo unto the deaf that will not hear; for they shall perish. 32 Wo unto the blind that will not see; for they shal perish also.
		TPJS—But listen to the explanation of the parable of the Sower: [Matt. 13:19]. Now mark the expression—that which was sown in his heart. This is he which receiveth seed by the way side. Men who have no principle of righteousness in themselves, and whose hearts are full of iniquity, and have no desire for the principles of truth, do not understand the world of truth when they hear it. The devil taketh away the word of truth out of their hearts, because there is no desire for righteousness in them. (p. 96)
11 Now the parable is this: the seed is the word of God.		1 Ne. 8:21 And I saw numberless concourses of people, many of whom were pressing forward, that they might obtain the path which led unto the tree by which I stood.
12 **Those** by the way side are they **that** hear; **then cometh** the devil, and taketh away the word out of their hearts, lest they should believe and be saved.	12 **That which fell** by the wayside are they **who** hear; **and** the devil **cometh** and taketh away the word out of their hearts, lest they should believe and be saved.	22 And it came to pass that they did come forth, and commence in the path which led to the tree. 23 And it came to pass that there arose a mist of darkness; yea, even an exceedingly great mist of darkness, insomuch that they who had commenced in the path did lose their way, that they wandered off and were lost. 24 And it came to pass that I beheld others pressing forward, and they came forth and caught hold of the end of the rod of iron; and they did press forward through the mist of darkness, clinging to the rod of iron, even until they did come forth and partake of the fruit of the tree.
13 **They** on the rock are they, **which**, when they hear, receive the word with joy;	13 **That which fell** on the rock are they, **who**, when they hear, receive the word with joy;	25 And after they had partaken of the fruit of the tree they did cast their eyes about as if they were ashamed.

Matt. 13	JST Matt. 13	Mark 4	JST Mark 4
21 Yet **hath he** not root in himself, **but** dureth for a while: for when tribulation or persecution ariseth because of the word, by and by he is offended.	yet **he hath** not root in himself, **and endureth but** for a while; for when tribulation or persecution ariseth because of the word, by and by he is offended.	17 And have no root in themselves, and so endure but for a time: afterward, when affliction or persecution ariseth for the word's sake, immediately they are offended.	and have no root in themselves, and so endure but for a time; **and** afterward, when affliction or persecution ariseth for the word's sake, immediately they are offended.
22 He also **that** received seed among the thorns is he that heareth the word;	20 He also **who** received seed among the thorns, is he that heareth the word;	18 And these are they **which are sown** among thorns; such as hear the word,	16 And these are they **who receive the word** among thorns; such as hear the word,
and the care of this world, and the deceitfulness of riches, choke the word, and he becometh unfruitful.	and the care of this world and the deceitfulness of riches, choke the word, and he becometh unfruitful.	19 And the cares of this world, and the deceitfulness of riches, and the lusts of other things entering in, choke the word, and it becometh unfruitful.	and the cares of this world, and the deceitfulness of riches, and the lusts of other things entering in, choke the word, and it becometh unfruitful.
23 But he that received seed into the good ground is he that heareth the word, and understandeth **it**; which also beareth fruit, and bringeth forth, some an hundredfold, some sixty, some thirty.	21 But he that received seed into the good ground, is he that heareth the word and understandeth **and endureth**; which also beareth fruit, and bringeth forth, some an hundred-fold, some sixty, **and** some thirty.	20 And these are they **which are sown** on good ground; such as hear the word, and receive it, and bring forth fruit, some thirtyfold, some sixty, and some an hundred.	17 And these are they **who receive the word** on good ground; such as hear the word, and receive it, and bring forth fruit; some thirty-fold, some sixty and some an hundred.
		21 ¶ And he said unto them, Is a candle brought to be put under a bushel, or under a bed? and not to be set on a candlestick?	18 And he said unto them, Is a candle brought to be put under a bushel, or under a bed, and not to be set on a candlestick? **I say unto you, Nay;**
		22 For there is nothing hid, which shall not be manifested; neither was any thing kept secret, but that it should come abroad. 23 If any man have ears to hear, let him hear. 24 And he said unto them, Take heed what ye hear: with what measure ye mete, it shall be measured to you: and unto you that **hear** shall more be given.	19 For there is nothing hid which shall not be manifested; neither was anything kept secret, but that it should **in due time** come abroad. If any man have ears to hear, let him hear. 20 And he said unto them, Take heed what ye hear; **for** with what measure ye mete, it shall be measured to you; and unto you that **continue to receive,** shall more be given; for he that **receiveth,** to him shall be given;
		25 For he that **hath,** to him shall be given: **and** he that **hath** not, from him shall be taken even that which he hath.	but he that **continueth** not **to receive,** from him shall be taken even that which he hath.

Luke 8	D&C JST Luke 8	B of M
	D&C 40:2 and he (James Covill) received the word with gladness, but straightway Satan tempted him; and the fear of persecution and the cares of the world caused him to reject the word.	1 Ne 8:26 And I also cast my eyes round about, and beheld, on the other side of the river of water, a great and spacious building; and it stood as it were in the air, high above the earth. 27 And it was filled with people, both old and young, both male and female; and their manner of dress was exceedingly fine; and they were in the attitude of mocking and pointing their fingers towards those who had come at and were partaking of the fruit.
14 And that which fell among thorns are they, **which**, when they have heard, go forth, and are choked with cares and riches and pleasures of this life, and bring no fruit to perfection	JST Lk 8:14 And that which fell among the thorns are they, **who**, when they have heard, go forth and are choked with cares, and riches, and pleasures of life, and bring no fruit to perfection.	28 And after they had tasted of the fruit they were ashamed, because of those that were scoffing at them; and they fell away into forbidden paths and were lost. 31 And he also saw other multitudes feeling their way towards that great and spacious building. 32 And it came to pass that many were drowned in the depths of the fountain; and many were lost from his view, wandering in strange roads.
15 But that on the good ground are they, **which** in an honest and good heart, having heard the word, keep **it**, and bring forth fruit with patience.	15 But that **which fell** on the good ground are they, **who receive the word** in an honest and good heart, having heard the word, keep **what they hear**, and bring forth fruit with patience.	33 And great was the multitude that did enter into that strange building. And after they did enter into that building they did point the finger of scorn at me and those that were partaking of the fruit also; but we heeded them not. 29 And now I, Nephi, do not speak all the words of my father.
		30 But, to be short in writing, behold, he saw other multitudes pressing forward; and they came and caught hold of the end of the rod of iron; and they did press their way forward, continually holding fast to the rod of iron, until they came forth and fell down and partook of the fruit of the tree.
16 ¶ No man, when he hath lighted a candle, covereth it with a vessel, or putteth it under a bed; but setteth it on a candlestick, that they **which** enter in may see the light.	16 **For** no man, when he hath lighted a candle, covereth it with a vessel, or putteth it under a bed; but setteth it on a candlestick, that they **who** enter in may see the light.	
17 for nothing is secret, **that** shall not be made manifest; neither **any thing** hid, **that** shall not be known and **come** abroad.	17 For nothing is secret, which shall not be made manifest; neither hid, which shall not be made known, and go abroad.	
18 Take heed therefore how ye hear:	18 Take heed therefore how ye hear;	
for whosoever **hath**, to him shall be given; and whosoever **hath** not, from him shall be taken even that which he seemeth to have.	for whosoever **receiveth**, to him shall be given; and whosoever **receiveth** not, from him shall be taken even that which he seemeth to have.	

Matt. 13	JST Matt. 13	Mark 4 D & C	TPJS

50 and 51. Parable of the Seed Growing by Itself and the Parable of the Wheat and the Tares. (These two parables are usually separated but are combined here on the assumption they are one and Mark did not give the full account.)

Matt. 13	JST Matt. 13	Mark 4 / D & C	TPJS
24 ¶ Another parable put he forth unto them, saying, The kingdom of heaven is likened unto a man which sowed good seed in his field:		26 And he said, So is the kingdom of God; as if a man should cast seed into the ground;	[This] parable has an allusion to the setting up of the Kingdom, in that age of the world also . . . we learn by this parable, not only the setting up of the Kingdom in the days of the Savior which is represented by the good seed, which produced fruit, but
25 But while **men** slept, his enemy came and sowed tares among the wheat, and went his way.	23 But while **he** slept, his enemy came and sowed tares among the wheat, and went his way.	27 And should sleep and rise, night and day, and the seed should spring and grow up, he knoweth not how;	
26 But when the blade **was** sprung up, and brought forth fruit, then appeared the tares also.	24 But when the blade sprung up, and brought forth fruit, then appeared the tares also.	28 For the earth bringeth forth fruit of herself, first the blade, then the ear, after that the full corn in the ear.	also the corruptions of the Church, which are represented by the tares, which were sown by the enemy,. . . (pp. 97-98)
27 So the servants of the householder came and said unto him, Sir, didst not thou sow good seed in thy field? **from** whence then hath it tares?	25 So the servants of the householder came and said unto him, Sir, didst not thou sow good seed in thy field? whence then hath it tares?		
28 He said unto them, An enemy hath done this. The servants said unto him, Wilt thou then that we go and gather them up?	26 He said unto them, An enemy hath done this. 27 **And** the servants said unto him, Wilt thou then that we go and gather them up?	D&C 101:65 Therefore, I must gather together my people, according to the parable of the wheat and the tares, that the wheat may be secured in the garners to possess eternal life, and be crowned with celestial glory, when I shall come in the kingdom of my Father to reward every man according as his work shall be;	His disciples would fain have plucked up [the tares], or cleansed the Church . . . if their views had been favored by the Savior. But He, knowing all things, says, Not so. As much as to say, your views are not correct, the Church is in its infancy, and if you take this rash step, you will destroy the wheat, or the Church, with the tares; therefore it is better to let them grow together until the harvest, or the end of the world, which means the destruction of the wicked, . . . (p. 98)
29 But he said, Nay; lest while ye gather up the tares, ye root up also the wheat with them.			
30 Let both grow together until the harvest: and in the time of harvest I will say to the reapers, Gather ye together first the **tares, and bind them in bundles to burn them: but gather the wheat into my barn.**	29 Let both grow together until the harvest, and in the time of harvest, I will say to the reapers, Gather ye together first the **wheat into my barn; and the tares are bound in bundles to be burned.**	66 While the tares shall be bound in bundles, and their bands made strong, that they may be burned with unquenchable fire.	
		29 But when the fruit is brought forth, immediately he putteth in the sickle, because the harvest is come.	

126

Matt. 13	JST Matt. 13	D & C	TPJS
36 Then Jesus sent the multitude away, and went into the house: and his disciples came unto him, saying, Declare unto us the parable of the tares of the field. 37 He answered and said unto them, He that soweth the good seed is the Son of man;		86:1 Verily, thus saith the Lord unto you my servants, concerning the parable of the wheat and of the tares:	
38 The field is the world; the good seed are the children of the kingdom; but the tares are the children of the wicked **one**; 39 The enemy that sowed them is the devil; the harvest is the end of the world;	37 The field is the world; the good seed are the children of the kingdom; but the tares are the children of the wicked. 38 The enemy that sowed them is the devil. 39 The harvest is the end of the world, **or the destruction of the wicked.**	2 Behold, verily I say, the field was the world, and the apostles were the sowers of the seed; 3 And after they have fallen asleep the great persecutor of the church, the apostate, the whore, even Babylon, that maketh all nations to drink of her cup, in whose hearts the enemy, even Satan, sitteth to reign--Behold he soweth the tares; wherefore, the tares choke the wheat and drive the church into the wilderness.	[Cites Matt. 13:38-40.] Now men cannot have any possible grounds to say that this is figurative, or that it does not mean what it says:. . . (p. 100) [T]he end of the world is the destruction of the wicked, . . . and the angels are to have something to do in this great work, for they are the reapers . . . [Matt. 13:40]; that is, as the servants of God go forth warning the nations, both priests and people, and as they harden their hearts and reject the light of truth ,. . . they are left in darkness, and delivered over unto the day of burning;. . . (p. 101).
and the reapers are the angels.	40 The reapers are the angels, **or the messengers sent of heaven.**	4 But behold, in the last days, even now while the Lord is beginning to bring forth the word, and the blade is springing up and is yet tender--	[Cites Matt. 13:41.] All these authoritative characters will come down and join hand in hand in bringing about this work (p. 159).
40 As therefore the tares are gathered and burned in the fire; so shall it be in this end of the world.	41 As, therefore, the tares are gathered and burned in the fire, so shall it be in the end of this world, **or the destruction of the wicked.**	5 Behold, verily I say unto you, the angels are crying unto the Lord day and night, who are ready and waiting to be sent forth to reap down the fields;	[Cites Matt. 13:41-42.] We understand that the work of gathering together of the wheat into barns, or garners, is to take place while the tares are being bound over, and preparing for the day of burning; that after the day of burnings, the righteous shall shine forth like the sun, in the Kingdom of their Father (p.101).
41 The Son of man shall send forth his angels,	42 **For in that day, before** the Son of Man **shall come, he** shall send forth his angels **and messengers of heaven.**	6 But the Lord saith unto them, pluck not up the tares while the blade is yet tender (for verily your faith is weak), lest you destroy the wheat also.	
and they shall gather out of his kingdom all things that offend, and them which do iniquity; 42 And shall cast them into a **furnace of fire**: there shall be wailing and gnashing of teeth.	43 And they shall gather out of his kingdom all things that offend, and them which do iniquity, and shall cast them **out among the wicked; and** there shall be wailing and gnashing of teeth. 44 **For the world shall be burned with fire.**	7 Therefore, let the wheat and the tares grow together until the harvest is fully ripe; then ye shall first gather out the wheat from among the tares, and after the gathering of the wheat, behold and lo, the tares are bound in bundles, and the	
43 Then shall the righteous shine forth as the sun in the kingdom of their Father. Who hath ears to hear, let him hear.			

127

Matt. 13	JST Matt. 13	D & C	
		field remaineth to be burned. 8 Therefore, thus saith the Lord unto you, with whom the priesthood hath continued through the lineage of your fathers-- 9 For ye are lawful heirs, according to the flesh, and have been hid from the world with Christ in God--	10 Therefore your life and the priesthood have remained, and must needs remain through you and your lineage until the restoration of all things spoken by the mouths of all the holy prophets since the world began.
JST Matt. 13	JST Mark 4	Luke 13	

52. Parables of Mustard Seed and Leaven

JST Matt. 13	JST Mark 4	Luke 13
30 ¶ **And** another parable put he forth unto them, saying, The kingdom of heaven is like to a grain of mustard seed, which a man took and sowed in his field; (JST added "**And**"). 31 Which indeed is the least of all seeds: but when it is grown, it is the geatest among herbs, and becometh a tree, so that the birds of the air come and lodge in the branches thereof.	24 And he said, Whereunto shall I liken the kingdom of God? or with what comparison shall we compare it? (JST changed "we" to "I"). 25 It is like a grain of mustard seed, which, when it is sown in the earth, is less than all the seeds that be in the earth: 26 But, when it is sown, it groweth up, and becometh greater than all herbs, and shooteth out great branches; so that the fowls of the air may lodge under the shadow of it.	18 Then said he, Unto what is the kingdom of God like? and whereunto shall I resemble it? 19 It is like a grain of mustard seed, which a man took, and cast into his garden; and it grew, and waxed a great tree; and the fowls of the air lodged in the branches of it.

TPJS-- [Cites Matt. 13:31-32.] Now we can discover plainly that this figure is given to represent the Church as it shall come forth in the last days. Behold, the Kingdom of Heaven is likened unto it. Now, what is like unto it?

Let us take the Book of Mormon, which a man took and hid in his field, securing it by his faith, to spring up in the last days, or in due time; let us behold it coming forth out of the ground, which is indeed accounted the least of all seeds, but behold it branching forth, yea, even towering, with lofty branches and God-like majesty, until it, like the mustard seed, becomes the greatest of all herbs. And it is truth, and it has sprouted and come forth out of the earth, and righteousness begins to look down from heaven, and God is sending down His powers, gifts and angels, to lodge in the branches thereof.

The Kingdom of Heaven is like unto a mustard seed. Behold, then is not this the Kingdom of Heaven that is raising its head in the last days in the majesty of its God, even the Church of the Latter-day Saints, like an impenetrable, immovable rock in the midst of the mighty deep, exposed to the storms and tempests of Satan, but has, thus far, remained steadfast, and is still braving the mountain waves of opposition . . . (p. 98-99).

Matt. 13	Mark 4 JST Matt. 13	Luke 13 Psalms	TPJS
33 ¶ Another parable spake he unto them; The kingdom of heaven is like unto leaven, which a woman took, and hid in three measures of meal, till the whole was leavened. 34 All these things spake Jesus unto the multitude in parables; and without a parable spake he not unto them: 35 That it might be fulfilled which was spoken by the prophet, saying, I will open my mouth in parables; I will utter things which have been kept secret from the foundation of the world.	33 And with many such parables spake he the word unto them, as they were able to **hear** it. (The JST reads **bear** it.) 34 But without a parable spake he not unto them: and when they were alone; he expounded all things to his disciples.	20 And again he said, Whereunto shall I liken the kingdom of God? 21 It is like leaven, which a woman took and hid in three measures of meal, till the whole was leavened. Psalm 78:2 I will open my mouth in a parable: I will utter dark sayings of old:	(Cites Matt. 13:33.) It may be understood that the Church of the Latter-day Saints has taken its rise from a little leaven that was put into three witnesses. Behold, how much this is like the parable! It is fast leavening the lump, and will soon leaven the whole. (p. 100)

53. Other Parables about the Kingdom of Heaven

Matt. 13	JST Matt. 13	Luke 13 / Psalms	TPJS
44 ¶ Again, the kingdom of heaven is like unto treasure hid in a field; **the which** when a man hath found, he **hideth**, and for joy thereof goeth and selleth all that he hath, and buyeth that field.	JST Matt. 13:46 Again, the kingdom of heaven is like unto **a** treasure hid in a field. **And** when a man hath found **a treasure which is hid**, he **secureth it**, and, **straightway**, for joy thereof, goeth and selleth all that he hath, and buyeth that field.	[T]o illustrate more clearly this gathering: We have another parable--[Matt. 13:44]. The Saints work after this pattern. See the Church of the Latter-day Saints, selling all that they have, and gathering themselves together unto a place that they may purchase for an inheritance, that they may be together and bear each other's afflictions in the day of calamity. (p. 101)
45 ¶ Again, the kingdom of heaven is like unto a merchant man, seeking goodly pearls; 46 Who, when he had found one pearl of great price, went and sold all that he had, and bought it.	47 **And** again, the kingdom of heaven is like unto a merchantman, seeking goodly pearls, who, when he had found one pearl of great price, **he** went and sold all that he had and bought it.	[Cites Matt. 13:45-46.] The Saints again work after this example. See men traveling to find places for Zion and her stakes or remnants, who, when they find the place for Zion, or the pearl of great price, straightway sell that they have, and buy it. (p.102)
47 Again, the kingdom of heaven is like unto a net, that was cast into the sea, and gathered of every kind: 48 Which, when it was full, they drew to shore, and sat down, and gathered the good into vessels, but cast the bad away. 49 **So shall it be at the end of the world:** the angels shall come forth, and sever the wicked from among the just,	50 **And the world is the children of the wicked. . .**	[Cites Matt. 13:47-48.] For the work of this pattern, behold the seed of Joseph, spreading forth the Gospel net upon the face of the earth, gathering of every kind, that the good may be saved in vessels prepared for that purpose, and the angels will take care of the bad. So shall it be at the end of the world--the angels shall come forth and sever the wicked from among the just, and cast them into the furnace of fire, and there shall be wailing and gnashing of teeth. (p. 102)	

129

Matt. 13	JST Matt. 13	TPJS
50 And shall cast them into the **furnace of fire**: there shall be wailing and gnashing of teeth.	and shall cast them **out into** the **world to be burned.** There shall be wailing and gnashing of teeth.	Matt. 13:53 And it came to pass, that when Jesus had finished these parables, he departed thence.
51 Jesus **saith** unto them, Have ye understood all these things? They say unto him, yeah, Lord.	52 **Then** Jesus **said** unto them, Have ye understood all these things? They say unto him, Yea, Lord.	[Cites Matt. 13:51.] And we say, yea, Lord; and well might they say, yea, Lord; for these things are so plain and so glorious, that every Saint in the last days must respond with a hearty Amen to them. (p. 102)
52 Then said he unto them, **Therefore** every scribe **which** is instructed **unto** the kingdom of heaven is like unto a **man that is an** householder, which bringeth forth out of his treasure **things** new and old. (Continued in columns 3 and 4.)	53 Then said he unto them, Every scribe **well** instructed **in the things of** the kingdom of heaven, is like unto a householder; **a man, therefore**, which bringeth forth out of his treasure **that which is** new and old.	[Cites Matt. 13:52] For the works of this example, see the Book of Mormon coming forth out of the treasure of the heart. Also the covenants given to the Latter-day Saints, also the translation of the Bible—thus bringing forth out of the heart things new and old, thus answering to three measures of meal undergoing the purifying touch by a revelation of Jesus Christ, and the ministering of angels, who have already commenced this work in the last days, which will answer to the leaven which leavened the whole lump. Amen. (p. 102)

Matt. 8	JST Matt. 8	Mark 4	JST Mark 4

54. Sea of Galilee—Jesus Calms the Sea

Matt. 8	JST Matt. 8	Mark 4	JST Mark 4
18 ¶ Now when Jesus saw great multitudes about him, he gave commandment to depart unto the other side.	18 Now when Jesus saw great multitudes about him, he gave commandment to depart unto the other side **of the sea**.	35 And the same day, when the even was come, he **saith** unto them, let us pass over unto the other side.	
23 ¶ And when he was entered into a ship, his disciples **followed** him.	23 And when he was entered into a ship, his disciples **came unto** him.	36 And when they had sent away the multitude, they took him even as he was in the ship. And there were also with him other little ships.	
24 And, behold, there arose a great tempest in the sea, insomuch that the ship was covered with the waves: but he was asleep.		37 And there arose a great storm of wind, and the waves beat into the ship, **so that it was now full.**	30 And there arose a great storm of wind, and the waves beat **over** into the ship;
25 And his disciples came to him, and awoke him, saying, Lord, save us: we perish.	25 And his disciples came **unto** him, and awoke him, saying, Lord, save us, **else** we perish.	38 And he was in the hinder part of the ship, asleep on a pillow: and they **awake** him, and **say** unto him, Master, carest thou not that we perish?	and he was in the hinder part of the ship asleep on a pillow; and they awoke him, and **said** unto him, Master, carest thou not that we perish?
26 And he **saith** unto them, Why are ye fearful, O ye of little faith? Then he arose, and rebuked the winds and the sea; and there was a great calm.		39 And he arose, and rebuked the wind, and said unto the sea, Peace, be still. And the wind ceased, and there was a great calm.	
		40 And he said unto them, Why are ye so fearful? how is it that ye have no faith?	

Luke 8	JST Luke 8		
22 ¶ Now it came to pass on a certain day, that he went into a ship with his disciples: and he said unto them, Let us go over unto the other side of the lake. And they launched forth.			
23 But as they sailed he fell asleep: and there came down a storm of wind on the lake; and they were filled with **water**, and were in **jeopardy**.	23 But as they sailed he fell asleep; and there came down a storm of wind on the lake; and they were filled with **fear**, and were in **danger**.		
24 And they came to him, and awoke him, saying, Master, master, we perish. Then he arose, and rebuked the wind and the raging of the water: and they ceased, and there was a calm. 25 And he said unto them, Where is your faith? And they being afraid wondered, saying one to ano-			

Matt. 8	JST Matt. 8	Mark 4 & 5	JST Mark 5
27 But the men marvelled, saying, What manner of man is this, that even the winds and the sea obey him!		41 And they feared exceedingly, and said one to another, What manner of man is this, that even the wind and the sea obey him?	

55. Country of the Gergesenes-- Devils Cast Out and Enter Swine

Matt. 8	JST Matt. 8	Mark 4 & 5	JST Mark 5
28 ¶ And when he was come to the other side into the country of the Gergesenes, there met him **two** possessed with devils, coming out of the tombs, exceeding fierce, so that no man **might** pass **by** that way.	29 And when he was come to the other side, into the country of the Gergesenes, there met him **a man** possessed with devils, coming out of the tombs, exceeding fierce, so that no man could pass that way.	Mark 5:1 And they came over unto the other side of the sea, into the country of the Gadarenes. 2 And when he was come out of the ship, immediately there met him out of the tombs a man with an unclean spirit, 3 Who had **his** dwelling among the tombs; and no man could bind him, no, not with chains: 4 Because that he had been often bound with fetters and chains, and the chains had been plucked asunder by him, and the fetters broken in pieces: neither could any man tame him. 5 And always, night and day, he was in the mountains, and in the tombs, crying, and cutting himself with stones.	2 And when he was come out of the ship, immediately there met him out of the tombs, a man with an unclean spirit, who had **been** dwelling among the tombs;
29 And, behold, **they** cried out, saying, What have we to do with thee, Jesus, thou Son of God? art thou come hither to torment us before the time?	30 And, behold, **he** cried out, saying, What have we to do with thee, Jesus, thou Son of God? Art thou come hither to torment us before the time?	6 But when he saw Jesus afar off, he ran and worshipped him, 7 And cried with a loud voice, and said, What have I to do with thee, Jesus, thou Son of the most high God? I adjure thee by God, that thou torment me not. 8 For he said unto him, Come out of the man, **thou** unclean spirit.	5 But when he saw Jesus afar off, he ran and worshipped him, and cried with a loud voice and said, What have I to do with thee, Jesus, thou Son of the most high·God? I adjure thee by God, that thou torment me not. For he said unto him, Come out of the man, unclean spirit.
		9 And he **asked** him, **What is** thy name? And he answered, saying, My	6 And he **commanded** him **saying, Declare** thy name. And he answered,

132

Luke 8	JST Luke 8	B of M	
ther, What manner of man is this! for he commandeth even the winds and water, and they obey him.		Jacob 4:6 Wherefore, we search the prophets, and we have many revelations and the spirit of prophecy; and having all these witnesses we obtain a hope, and our faith becometh unshaken, insomuch that we truly can command in the name of Jesus and the very trees obey us, or the mountains, or the waves of the sea (See also Helaman 12:7-22).	
26 ¶ And they arrived at the country of the Gadarenes, which is over against Galilee.			
27 And when he went forth to land, there met him out of the city a certain man, which had devils long time, and **ware** no clothes, neither abode in **any** house, but in the tombs.	27 And when he went forth to land, there met him out of the city a certain man, who had devils **for a** long time, and **he would wear** no clothes, neither abode in a house, but in the tombs.		
28 When he saw Jesus, he cried out, and fell down before him, and with a loud voice said, What have I to do with thee, Jesus, thou Son of God most high? I beseech thee, torment me not.		TPJS—It would seem also, that wicked spirits have their bounds, limits, and laws by which they are governed or controlled, and know their future destiny; hence, those that were in the maniac said to our Savior. "Art thou come to torment us before the time?" (p. 208)	
29 (For he had commanded the unclean spirit to come out of the man. For oftentimes it had caught him: and he was kept bound with chains and in fetters: and he brake the bands, and was driven of the devil into the wilderness.)			
30 **And** Jesus asked him, saying, What is thy name? And he said, Legion:	30 Jesus asked him, saying, What is thy name? And he said, Legion;		

Matt. 8	JST Matt. 8	Mark 5	JST Mark 5
		name is Legion: for we are many. 10 And he besought him much that he would not send them away out of the country.	saying, My name is Legion; for we are many.
30 And there was a good way off from them an herd of many swine feeding.	31 And there was, a good way off from them, a herd of many swine, feeding.	11 Now there was there nigh unto the mountains a great herd of swine feeding.	
31 So the devils besought him, saying, If thou cast us out, suffer us to go **away** into the herd of swine. 32 And he said unto them, Go. And when they were come out, they went into the herd of swine: and, behold, the whole herd of swine ran violently down a steep place into the sea, and perished in the waters.	32 So the devils besought him, saying, If thou cast us out, suffer us to go into the herd of swine.	12 And all the devils besought him, saying, Send us into the swine, that we may enter into them. 13 And forthwith Jesus gave them leave. And the unclean spirits went out, and entered into the swine: and the herd ran violently down a steep place into the sea, (they were about two thousand;) and were choked in the sea.	
33 And they that kept them fled, and went their ways into the city, and told every thing, and what was befallen to the possessed of the devils.	34 And they that kept them fled, and went their way into the city, and told everything **which took place,** and what was befallen the possessed of the devils.	14 And they that fed the swine fled, and told it in the city, and in the country. And they went out to see what it was that was done.	11 And they that fed the swine fled, and told **the people** in the city, and in the country, **all that was done unto the swine.**
And, behold, the whole city came out to meet Jesus:		15 And they **come** to Jesus, and **see** him that was possessed with the devil, and had the legion, sitting, and clothed, and in his right mind: and they were afraid. 16 And they that saw **it** told them how it befell **to** him that was possessed with the devil, and **also** concerning the swine.	12 ... And they **came** to Jesus, and **saw** him that was possessed with the devil, and had the Legion, sitting, and clothed, and in his right mind; and they were afraid. 13 And they that saw **the miracle** told them **that came out,** how it befell him that was possessed with the devil, **and how the devil was cast out,** and concerning the swine.
and when they saw him, they besought him that he would depart out of their coasts.		17 And they began to pray him to depart out of their coasts.	14 And they began im-**mediately** to pray him to depart out of their coasts.

Luke 8	JST Luke 8	Joseph Smith
because many devils were entered into him. **31 And they besought him that he would not command them to go out into the deep.** 32 And there was there an herd of many swine feeding on the mountain: and they besought him that he would suffer them to enter into **them**. And he suffered them.	because many devils were entered into him. 31 And there was there a herd of many swine, feeding on the mountain. 32 And they besought him that he would suffer them to enter into **the swine, and** he suffered them. 33 **And they besought him also, that he would not command them to go out into the deep. And he said unto them, Come out of the man.**	TPJS-- We came to this earth that we might have a body and present it pure before God in the celestial kingdom. The great principle of happiness consists in having a body. The devil has no body, and herein is his punishment. He is pleased when he can obtain the tabernacle of man, and when cast out by the Savior he asked to go into the herd of swine, showing that he would prefer a swine's body to having none. All beings who have bodies have power over those who have not. The devil has no power over us only as we permit him. The moment we revolt at anything which comes from God, the devil takes power (p. 181). WJS-- ... for the devil knew they were a covetous people and if he could kill their hogs that would drive Jesus out of their coasts and he then would have tabernacle enough (p 68).
33 Then went the devils out of the man, and entered into the swine: and the herd ran violently down a steep place into the lake, and were choked. 34 When they **that** fed them saw what was done, they fled, and went and told it in the city and in the country.	35 When they **who** fed the swine saw what was done, they fled, and went and told **the people** in the city and in the country.	
35 Then they went out to see what was done; and came to Jesus, and found the man, out of whom the devils were departed, sitting at the feet of Jesus, clothed, and in his right mind: and they were afraid. 36 They also **which** saw **it** told them by what means he **that** was possessed of the devils was healed.	37 They also **who** saw **the miracle**, told them by what means he **who** was possessed of the devils was healed.	
37 ¶ Then the whole multitude of the country of the Gadarenes round about besought **him** to depart from them; for they were taken with great fear:	38 Then the whole multitude of the country of the Gadarenes round about, besought **Jesus** to depart from them; for they were taken with great fear.	

Matt. 9	JST Matt. 9	Mark 5	JST Mark 5
		18 And when he was come into the ship,	15 And when he was come into the ship,
		he that had been possessed with the devil prayed him that he might be with him.	he that had been possessed with the devil, **spoke to Jesus, and** prayed him that he might be with him.
		19 Howbeit Jesus suffered him not, but saith unto him, Go home to thy friends, and tell them how great things the Lord hath done for thee, and hath had compassion on thee.	
		20 And he departed, and began to publish in Decapolis how great things Jesus had done for him: and all **men** did marvel.	17 And he departed, and began to publish in Decapolis, how great things Jesus had done for him; and all **that heard him** did marvel.

56. Capernaum

Matt. 9	JST Matt. 9	Mark 5	JST Mark 5
And **he** entered into a ship, and passed over, and came into his own city.	And **Jesus** entered into a ship, and passed over, and came into his own city.	21 And when Jesus **was** passed over again by ship unto the other side, much people gathered unto him: and he was nigh unto the sea.	18 And when Jesus **had** passed over again by ship unto the other side, much people gathered unto him; and he was nigh unto the sea.

57. Jairus seeks Jesus to Heal His Daughter

Matt. 9	JST Matt. 9	Mark 5	JST Mark 5
18 ¶ While he spake these things unto them, behold, there came a certain ruler, and worshipped him,	24 While he spake these things unto them, behold, there came a certain ruler and worshipped him,	22 And, behold, there cometh one of the rulers of the synagogue, Jairus by name; and when he saw him, he fell at his feet.	19 And behold there cometh one of the rulers of the synagogue, Jairus by name; and when he saw him he fell at his feet,
saying, My daughter is even now **dead**: but come and lay thy hand upon her, and she shall live.	saying, My daughter is even now **dying**; but come and lay thy hand upon her and she shall live.	23 And besought him greatly, saying, My little daughter lieth at the point of death: **I pray thee,** come and lay thy hands on her, that she may be healed; and she shall live.	and besought him greatly, saying, My little daughter lieth at the point of death; come and lay thy hands on her that she may be healed; and she shall live.
19 And Jesus arose, and followed him, and so **did** his disciples.	25 And Jesus arose and followed him, and **also** his disciples, **and much people thronged him.**	24 And **Jesus** went with him; and much people followed him, and thronged him.	20 And **he** went with him; and much people followed him, and thronged him.

136

Luke 8	JST Luke 8		
and **he** went up into the ship, and returned back again. 38 Now the man out of whom the devils were departed besought him that he might be with him: but Jesus sent him away, saying, 39 Return to thine own house, and shew how great things God hath done unto thee. And he went his way, and published throughout the whole city how great things Jesus had done unto him.	And **Jesus** went up into the ship, and returned back again.		
40 And it came to pass, that, when Jesus was returned, the people **gladly** received him: for they were all waiting for him.	41 And it came to pass, that, when Jesus was returned, the people received him; for they were all waiting for him.		
41 ¶ And, behold, there came a man named Jairus, and he was a ruler of the synagogue: and he fell down at Jesus' feet, and besought him that he would come into his house: 42 For he had **one** only daughter, about twelve years of age, and she lay a dying. But as he went the people thronged him.	43 For he had **an** only daughter, about twelve years of age, and she lay a-dying.		

Matt. 9		Mark 5	JST Mark 5

58. Woman Touches Garment

Matt. 9		Mark 5	JST Mark 5
20 ¶ And, behold, a woman, which was diseased with an issue of blood twelve years,		25 And a certain woman, which had an issue of blood twelve years,	
		26 And had suffered many things of many physicians, and had spent all that she had, and was nothing bettered, but rather grew worse,	
came behind him, and touched the hem of his garment:		27 When she had heard of Jesus, came in the press behind, and touched his garment.	21 . . . when she had heard of Jesus, she came in the press behind, and touched his garment;
21 For she said within herself, If I may but touch his garment, I shall be whole.		28 For she said, If I may touch but his clothes, I shall be whole.	
		29 And straightway the fountain of her blood was dried up; and she felt in her body that she was healed of that plague.	
		30 And Jesus, immediately knowing in himself that virtue had gone out of him, turned him about in the press, and said, Who touched my clothes?	
		31 And his disciples said unto him, Thou seest the multitude thronging thee, and sayest thou, Who touched me?	
		32 And he looked round about to see her that had done this thing.	
		33 But the woman fearing and trembling, knowing what was done in her, came and fell down before him, and told him all the truth.	
22 But Jesus turned him about, and when he saw her, he said, Daughter, be of good comfort; thy faith hath made thee whole. And the woman was made whole from that hour.		34 And he said unto her, Daughter, thy faith hath made thee whole; go in peace, and be whole of thy plague.	

Luke 8	JST Luke 8		

43 ¶ And a woman having an issue of blood twelve years, **which** had spent all her living upon physicians, neither could be healed of any,

44 And a woman, having an issue of blood twelve years, **who** had spent all her living upon physicians, neither could be healed of any,

44 Came behind **him**, and touched the border of his garment:

44 Came behind **Jesus**, and touched the border of his garment;. . .

and immediately her issue of blood stanched.

45 And Jesus said, Who touched me? When all denied, Peter and they **that** were with him said, Master, the multitude throng thee and press thee, and sayest thou, Who touched me?

45 And Jesus said, Who touched me? When all denied, Peter and they **who** were with him, said, Master, the multitude throng thee and press **upon** thee, and sayest thou, Who touched me?

46 And Jesus said, Some-**body** hath touched me: for I perceive that virtue is gone out of me.

46 And Jesus said, Some **one** hath touched me; for I perceive that virtue is gone out of me.

47 And when the woman **saw** that she was not hid, she came trembling, and falling down before him, she declared unto him before all the people for what cause she had touched him, and how she was healed immediately.

47 And when the woman **found** that she was not hid, she came trembling, and falling down before him, she declared unto him before all the people for what cause she had touched him, and how she was healed immediately.

48 And he said unto her, Daughter, be of good comfort: thy faith hath made thee whole; go in peace.

TPJS-- Elder Jedediah M. Grant enquired of me the cause of my turning pale and losing strength last night while blessing children. I told him that I saw that Lucifer would exert his influence to destroy the children that I was blessing, and I strove with all the faith and spirit that I had to seal upon them a blessing that would secure their lives upon the earth; and so much virtue went out of me into the children, that I became weak, from which I have not yet recovered; and I referred to the case of the woman touching the hem of the garment of Jesus. (Luke, 8th chapter.) The virtue here referred to is the spirit of life; and a man who exercises great faith in administering to the sick, blessing little children, or confirming, is liable to become weakened. (pp. 280-281)

139

Matt. 9	JST Matt. 9	Mark 5	JST Mark 5

59. Jairus' Daughter Raised

Matt. 9	JST Matt. 9	Mark 5	JST Mark 5
		35 While he yet spake, there came from the ruler of the synagogue's house **certain which** said, Thy daughter is dead: why troublest thou the Master any further?	27 While he yet spake, there came from the ruler of the synagogue's house, **a man who** said, Thy daughter is dead; why troublest thou the Master any further?
		36 As soon as Jesus heard the word that was spoken, **he saith** unto the ruler of the synagogue, Be not afraid, only believe.	28 As soon as **he spake**, Jesus heard the word that was spoken, **and** said unto the ruler of the synagogue, Be not afraid, only believe.
		37 And he suffered no man to follow him, save Peter, and James, and John the brother of James.	
23 And when Jesus came into the ruler's house, and saw the minstrels and the people making a noise,		38 And he cometh to the house of the ruler of the synagogue, and seeth the tumult, and them that wept and wailed greatly.	
24 He said unto them, Give place: for the maid is not dead, but sleepeth. And they laughed him to scorn.		39 And when he was come in, he saith unto them, Why make ye this ado, and weep? the damsel is not dead, but sleepeth.	
25 But when the people were put forth,		40 And they laughed him to scorn. But when he had put them all out, he taketh the father and the mother of the damsel, and them that were with him, and entereth in where the damsel was lying.	
he went in, and took her by the hand,		41 And he took the damsel by the hand, and said unto her, Talitha cumi; which is, being interpreted, Damsel, I say unto thee, arise.	
and the maid arose.		42 And straightway the damsel arose, and walked; for she was **of the age of** twelve years. And they were astonished with a great astonishment.	34 And straightway the damsel arose and walked; for she was twelve years **old**. And they were astonished with a great astonishment.
26 And the fame **hereof** went abroad into all that land.	32 And the fame **of Jesus** went abroad into all that land.	43 And he charged them straitly that no man should know it; and commanded that something should be given her to eat.	

Luke 8	JST Luke 8		
49 ¶ While he yet spake, there cometh one from the ruler of the synagogue's house, saying to him, Thy daughter is dead; trouble not the Master.			
50 But **when** Jesus heard it, he **answered him saying,** Fear not: believe only and she shall be made whole.	51 But Jesus heard **him, and** he **said unto the ruler of the synagogue,** Fear not; believe only, and she shall be made whole. . .		
51 And when he came into the house, he suffered no man to go in, save Peter, and James, and John, and the father and the mother of the maiden.			
52 And all wept, and bewailed her: but he said, Weep not; she is not dead, but sleepeth.	52 And all wept and bewailed her; but he said, Weep not; **for** she is not dead, but sleepeth.		
53 And they laughed him to scorn, knowing that she was dead.			
54 And he put them all out, and took her by the hand, and called, saying, Maid, arise.	53 And he put them all out, and took her by the hand, and **he** called, saying, Maid, arise.		
55 And her spirit came again, and she arose straightway: and he commanded to give her meat.			
56 And her parents were astonished: but he charged them that they should tell no man what was done.			

Matt. 9	JST Matt. 9	Matt. 9	JST Matt. 9

60. Blind Men Healed-- Devil Cast Out

27 ¶ And when Jesus departed thence, two blind men followed him, crying, and saying, Thou Son of David, have mercy on us.	33 And when Jesus departed thence, two blind men followed him, crying, and saying, **Jesus**, Thou Son of David, have mercy on us.	32 ¶ As they went out, behold, they brought to him a dumb man possessed with a devil.	38 **And** as they went out, behold, they brought to him a dumb man possessed with a devil.
28 And when he was come into the house, the blind men came to them: and Jesus saith unto them, Believe ye that I am able to do this? They said unto him, Yea, Lord.		33 And when the devil was cast out, the dumb spake: and the multitudes marvelled, saying, It was never so seen in Israel.	39 And when the devil was cast out, the dumb **man** spake. And the multitudes marvelled, saying, It was never so seen in Israel.
29 Then touched he their eyes, saying, According to your faith be it done unto you.		34 But the Pharisees said, He casteth out devils through the prince of devils.	34 But the Pharisees said, He casteth out **the** devils, through the prince of the devils.
30 And their eyes were opened; and **Jesus** straitly charged them, saying,	36 And their eyes were opened; and straitly **h e** charged them, saying, **Keep my commandments, and see ye tell no man in this place,** that no man know it.		
See that no man know it.			
31 But they, when they were departed, spread abroad his fame in all that country.			
(continued in column 3)	(continued in column 4)		

Matt. 13	JST Matt. 13	Mark 6	JST Mark 6

61. Nazareth-- Second Rejection

54 And when he was come into his own country,	55 And when he was come into his own country,	And he went out from thence, and came into his own country; and his disciples follow him.	
		2 And when the sabbath day was come, he began to teach in the synagogue: and many hearing **h i m** were astonished, saying, From whence hath this man these things? and what wisdom is this **which** is given unto him, that even such mighty works are wrought by his hands?	2 And when the Sabbath day was come, he began to teach in the synagogue; and many hearing, were astonished **at his words**, saying, From whence hath this man these things?
he taught them in their synagogue, insomuch that they were astonished, and said, Whence hath this **m a n** this wisdom, and these mighty works?	he taught them in their synagogues, insomuch that they were astonished, and said, Whence hath this **Jesus** this wisdom and these mighty works?		3 And what wisdom is this **that** is given unto him, that even such mighty works are wrought by his hands?

Matt. 13	JST Matt. 13 Psalms	Mark 6	JST Mark 6
55 Is not this the carpenter's son? is not his mother called Mary? and his brethren, James, and Joses, and Simon, and Judas?		3 Is not this the carpenter, the son of Mary, the brother of James, and Joses, and of Juda, and Simon?	
56 And his sisters, are they not all with us? Whence then hath this man all these things?		and are not his sisters here with us?	
57 And they were offended **in** him.	57 And they were offended **at** him. . .	And they were offended at him.	6 But Jesus said unto them, A prophet is not without honor, **save** in his own country, and among his own kin, and in his own house.
But Jesus said unto them, A prophet is not without honour, save in his own country, and in his own house.	Psalm 69:8 I am become a stranger unto my brethren, and an alien unto my mother's children.	4 But Jesus said unto them, A prophet is not without honour, **but** in his own country, and among his own kin, and in his own house.	
58 And he did not many mighty works there because of their unbelief.		5 And he could **there** do no mighty work, save that he laid his hands upon a few sick folk, and healed **them.**	7 And he could do no mighty work **there**, save that he laid his hands upon a few sick folk and **they were** healed.
		6 And he marvelled because of their unbelief. . .	

Matt. 9	JST Matt. 9	Mark 6	

62. Galilee-- Jesus' Third Tour

35 And Jesus went about all the cities and villages, teaching in their synagogues, and preaching the gospel of the kingdom, and healing every sickness and **every** disease among the people.	41 And Jesus went about all the cities and villages, teaching in their synagogues, and preaching the gospel of the kingdom, and healing every sickness and disease among the people.	6. . . And he went round about the villages, teaching.	
36 ¶ But when he saw the multitudes, he was moved with compassion on them, because they fainted, and were scattered abroad, as sheep having no shepherd.			
37 Then saith he unto his disciples, The harvest truly is plenteous, but the labourers are few;			
38 Pray ye therefore the Lord of the harvest, that he will send forth labourers into his harvest.			

143

Matt. 10	JST Matt. 10	Mark 6	JST Mark 6

63. Twelve Sent on Missions

Matt. 10	JST Matt. 10	Mark 6	JST Mark 6
And when he had called unto him his twelve disciples, he gave them power **against** unclean spirits, to cast them out, and to heal all manner of sickness and all manner of disease. 5 These twelve Jesus sent forth, and commanded them, saying, Go not into the way of the Gentiles, and into any city of the Samaritans **enter ye not:**	And when he had called unto him his twelve disciples, he gave them power **over** unclean spirits, to cast them out, and to heal all manner of sickness and all manner of disease. 3 These twelve Jesus sent forth, and commanded them, saying, 4 Go not into the way of the Gentiles, and **enter ye not** into any city of the Samaritans.	7 ¶ And he called **unto him** the twelve, and began to send them forth by two and two; and gave them power over unclean spirits;	9 And he called the twelve, and began to send them forth by two and two; and gave them power over unclean spirits;
6 But **go** rather to the lost sheep of the house of Israel. 7 And as ye go, preach, saying, The kingdom of heaven is at hand. 8 Heal the sick, cleanse the lepers, raise the dead, cast out devils: freely ye have received, freely give. 9 Provide neither gold, nor silver, nor brass in your purses, 10 Nor scrip for your journey, neither two coats, neither shoes, nor yet staves: for the workman is worthy of his meat. 11 And into whatsoever city or town ye shall enter, enquire who in it is worthy; and there abide until ye go thence.	5 But rather **go** to the lost sheep of the house of Israel.	8 And commanded them that they should take nothing for their journey, save a staff only; no scrip, no bread, no money in their purse: 9 But be shod with sandals; and not **put on** two coats. 10 And he said unto them, In **what** place soever ye enter into **an** house, there abide till ye depart from that place.	and commanded them that they should take nothing for their journey, save a staff only; no scrip, nor bread, nor money in their purse; but **should** be shod with sandals, and not **take** two coats. 10 And he said unto them, In **whatsoever** place ye enter into a house, there abide till ye depart from that place.
12 And when ye come into **an** house, salute it. 13 And if the house be worthy, let your peace come upon it: but if it be not worthy, let your peace return to you.	11 And when ye come into a house, salute it.		
14 And whosoever shall not receive you, nor hear your words, when ye depart out of that house or city, shake off the dust of your feet.	12 And whosoever shall not receive you, nor hear your words, when ye depart out of that house, or city, shake off the dust of your feet **for a testimony against them.**	11 And whosoever shall not receive you, nor hear you, when ye depart thence, shake off the dust **under** your feet for a testimony against them . . .	11 And whosoever shall not receive you, nor hear you; when ye depart thence shake off the dust **of** your feet for a testimony against them.

Luke 9	JST Luke 9	D & C	D & C
Then he called his twelve disciples together, and gave them power and authority over all devils, and to cure diseases. 2 And he sent them to preach the kingdom of God, and to heal the sick.	Then he called his twelve disciples together, and **he** gave them power and authority over all devils, and to cure diseases.		42:6 And ye shall go forth in the power of my Spirit, preaching my gospel, two by two, in my name, lifting up your voices as with the sound of a trump, declaring my word like unto angels of God. (See also D&C 52:10.)
3 And he said unto them, Take nothing for your journey, neither staves, nor scrip, neither bread, neither money; neither have two coats apiece. 4 And whatsoever house ye enter **into**, there abide, **and** thence **depart**.	4 And **into** whatsoever house ye enter, there abide **until ye depart** thence.	84:77 And again I say unto you, my friends, for from henceforth I shall call you friends, it is expedient that I give unto you this commandment, that ye become even as my friends in days when I was with them, traveling to preach the gospel in my power; 78 For I suffered them not to have purse or scrip, neither two coats. 79 Behold, I send you out to prove the world, and the laborer is worthy of his hire. (See also D&C 24:18.)	75:19 And in whatsoever house ye enter, and they receive you, leave your blessing upon that house.
5 And whosoever will not receive you, when ye go out of that city, shake off the very dust from your feet for a testimony against them.			20 And in whatsoever house ye enter, and they receive you not, ye shall depart speedily from that house, and shake off the dust of your feet as a testimony against them.

145

Matt. 10	JST Matt. 10	Mark 6	D & C
			75:21 And you shall be filled with joy and gladness; and know this, that in the day of judgment you shall be judges of that house, and condemn them;
15 Verily I say unto you, It shall be more tolerable for the land of Sodom and Gomorrha in the day of judgment, than for that city.	13 **And**, verily, I say unto you, it shall be more tolerable for the land of Sodom and Gomorrah in the day of judgment, than for that city.	11 . . . Verily I say unto you, It shall be more tolerable for Sodom and Gomorrha in the day of judgment, than for that city. (JST spells "Gomorrah")	22 And it shall be more tolerable for the heathen in the day of judgment, than for that house; therefore, gird up your loins and be faithful, and ye shall overcome all things, and be lifted up at the last day. Even so. Amen. (See also D&C 24:15; 60:15; 84:92-95; 109:39.)
16 ¶ Behold, I send you forth as sheep in the midst of wolves: be ye therefore wise **as serpents,** and harmless as doves.	14 Behold, I send you forth as sheep in the midst of wolves; be ye therefore wise **servants, and as** harmless as doves.		111:11 Therefore, be ye as wise as serpents and yet without sin; and I will order all things for your good, as fast as ye are able to receive them. Amen.
17 But beware of men: for they will deliver you up to the councils, and they will scourge you in their synagogues;			
18 And ye shall be brought before governors and kings for my sake, for a testimony against them and the Gentiles.			100:5 Therefore, verily I say unto you, lift up your voices unto this people; speak the thoughts that I shall put into your hearts, and you shall not be confounded before men;
19 But when they deliver you up, take no thought how or what ye shall speak: for it shall be given you in that same hour what ye shall speak.			6 For it shall be given you in the very hour, yea, in the very moment, what ye shall say.
20 For it is not ye that speak, but the Spirit of your Father which speaketh in you.			
21 And the brother shall deliver up the brother to death, and the father the child: and the children shall rise up against their parents, and cause them to be put to death.			
22 And ye shall be hated of all **men** for my name's sake: but he that endureth to the end shall be saved.	19 And ye shall be hated of all **the world** for my name's sake; but he that endureth to the end shall be saved.		
23 But when they persecute you in **this** city, flee ye into another: for verily I	20 But when they persecute you in **one** city, flee ye into another; for verily,		

Matt. 10	JST Matt. 10		
say unto you, Ye shall not have gone over the cities of Israel, till the Son of man be come.			
24 The disciple is not above his master, nor the servant above his lord.	21 **Remember**, the disciple is not above his master; nor the servant above his lord.		
25 It is enough **for the** disciple **that he** be as his master, and the servant as his lord. If they have called the master of the house Beelzebub, how much more shall they call them of his household?	It is enough **that** the disciple be as his master, and the servant as his lord.		
26 Fear them not therefore: for there is nothing covered, that shall not be revealed; and hid, that shall not be known.			
27 What I tell you in darkness, **that speak** ye in light: and what ye hear in the ear, **that** preach ye upon the housetops.	24 What I tell you in darkness, **preach** ye in light; and what ye hear in the ear, preach ye upon the housetops.		
28 And fear not them **which** kill the body, but are not able to kill the soul: but rather fear him **which** is able to destroy both soul and body in hell.	25 And fear not them **who are able to** kill the body, but are not able to kill the soul; but rather fear him **who** is able to destroy both soul and body in hell.		
29 Are not two sparrows sold for a farthing? and one of them shall not fall on the ground without your Father.	26 Are not two sparrows sold for a farthing? And one of them shall not fall on the ground without your Father **knoweth it.**		
30 **But** the very hairs of your head are all numbered.	27 **And** the very hairs of your head are all numbered.		
31 Fear ye not therefore, ye are of more value than many sparrows.			
32 Whosoever therefore shall confess me before men, him will I confess also before my Father **which** is in heaven.	28 Whosoever, therefore, shall confess me before men, him will I confess also before my Father **who** is in heaven.		
33 But whosoever shall deny me before men, him will I also deny before my Father **which** is in heaven.	29 But whosoever shall deny me before men, him will I also deny before my Father **who** is in heaven.		
34 Think not that I am come to send peace on earth: I came not to send peace, but a sword.			

Matt. 10 & 11	JST Matt. 10 Luke 9	D & C Mark 6	D & C JST Mark 6
35 For I am come to set a man at variance against his father, and the daughter against her mother, and the daughter in law against her mother in law. 36 And a man's foes shall be they of his own household.			
37 He **that** loveth father **or** mother more than me is not worthy of me: and he **that** loveth son or daughter more than me is not worthy of me.	32 He **who** loveth father **and** mother more than me, is not worthy of me; and he **who** loveth son or daughter more than me, is not worthy of me.	D&C 84:87 Behold, I send you out to reprove the world of all their unrighteous deeds, and to teach them of a judgment which is to come.	
38 And he **that** taketh not his cross, and followeth after me, is not worthy of me.	33 And he **who** taketh not his cross and followeth after me, is not worthy of me.		
39 He **that findeth** his life shall lose it: and he **that** loseth his life for my sake shall find it.	34 He **who seeketh to save** his life shall lose it; and he **who** loseth his life for my sake shall find it.	88 And whoso receiveth you, there I will be also, for I will go before your face. I will be on your right hand and on your left, and my Spirit shall be in your hearts, and mine angels round about you, to bear you up.	D&C 103:27 Let no man be afraid to lay down his life for my sake; for whoso layeth down his life for my sake shall find it again.
40 ¶ He **that** receiveth you receiveth me, and he **that** receiveth me receiveth him **that** sent me.	35 He **who** receiveth you, receiveth me; and he **who** receiveth me, receiveth him **who** sent me.	89 Whoso receiveth you receiveth me; and the same will feed you, and clothe you, and give you money.	28 And whoso is not willing to lay down his life for my sake is not my disciple. (See also D&C 98:13-15.)
41 He that receiveth a prophet in the name of a prophet shall receive a prophet's reward; **and he** that receiveth a righteous man in the name of a righteous man shall receive a righteous man's reward.	37 He that receiveth a righteous man, in the name of a righteous man, shall receive a righteous man's reward.	90 And he who feeds you, or clothes you, or gives you money, shall in nowise lose his reward.	
42 And whosoever shall give to drink unto one of these little ones a cup of cold water only in the name of a disciple, verily I say unto you, he shall in no wise lose his reward.		91 And he that doeth not these things is not my disciple; by this you may know my disciples. (See also D&C 84:36-38; 39:22; 99:2; 112: 20-21.)	

TPJS-- Remember that he that gives a cup of cold water in the name of a disciple, to one of the saints in prison, or secluded from friends by reason of vexatious law suits, intended for persecution, shall in no wise lose his reward. (p. 261)

Matt. 11:1 And it came to pass, when Jesus had made an end of commanding his twelve disciples, he departed thence to teach and to preach in their cities.	Luke 9:6 And they departed, and went through the towns, preaching the gospel, and healing every where.	Mark 6:12 And they went out, and preached that men should repent. 13 And they cast out many devils, and anointed with oil many that were sick, and healed **them**.	JST Mark 6:14 And they cast out many devils, and anointed with oil many that were sick, and **they were** healed.

Matt. 14	JST Matt. 14 TPJS	Mark 6	JST Mark 6

64. Jerusalem-- John the Baptist Beheaded

Matt. 14	JST Matt. 14 TPJS	Mark 6	JST Mark 6
6 But when Herod's birthday was kept,		21 **And** when **a convenient day was come, that** Herod **on his** birthday made a supper **to** his lords, high captains, and chief **estates** of Galilee;	21 **But** when Herod's birthday **was come, h e** made a supper **for** his lords, high captains, and the chief **priests** of Galilee.
the daughter of Herodias danced before them, and pleased Herod.		22 And when the daughter of **the said** Herodias came in, and danced, and pleased Herod and them that sat with him, the king said unto the damsel, Ask of me whatsoever thou wilt, and I will give it thee.	23 And when the daughter of Herodias came in, and danced, and pleased Herod and them that sat with him, the king said unto the damsel, Ask of me whatsoever thou wilt, and I will give it thee.
7 Whereupon he promised with an oath to give her whatsoever she would ask.	6 Whereupon he promised with an oath to give her whatever she would ask.	23 And he sware unto her, Whatsoever thou shalt ask of me, I will give it thee, unto the half of my kingdom. 24 And she went forth, and said unto her mother, What shall I ask? And she said, The head of John the Baptist. 25 And she came in straightway with haste unto the king, and asked, saying, I will that thou give me by and by in a charger the head of John the Baptist.	
8 And she, being before instructed of her mother, said, Give me here John Baptist's head in a charger. 9 And the king was sorry: nevertheless for the oath's sake, and them which sat with him at meat, he commanded it to be given **her.**	8 And the king was sorry; nevertheless for the oath's sake, and them which sat with him at meat, he commanded it to be given.	26 And the king was exceedingly sorry; **yet** for his oath's sake, and for their sakes which sat with him, he would not reject her. 27 And immediately the king sent an executioner, and commanded his head to be brought: and he went and beheaded him in the prison,	26 And the king was exceedingly sorry; **but** for his oath's sake, and for their sakes which sat with him, he would not reject her.
10 And he sent, and beheaded John in the prison. 11 And his head was brought in a charger, and given to the damsel: and she brought it to her mother. 12 And his disciples came, and took up the body, and buried it, and went and told Jesus.	TPJS-- John's head was taken to Herod, the son of this infant murderer, in a charger--notwithstanding there was never a greater prophet born of woman than him! (p. 261)	28 And brought his head in a charger, and gave it to the damsel: and the damsel gave it to her mother. 29 And when **the** disciples heard of it, they came and took up his corpse, and laid it in a tomb.	30 And when **John's** disciples heard of it, they came and took up his corpse and laid it in a tomb.

Matt. 14	JST Matt. 14	Mark 6	JST Mark 6

65. Sea of Galilee-- Jesus and Apostles Travel to a Solitary Place

Matt. 14	JST Matt. 14	Mark 6	JST Mark 6
		30 **And** the apostles gathered themselves together unto Jesus, and told him all things, both what they had done, and what they had taught.	31 **Now** the apostles gathered themselves together unto Jesus, and told him all things;both what they had done, and what they had taught.
13 ¶ When Jesus heard of it,	12 When Jesus heard **that John was beheaded,**	31 And he said unto them, Come ye yourselves apart into a **desert** place, and rest a while: for there were many coming and going, and they had no leisure so much as to eat.	32 And he said unto them, Come ye yourselves apart into a **solitary** place, and rest a while; for there were many coming and going, and they had no leisure, **not** so much as to eat.
he departed thence by ship into a desert place apart:	he departed thence by ship into a desert place apart;	32 And they departed into a **desert** place by ship privately.	33 And they departed into a **solitary** place by ship, privately.
and when the people had heard **thereof**, they followed him on foot out of the cities.	and when the people had heard **of him**, they followed him on foot out of the cities.	33 And the people saw them departing, and many knew **him**, and ran afoot thither out of all cities, and **outwent** them, and came together unto him.	34 And the people saw them departing; and many knew **Jesus**, and ran afoot thither out of all cities, and **outran** them, and came together unto him.

The Third Year of Jesus' Ministry

66. Mountain (Bethsaida)-- Feeds 5,000

Matt. 14	JST Matt. 14	Mark 6	JST Mark 6
14 And Jesus went forth, and saw a great multitude, and was moved with compassion toward them, and he healed their sick.		34 And Jesus, when he came out, saw much people, and was moved with compassion toward them, because they were as sheep not having a shepherd: and he began to teach them many things.	
15 ¶ And when it was evening, his disciples came to him, saying, This is a desert place, and the time is now past;		35 And when the day was now far spent, his disciples came unto him, and said, This is a **desert** place, and now the time **is far passed:**	36 And when the day was now far spent, his disciples came unto him and said, This is a **solitary** place, and now the time **for departure is come,**
send the multitude away, that they may go into the villages, and buy themselves victuals.		36 Send them away, that they may go into the country round about, and into the villages, and buy themselves bread: for they have nothing to eat.	

Luke 9	JST Luke 9	John 6	

10 ¶ And the apostles, when they **were** returned, told him all that they had done.

10 And the apostles, when they returned, told **Jesus** all that they had done.

And he took them, and went aside privately into a **desert** place belonging to the city called Bethsaida.
11 And the people, when they knew it, followed him:

And he took them, and went aside privately into a **solitary** place belonging to the city called Bethsaida.
11 And the people, when they knew it, followed him;

After these things Jesus went over the sea of Galilee, which is the sea of Tiberias.
2 And a great multitude followed him, because they saw his miracles which he did on them that were diseased.

and he received them, and spake unto them of the kingdom of God, and healed them **that** had need of healing.

and he received them, and spake unto them of the kingdom of God, and healed them **who** had need of healing.

3 And Jesus went up into a mountain, and there he sat with his disciples.
4 And the passover, a feast of the Jews, was nigh.

12 And when the day began to wear away, then came the twelve, and said unto him,

12 And when the day began to wear away, then came the twelve, and said unto him,

Send the multitude away, that they may go into the towns and country round about, and lodge, and get victuals: for we are here in a **desert** place.

Send the multitude away, that they may go into the towns and country round about, and lodge, and get victuals; for we are here in a **solitary** place.

151

Matt. 14	JST Matt. 14	Mark 6	JST Mark 6
16 But Jesus said unto them, They need not depart; give ye them to eat.		37 He answered and said unto them, Give ye them to eat. And they say unto him, Shall we go and buy two hundred pennyworth of bread, and give them to eat? 38 And he saith unto them, How many loaves have ye? go and see. And when they knew, they say, Five, and two fishes.	
17 And they said unto him, We have here but five loaves, and two fishes. 18 He said, Bring them hither to me. 19 And he commanded the multitude to sit down on the grass,	17 And he commanded the multitude to sit down on the grass;	39 And he commanded them to make all sit down by companies upon the green grass. 40 And they sat down in ranks, by hundreds, and by fifties.	
and took the five loaves, and the two fishes, and looking up to heaven, he blessed, and break, and gave the loaves to **his** disciples, and the disciples to the multitude.	and he took the five loaves and the two fishes, and looking up to heaven, he blessed and break and gave the loaves to **the** disciples, and the disciples, to the multitude.	41 And when he had taken the five loaves and the two fishes, he looked up to heaven, and blessed, and brake the loaves, and gave them to his disciples to set before **them**; and the two fishes divided he among them all.	43 And when he had taken the five loaves and two fishes, he looked up to heaven, and blessed, and break the loaves, and gave to his disciples to set before **the multitude**; and the two fishes divided he among them all.
20 And they did all eat, and were filled:	18 And they did all eat, and were filled.	42 And they did all eat, and were filled.	
and they took up of the fragments that remained twelve **baskets full**.	And they took up of the fragments that remained, twelve **basketsful**.	43 And they took up twelve **baskets full** of the fragments, and of the fishes.	45 And they took up twelve **basketsful** of the fragments, and of the fishes.
21 And they that had eaten were about five thousand men, beside women and children.	And they that had eaten were about five thousand men, besides women and children.	44 And they that did eat of the loaves were about five thousand men.	

Luke 9	JST Luke 9	John 6	JST John 6
		5 ¶ When Jesus then lifted up his eyes, and saw a great company come unto him, he saith unto Philip, Whence shall we buy bread, that these may eat?	
		6 And this he said to prove him: for he himself knew what he would do.	
13 But he said unto them, Give ye them to eat.	13 But he said unto them, Give ye them to eat.	7 Philip answered him, Two hundred pennyworth of bread is not sufficient for them, that every one of them may take a little.	
		8 One of his disciple, Andrew, Simon Peter's brother, saith unto him,	
And they said, We have **no more** but five loaves and two fishes; except we should go and buy meat for all this **people**.	And they said, We have but five loaves and two fishes; **and** except we should go and buy meat, **we can provide no more food** for all this **multitude**.	9 There is a lad here, which hath five barley loaves, and two small fishes: but what are they among so many?	
14 For they were about five thousand men. And **he** said to his disciples, Make them sit down by fifties in a company.	14 For they were **in number** about five thousand men. And **Jesus** said **un**to his disciples, Make them sit down by fifties in a company.	10 And Jesus said, Make the men sit down. Now there was much grass in the place. So the men sat down, in number about five thousand.	
15 And they did so, and made them all sit down.			
16 Then he took the five loaves and the two fishes, and looking up to heaven, he blessed them, and brake, and gave to the disciples to set before the multitude.		11 And Jesus took the loaves; and when he had given thanks, he distributed to the disciples, and the disciples to them that were set down; and likewise of the fishes as much as they would.	
		12 When they **were filled**, he said unto his disciples, Gather up the fragments that remain, that nothing be lost.	12 When they **had eaten and were satisfied**, he said unto his disciples, Gather up the fragments that remain, that nothing be lost.
17 And they did eat, and were all filled:	17 And they did eat, and were all filled.		
and there was taken up of the fragments **that remained to them** twelve baskets.	And there was taken up of the fragments **which** remained, twelve baskets.	13 Therefore they gathered them together, and filled twelve baskets with the fragments of the barley loaves, which remained over and above unto them that had eaten.	
		14 Then those men, when they had seen the miracle that Jesus did, said, This is of a truth that prophet that should come into the world.	

Matt. 14	JST Matt. 14	Mark 6	JST Mark 6

67. Mountain-- Jesus Prays

Matt. 14	JST Matt. 14	Mark 6	JST Mark 6
22 ¶ And straightway Jesus constrained his disciples to get into a ship, and to go before him unto the other side, while he sent the multitudes away. 23 And when he had sent the multitudes away, he went up into a mountain apart to pray: and when the evening was come, he was there alone.		45 And straightway he constrained his disciples to get into the ship, and to go to the other side before unto Bethsaida, while he sent away the people. 46 And when he had sent them away, he departed into a mountain to pray.	47 And straightway he constrained his disciples to get into the ship, and to go to the other side before **him**, unto Bethsaida, while he sent away the people.

68. Sea of Galilee-- Jesus Walks on Water

Matt. 14	JST Matt. 14	Mark 6	JST Mark 6
		47 And when even was come, the ship was in the midst of the sea, and he alone on the land.	
24 But the ship was now in the midst of the sea, tossed with waves: for the wind was contrary. 25 And in the fourth watch of the night Jesus went unto them, walking on the sea. 26 And when the disciples saw him walking on the sea, they were troubled, saying, It is a spirit; and they cried out for fear.	20 . . . But the ship was now in the midst of the sea, tossed with **the** waves: for the wind was contrary.	48 And he saw them toiling in rowing; for the wind was contrary unto them: and about the fourth watch of the night he cometh unto them, walking upon the sea, **and** would have passed by them. 49 **But** when they saw him walking upon the sea, they supposed it had been a spirit, and cried out:	50 And about the fourth watch of the night he cometh unto them, walking upon the sea, **as if he** would have passed by them. 51 **And** when they saw him walking upon the sea, they supposed it had been a spirit, and cried out;
27 But straightway Jesus spake unto them, saying; Be of good cheer; it is I; be not afraid. 28 And Peter answered him and said, Lord, if it be thou, bid me come unto thee on the water. 29 And he said, Come. And when Peter was come		50 For they all saw him, and were troubled. And immediately he talked with them, and saith unto them, Be of good cheer: it is I; be not afraid.	

154

		John 6	JST John 6

15 ¶ When Jesus therefore perceived that they would come and take him by force, to make him a king,

he departed again into a mountain himself alone.

16 And when even was now come, his disciples went down unto the sea,
17 And entered into a ship, and went over the sea toward Capernaum. And it was now dark, and Jesus **was** not come to them.
18 And the sea arose by reason of a great wind that blew.

17 And entered into a ship, and went over the sea toward Capernaum. And it was now dark, and Jesus **had** not come to them.

19 So when they had rowed about five and twenty or thirty furlongs, they **see** Jesus walking on the sea, and drawing nigh unto the ship: and they were afraid.

19 So when they had rowed about five and twenty or thirty furlongs, they **saw** Jesus walking on the sea, and drawing nigh unto the ship; and they were afraid.

20 But he saith unto them, It is I; be not afraid.

Matt. 14	Mark 6	JST Mark 6	John 6
down out of the ship, he walked on the water, to go to Jesus. 30 But when he saw the wind boisterous, he was afraid; and beginning to sink, he cried, saying, Lord, save me. 31 And immediately Jesus stretched forth his hand, and caught him, and said unto him, O thou of little faith, wherefore didst thou doubt? 32 And when they were come into the ship, the wind ceased.	51 And he went up unto them in the ship; and the wind ceased: and they were sore amazed in themselves beyond measure, and wondered.		21 Then they willingly received him into the ship:
33 Then they that were in the ship came and worshipped him, saying, Of a truth thou art the Son of God.			
	52 For they considered not the **miracle of the** loaves: for their heart **was** hardened.	55 For they considered not of the loaves; for their hearts were hardened.	and immediately the ship was at the land whither they went.

John 6	JST John 6	John 6	JST John 6

69. Capernaum-- Bread of Life Sermon

22 ¶ The day following, when the people which stood on the other side of the sea saw that there was none other boat there, save that one whereinto his disciples were entered, and that Jesus went not with his disciples into the boat, but that his disciples were gone away alone;

23 (Howbeit there came other boats from Tiberias nigh unto the place where they did eat bread, after that the Lord had given thanks:)

24 When the people therefore saw that Jesus was not there, neither his disciples, they also took shipping, and came to Capernaum, seeking for Jesus.

25 And when they had found him on the other side of the sea, they said unto him, Rabbi, **when** camest thou hither?

26 Jesus answered them and said, Verily, verily, I say unto you, Ye seek me, not because ye saw the miracles, but because ye did eat of the loaves, and were filled.

27 Labour not for the meat which perisheth, but for that meat which endureth unto everlasting life, which the Son of man **shall** give unto you: for him hath God the Father sealed.

28 Then said they unto him, What shall we do, that we might work the works of God?

29 Jesus answered and said unto them, This is the (continued in column 3)

25 And when they had found him on the other side of the sea, they said unto him, Rabbi, **how** camest thou hither?

26 Jesus answered them and said, Verily, verily, I say unto you, Ye seek me, not because ye **desire to keep my sayings, neither because ye** saw the miracles, but because ye did eat of the loaves, and were filled.

27 Labor not for the meat which perisheth, but for that meat which endureth unto everlasting life, which the Son of Man **hath power to** give unto you; for him hath God the Father sealed.

work of God, that ye believe on him whom he hath sent.

30 They said therefore unto him, What sign shewest thou then, that we may see, and believe thee? what dost thou work?

31 Our fathers did eat manna in the desert; as it is written, He gave them bread from heaven to eat.

32 Then Jesus said unto them, Verily, verily, I say unto you, Moses gave you not that bread from heaven; but my Father giveth you the true bread from heaven.

33 For the bread of God is he which cometh down from heaven, and giveth life unto the world.

34 Then said they unto him, Lord, evermore give us this bread.

35 And Jesus said unto them, I am the bread of life: he that cometh to me shall never hunger; and he that believeth on me shall never thirst.

36 But I said unto you, That ye also have seen me, and believe not.

37 All that the Father giveth me shall come to me; and him that cometh to me I will in no wise cast out.

38 For I came down from heaven, not to do mine own will, but the will of him that sent me.

39 And this is the Father's will which hath sent me, that of all which he hath given me I should lose nothing, but should raise it up again at the last day.

40 And this is the will of him that sent me, that everyone which seeth the

40 And this is the will of him that sent me, that everyone which seeth the

John 6	JST John 6	John 6	JST John 6
Son, and believeth on him, may have everlasting life: and I will raise him up at the last day.	Son, and believeth on him, may have everlasting life; and I will raise him up **in the resurrection of the just** at the last day.	51 I am the living bread which came down from heaven: if any man eat of this bread, he shall live forever: and the bread that I will give is my flesh, which I will give for the life of the world.	51 **But** I am the living bread which came down from heaven; if any man eat of this bread, he shall live for ever; and the bread that I will give is my flesh, which I will give for the life of the world.
41 The Jews then murmured at him, because he said, I am the bread which came down from heaven.		52 The Jews therefore strove among themselves, saying, How can this man give us his flesh to eat?	
42 And they said, Is not this Jesus, the son of Joseph, whose father and mother we know? how is it then that he saith, I came down from heaven?		53 Then Jesus said unto them, Verily, verily, I say unto you, Except ye eat the flesh of the Son of man, and drink his blood, ye have no life in you.	
43 Jesus therefore answered and said unto them, Murmur not among yourselves.			
44 No man can come to me, except the Father **which** hath sent me **draw him**: and	44 No man can come unto me, except **he doeth** the **will** of my Father **who** hath sent me. And **this is the will of him who hath sent me, that ye receive the Son; for the Father beareth record of him; and he who receiveth the testimony, and doeth the will of him who sent me, I will raise up in the resurrection of the just.**	54 Whoso eateth my flesh, and drinketh my blood, hath eternal life; and I will raise him up at the last day.	54 Whoso eateth my flesh, and drinketh my blood, hath eternal life; and I will raise him up **in the resurrection of the just** at the last day.
		55 For my flesh is meat indeed, and my blood is drink indeed.	
		56 He that eateth my flesh, and drinketh my blood, dwelleth in me, and I in him.	
I will raise **him** up **at the last day.**		57 As the living Father hath sent me, and I live by the Father: so he that eateth me, even he shall live by me.	
45 It is written in the prophets, And **they** shall **be all** taught of God. Every man therefore that hath heard, and hath learned of the Father, cometh unto me.	45 **For** it is written in the prophets, And **these** shall **all be** taught of God. Every man therefore that hath heard, and hath learned of the Father, cometh unto me.	58 This is that bread which came down from heaven: not as your fathers did eat manna, and are dead: he that eateth of this bread shall live for ever.	
46 Not that any man hath seen the father, save he which is of God, he hath seen the Father.		59 These things said he in the synagogue, as he taught in Capernaum.	
47 Verily, verily, I say unto you, He that believeth on me hath everlasting life.		60 Many therefore of his disciples, when they had heard this, said, This is an hard saying; who can hear it?	
48 I am that bread of life.			
49 Your fathers did eat manna in the wilderness, and are dead.	(Vss. 49 and 50 are reversed in the JST.)	61 When Jesus knew in himself that his disciples murmured at it, he said unto them, Doth this offend you?	
50 This is the bread which cometh down from heaven, that a man may eat thereof, and not die.			
(continued in column 3)	(continued in column 4)		

John 6 & 7	JST John 6		
62 What and if ye shall see the Son of man ascend up where he was before? 63 It is the spirit that quickeneth; the flesh profiteth nothing: the words that I speak unto you, they are spirit, and they are life. 64 But there are some of you that believe not. For Jesus knew from the beginning who they were that believed not, and who should betray him. 65 And he said, Therefore said I unto you, that no man can come unto me, except **it were given unto him** of my Father. 66 ¶ From that time many of his disciples went back, and walked no more with him. 67 Then said Jesus unto the twelve, Will ye also go away? 68 Then Simon Peter answered him, Lord, to whom shall we go? thou hast the words of eternal life. 69 And we believe and are sure that thou art that Christ, the Son of the living God. 70 Jesus answered them, Have not I chosen you twelve, and one of you is a devil? 71 He spake of Judas Iscariot the son of Simon: for he it was that should betray him, being one of the twelve. 7:1 After these things Jesus walked in Galilee: for he would not walk in Jewry, because the Jews sought to kill him.	65 And he said, Therefore said I unto you, that no man can come unto me, except **he doeth the will** of my Father **who hath sent me**.		

Matt. 14		Mark 6	JST Mark 6

70. Gennesaret-- People Healed

34 ¶ And when they were gone over, they came into the land of Gennesaret.

35 And when the men of that place had knowledge of him, they sent out into all that country round about, and brought unto him all that were diseased;

36 And besought him that they might only touch the hem of his garment: and as many as touched were made perfectly whole.

53 And when they had passed over, they came into the land of Gennesaret, and drew to the shore.

54 And when they were come out of the ship, straightway **they knew** him,

55 And ran through that whole region round about, and began to carry about in beds those that were sick, where they heard he was.

56 And whithersoever he entered, into villages, or cities, or country, they laid the sick in the streets, and besought him that they might touch if it were but the border of his garment: and as many as touched him were made whole.

57 And when they were come out of the ship, straightway **the people** knew him, and ran through that whole region round about, and began to carry about in beds, those that were sick, where they heard he was.

Matt. 15	JST Matt. 15	Mark 7	JST Mark 7

71. Pharisees and Scribes from Jerusalem-- Cleanliness

Matt. 15	JST Matt. 15	Mark 7	JST Mark 7
Then came to Jesus scribes and Pharisees, which were of Jerusalem, saying,		Then came together unto him the Pharisees, and certain of the scribes, which came from Jerusalem.	
		2 And when they saw some of his disciples eat bread with defiled, that is to say, with unwashen, hands, they found fault.	
		3 For the Pharisees, and all the Jews, except they wash **their** hands oft, eat not, holding the tradition of the elders.	3 For the Pharisees, and all the Jews, except they wash hands oft, eat not; holding the tradition of the elders.
		4 And when they come from the market, except they wash, they eat not. And many other things there be, which they have received to hold, as the washing of cups, and pots, brasen vessels, and of tables.	4 And when they came from the market, except they wash **their bodies**, they eat not.
2 Why do thy disciples transgress the tradition of the elders? for they wash not their hands when they eat bread.		5 **Then** the Pharisees and scribes asked him, Why walk not thy disciples according to the tradition of the elders, but eat bread with unwashen hands?	6 **And** the Pharisees and scribes asked him, Why walk not thy disciples according to the **traditions of** the elders, but eat bread with unwashen hands?
7 Ye hypocrites, well did Esaias prophesy of you, saying,	7 **O** ye hypocrites! well did Esaias prophesy of you, saying, This people draw nigh unto me with their mouth, and honoreth me with their lips; but their heart is far from me.	6 He answered and said unto them, Well hath **Esaias** prophesied of you hypocrites, as it is written, This people honoureth me with their lips, but their heart is far from me.	7 He answered and said unto them, Well hath **Isaiah** prophesied of you hypocrites, as it is written, This people honoreth me with their lips, but their heart is far from me.
8 This people **draweth** nigh unto me with their mouth, and honoureth me with their lips; but their heart is far from me.			
9 But in vain they do worship me, teaching **for** doctrines the commandments of men.	8 But in vain do they worship me, teaching **the** doctrines **a n d t h e** commandments of men.	7 Howbeit in vain do they worship me, teaching **for** doctrines **the** commandments of men.	Howbeit, in vain do they worship me, teaching **the** doctrines **and** commandments of men.
		8 For laying aside the commandment of God, ye hold the tradition of men, **as** the washing of pots and cups: and many other such like things ye do.	8 For laying aside the commandment of God, ye hold the tradition of men; the washing of pots and **of** cups; and many other such like things ye do.
3 But he answered and said unto them, Why do ye also transgress the commandment of God by your tradition?		9 And he said unto them, **Full well** ye reject the commandment of God, that ye may keep your own tradition.	9 And he said unto them, **Yea, altogether** ye reject the commandment of God, that ye may keep your own tradition.

161

Matt. 15	JST Matt. 15	Mark 7	JST Mark 7
			10 **Full well is it written of you, by the prophets whom ye have rejected.** 11 **They testified these things of a truth, and their blood shall be upon you.** 12 **Ye have kept not the ordinances of God**; for Moses said, Honor thy father and thy mother; and whoso curseth father or mother, let him die the death **of the transgressor, as it is written in your law; but ye keep not the law.**
4 For God commanded, saying, Honour thy father and mother: and, He that curseth father or mother, let him die the death.	4 For God commanded, saying, Honor thy father and mother; and, He that curseth father or mother, let him die the death **which Moses shall appoint.**	10 For Moses said, Honour thy father and thy mother; and, Whoso curseth father or mother, let him die the death:	
5 But ye say, Whosoever shall say to **his** father or **his** mother, **It is a gift**, by whatsoever thou mightest be profited by me;	5 But ye say, Whosoever shall say to father or mother, By whatsoever thou mightest be profited by me, **it is a gift from me**	11 **But** ye say, If a man shall say to his father or mother, **It is Corban, that is to say, a gift**, by whatsoever thou mightest be profited by me;	13 Ye say, If a man shall say to his father or mother, Corban, that is to say, a gift, by whatsoever thou mightest be profited by me,
6 And honour not his father or his mother, **he shall be free.**	and honor not his father or mother, it is well.	he **shall be free.**	he **is of age.**
		12 And ye suffer him no more to do ought for his father or his mother;	
Thus ye have made the commandment of God of none effect by your tradition.		13 Making the word of God of none effect through your tradition, which ye have delivered: and many such like things do ye.	
		14 ¶ And when he had called all the people **unto him**, he said unto them, Hearken unto me every one **of you**, and understand:	14 And when he had called all the people, he said unto them, Hearken unto me every one, and understand;
10 ¶ And he called the multitude, and said unto them, Hear, and understand:			
11 Not that which goeth into the mouth defileth a man, but that which cometh out of the mouth, this defileth **a man.**	10 Not that which goeth into the mouth defileth a man; but that which cometh out of the mouth, this defileth **the man.**	15 There is nothing from without **a man**, that entering into **him** can defile him: but the things which come out of him, those are they that defile the man.	15 There is nothing from without, that entering into **a man**, can defile him, **which is food**; but the things which come out of him; those are they that defile the man, **that proceedeth forth out of the heart.**
		16 If any man have ears to hear, let him hear.	
12 Then came his disciples, and said unto him, Knowest thou that the Pharisees were offended,			

162

Matt. 15	JST Matt. 15	Mark 7	JST Mark 7
after they heard this saying?			
13 But he answered and said, Every plant, which my heavenly Father hath not planted, shall be rooted up.			
14 Let them alone: they be blind leaders of the blind. And if the blind lead the blind, both shall fall into the ditch.			
		17 And when he was entered into the house from the people, his disciples asked him concerning the parable.	17 And when he was entered into the house from **among** the people, his disciples asked him concerning the parable.
15 Then answered Peter and said unto him, Declare unto us this parable.			
16 And Jesus said, Are ye also yet without understanding?		18 And he **saith** unto them, Are ye **so** without understanding also? Do ye not perceive, that whatsoever thing from without entereth into the man, **it** cannot defile him;	18 And he **said** unto them, Are ye without understanding also? Do ye not perceive, that whatsoever thing from without entereth into the man, cannot defile him;
17 Do **not** ye yet understand, that whatsoever entereth in at the mouth goeth into the belly, and is cast **out** into the draught?	16 Do **ye** **not** yet understand, that whatsoever entereth in at the mouth goeth into the belly, and is cast into the draught?	19 Because it entereth not into his heart, but into the belly, and goeth out into the draught, purging all meats?	
18 But those things which proceed out of the mouth come forth from the heart; and they defile the man.		20 And he said, That which cometh out of **the** man, **that** defileth the man.	19 And he said, That which cometh out of **a** man, defileth the man.
19 For out of the heart proceed evil thoughts, murders, adulteries, fornications, thefts, false witness, blasphemies:		21 For from within, out of the heart of men, proceed evil thoughts, adulteries, fornications, murders,	
		22 Thefts, covetousness, wickedness, deceit, lasciviousness, an evil eye, blasphemy, pride, foolishness:	
20 These are the things which defile a man: but to eat with unwashen hands defileth not a man.		23 All these evil things come from within, and defile the man.	

72. Coasts of Tyre and Sidon-- Gentile's Daughter Healed

Matt. 15	JST Matt. 15	Mark 7	JST Mark 7
21 ¶ Then Jesus went thence, and departed into the coasts of Tyre and Sidon.		24 ¶ And from thence he arose, and went into the borders of Tyre and Sidon, and entered into an house, and would **have** no man	22 And from thence he arose, and went into the borders of Tyre and Sidon, and entered into a house, and would **that** no man

Matt. 15	JST Matt. 15	Mark 7	JST Mark 7
		know it: but he could not be hid.	should come unto him.
			23 But he could not deny them; for he had compassion upon all men.
		25 For a certain woman, whose young daughter had an unclean spirit, heard of him, and came and fell at his feet:	25 For a woman, whose young daughter had an unclean spirit, heard of him and came and fell at his feet.
22 And, behold, a woman of Canaan came out of the same coasts, and cried unto him, saying, Have mercy on me, O Lord, thou Son of David; my daughter is grievously vexed with a devil.		26 The woman was a Greek, a Syrophenician by nation; and she besought him that he would cast forth the devil out of her daughter.	
23 But he answered her not a word. And his disciples came and besought him, saying, Send her away; for she crieth after us.			
24 But he answered and said, I am not sent but unto the lost sheep of the house of Israel.	23 He answered, I am not sent but unto the lost sheep of the house of Israel.		
25 Then came she and worshipped him, saying, Lord, help me.			
26 But he answered and said, It is not meet to take the children's bread, and to cast it to dogs.		27 But Jesus said unto her, Let the children first be filled: for it is not meet to take the children's bread, and to cast it unto the dogs.	26 But Jesus said unto her, Let the children of the kingdom first be filled; for it is not meet to take the children's bread, and to cast it unto the dogs.
27 And she said, Truth, Lord: yet the dogs eat of the crumbs which fall from their masters' table.	26 And she said, Truth, Lord; yet the dogs eat the crumbs that fall from the master's table.	28 And she answered and said unto him, Yes, Lord: yet the dogs under the table eat of the children's crumbs.	27 And she answered and said unto him, Yes, Lord; thou sayest truly, yet the dogs under the table eat of the children's crumbs.
28 Then Jesus answered and said unto her, O woman, great is thy faith: be it unto thee even as thou wilt. And her daughter was made whole from that very hour.		29 And he said unto her, For this saying go thy way; the devil is gone out of thy daughter.	
		30 And when she was come to her house, she found the devil gone out, and her daughter laid upon the bed.	29 And when she was come to her house, she found that the devil had gone out, and her daughter was laid upon the bed.

Matt. 15	JST Matt. 15	Mark 7	JST Mark 7

73. Mountain by Galilee-- Many Healed

Matt. 15	JST Matt. 15	Mark 7	JST Mark 7
29 And Jesus departed from thence, and came nigh unto the sea of Galilee; and went up into a mountain, and sat down there.		31 ¶ And again, departing from the coasts of Tyre and Sidon, he came unto the sea of Galilee, through the midst of the coasts of Decapolis.	
30 And great multitudes came unto him, having with them **those that were** lame, blind, dumb, maimed, and many others, and cast them down at Jesus' feet; and he healed them:	29 And great multitudes came unto him, having with them **some** lame, blind, dumb, maimed, and many others, and cast them down at Jesus' feet; and he healed them;		
		32 And they **bring** unto him one that was deaf, and had an impediment in his speech; and they **beseech** him to put his hand upon him.	31 And they **brought** unto him one that was deaf, and had an impediment in his speech; and they **besought** him to put his hand upon him.
		33 And he took him aside from the multitude, and put his fingers into his ears, and he spit, and touched his tongue.	
		34 And looking up to heaven, he sighed, and saith unto him, Ephphatha, that is, Be opened.	
		35 And straightway his ears were opened, and the string of his tongue was loosed, and he spoke plain.	
		36 And he charged them that they should tell no man: but the more he charged them, so much the more a great deal they published **it**;	35 And he charged them that they should tell no man; but the more he charged them, so much the more a great deal they published **him**;
31 Insomuch that the multitude wondered, when they saw the dumb to speak, the maimed to be whole, the lame to walk, and the blind to see: and they glorified the God of Israel.		37 And were beyond measure astonished, saying, He hath done all things well: he maketh both the deaf to hear, and the dumb to speak.	

Matt. 15	JST Matt. 15	Mark 8	JST Mark 8
		74. 4,000 Miraculously Fed	
		In those days the multitude being very great, and having nothing to eat, Jesus called his disciples **unto him** and **saith** unto them,	In those days, the multitude being very great, and having nothing to eat, Jesus called his disciples, and **said** unto them,
32 ¶ Then Jesus called his disciples **unto him**, and said, I have compassion on the multitude, because they continue with me now three days, and have nothing to eat: and I will not send them away fasting, lest they faint in the way.	30 Then Jesus called his disciples and said, I have compassion on the multitude, because they continue with me now three days, and have nothing to eat; and I will not send them away fasting; lest they faint in the way.	2 I have compassion on the multitude, because they have now been with me three days, and have nothing to eat:	
		3 And if I send them away fasting to their own houses, they will faint by the way: for divers of them came from far.	
33 And his disciples say unto him, Whence should we have so much bread in the wilderness, as to fill so great a multitude?		4 And his disciples answered him, From whence can a man satisfy these **men** with bread here in the wilderness?	3 And his disciples answered him, From whence can a man satisfy these, **so great a multitude**, with bread, here in the wilderness?
34 And Jesus **saith** unto them, How many loaves have ye? And they said, Seven, and a few little fishes.		5 And he asked them, How many loaves have ye? And they said, Seven.	
35 And he commanded the multitude to sit down on the ground. 36 And he took the seven loaves and the fishes, and gave thanks, and brake **them**, and gave to his disciples, and the disciples to the multitude.	34 and he took the seven loaves, and the fishes, and gave thanks, and brake **the bread**, and gave to his disciples, and the disciples, to the multitude.	6 And he commanded the people to sit down on the ground: and he took to seven loaves, and gave thanks, and brake, and gave to his disciples to set before **them**; and they did set them before the people.	5 And he commanded the people to sit down on the ground; and he took the seven loaves, and gave thanks, and brake, and gave to his disciples to set before **the people**; and they did set them before the people.
		7 And they had a few small fishes: and he blessed, and commanded to set them also before **them**.	6 And they had a few small fishes; and he blessed **them**, and commanded to set them also before **the people, that they should eat**.
37 And they did all eat, and were filled: and they took up of the broken meat **that was left** seven baskets full.	35 And they did all eat, and were filled. And they took up of the broken meat seven baskets full.	8 So they did eat, and were filled: and they took up of the broken **meat** that was left seven baskets.	7 So they did eat and were filled, and they took up of the broken **bread** that was left, seven baskets.

Matt. 15 & 16	JST Matt. 16	Mark 8	JST Mark 8

75. Coasts of Magdala (Dalmanutha)-- Discourse on Signs

Matt. 15 & 16	JST Matt. 16	Mark 8	JST Mark 8
15:39 And he sent away the multitude, and took ship, and came into the coasts of Magdala. 16:1 The Pharisees also with the Sadducees came, and tempting desired him that he would shew them a sign from heaven. 2 He answered and said unto them, When it is evening, ye say, **It will be fair** weather: for the sky is red. 3 And in the morning, **It will be foul** weather to day: for the sky is red and lowring, O **ye** hypocrites, ye can discern the face of the sky; but **can ye not discern** the signs of the times? 4 A wicked and adulterous generation seeketh after a sign; and there shall no sign be given unto it, but the sign of the prophet Jonas.	The Pharisees also, with the Sadducees, came, and tempting **Jesus**, desired him that he would show them a sign from heaven. 2 **And** he answered and said unto them, When it is evening ye say, **The weather is fair**, for the sky is red; and in the morning **ye say**, **The** weather **is foul** today; for the sky is red and lowering. 3 O hypocrites! ye can discern the face of the sky; but ye **cannot tell** the signs of the times.	10 ¶ And straightway he entered into a ship with his disciples, and came into the parts of Dalmanutha. 11 And the Pharisees came forth, and began to question with him, seeking of him a sign from heaven, tempting him. 12 And he sighed deeply in his spirit, and saith, Why doth this generation seek after a sign? verily I say unto you, There shall no sign be given unto this generation.	12 Verily I say unto you, There shall no sign be given unto this generation, **save the sign of the prophet Jonah; for as Jonah was three days and three nights in the whale's belly, so likewise shall the Son of Man be buried in the bowels of the earth.**

TPJS-- [W]henever you see a man seeking after a sign, you may set it down that he is an adulterous man. (p. 157)

When I was preaching in Philadelphia, a Quaker called out for a sign. I told him to be still. After the sermon, he again asked for a sign. I told the congregation the man was an adulterer; that a wicked and adulterous generation seeketh after a sign; and that the Lord had said to me in a revelation, that any man who wanted a sign was an adulterous person. "It is true," cried one, "for I caught him in the very act," which the man afterwards confessed when he was baptized. (p. 278)

Matt. 15 & 16	JST Matt. 16	Mark 8	JST Mark 8
And he left them, and departed. 5 And when his disciples were come to the other side, they had forgotten to take bread.		13 And he left them, and entering into the ship again departed to the other side. 14 ¶ Now the **disciples** had forgotten to take bread, neither had they in the ship with them more than one loaf.	13 And he left them, and entering into the ship again **he** departed to the other side. 14 Now the **multitude** had forgotten to take bread; neither had they, in the ship with them, more than one loaf.

Matt. 16	JST Matt. 16	Mark 8	JST Mark 8
6 ¶ Then Jesus said unto them, Take heed and beware of the leaven of the Pharisees and of the Sadducees.		15 And he charged them, saying, Take heed, beware of the leaven of the Pharisees, and of the leaven of Herod.	15 And he charged them, saying, Take heed, **and** beware of the leaven of the Pharisees, and the leaven of Herod.
7 And they reasoned among themselves, saying, It is because we have taken no bread.	8 And they reasoned among themselves, saying, **He said this** because we have taken no bread.	16 And they reasoned among themselves, saying, It is because we have no bread.	16 And they reasoned among themselves, saying, **He hath said this**, because we have no bread.
	9 **And** when **they reasoned among themselves,** Jesus perceived **it; and he** said unto them, O ye of little faith! why reason ye among yourselves, because ye have brought no bread?		17 And when **they said this among themselves,** Jesus knew it, **and he said** unto them,
8 **Which** when Jesus perceived, he said unto them, O ye of little faith, why reason ye among yourselves, because ye have brought no bread?		17 And when Jesus knew it, he saith unto them,	
9 Do ye not yet understand,		Why reason ye, because ye have no bread? perceive ye not yet, neither understand? **have ye your** heart yet hardened?	18 Why reason ye because ye have no bread? Perceive ye not yet, neither understand **ye**? Are your hearts yet hardened?
		18 Having eyes, see ye not? and having ears, hear ye not? and do ye not remember?	
neither remember the five loaves of the five thousand, and how many baskets ye took up?		19 When I brake the five loaves among five thousand, how many baskets full of fragments took ye up? They say unto him, Twelve.	20 When I brake the five loaves among **the** five thousand, how many baskets full of fragments took ye up? They say unto him, Twelve.
10 Neither the seven loaves of the four thousand, and how many baskets ye took up?		20 And when the seven among four thousand, how many baskets full of fragments took ye up? And they said, Seven.	21 And when the seven among **the** four thousand, how many baskets full of fragments took ye up? And they said, Seven.
11 How is it that ye do not understand that I spake **it** not to you concerning bread, that ye should beware of the leaven of the Pharisees and of the Sadducees?	12 How is it that ye do not understand, that I spake not **unto** you concerning bread, that ye should beware of the leaven of the Pharisees and of the Sadducees?	21 And he said unto them, How is it that ye do not understand?	
12 Then understood they how that he bade them not beware of the leaven of bread, but of the doctrine of the Pharisees and of the Sadducees.			

		Mark 8	JST Mark 8

76. Blind Man Healed

		Mark 8	JST Mark 8
		22 ¶ And he cometh to Bethsaida; and they bring a blind man unto him, and besought him to touch him.	
		23 And he took the blind man by the hand, and led him out of the town; and when he had spit on his eyes, and put his hands upon him, he asked him if he saw ought.	24 And he took the blind man by the hand, and led him out of the town; and when he had spit **upon** his eyes, and put his hands upon him, he asked him if he saw **aught**?
		24 And he looked up, and said, I see men as trees, walking.	
		25 After that he put his hands again upon his eyes, and made him look up: and he was restored, and saw every man clearly.	
		26 And he sent him away to his house, saying, Neither go into the town, nor tell **it** to any in the town.	27 And he sent him away to his house, saying, Neither go into the town, nor tell **what is done**, to any in the town.

Matt. 14		Mark 6	JST Mark 6

77. Jerusalem-- Herod Wonders if John the Baptist is Risen

At that time Herod the tetrarch heard of the fame of Jesus, 2 And said unto his servants, This is John the Baptist; he is risen from the dead; and therefore mighty works do shew forth themselves in him.		14 And king Herod heard of **him**; (for his name was spread abroad:) and he said, That John the Baptist was risen from the dead, and therefore mighty works do shew forth themselves in him. 15 Others said, That is Elias. And others said, That it is a prophet, or as one of the prophets. 16 But when Herod heard **thereof**, he said, It is John, whom I beheaded: he is risen from the dead.	15 And **King** Herod heard of **Jesus**; for his name was spread abroad; and he said, That John the Baptist was risen from the dead, and therefore, mighty works do show forth themselves in him. 17 But when Herod heard **of him**, he said, It is John whom I beheaded; he is risen form the dead.

Matt. 16	JST Matt. 16	Mark 8	JST Mark 8

78. Coast of Cæsarea Philippi-- Peter's Testimony of Christ

13 ¶ When Jesus came into the coasts of Cæsarea Philippi, he asked his disciples, saying, Whom do men say that I the Son of man am? 14 And they said, Some say **that thou art** John the Baptist; some, Elias; and others, Jeremias, or one of the prophets. 15 He saith unto them, But whom say ye that I am? 16 And Simon Peter answered and said, Thou art the Christ, the Son of the living God. 17 And Jesus answered and said unto him, Blessed art thou, Simon Bar-jona: for flesh and blood hath not revealed **it** unto thee, but my Father **which** is in heaven. 18 And I say also unto	14 **And** when Jesus came into the coasts of Cæsarea Philippi, he asked his disciples, saying, Whom do men say that I, the Son of Man, am? 15 And they said, Some say John the Baptist; some Elias; and others Jeremias; or one of the prophets. 18 And Jesus answered and said unto him, Blessed art thou, Simon Bar-Jona; for flesh and blood hath not revealed **this** unto thee, but my Father **who** is in heaven.	27 ¶ And Jesus went out, and his disciples, into the towns of Cæsarea Philippi: and by the way he asked his disciples, saying unto them, Whom do men say that I am? 28 And they answered, John the Baptist: but some say, Elias; and others, One of the prophets. 29 And he saith unto them, But whom say ye that I am? And Peter answereth and saith unto him, Thou art the Christ.	31 And Peter answered and said unto him, Thou art the Christ, **the Son of the living God.**

Luke 9	JST Luke 9		

7 ¶ Now Herod the tetrarch heard of all that was done by **him**: and he was perplexed, because that it was said of some, that John was risen from the dead;

7 Now Herod the tetrarch heard of all that was done by **Jesus**; and he was perplexed, because that it was said of some, That John was risen from the dead;

8 And of some, that Elias had appeared; and of others, that one of the old prophets was risen again.

9 And Herod said, John have I beheaded: but who is this, of whom I hear such things? And he desired to see him.

18 ¶ And it came to pass, as he **was alone praying, his disciples were with him: and** he asked them, saying, Whom say the people that I am?

18 And it came to pass, as he **went** alone **with his disciples to pray,** he asked them, saying, Who say the people that I am?

19 They answering said, John the Baptist; but **some** say, Elias; and others **say,** that one of the old prophets is risen again.

19 They answering said, **Some say,** John the Baptist; but **others** say, Elias; and others, That one of the old prophets is risen again.

20 He said unto them, But **whom** say ye that I am?

20 He said unto them, But **who** say ye that I am?

Peter answering said, The Christ of God.

Peter answering said, The Christ, **the Son** of God.

Matt. 16	JST Matt. 16	Mark 8	JST Mark 8
thee, That thou art Peter, and upon this rock I will build my church; and the gates of hell shall not prevail against it.			

TPJS-- "Upon this rock I will build my Church, and the gates of hell shall not prevail against it." What rock? Revelation. (p. 274)

Christ was the head of the Church, the chief corner stone, the spiritual rock upon which the church was built, and the gates of hell shall not prevail against it. He built up the Kingdom, chose Apostles, and ordained them to the Melchizedek Priesthood, giving them power to administer in the ordinances of the Gospel. John was a priest after the order of Aaron before Christ. (p. 318)

Matt. 16	JST Matt. 16	Mark 8	JST Mark 8
19 And I will give unto thee the keys of the kingdom of heaven: and whatsoever thou shalt bind on earth shall be bound in heaven: and whatsoever thou shalt loose on earth shall be loosed in heaven.			
20 Then charged he his disciples that they should tell no man that he was Jesus the Christ.		30 And he charged them that they should tell no man of him.	

79. Jesus Fortells His Death and Resurrection

Matt. 16	JST Matt. 16	Mark 8	JST Mark 8
21 ¶ From that time forth began Jesus to shew unto his disciples, how that he must go unto Jerusalem, and suffer many things of the elders and chief priests and scribes, and be killed, and be raised again the third day.	22 From that time forth began Jesus to show unto his disciples, how that he must go to Jerusalem, and suffer many things of the elders and chief priests, and Scribes, and be killed, and be raised again the third day.	31 And he began to teach them, that the Son of man must suffer many things, and be rejected of the elders, and of the chief priests, and scribes, and be killed, and after three days rise again.	33 And he began to teach them, that the Son of Man must suffer many things, and be rejected of the elders, and the chief priests, and scribes, and be killed, and after three days rise again.
22 Then Peter took him, and began to rebuke him, saying, Be it far from thee, Lord: this shall not be unto thee.	23 Then Peter took him, and began to rebuke him, saying, Be it far from thee, Lord; this shall not be **done** unto thee.	32 And he spake that saying openly. And Peter took him, and began to rebuke him.	
23 But he turned, and said unto Peter, Get thee behind me, Satan: thou art an offence unto me: for thou savourest not the things that be of God, but those that be of men.		33 But when he had turned about and looked on his disciples, he rebuked Peter, saying, Get thee behind me, Satan: for thou savourest not the things that be of God, but the things that be of men.	35 But when he had turned about and looked upon his disciples, he rebuked Peter, saying, Get thee behind me, Satan; for thou savorest not the things that be of God, but the things that be of man.
24 ¶ Then said Jesus unto his disciples, If any man will come after me, let him		34 ¶ And when he had called the people unto him with his disciples also, he said unto them, Whosoever will come after me, let him	36 And when he had called the people, with his disciples also, he said unto them, Whosoever will come after me, let him

172

Luke 9	JST Luke 9	B of M	D & C
			10:69 And now, behold, whosoever is of my church, and endureth of my church to the end, him will I establish upon my rock, and the gates of hell shall not prevail against them. (See also D&C 21:6; 33:13; 98:27.)
		Hel. 10:7 Behold, I give unto you power, that whatsoever ye shall seal on earth shall be sealed in heaven; and whatsoever ye shall loose on earth shall be loosed in heaven; and thus shall ye have power among this people.	132:49 For I am the Lord thy God, and will be with thee even unto the end of the world, and through all eternity; for verily I seal upon you your exaltation, and prepare a throne for you in the kingdom of my Father, with Abraham your father. (See also D&C 124:93; 127:7; 128:8,10.)
21 And he straitly charged them, and commanded them to tell no man **that thing;**	21 And he straitly charged them, and commanded them to tell no man **o f him,**		
22 Saying, The Son of man must suffer many things, and be rejected of the elders and chief priests and scribes, and be slain, and be raised the third day.			
23 ¶ And he said to them all, If any man will come after me, let him deny			56:2 And he that will not take up his cross and follow me, and keep my

Matt. 16	JST Matt. 16	Mark 8	JST Mark 8
deny himself, and take up his cross, and follow me.		deny himself, and take up his cross, and follow me.	deny himself, and take up his cross, and follow me.
	26 And now for a man to take up his cross, is to deny himself all ungodliness, and every worldly lust, and keep my commandments. **27 Break not my commandments for to save your lives;** for whosoever will save his life **in this world,** shall lose it **in the world to come.**		
25 For whosoever will save his life shall lose it:		35 For whosoever will save his life shall lose it;	37 For whosoever will save his life, shall lose it; **or whosoever will save his life, shall be willing to lay it down for my sake; and if he is not willing to lay it down for my sake, he shall lose it.**
and whosoever will lose his life for my sake shall find it.	28 And whosoever will lose his life **in this world,** for my sake, shall find it **in the world to come.**	but whosoever shall lose his life for my sake and the gospel's, the same shall save it.	38 But whosoever shall **be willing to** lose his life for my sake, and the gospel, the same shall save it.

TPJS-- And now dear and well beloved brethren--and when we say brethren, we mean those who have continued faithful in Christ, men, women and children--we feel to exhort you in the name of the Lord Jesus, to be strong in the faith in the new and everlasting covenant, and nothing frightened at your enemies. For what has happened unto us is an evident token to them of damnation; but unto us, of salvation, and that of God. Therefore hold on even unto death; for "he that seeks to save his life shall lose it; and he that loses his life for my sake, and the Gospel's, shall find it," saith Jesus Christ. (pp. 128-129)

Matt. 16	JST Matt. 16	Mark 8	JST Mark 8
	29 Therefore, forsake the world, and save your souls; for what is a man profited, if he shall gain the whole world, and lose his own soul? Or what shall a man give in exchange for his soul?	36 For what shall it profit a man, if he shall gain the whole world, and lose his own soul? 37 Or what shall a man give in exchange for his soul?	
26 For what is a man profited, if he shall gain the whole world, and lose his own soul? or what shall a man give in exchange for his soul?			
			40 Therefore deny yourselves of these, and be not ashamed of me.
		38 Whosoever **therefore** shall be ashamed of me and of my words in this adulterous and sinful generation; of him also shall the Son of man be ashamed, when he cometh in the glory of his Father with the holy angels.	41 Whosoever shall be ashamed of me, and of my words, in this adulterous and sinful generation, of him also shall the Son of Man be ashamed, when he cometh in the glory of his Father with the holy angels.
27 For the Son of man shall come in the glory of his Father with his angels; and then he shall reward every man according to his works.			**42 And they shall not have part in that resurrection when he cometh.** **43 For verily I say unto you, That he shall come; and he that layeth down**

174

Luke 9	JST Luke 9	Romans	D & C
himself, and take up his cross daily, and follow me.			commandments, the same shall not be saved. (See also D&C 112: 14.)
24 For whosoever will save his life **shall** lose it:	24 For whosoever will save his life, **must be willing** to lose it **for my sake;**		
but whosoever will lose his life for my sake, the same shall save it.	**and** whosoever will **be willing to** lose his life for my sake, the same shall save it.		
25 For what **is** a man **advantaged**, if he gain the whole world, and lose himself, **or be cast away?**	25 For what **doth it profit** a man if he gain the whole world, **and yet he receive him not whom God hath ordained,** and he lose **his own soul, and he** himself be **a castaway?**		
26 For whosoever shall be ashamed of me and of my words, of him shall the Son of man be ashamed, when he shall come in his own **glory, and** in his Father's, **and** of the holy angels.	26 For whosoever shall be ashamed of me, and of my words, of him shall the Son of Man be ashamed, when he shall come in his own **kingdom, clothed in the glory of** his Father, **with** the holy angels.	1:16 For I am not ashamed of the gospel of Christ: for it is the power of God unto salvation to every one that believeth; . . .	

175

Matt. 16 & 17	JST Matt. 17	Mark 9	JST Mark 8 & 9
		And he said unto them, Verily I say unto you, That there be some of them that stand here, which shall not taste of death, till they have seen the kingdom of God come with power.	**his life for my sake and the gospel's, shall come with him, and shall be clothed with his glory in the cloud, on the right hand of the Son of Man.** 44 And he said unto them **again,** Verily I say unto you, That there be some of them that stand here, which shall not taste of death, till they have seen the kingdom of God come with power.
28 Verily I say unto you, There be some standing here, which shall not taste of death, till they see the Son of man coming in his kingdom.			

80. High Mountain in Galilee-- Transfiguration

Matt. 16 & 17	JST Matt. 17	Mark 9	JST Mark 8 & 9
17:1 And after six days Jesus taketh Peter, James, and John his brother,		2 ¶ And after six days Jesus taketh **with him** Peter, and James, and John,	9:1 And after six days Jesus taketh Peter, and James, and John, **w h o asked him many questions concerning his sayings; and Jesus** leadeth them up into a high mountain apart by themselves. And he was transfigured before them.
and bringeth them up into an high mountain apart, 2 And was transfigured before them: and his face did shine as the sun, and his raiment was white as the light.		and leadeth them up into an high mountain apart by themselves: and he was transfigured before them. 3 And his raiment became shining, exceeding white as snow; so as no fuller on earth **can white** them.	2 And his raiment became shining, exceeding white, as snow; so **white** as no fuller on earth **could whiten** them.
3 And, behold, there appeared unto them Moses and Elias		4 And there appeared unto them Elias with Moses:	3 And there appeared unto them Elias with Moses, **or in other words, John the Baptist and Moses; and** they were talking with Jesus.
talking with him.		and they were talking with Jesus.	
4 Then answered Peter, and said unto Jesus, Lord, it is good for us to be here: if thou wilt, let us make here three tabernacles; one for thee, **and** one for Moses, and one for Elias.	3 Then answered Peter, and said unto Jesus, Lord, it is good for us to be here; if thou wilt, let us make here three tabernacles; one for thee, one for Moses, and one for Elias.	5 And Peter answered and said to Jesus, Master, it is good for us to be here: and let us make three tabernacles; one for thee, and one for Moses, and one for Elias.	

Luke 9	JST Luke 9		D & C
27 **But** I tell you of a truth, there **be** some standing here, **which** shall not taste of death, till they see the kingdom of God.	27 **Verily**, I tell you of a truth, there **are** some standing here **who** shall not taste of death, **until** they see the kingdom of God **coming in power**.		
28 ¶ And it came to pass **about an** eight days after these sayings, he took Peter and John and James,	28 And it came to pass, eight days after these sayings, **that** he took Peter and John and James,		
and went up into a mountain to pray. 29 And as he prayed, the fashion of his countenance was **altered**, and his raiment **was** white and **glistering**.	and went up into a mountain to pray. 29 And as he prayed, the fashion of his countenance was **changed**, and his raiment **became** white and **glittering**.		
30 And, behold, there talked with him two men, **which were** Moses and Elias: 31 Who appeared in glory, and spake of his **decease** which he should accomplish at Jerusalem. 32 But Peter and they **that** were with him were heavy with sleep: and when they were awake, they saw his glory, and the two men **that** stood with him. 33 And **it came to pass, as they** departed from him, Peter said unto Jesus, Master, it is good for us to be here: **and** let us make three tabernacles; one for thee, and one for Moses, and one for Elias:	30 And behold, there **came and** talked with him two men, **even** Moses and Elias, 31 Who appeared in glory, and spake of his **death, and also his resurrection,** which he should accomplish at Jerusalem. 32 But Peter and they **who** were with him were heavy with sleep, and when they were awake they saw his glory, and the two men **who** stood with him. 33 And **after the two men** departed from him, Peter said unto Jesus, Master, it is good for us to be here; let us make three tabernacles; one for thee, and one for Moses, and one for Elias;		138:45 Elias, who was with Moses on the Mount of Transfiguration . . .

Matt. 17	JST Matt. 17	Mark 9	JST Mark 9
		6 For he **wist** not what to say; for they were sore afraid. 7 And there was a cloud that overshadowed them:	4 . . . for he **knew** not what to say; for they were sore afraid.
5 While he yet spake, behold, a bright cloud overshadowed them: and behold a voice out of the cloud, which said, This is my beloved Son, in whom I am well pleased; hear ye him.		and a voice came out of the cloud, saying, This is my beloved Son: hear him.	

TPJS-- The Savior, Moses, and Elias, gave the keys to Peter, James and John, on the mount, when they were transfigured before him. (p. 158)

Now for the secret and grand key. Though they might hear the voice of God and know that Jesus was the Son of God, this would be no evidence that their election and calling was made sure, that they had part with Christ, and were joint heirs with Him. They then would want that more sure word of prophecy, that they were sealed in the heavens and had the promise of eternal life in the kingdom of God. Then, having this promise sealed unto them, it was an anchor to the soul, sure and steadfast. Though the thunders might roll and lightnings flash, and earthquakes bellow, and war gather thick around, yet this hope and knowledge would support the soul in every hour of trial, trouble and tribulation. Then knowledge through our Lord and Savior Jesus Christ is the grand key that unlocks the glories and mysteries of the kingdom of heaven. (p. 298)

It is one thing to be on the mount and hear the excellent voice, etc., and another to hear the voice declare to you, You have a part and lot in that kingdom. (p. 306)

Matt. 17	JST Matt. 17	Mark 9	JST Mark 9
6 And when the disciples heard **it**, they fell on their face, and were sore afraid.	5 And when the disciples heard **the voice**, they fell on their faces, and were sore afraid.		
7 And Jesus came and touched them, and said, Arise, and be not afraid. 8 And when they had lifted up their eyes,		8 And suddenly, when they had looked round about, they saw no man any	6 And suddenly, when they had looked round about **with great astonishment**, they saw no man
they saw no man, save Jesus only.		more, save Jesus only with themselves.	any more, save Jesus only, with themselves. **And immediately they departed.**
9 And as they came down from the mountain, Jesus charged them, saying, Tell the vision to no man, until the Son of **man** be risen again from the dead.	8 And as they came down from the mountain, Jesus charged them, saying, Tell the vision to no man, until the Son of **Man** be risen again from the dead.	9 And as they came down from the mountain, he charged them that they should tell no man what things they had seen, till the Son of **man were** risen from the dead.	7 And as they came down from the mountain, he charged them that they should tell no man what things they had seen till the Son of **Man was** risen from the dead.

Luke 9	JST Luke 9	JST 2 Peter	D & C
not knowing what he said.	not knowing what he said.	1:16 For we have not followed cunningly devised fables, when we made known unto you the power and coming of our Lord Jesus Christ, but were eye-witnesses of his majesty.	
34 While he thus spake, there came a cloud, and overshadowed them: and they feared as they entered into the cloud.	34 While he thus spake, there came a cloud, and overshadowed them **all**; and they feared as they entered into the cloud.	17 For he received from God the Father honor and glory, when there came such a voice to him from the excellent glory, This is my beloved Son, in whom I am well pleased.	
35 And there came a voice out of the cloud, saying, This is my beloved Son: hear him.		18 And this voice which came from heaven we heard, when we were with him in the holy mount.	63:20 Nevertheless, he that endureth in faith and doeth my will, the same shall overcome, and shall receive an inheritance upon the earth when the day of transfiguration shall come;
		19 We have **therefore** a more sure **knowledge of the** word of prophecy, **to which word of prophecy** ye do well that ye take heed, as unto a light **which** shineth in a dark place, until the day-dawn, and the day-star arise in your hearts;	21 When the earth shall be transfigured, even according to the pattern which was shown unto mine apostles upon the mount; of which account the fulness ye have not yet received.
			27:12 And also with Peter, and James, and John, whom I have sent unto you, by whom I have ordained you and confirmed you to be apostles, and especial witnesses of my name, and bear the keys of your ministry and of the same things which I revealed unto them;
36 And when the voice was past, Jesus was found alone.			

179

Matt. 17	JST Matt. 17	Mark 9	JST Mark 9

TPJS-- [T]hey ['the Seers and Prophets'] saw the glory of the Lord when he showed the transfiguration of the earth on the mount; they saw every mountain laid low and every valley exalted when the Lord was taking vengeance upon the wicked; they saw truth spring out of the earth, and righteousness look down from heaven in the last days, before the Lord came the second time to gather his elect; they saw the end of wickedness on earth, and the Sabbath of creation crowned with peace; they saw the end of the glorious thousand years, when Satan was loosed for a little season; they saw the day of judgment when all men received according to their works, and they saw the heaven and the earth flee away to make room for the city of God, when the righteous receive an inheritance in eternity. And, fellow sojourners upon earth, it is your privilege to purify yourselves and come up to the same glory, and see for yourselves, and know for yourselves. Ask, and it shall be given you; seek and ye shall find; knock, and it shall be opened unto you. (p. 13)

Matt. 17	JST Matt. 17	Mark 9	JST Mark 9
		10 And they kept that saying with themselves, questioning one with another what the rising from the dead should mean.	
10 And his disciples asked him, saying, Why then say the scribes that Elias must first come?		11 ¶ And they asked him, saying, Why say the scribes that Elias must first come?	
11 And Jesus answered and said unto them, Elias truly shall first come, and restore all things.	10 And Jesus answered and said unto them, Elias truly shall first come, and restore all things, **as the prophets have written,**	12 And he answered and told them, Elias verily cometh first, and **restoreth** all things; and how it is written of the Son of man, that he must suffer many things, and be set at nought.	10 And he answered and told them, **saying,** Elias verily cometh first, and **prepareth** all things; and **teacheth you of the prophets;** how it is written of the Son of Man, that he must suffer many things, and be set at naught.
12 **But I say unto you,** That Elias **is** come already,	11 **And again I** say unto you that Elias **has** come already, **concerning whom it is written, Behold, I will send my messenger, and he shall prepare the way before me;**	13 **But** I say unto you, That Elias is indeed come, **and** they have done unto him whatsoever they listed, as it is written of him.	11 **Again** I say unto you, That Elias is indeed come, **but** they have done unto him whatsoever they listed; **and even** as it is written of him; **and he bore record of me, and they received him not. Verily this was Elias.**
and they knew him not, **but have done unto him** whatsoever they listed. Likewise shall also the Son of man suffer of them.	and they knew him not, **and** have done unto him, whatsoever they listed. 12 Likewise shall also the Son of Man suffer of them. 13 **But I say unto you, Who is Elias? Behold, this is Elias, whom I send to prepare the way before me.**		
13 Then the disciples understood that he spake unto them of John the Baptist.	14 Then the disciples understood that he spake unto them of John the Baptist, **and also of another who should come and restore all things, as it is written by the prophets.**		

Luke 9	JST Luke 9		
And they kept **it** close, and told no man in those days any of **those** things which they had seen.	36 . . . And **these things** they kept close, and **they** told no man, in those days, any of **the** things which they had seen.		

Matt. 17	JST Matt. 17	Mark 9	JST Mark 9

81. Demonic Boy Healed

Matt. 17	JST Matt. 17	Mark 9	JST Mark 9
14 ¶ And when they were come to the multitude,	15 And when they were come to the multitude,	14 ¶ And when he came to his disciples, he saw a great multitude about them, and the scribes questioning with them. 15 And straightway all the people, when they beheld him, were greatly amazed and, running to him saluted him.	12 And when he came to the disciples, he saw a great multitude about them, and the scribes questioning with them.
		16 And he asked the scribes, What question ye with them?	14 And Jesus asked the scribes, What questioned ye with them?
there came to him a certain man, kneeling down to him, and saying,	there came to him a man kneeling down to him, and saying,	17 And one of the multitude answered and said, Master, I have brought unto thee my son, which hath a dumb spirit;	15 And one of the multitude answered, and said, Master, I have brought unto thee my son, who hath a dumb spirit that is a devil;
15 Lord, have mercy on my son: for he is lunatick, and sore vexed: for ofttimes he falleth into the fire, and oft into the water.			
		18 And wheresoever he taketh him, he teareth him: and he foameth, and gnasheth with his teeth, and pineth away: and I spake to thy disciples that they should cast him out; and they could not.	and when he seizeth him, he teareth him; and he foameth and gnasheth with his teeth, and pineth away; and I spake to thy disciples that they might cast him out, and they could not.
16 And I brought him to thy disciples, and they could not cure him.			
17 Then Jesus answered and said, O faithless and perverse generation, how long shall I be with you? how long shall I suffer you? bring him hither to me.		19 He answereth him, and saith, O faithless generation, how long shall I be with you? how long shall I suffer you? bring him unto me.	16 Jesus spake unto him and said, O faithless generation! how long shall I be with you? How long shall I suffer you? Bring him unto me. And they brought him unto Jesus.
		20 And they brought him unto him: and when he saw him, straightway the spirit tare him; and he fell on the ground, and wallowed foaming.	17 And when the man saw him, immediately he was torn by the spirit; and he fell on the ground and wallowed, foaming.
		21 And he asked his father, How long is it ago since this came unto him? And he said, Of a child.	18 And Jesus asked his father, How long a time is it since this came unto him? and his father said, When a child;
		22 And ofttimes it hath cast him into the fire, and into the waters, to destroy him: but if thou canst do any thing, have compassion on us, and help us.	19 And ofttimes it hath cast him into the fire and into the waters, to destroy him, but if thou canst, I ask thee to have compassion on us, and help us.

Luke 9	JST Luke 9		

37 ¶ And it came to pass, that on the next day, when they were come down from the hill, much people met him.

38 And, behold, a man of the company cried out, saying, Master, I beseech thee, look upon my son: for he is mine only child.

39 And, lo, a spirit taketh him, and he suddenly crieth out; and it teareth him that he foameth **again**, and bruising him hardly departeth from him.

40 And I besought thy disciples to cast him out; and they could not.

41 And Jesus answering said, O faithless and perverse generation, how long shall I be with you, and suffer you? Bring thy son hither.

39 And, lo, a spirit taketh him, and he suddenly crieth out; and it teareth him, that he foameth, and bruising him hardly, departeth from him.

Matt. 17	JST Matt. 17	Mark 9	JST Mark 9
		23 Jesus said unto him, If thou **canst** believe, all things **are** possible to him that believeth.	20 Jesus said unto him, If thou **wilt** believe all things **I shall say unto you, this** is possible to him that believeth.
		24 And **straightway** the father of the child cried out, and said with tears, Lord, I believe; help thou mine unbelief.	21 And **immediately** the father of the child cried out, and said, with tears, Lord, I believe; help thou mine unbelief.
		25 When Jesus saw that the people came running together, he rebuked the foul spirit, saying unto him, **Thou dumb and deaf spirit**, I charge thee, come out of him, and enter no more into him.	22 When Jesus saw that the people came running together, he rebuked the foul spirit, saying unto him, I charge thee **t o** come out of him, and enter no more into him.
18 And Jesus rebuked the devil; and he departed out of him: and the child was cured from that very hour.		26 **And** the spirit cried, and rent him sore, and came out of him: and he was as one dead; insomuch that many said, He is dead.	23 **Now the dumb and deaf** spirit cried, and rent him sore, and came out of him; and he was as one dead, insomuch that many said, He is dead.
		27 But Jesus took him by the hand, and lifted him up; and he arose.	
19 Then came the disciples to Jesus apart, and said, Why could not we cast him out?		28 **And** when he was come into the house, his disciples asked him privately, Why could not we cast him out?	25 When **Jesus** was come into the house, his disciples asked him privately, Why could not we cast him out?
20 And Jesus said unto them, Because of your unbelief: for verily I say unto you, If ye have faith as a grain of mustard seed, ye shall say unto this mountain, Remove **hence** to yonder place; and it shall remove; and nothing shall be impossible unto you.	20 And Jesus said unto them, Because of your unbelief; for, verily, I say unto you, If ye have faith as a grain of mustard seed, ye shall say unto this mountain, Remove to yonder place, and it shall remove; and nothing shall be impossible unto you.		
21 Howbeit this kind goeth not out but by prayer and fasting.		29 And he said unto them, This kind can come forth by nothing, but by prayer and fasting.	

Luke 9	JST Luke 9	B of M	
42 And as he was **yet a** coming, the devil threw him down, and tare him. And Jesus rebuked the unclean spirit,	42 And as he was coming, the devil threw him down, and tare him **again**. And Jesus rebuked the unclean spirit,		
and healed the child, and delivered him again to his father.	and healed the child, and delivered him again to his father.		
43 ¶ And they were all amazed at the mighty power of God.			
		Ether 12:30 for the brother of Jared said unto the mountain Zerin, Remove—and it was removed. And if he had not had faith it would not have moved; wherefore thou workest after men have faith. (See also Jacob 4:6, quoted on p. 133).	

185

Matt. 17	JST Matt. 17	Mark 9	JST Mark 9

82. Galilee-- Again Fortells His Death and Resurrection

Matt. 17	JST Matt. 17	Mark 9	JST Mark 9
		30 ¶ And they departed thence, and passed through Galilee; **and** he would not that any man should know it.	27 And they departed thence, and passed through Galilee **privately; for** he would not that any man should know it.
22 ¶ And while they abode in Galilee, Jesus said unto them, The Son of man shall be betrayed into the hands of men:	22 And while they abode in Galilee, Jesus said unto them, The Son of M a n shall be betrayed into the hands of men . . .	31 For he taught his disciples, and said unto them, The Son of man is delivered into the hands of men, and they shall kill him; and after that he is killed, he shall rise the third day.	28 And he taught his disciples, and said unto them, The Son of Man is delivered into the hands of men, and they shall kill him; and after that he is killed, he shall rise the third day.
23 And they shall kill him, and the third day he shall be raised again. And they were exceedingly sorry.		32 But they understood not that saying, and were afraid to ask him.	
24 ¶ And when they were come to Capernaum, they that received tribute **money** came to Peter, and said, Doth not your master pay tribute?	23 And when they were come to Capernaum, they that received tribute came to Peter, and said, Doth not your master pay tribute?	33 ¶ And he came to Capernaum . . .	
25 He saith, **Yes.** And when he was come into the house, Jesus **prevented** him, saying, What thinkest thou, Simon? of whom do the kings of the earth take custom or tribute? of their own children, or of strangers?	He said, **Yea.** 24 And when he was come into the house, Jesus **rebuked** him, saying,		
26 Peter saith unto him, Of strangers. Jesus saith unto him, Then are the children free.			
27 Notwithstanding, lest we should offend them, go thou to the sea, and cast **an** hook, and take up the fish that first cometh up; and when thou hast opened his mouth, thou shalt find a piece of money: that take, and give unto them for me and thee.	26 . . . Notwithstanding, lest we should offend them, go thou to the sea, and cast **a** hook, and take up the fish, that first cometh up; and when thou hast opened his mouth, thou shalt find a piece of money: that take and give unto them for me and thee.		

Luke 9	JST Luke 9		

But while they wondered every one at all the things which Jesus did, he said unto his disciples,

44 Let these sayings sink down into your **ears**: for the Son of **m**an shall be delivered into the hands of men.

45 But they understood not this saying, and it was hid from them, that they perceived it not: and they feared to ask him of that saying.

44 Let these sayings sink down into your **hearts**; for the Son of **M**an shall be delivered into the hands of men.

Matt. 18		Mark 9	JST Mark 9

83. Discourses on Humility

Matt. 18		Mark 9	JST Mark 9
		33 . . . and being in the house he asked them, **What** was it that ye disputed among yourselves by the way?	30 . . . and being in the house, he asked them, **W h y** was it that ye disputed among yourselves by the way?
At the same time came the disciples unto Jesus, saying, Who is the greatest in the kingdom of heaven?		34 But they held their peace: for by the way they had disputed among themselves, who **should be** the greatest.	31 But they held their peace, **being afraid**, for by the way they had disputed among themselves, who **was** the greatest **among them**.
		35 **And he** sat down, and called the twelve, and **saith** unto them, If any man desire to be first, **the same** shall be the last of all, and servant of all.	32 **Now Jesus** sat down and called the twelve, and said unto them, If any man desire to be first, **he shall** be the last of all, and servant of all.
2 And Jesus called a little child unto him, and set him in the midst of them,		36 And he took a child, and **set him** in the midst of them: and when he had taken **him** in his arms, he said unto them,	33 And he took a child, and **sat** in the midst of them; and when he had taken **the child** in his arms, he said unto them,
3 And said, Verily I say unto you, Except ye be converted, and become as little children, ye shall not enter into the kingdom of heaven.			
4 Whosoever therefore shall humble himself as this little child, the same is greatest in the kingdom of heaven.			
5 And whoso shall receive one such little child in my name receiveth me.		37 Whosoever shall **receive** one of **such** children **in my name**, receiveth me:	34 Whosoever shall **humble himself like** one of these children, **and** receiveth me, ye **shall receive in my name**.
		and whosoever shall receive me, receiveth not me, but him that sent me.	35 And whosoever shall receive me, receiveth not me **only**, but him that sent me, **even the Father**.
		38 ¶ And John **answered** him, saying, Master, we saw one casting out devils in thy name, and he **followeth** not us: and we forbad him, because he **followeth** not us.	36 And John **spake unto** him, saying, Master, we saw one casting out devils in thy name, and he **followed** not us; and we forbade him, because he followed not us.
		39 But Jesus said, Forbid him not: for there is no man which shall do a miracle in my name, that can	37 But Jesus said, Forbid him not; for there is no man which shall do a miracle in my name, that can

188

Luke 9	JST Luke 9		D & C
46 ¶ Then there arose a reasoning among them, **which** of them should be greatest.	46 Then there arose a reasoning among them, **who** of them should be **the** greatest.		
47 And Jesus, perceiving the thought of their heart, took a child, and set him **by him**,	47 And Jesus perceiving the thoughts of their hearts, took a child and set him **in the midst**;		
48 And said unto them, Whosoever shall receive this child in my name receiveth me: and whosoever shall receive me receiveth him **that** sent me: for he **that** is least among you all, the same shall be great.	48 And said unto them, Whosoever shall receive this child in my name, receiveth me; and whosoever shall receive me, receiveth him **who** sent me; for he **who** is least among you all, the same shall be great.		99:3 And who receiveth you as a little child, receiveth my kingdom; and blessed are they, for they shall obtain mercy.
49 ¶ And John **answered** and said, Master, we saw one casting out devils in thy name; and we forbad him, because he followeth not with us.	49 And John **spake** and said, Master, we saw one casting out devils in thy name; and we forbade him, because he followeth not with us.		
50 And Jesus said unto him, Forbid **him** not:	50 And Jesus said unto him, Forbid not **any**;		

Matt. 18	JST Matt. 18	Mark 9	JST Mark 9
		lightly speak evil of me. 40 For he that is not against us is on our part. 41 **For** whosoever shall give you a cup of water to drink in my name, because ye belong to Christ, verily I say unto you, he shall not lose his reward.	speak evil of me. For he that is not against us is on our part. 38 **And** whosoever shall give you a cup of water to drink, in my name, because ye belong to Christ, verily I say unto you, He shall not lose his reward.
6 But whoso shall offend one of these little ones which believe in me, it were better for him that a millstone were hanged about his neck, and **that** he were drowned in the depth of the sea. 7 ¶ Woe unto the world because of offences! for it must needs be that offences come; but woe to that man by whom the offence cometh!	5 But whoso shall offend one of these little ones which believe in me, it were better for him that a millstone were hanged about his neck and he were drowned in the depth of the sea.	42 And whosoever shall offend one of these little ones that believe in me, it is better for him that a millstone were hanged about his neck, and he were cast into the sea.	

TPJS-- But remember, brethren, he that offends one of the least of the saints, would be better off with a millstone tied to his neck and he and the stone plunged into the depth of the sea! (p. 261)

Matt. 18	JST Matt. 18	Mark 9	JST Mark 9
8 Wherefore if thy hand or thy foot offend thee, cut **them** off, and cast **them** from thee: it is better for thee to enter into life halt or maimed, rather than having two hands or two feet to be cast into everlasting fire.	7 Wherefore if thy hand or thy foot offend thee, cut **it** off and cast **it** from thee; **for** it is better for thee to enter into life halt or maimed, rather than having two hands or two feet to be cast into everlasting fire.	43 **And** if thy hand offend thee, cut it off: it is better for thee to enter into life maimed, than having two hands to go into hell, into the fire that never shall be quenched: 44 Where their worm dieth not, and the fire is not quenched. 45 And if thy foot offend thee, cut it off: it is better for thee to enter halt into life, than having two feet to be cast into hell, into the fire that never	40 **Therefore**, if thy hand offend thee, cut it off; **or if thy brother offend thee and confess not and forsake not, he shall be cut off.** It is better for thee to enter into life maimed, than having two hands, to go into hell. 41 **For it is better for thee to enter into life without thy brother, than for thee and thy brother to be cast into hell;** into the fire that never shall be quenched, where their worm dieth not, and the fire is not quenched. 42 And **again**, if thy foot offend thee, cut it off; **for he that is thy standard, by whom thou walkest, if he become a transgressor, he shall be cut off.** 43 It is better for thee, to enter halt into life, than having two feet to be cast into hell; into the fire that

Luke 9	JST Luke 9		D & C
for he **that** is not against us is for us.	for he **who** is not against us is for us.		
			121:19 Wo unto them; because they have offended my little ones they shall be severed from the ordinances of mine house.
			20 Their basket shall not be full, their houses and their barns shall perish, and they themselves shall be despised by those that flattered them.
			21 They shall not have right to the priesthood, nor their posterity after them from generation to generation.
			22 It had been better for them that a millstone had been hanged about their necks, and they drowned in the depth of the sea. (See also D&C 54:4-5.)

Matt. 18	JST Matt. 18	Mark 9	JST Mark 9
		shall be quenched: 46 Where their worm dieth not, and the fire is not quenched.	never shall be quenched.
			44 Therefore, let every man stand or fall, by himself, and not for another; or not trusting another. 45 Seek unto my Father, and it shall be done in that very moment what ye shall ask, if ye ask in faith, believing that ye shall receive.
9 And if thine eye		47 And if thine eye	46 And if thine eye **which seeth for thee, him that is appointed to watch over thee to show thee light, become a transgressor and** offend thee, **pluck him** out.
offend thee, pluck it out, and cast it from thee: it is better for thee to enter into life with one eye, rather than having two eyes to be cast into hell fire.		offend thee, pluck it out: it is better for thee to enter into the kingdom of God with one eye, than having two eyes to be cast into hell fire:	
	9 **And a man's hand is his friend, and his foot, also; and a man's eye, are they of his own household.**		
			48 **For it is better that thyself should be saved, than to be cast into hell with thy brother,** where their worm dieth not, and **where** the fire is not quenched.
		48 Where their worm dieth not, and the fire is not quenched. 49 For every one shall be salted with fire, and every sacrifice shall be salted with salt. 50 Salt **is** good: **but** if the salt have lost his saltness, wherewith will ye season it?	49 For every one shall be salted with fire; and every sacrifice shall be salted with salt; but the salt **must be** good. 50 **For** if the salt have lost his saltness, wherewith will ye season it? (**the sacrifice;**) therefore it must **needs be that** ye have salt in yourselves, and have peace one with another.
		Have salt in yourselves, and have peace one with another.	
10 Take heed that ye despise not one of these little ones; for I say unto you, That in heaven their angels do always behold the face of my Father **which** is in heaven.	10 Take heed that ye despise not one of these little ones; for I say unto you, that in heaven their angels do always behold the face of my Father **who** is in heaven.		

Matt. 18	JST Matt. 18	Deut.	D & C
11 For the son of man is come to save that which was lost.	11 For the Son of Man is come to save that which was lost, **and to call sinners to repentance; but these little ones have no need of repentance, and I will save them.**		18:10 Remember the worth of souls is great in the sight of God; 11 For, behold, the Lord your Redeemer suffered death in the flesh; wherefore he suffered the pain of all men, that all men might repent and come unto him.
12 How think ye? if a man have **an** hundred sheep, and one of them be gone astray, doth he not leave the ninety and nine, and goeth into the mountains, and seeketh that which is gone astray?			12 And he hath risen again from the dead, that he might bring all men unto hi, on conditions of repentance.
13 And if so be that he find it, verily I say unto you, he rejoiceth more **of** that **sheep**, and **of** the ninety and nine which went not astray.	13 And if **it** so be that he find it, verily, I say unto you, he rejoiceth more **over** that **which was lost,** than **over** the ninety and nine which went not astray.		13 And how great is his joy in the soul that repententh! 14 Wherefore, you are called to cry repentance unto this people.
14 Even so it is not the will of your Father which is in heaven, that one of these little ones should perish.			15 And if it so be that you should labor all your days in crying repentance unto this people, and bring, save it be one soul unto me, how great shall be your joy with him in the kingdom of my Father!
15 ¶ Moreover if thy brother shall trespass against thee, go and tell him his fault between thee and him alone: if he shall hear thee, thou hast gained thy brother.			16 And now, if your joy will be great with one soul that you have brought unto me into the kingdom of my Father, how great will be your joy if you should bring many souls unto me!
16 But if he will not hear thee, then take with thee one or two more, that in the mouth of two or three witnesses every word may be established.			
17 And if he shall neglect to hear them, tell it unto the church: but if he neglect to hear the church, let him be unto thee as **an** heathen man and a publican.		Deut. 19:15 . . . at the mouth of two witnesses, or at the mouth of three witnesses, shall the matter be established. (See also 2 Cor. 13:1.)	6:28 And now, behold, I give unto you and also unto my servant Joseph, the keys of this gift, which shall bring to light this ministry; and in the mouth of two or three witnesses shall every word be established. (See also 128:3.)
18 Verily I say unto you, Whatsoever ye shall bind on earth shall be bound in heaven: and whatsoever ye shall loose on earth shall be loosed in heaven.			
19 Again I say unto you, That if two of you shall agree on earth as touching	19 Again, I say unto you, That if two of you shall agree on earth as touching		

Matt. 18	JST Matt. 18	D & C	Matt. 18
any thing that they shall ask, it shall be done for them of my Father which is in heaven. 20 For where two or three are gathered together in my name, there am I in the midst of them. 21 ¶ Then came Peter to him, and said, Lord, how oft shall my brother sin against me, and I forgive him? till seven times? 22 Jesus **saith** unto him, I say not unto thee, Until seven times: but, Until seventy times seven.	any thing that they shall ask, **that they may not ask amiss**, it shall be done for them of my Father which is in heaven.		28 But the same servant went out, and found one of his fellowservants, which owed him an hundred pence: and he laid hands on him, and took him by the throat, saying, Pay me that thou owest. 29 And his fellowservant fell down at his feet, and besought him, saying, Have patience with me, and I will pay thee all. 30 And he would not: but went and cast him into prison, till he should pay the debt.
		98:39 And again, verily I say unto you, if after thine enemy has come upon thee the first time, he repent and come unto thee praying thy forgiveness, thou shalt forgive him, and shalt hold it no more as a testimony against thine enemy-- 40 And so on unto the second and third time; and as oft as thine enemy repenteth of the trespass wherewith he has trespassed against thee, thou shalt forgive him, until seventy times seven. (see also vv. 41-48.)	31 So when his fellowservants saw what was done, they were very sorry, and came and told unto their lord all that was done. 32 Then his lord, after that he had called him, said unto him, O thou wicked servant, I forgave thee all that debt, because thou desiredst me: 33 Shouldest not thou also have had compassion on thy fellowservant, even as I had pity on thee? 34 And his lord was wroth, and delivered him to the tormentors, till he should pay all that was due unto him. 35 So likewise shall my heavenly Father do also unto you, if ye from your hearts forgive not every one his brother their trespasses.

TPJS-- With deep feeling he said that they are fellow mortals, we loved them once, shall we not encourage them to reformation? We have not yet forgiven them seventy times seven, as our Savior directed; perhaps we have not forgiven them once. (p. 238)

23 ¶ Therefore is the kingdom of heaven likened unto a certain king, **which** would take account of his servants. 24 And when he had begun to reckon, one was brought unto him, **which** owed him ten thousand talents. 25 But forasmuch as he had not to pay, his lord commanded him to be sold, and his wife, and children, and all that he had, and payment to be made. 26 The servant **therefore fell down, and worshipped** him, saying, Lord, have patience with me, and I will pay thee all. 27 Then the lord of that servant was moved with compassion, and loosed him, and forgave him the debt.	23 Therefore is the kingdom of heaven likened unto a certain king, **who** would take account of his servants. 24 And when he had begun to reckon, one was brought unto him **who** owed him ten thousand talents. 26 **And** the servant **besought** him, saying, Lord, have patience with me, and I will pay thee all. 27 Then the lord of that servant was moved with compassion, and loosed him, and forgave him the debt. **The servant, therefore, fell down and worshipped him.**		

(continued in column 4)

		Luke 10	JST Luke 10

84. Seventy Sent Forth

		Luke 10	JST Luke 10
		After these things the Lord appointed other seventy also, and sent them two by two before his face into every city and place, **whither** he himself would come.	After these things the Lord appointed other seventy also, and sent them two and two before his face, into every city and place **where** he himself would come.
		2 **Therefore** said **he** unto them, The harvest truly is great, but the labourers **are** few: pray ye therefore the Lord of the harvest, that he would send forth labourers into his harvest.	2 **And he** said unto them, The harvest truly is great, but the laborers few; pray ye therefore the Lord of the harvest, that he would send forth laborers into his harvest.
		3 Go your ways: behold, I send you forth as lambs among wolves.	
		4 Carry neither purse, nor scrip, nor shoes: **and** salute **no** man by the way.	4 Carry neither purse, nor scrip, nor shoes; **nor** salute **any** man by the way.
		5 And into whatsoever house ye enter, first say, Peace **be** to this house.	5 And into whatsoever house ye enter, first say, Peace to this house.
		6 And if the son of peace be there, your peace shall rest upon it: if not, it shall turn to you again.	
		7 And in **the same** house remain, eating and drinking such things as they give: for the labourer is worthy of his hire. Go not from house to house.	7 And into **whatsoever** house **they receive you**, remain, eating and drinking such things as they give; for the laborer is worthy of his hire. Go not from house to house.
		8 And into whatsoever city ye enter, and they receive you, eat such things as are set before you:	
		9 And heal the sick that are therein, and say **unto them**, The kingdom of God is come nigh unto you.	9 And heal the sick that are therein, and say, The kingdom of God is come nigh unto you.
		10 But into whatsoever city ye enter, and they receive you not, go your ways out into the streets of the same, and say,	
		11 Even the very dust of your city, which cleaveth on us, we do wipe off against you: notwithstanding be **ye** sure of this, that	11 Even the very dust of your city which cleaveth on us, we do wipe off against you; notwithstanding, be sure of this, that the

Matt. 11	JST Matt. 11	B of M	TPJS
20 ¶ Then began he to upbraid the cities wherein most of his mighty works were done, because they repented not:			
21 Woe unto thee, Chorazin! woe unto thee, Bethsaida! for if the mighty works, which were done in you, had been done in Tyre and Sidon, they would have repented long ago in sackcloth and ashes.	23 Woe unto thee, Chorazin! Woe unto thee, Bethsaida! For if the mighty works which were done in you, had been done in Tyre and Sidon, they would have repented long **since** in sackcloth and ashes.		
22 But I say unto you, It shall be more tolerable for Tyre and Sidon at the day of judgment, than for you.			
23 And thou, Capernaum, which are exalted unto heaven, shalt be brought down to hell: for if the mighty works, which have been done in thee, had been done in Sodom, it would have remained until this day.		2 Nephi 10:3 Wherefore, as I said unto you, it must needs be expedient that Christ—for in the last night the angel spake unto me that this should be his name—should come among the Jews, among those who are the more wicked part of the world: and they shall crucify him—for thus it behooveth our god, and there is none other nation on earth that would crucify our God.	I prophesy, in the name of the Lord God of Israel, anguish and wrath and tribulation and the withdrawing of the Spirit of God from the earth await this generation, until they are visited with utter desolation. This generation is as corrupt as the generation of the Jews that crucified Christ; and if He were here today, and should preach the same doctrine He did then, they would put Him to death. I defy all the world to destroy the work of God: and I prophesy they never will have power to kill me till my work is accomplished, and I am ready to die (p. 328).
24 But I say unto you, **That** it shall be more tolerable for the land of Sodom in the day of judgment, than for thee.	26 But I say unto you, it shall be more tolerable for the land of Sodom in the day of judgment, than for thee.		

Luke 10	JST Luke 10		D & C
the kingdom of God is come nigh unto you. 12 But I say unto you, that it shall be more tolerable in **that** day for Sodom, than for that city.	kingdom of God is come nigh unto you. 12 But I say unto you, That it shall be more tolerable in **the** day **of judgment** for Sodom, than for that city. 13 **Then began he to upbraid the people in every city wherein his mighty works were done, who received him not, saying,**		
13 Woe unto thee, Chorazin! woe unto thee, Bethsaida! for if the mighty works had been done in Tyre and Sidon, which have been done in you, they **had a great while ago** repented, sitting in sackcloth and ashes. 14 But it shall be more tolerable for Tyre and Sidon **at** the judgment, than for you. 15 And thou, Capernaum, which art exalted to heaven, shalt be **thrust** down to hell.	14 Woe unto thee, Chorazin! Woe unto thee, Bethsaida! For if the mighty works, had been done in Tyre and Sidon, which have been done in you, they **would have** repented, sitting in sackcloth and ashes. 15 But it shall be more tolerable for Tyre and Sidon **in the day of** judgment, than for you. 16 And thou, Capernaum, which art exalted to heaven, shall be **cast** down to hell.		75:21 And you shall be filled with joy and gladness; and know this, that in the day of judgment you shall be judges of that house, and condemn them; 22 And it shall be more tolerable for the heathen in the day of judgment, than for that house; therefore, gird up your loins and be faithful, and ye shall overcome all things, and be lifted up at the last day. Even so. Amen.
16 He that heareth you heareth me; and he that despiseth you despiseth me; and he that despiseth me despiseth him **that** sent me.	17 **And he said unto his disciples,** He that heareth you, heareth me; and he that despiseth you, despiseth me; and he that despiseth me, despiseth him **who** sent me.		

197

	Psalms	John 7	JST John 7

Later Judean Ministry

85. Galilee-- The Feast of the Tabernacles at Hand

	Psalms	John 7	JST John 7
	69:8 I am become a stranger unto my brethren, and an alien unto my mother's children.	2 Now the Jews' feast of tabernacles was at hand. 3 His brethren therefore said unto him, Depart hence, and go into Judæa, that thy disciples also may see the works that thou doest. 4 For there is no man that doeth any thing in secret, **and** he himself seeketh to be known openly. If thou do these things, shew thyself to the world. 5 For neither did his brethren believe in him. 6 Then Jesus said unto them, My time is not yet come: but your time is alway ready. 7 The world cannot hate you; but me it hateth, because I testify of it, that the works thereof are evil. 8 Go ye up unto this feast: I go not up yet unto this feast; for my time is not yet full come. 9 When he had said these words unto them, he **abode** still in Galilee.	3 His brethren therefore said unto him, Depart hence, and go into Judea, that thy disciples **there** also may see the works that thou doest. 4 For there is no man that doeth any thing in secret, **but** he himself seeketh to be known openly. If thou do these things, show thyself to the world. 9 When he had said these words unto them, he **continued** still in Galilee.

Luke 9	JST Luke 9	John 7	JST John 7

86. Jesus Attends the Feast

Luke 9	JST Luke 9	John 7	JST John 7
51 ¶ And it came to pass, when the time was come that he should be received up, he stedfastly set his face to go to Jerusalem,			
52 And sent messengers before his face: and they went, and entered into a village of the Samaritans, to make ready for him.			
		10 ¶ But **when** his brethren were gone up, then went he also up unto the feast, not openly, but as it were in secret.	10 But **after** his brethren were gone up, then went he up also unto the feast, not openly, but as it were in secret.
53 And **they did** not receive him, because his face was as though he would go to Jerusalem.	53 And **the Samaritans would** not receive him, because his face was **turned** as though he would go to Jerusalem.		
54 And when his disciples James and John saw **this**, they said, Lord, wilt thou that we command fire to come down from heaven, and consume them, even as Elias did?	54 And when his disciples, James and John, saw **that they would not receive him**, they said, Lord, wilt thou that we command fire to come down from heaven and consume them, even as Elias did?		
55 But he turned, and rebuked them, and said, Ye know not what manner of spirit ye are of.			
56 For the Son of **man** is not come to destroy men's lives, but to save them. And they went to another village.	56 For the Son of **Man** is not come to destroy men's lives, but to save them. And they went to another village.		

Matt. 8	JST Matt. 8		
19 And a certain scribe came, and said **unto him**, Master, I will follow thee withersoever thou goest. 20 And Jesus saith unto him, The foxes have holes, and the birds of the air have nests; but the Son of man hath not where to lay his head. 21 And another of his disciples said unto him, Lord, suffer me first to go and bury my father. 22 But Jesus said unto him, Follow me; and let the dead bury their dead.	19 And a certain scribe came **unto him** and said, Master, I will follow thee withersoever thou goest.		

Luke 9	JST Luke 9	John 7	

Luke 9	JST Luke 9	John 7
57 ¶ And it came to pass, **that**, as they went in the way, a certain man said unto him, Lord, I will follow thee withersoever thou goest.	57 And it came to pass, as they went in the way, a certain man said unto him, Lord, I will follow thee withersoever thou goest.	
58 And Jesus said unto him, Foxes have holes, and birds of the air have nests; but the Son of **m**an hath not where to lay his head.	58 And Jesus said unto him, **The** foxes have holes, and **the** birds of the air have nests; but the Son of **Man** hath not where to lay his head.	
59 And he said unto another, Follow me. But he said, Lord, suffer me first to go and bury my father.		
60 Jesus said unto him, Let the dead bury their dead: but go thou and preach the kingdom of God.		
61 And another also said, Lord, I will follow thee; but let me first go bid them farewell, **which** are **at home** at my house.	61 And another also said, Lord, I will follow thee; but let me first go and bid them farewell **who** are at my house.	
62 And Jesus said unto him, No man, having put his hand to the plough, and looking back, is fit for the kingdom of God.		
		11 Then the Jews sought him at the feast, and said, Where is he?
		12 And there was much murmuring among the people concerning him: for some said, He is a good man: others said, Nay; but he deceiveth the people.
		13 Howbeit no man spake openly of him for fear of the Jews.

87. Jesus Teaches in the Temple

Luke 9	JST Luke 9	John 7
		14 ¶ Now about the midst of the feast Jesus went up into the temple, and taught.
		15 And the Jews marvelled, saying, How knoweth this man letters, having never learned?
		16 Jesus answered them, and said, My doctrine is

John 7	JST John 7	John 7	
not mine, but his that sent me. 17 If any man will do his will, he shall know of the doctrine, whether it be of God, or whether I speak of myself. 18 He that speaketh of himself seeketh his own glory: but he that seeketh his glory that sent him, the same is true, and no unrighteousness is in him. 19 Did not Moses give you the law, and yet none of you keepeth the law? Why go ye about to kill me? 20 The people answered and said, Thou hast a devil: who goeth about to kill thee? 21 Jesus answered and said unto them, I have done one work, and ye all marvel. 22 Moses therefore gave unto you circumcision; (not because it is of Moses, but of the fathers;) and ye on the sabbath day circumcise a man. 23 If a man on the sabbath day receive circumcision, that the law of Moses should not be broken; are ye angry at me, because I have made a man every whit whole on the sabbath day? 24 Judge not according to **the appearance**, but judge righteous judgment. 25 Then said some of them of Jerusalem, Is not this he, whom they seek to kill? 26 But, lo, he speaketh boldly, and they say nothing unto him. Do the rulers know indeed that this is the very Christ? 27 Howbeit we know this man whence he is: but when Christ cometh, no (continued in column 3)	24 Judge not according to **your traditions**, but judge righteous judgment.	man knoweth whence he is. 28 Then cried Jesus in the temple as he taught, saying, Ye both know me, and ye know whence I am: and I am not come of myself, but he that sent me is true, whom ye know not. 29 But I know him: for I am from him, and he hath sent me. 30 Then they sought to take him: but no man laid hands on him, because his hour was not yet come. 31 And many of the people believed on him, and said, When Christ cometh, will he do more miracles than these which this man hath done? 32 ¶ The Pharisees heard that the people murmured such things concerning him; and the Pharisees and the chief priests sent officers to take him. 33 Then said Jesus unto them, Yet a little while am I with you, and then I go unto him that sent me. 34 Ye shall seek me, and shall not find me: and where I am, thither ye cannot come. 35 Then said the Jews among themselves, Whither will he go, that we shall not find him? will he go unto the dispersed among the Gentiles, and teach the Gentiles? 36 What manner of saying is this that he said, Ye shall seek me, and shall not find me: and where I am, thither ye cannot come?	

88. The Last Day of the Feast

37 In the last day, that great day of the feast, Jesus stood and cried, saying, If any man thirst, let him come unto me, and drink.

38 He that believeth on me, as the scripture hath said, out of his belly shall flow rivers of living water.

39 (But this spake he of the Spirit, which they that believe on him should receive: for the Holy Ghost was **not yet given; because** that Jesus was **not yet** glorified.)

40 ¶ Many of the people therefore, when they heard this saying, said, Of a truth this is the Prophet.

41 Others said, This is the Christ. But some said, Shall Christ come out of Galilee?

42 Hath not the scripture said, That Christ cometh of the seed of David, and out of the town of Bethlehem, where David was.

43 So there was a division among the people because of him.

44 And some of them would have taken him; but no man laid hands on him.

45 ¶ Then came the officers to the chief priests and Pharisees; and they said unto them, Why have ye not brought him?

46 The officers answered, Never man spake like this man.

47 Then answered them the Pharisees, Are ye also deceived?

48 Have any of the rulers or of the Pharisees believed on him?

(continued in column 3)

39 (But this spake he of the Spirit, which they that believe on him should receive; for the Holy Ghost was **promised unto them who believe, after** that Jesus was glorified.)

49 But this people who knoweth not the law are cursed.

50 Nicodemus saith unto them, (he that came to Jesus by night, being one of them,)

51 Doth our law judge any man, before it hear him, and know what he doeth?

52 They answered and said unto him, Art thou also of Galilee? Search, and look: for out of Galilee ariseth no prophet.

53 And every man went unto his own house.

John 8	JST John 8 Deut.	John 8	JST John 8 B of M

89. Mount of Olives-- Woman Taken in Adultery

Jesus went unto the mount of Olives.

2 **And** early in the morning he came again into the temple, and all the people came unto him; and he sat down, and taught them.

3 And the scribes and Pharisees brought unto him a woman taken in adultery; and when they had set her in the midst,

4 They say unto him, Master, this woman was taken in adultery, in the very act.

5 Now Moses in the law commanded us, that such should be stoned: but what sayest thou?

6 This they said, tempting him, that they might have to accuse him. But Jesus stooped down, and with his finger wrote on the ground, as though he heard them not.

7 So when they continued asking him, he lifted up himself, and said unto them, He that is without sin among you, let him first cast a stone at her.

8 And again he stooped down, and wrote on the ground.

9 And they which heard it, being convicted by their own conscience, went out one by one, beginning at the eldest, even unto the last: and Jesus was left alone, and the woman standing in the midst.

10 When Jesus had **lifted** up himself, and saw none **but** the woman, he said unto her, Woman, where are those thine accusers? hath no man condemned
(continued in column 3)

And Jesus went unto the mount of Olives.

2 Early in the morning he came again into the temple, and all the people came unto him; and he sat down, and taught them.

3 And the scribes and Pharisees brought unto him a woman taken in adultery; and when they had set her in the midst **of the people,**

Deut. 17:7 The hands of the witnesses shall be first upon him to put him to death, and afterward the hands of all the people. So thou shalt put the evil away from among you.

9 And they which heard it, being convicted by their own conscience, went out one by one, beginning at the eldest, even unto the last; and Jesus was left alone, and the woman standing in the midst **of the temple.**

10 When Jesus had **raised** up himself, and saw none **of her accusers, and** the woman **standing,** he said unto her, Woman, where are those thine accusers?
(continued in column 4)

thee?

11 She said, No man, Lord. And Jesus said unto her, Neither do I condemn thee: go, and sin no more.

12 ¶ Then spake Jesus again unto them, saying, I am the light of the world: he that followeth me shall not walk in darkness, but shall have the light of life.

13 The Pharisees therefore said unto him, Thou bearest record of thyself; thy record is not true.

14 Jesus answered and said unto them, Though I bear record of myself, yet my record is true: for I know whence I came, and whither I go; but ye cannot tell whence I come, and whither I go.

15 Ye judge after the flesh; I judge no man.

16 And yet if I judge, my judgment is true: for I am not alone, but I and the Father that sent me.

17 It is also written in your law, that the testimony of two men is true.

18 I am one that bear witness of myself, and the Father that sent me beareth witness of me.

19 Then said they unto him, Where is thy Father? Jesus answered, Ye neither know me, nor my Father: if ye had known me, ye should have known my Father also.

20 These words spake Jesus in the treasury, as he taught in the temple: and no man laid hands on him;

hath no man condemned thee?

11 She said, No man, Lord. And Jesus said unto her, Neither do I condemn thee; go, and sin no more. **And the woman glorified God from that hour, and believed on his name.**

3 Ne. 9:18 I am the light and the life of the world. . .
(See also 3 Ne. 11:11, Eth. 4:14.)

for his hour was not yet come.

21 Then said Jesus again unto them, I go my way, and ye shall seek me, and shall die in your sins: whither I go, ye cannot come.

22 Then said the Jews, Will he kill himself? because he saith, Whither I go, ye cannot come.

23 And he said unto them, Ye are from beneath; I am from above: ye are of this world; I am not of this world.

24 I said therefore unto you, that ye shall die in your sins: for if ye believe not that I am he, ye shall die in your sins.

25 Then said they unto him, Who art thou? And Jesus saith unto them, Even the same that I said unto you from the beginning.

26 I have many things to say and to judge of you: but he that sent me is true; and I speak to the world those things which I have heard of him.

27 They understood not that he spake to them of the Father.

28 Then said Jesus unto them, When ye have lifted up the Son of man, then shall ye know that I am he, and that I do nothing of myself; but as my Father hath taught me, I speak these things.

29 And he that sent me is with me: the Father hath not left me alone; for I do always those things that please him.

30 As he spake these words, many believed on him.

31 Then said Jesus to those Jews which believed on him, If ye continue in

(continued in column 3)

my word, then are ye my disciples indeed;

32 And ye shall know the truth, and the truth shall make you free.

33 ¶ They answered him, We be Abraham's seed, and were never in bondage to any man: how sayest thou, Ye shall be made free?

34 Jesus answered them, Verily, verily, I say unto you, Whosoever committeth sin is the servant of sin.

35 And the servant abideth not in the house for ever: but the Son abideth ever.

36 If the Son therefore shall make you free, ye shall be free indeed.

37 I know that ye are Abraham's seed; but ye seek to kill me, because my word hath no place in you.

38 I speak that which I have seen with my Father: and ye do that which ye have seen with your father.

39 They answered and said unto him, Abraham is our father. Jesus saith unto them, If ye were Abraham's children, ye would do the works of Abraham.

40 But now ye seek to kill me, a man that hath told you the truth, which I have heard of God: this did not Abraham.

41 Ye do the deeds of your father. Then said they to him, We be not born of fornication; we have one Father, even God.

42 Jesus said unto them, If God were your Father, ye would love me: for I proceeded forth and came from God; neither came I of myself, but he sent me.

John 8	JST John 8	John 8	B of M D & C
43 Why do ye not under-stand my speech? even be-cause ye cannot **hear** my word. 44 Ye are of your father the devil, and the lusts of your father ye will do. He was a murderer from the beginning, and abode not in the truth, because there is no truth in him. When he speaketh a lie, he speak-eth of his own: for he is a liar, and the father of it. 45 And because I tell you the truth, ye believe me not. 46 Which of you convinc-eth me of sin? And if I say the truth, why do ye not believe me? 47 He that is of God **hear-eth** God's words: ye there-fore **hear** them not, be-cause ye are not of God. 48 Then answered the Jews, and said unto him, Say we not well that thou art a Samaritan, and hast a devil? 49 Jesus answered, I have not a devil; but I honour my Father, and ye do dis-honour me. 50 And I seek not mine own glory: there is one that seeketh and judgeth. 51 Verily, verily, I say un-to you, If a man keep my saying, he shall never see death. 52 Then said the Jews un-to him, Now we know that thou hast a devil. Abraham is dead, and the prophets; and thou sayest, If a man keep my saying, he shall never taste of death. 53 Art thou greater than our father Abraham, which is dead? and the prophets are dead: whom makest thou thyself? 54 Jesus answered, If I honour myself, my hon- (continued in column 3)	43 Why do ye not under-stand my speech? even be-cause ye cannot **bear** my word. 47 He that is of God **re-ceiveth** God's words: ye therefore **receive** them not, because ye are not of God.	our is nothing: it is my Father that honoureth me; of whom ye say, that he is your God: 55 Yet ye have not known him; but I know him: and if I should say, I know him not, I shall be a liar like unto you: but I know him, and keep his saying. 56 Your father Abraham rejoiced to see my day: and he saw it, and was glad. 57 Then said the Jews un-to him, Thou art not yet fifty years old, and hast thou seen Abraham? 58 Jesus said unto them, Verily, verily I say unto you, Before Abraham was, I am. 59 Then took they up stones to cast at him: but Jesus hid himself, and went out of the temple, going through the midst of them, and so passed by.	Hel 8:17 Yea, and behold, Abraham saw of his com-ing, and was filled with gladness and did rejoice. D&C 39:1 Hearken and listen to the voice of him who is from all eternity to all eternity, the Great I AM, even Jesus Christ--

John 9	JST John 9 Moses	John 9	JST John 9

90. Jerusalem—Man Born Blind

John 9	JST John 9 Moses	John 9	JST John 9
And as Jesus passed by he saw a man which was blind from birth.		went and washed, and I received sight.	
2 And his disciples asked him, saying, Master, who did sin, this man, or his parents, that he was born blind?		12 Then said they unto him, Where is he? He said, I know not.	
3 Jesus answered, neither hath this man sinned, nor his parents; but that the work of God should be made manifest in him.		13 ¶ They brought **to the Pharisees** him **that aforetime was** blind.	13 **And** they brought him **who had been** blind **to the Pharisees.**
4 I must work the works of him that sent me, while **it is day**: the **night** cometh, when **no man can** work.	4 I must work the works of him that sent me, while **I am with you**; the **time** cometh when **I shall have finished my** work, **then I go unto the Father.**	14 And it was the sabbath day when Jesus made the clay, and opened his eyes.	
5 As long as I am in the world, I am the light of the world.		15 Then again the Pharisees also asked him how he had received his sight. He said unto them, He put clay upon my eyes, and I washed, and so see.	
6 When he has thus spoken, he spat on the ground, and made clay of the spittle, and he anointed the eyes of the blind man with the clay.		16 Therefore said some of the Pharisees, This man is not of God, because he keepeth not the sabbath day. Others said, How can a man that is a sinner do such miracles? And there was a division among them.	
7 And said unto him, go, wash in the pool of Siloam, (which is by interpretation, Sent.) He went his way therefore, and washed, and came seeing.	Moses 6:35 And the Lord spake unto Enoch, and said unto him: Anoint thine eyes with clay, and wash them, and thou shalt see. And he did so.	17 They say unto the blind man again, What sayest thou of him, **that he** hath opened thine eyes? He said, He is a prophet.	17 They say unto the blind man again, What sayest thou of him **who** hath opened thine eyes? He said, He is a prophet.
8 ¶ The neighbors therefore, and they which before had seen him that he was blind, said, Is not this he that sat and begged?		18 But the Jews did not believe concerning him, that he had been blind, and received his sight, until they called the parents of him that had received his sight.	
9 Some said, This is he: others said, He is like him: but he said, I am he.		19 And they asked them, saying, Is this your son, who ye say was born blind? how then doth he now see?	
10 Therefore said they unto him, How were thine eyes opened?		20 His parents answered them and said, We know that this is our son, and that he was born blind:	
11 He answered and said, A man that is called Jesus made clay, and anointed mine eyes, and said unto me, Go to the pool of Siloam, and wash: and I		21 But by what means he now seeth, we know not; or who hath opened his eyes, we know not: he is of	
(continued in column 3)	(continued in column 4)		

John 9	JST John 9	John 9	JST John 9
age; ask him: he shall speak for himself.		one that was born blind.	one that was born blind, **except he be of God**.
22 These words spake his parents, because they feared the Jews: for the Jews had agreed already, that if any man did confess that he was Christ, he should be put out of the synagogue.		33 If this man were not of God, he could do nothing.	
23 Therefore said his parents, He is of age; ask him.		34 They answered and said unto him, Thou wast altogether born in sins, and dost thou teach us? And they cast him out.	
24 Then again called they the man that was blind, and said unto him, Give God the praise: we know that this man is a sinner.		35 Jesus heard that they had cast him out; and when he had found him, he said unto him, Dost thou believe on the Son of God?	
25 He answered and said, Whether he be a sinner or no, I know not: one thing I know, that, whereas I was blind, now I see.		36 He answered and said, Who is he, Lord, that I might believe on him?	
26 Then said they to him again, What did he to thee? how opened he thine eyes?		37 And Jesus said unto him, Thou hast both seen him, and it is he that talketh with thee.	
27 He answered them, I have told you already, and ye did not **hear**: wherefore would ye **hear it** again? will ye also be his disciples?	27 He answered them, I have told you already, and ye did not **believe**; wherefore would you **believe if I should tell you** again? **and would you** be his disciples?	38 And he said, Lord, I believe. And he worshipped him.	
28 Then they reviled him, and said, Thou art his disciple; but we are Moses' disciples.		39 ¶ And Jesus said, For judgment I am come into this world, that they which see not might see; and that they which see might be made blind.	
29 We know that God spake unto Moses: as for this **fellow**, we know not from whence he is.	29 We know that God spake unto Moses; as for this **man**, we know not from whence he is.	40 And some of the Pharisees which were with him heard these words, and said unto him, Are we blind also?	
30 The man answered and said unto them, Why herein is a marvellous thing, that ye know not from whence he is, and yet he hath opened mine eyes.		41 Jesus said unto them, If ye were blind, ye should have no sin: but now ye say, We see; therefore your sin remaineth.	
31 Now we know that God heareth not sinners: but if any man be a worshipper of God, and doeth his will, him he heareth.			
32 Since the world began was it not heard that any man opened the eyes of (continued in column 3)	32 Since the world began was it not heard that any man opened the eyes of (continued in column 4)		

	TPJS	John 10	JST John 10

91. Jesus is the Good Shepherd

	TPJS	John 10	JST John 10
	TPJS- Surely, then, if it became John and Jesus Christ, the Savior, to fulfil all righteousness to be baptized-- so surely, then, it will become every other person that seeks the kingdom of heaven to go and do likewise; for he is the door, and if any person climbs up any other way, the same is a thief and a robber! (p. 266)	Verily, verily, I say unto you, He that entereth not by the door into the sheepfold, but climbeth up some other way, the same is a thief and a robber. 2 But he that entereth in by the door is the shepherd of the sheep. 3 To him the porter openeth; and the sheep hear his voice: and he calleth his own sheep by name, and leadeth them out. 4 And when he putteth forth his own sheep, he goeth before them, and the sheep follow him: for they know his voice. 5 And a stranger will they not follow, but will flee from him: for they know not the voice of strangers. 6 This parable spake Jesus unto them: but they understood not what things they were which he spake unto them. 7 Then said Jesus unto them again, Verily, verily, I say unto you, I am the door of the sheep. 8 All that ever came before me are thieves and robbers: but the sheep did not hear them. 9 I am the door: by me if any man enter in, he shall be saved, and shall go in and out, and find pasture. 10 The thief cometh not, but for to steal, and to kill, and to destroy: I am come that they might have life, and that they might have it more abundantly. 11 I am the good shepherd: the good shepherd giveth his life for **the** sheep. 12 **But** he **that** is **a n** hireling, **and** **not** **the**	7 Then said Jesus unto them again, Verily, verily, I say unto you, I am the door of the sheep**fold**. 8 All that ever came before me **who testified not of me** are thieves and robbers; but the sheep did not hear them. 11 I am the good shepherd; the good shepherd giveth his life for **his** sheep. 12 **And the shepherd** is **not as a** hireling, whose

John 10	JST John 10	B of M	D & C
shepherd, whose own the sheep are not, seeth the wolf coming, and leaveth the sheep, and fleeth: and the wolf catcheth **them,** and scattereth **the sheep.** 13 **The** hireling fleeth, because he is **an** hireling, and careth not for the sheep. 14 I am the good shepherd, and know my sheep, and am known of mine. 15 As the Father knoweth me, even so know I the Father: and I lay down my life for the sheep. 16 And other sheep I have, which are not of this fold: them also I must bring, and they shall hear my voice; and there shall be one fold, and one shepherd. 17 Therefore doth my Father love me, because I lay down my life, that I might take it again. 18 No man taketh it from me, but I lay it down of myself. I have power to lay it down, and I have power to take it again. This commandment have I received of my Father.	own the sheep are not, **who** seeth the wolf coming, and leaveth the sheep, and fleeth; and the wolf catcheth **the sheep** and scattereth **them.** 14 **But he who is a** hireling fleeth, because he is **a** hireling, and careth not for the sheep. 13 **For** I am the good shepherd, and know my sheep, and am known of mine.		50:44 Wherefore, I am in your midst, and I am the good shepherd, and the stone of Israel. He that buildeth upon this rock shall never fall.
		3 Ne. 15:21 And verily I say unto you, that ye are they of whom I said: Other sheep I have which are not of this fold; them also I must bring, and they shall hear my voice; and there shall be one fold, and one shepherd. 22 And they understood me not for they supposed it had been the Gentiles; for they understood not that the Gentiles should be converted through their preaching.	10:59 I am he who said-- Other sheep have I which are not of this fold-- unto my disciples, and many there were that understood me not. 60 And I will show unto this people that I had other sheep, and that they were a branch of the house of Jacob;

TPJS-- As the Father hath power in Himself, so hath the Son power in Himself, to lay down His life and take it again, so He has a body of His own. The Son doeth what He hath seen the Father do: then the Father hath some day laid down His life and taken it again; so He has a body of His own; each one will be in His own body; and yet the sectarian world believe the body of the Son is identical with the Father's. (p. 312)

19 ¶ There was a division therefore again among the Jews for these sayings. 20 And many of them said, He hath a devil, and is mad; why hear ye him? 21 Others said, These are not the words of him that hath a devil. Can a devil open the eyes of the blind?		23 And they understood me not that I said they shall hear my voice; and they understood me not that the Gentiles should not at anytime hear my voice-- that I should not manifest myself unto them save it were by the Holy Ghost. 24 But behold, ye have both heard my voice, and seen me; and ye are my sheep, and ye are numbered among those whom the Father hath given me. (See also 3 Ne. 15:14-20; 16:1-4; 17:4; 1 Ne. 22:25.)	

Luke 10	JST Luke 10	Luke 10	JST Luke 10

92. Parable of the Good Samaritan

25 ¶ And, behold, a certain lawyer stood up, and tempted him, saying, Master, what shall I do to inherit eternal life?

26 He said unto him, What is written in the law? how readest thou?

27 And he answering said, Thou shalt love the Lord thy God with all thy heart, and with all thy soul, and with all thy strength, and with all thy mind; and thy neighbour as thyself.

28 And he said unto him, Thou hast answered right: this do, and thou shalt live.

29 But he, willing to justify himself, said unto Jesus, And who is my neighbor?

30 And Jesus answering said, A certain man went down from Jerusalem to Jericho, and fell among thieves, **which** stripped him of his raiment, and wounded him, and departed, leaving him half dead.

31 And by chance there came down a certain priest that way: and when he saw him, he passed by on the other side.

(continued in column 3)

31 And Jesus answering, said, A certain man went down from Jerusalem to Jericho, and fell among thieves, **who** stripped him of his raiment and wounded him, and departed, leaving him half dead.

32 And by chance, there came down a certain priest that way; and when he saw him, he passed by on the other side **of the way**.

(continued in column 4)

32 And likewise a Levite, when he was at the place, came and looked on him, and passed by on the other side.

33 But a certain Samaritan, as he journeyed, came where he was: and when he saw him, he had compassion on him,

34 And went to him, and bound up his wounds, pouring in oil and wine, and set him on his own beast, and brought him to an inn, and took care of him.

35 And on the morrow when he departed, he took **out two pence**, and gave **them** to the host, and said unto him, Take care of him; and whatsoever thou spendest more, when I come again, I will repay thee.

36 **Which** now of these three, thinkest thou, was neighbour unto him **that** fell among the thieves?

37 And he said, He **that** shewed mercy on him. Then said Jesus unto him, Go, and do **thou** likewise.

33 And likewise a Levite, when he was at the place, came and looked **upon** him, and passed by on the other side **of the way; for they desired in their hearts that it might not be known that they had seen him.**

36 And on the morrow, when he departed, he took **money**, and gave to the host, and said unto him, Take care of him, and whatsoever thou spendest more, when I come again, I will repay thee.

37 **Who** now of these three, thinkest thou, was neighbor unto him **who** fell among the thieves?

38 And he said, He **who** showed mercy on him. Then said Jesus unto him, Go and do likewise.

93. Bethany-- Visits Mary and Martha

38 ¶ Now it came to pass, as they went, **that he** entered into a certain village: and a certain woman named Martha received him into her house.

39 And she had a sister called Mary, **which** also sat at Jesus' feet, and heard his word.

40 But Martha was cumbered about much serving, and came to him, and

(continued in column 3)

39 Now it came to pass, as they went, **they** entered into a certain village; and a certain woman named Martha received him into her house.

40 And she had a sister, called Mary, **who** also sat at Jesus' feet, and heard his words.

said, Lord, dost thou not care that my sister hath left me to serve alone? bid her therefore that she help me.

41 And Jesus answered and said unto her, Martha, Martha, thou art careful and troubled about many things:

42 But one thing is needful: and Mary hath chosen that good part, which shall not be taken away from her.

94. "A Certain Place"-- Teaches Disciples to Pray

Luke 11	JST Luke 11	Luke 11	JST Luke 11
And it came to pass, **that,** as **he** was praying in a certain place, when he ceased, one of his disciples said unto him, Lord, teach us to pray, as John also taught his disciples. 2 And he said unto them, When ye pray, say, Our Father **which** art in heaven, Hallowed be thy name. Thy kingdom come. Thy will be done, as in heaven, so in earth. 3 Give us day by day our daily bread. 4 And forgive us our sins; for we also forgive every one **that** is indebted to us. And **lead** us not into temptation; but deliver us from evil. 5 And he said unto them,	And it came to pass, as **Jesus** was praying in a certain place, when he ceased, one of his disciples said unto him, Lord, teach us to pray, as John also taught his disciples. 2 And he said unto them, When ye pray, say, Our Father **who** art in heaven, hallowed be thy name. Thy kingdom come. Thy will be done as in heaven, so in earth. 4 And forgive us our sins; for we also forgive every one **who** is indebted to us. And **let** us not **be lead** unto temptation; but deliver us from evil; **for thine is the kingdom and power. Amen.** 5 And he said unto them, **Your heavenly Father will not fail to give unto you whatsoever ye ask of him. And he spake a parable, saying,**	and give him as many as he needeth. 9 And I say unto you, Ask, and it shall be given you; seek, and ye shall find; knock, and it shall be opened unto you. 10 For every one **that** asketh receiveth; and he that seeketh findeth; and to him that knocketh it shall be opened. 11 If a son shall ask bread of any of you **that** is a father, will he give him a stone? or if he ask a fish, will he for a fish give him a serpent? 12 Or if he shall ask an egg, will he offer him a scorpion? 13 If ye then, being evil, know how to give good gifts unto your children: how much more shall your heavenly Father give the Holy Spirit to them **that** ask him?	11 For every one **who** asketh, receiveth; and he that seeketh, findeth; and to him that knocketh, it shall be opened. 12 If a son shall ask bread of any of you **who** is a father, will he give him a stone? or, if a fish, will he for a fish give him a serpent? 14 If ye then, being evil, know how to give good gifts unto your children, how much more shall your heavenly Father give **good gifts, through** the Holy Spirit, to them **who** ask him.
Which of you shall have a friend, and shall go unto him at midnight, and say unto him, Friend, lend me three loaves; 6 For a friend of mine **in his journey is** come to me, and I have nothing to set before him? 7 And he from within shall answer and say, Trouble me not: the door is now shut, and my children are with me in bed; I cannot rise and give thee. 8 I say unto you, Though he will not rise and give him, because he is his friend, yet because of his importunity he will rise (continued in column 3)	7 For a friend of mine **has** come to me **in his journey,** and I have nothing to set before him; (continued in column 4)		

95. Judea-- Casts Out a Devil

14 ¶ And he was casting out a devil, and it was dumb. And it came to pass, when the devil was gone out, the dumb spake; and the people wondered.

15 But some of them said, He casteth out devils through Beelzebub the chief of the devils.

16 And others, tempting him, sought of him a sign from heaven.

17 But he, knowing their thoughts, said unto them, Every kingdom divided against itself is brought to desolation; and a house divided **against a house** falleth.

18 If Satan also be divided against himself, how **shall** his kingdom stand? because ye say **that** I cast out devils through Beelzebub.

19 And if I by Beelzebub cast out devils, by whom do your sons cast **them** out? therefore shall they be your judges.

20 But if I with the finger of God cast out devils, no doubt the kingdom of God is come upon you.

21 When a strong man armed keepeth his palace, his goods are in peace:

22 But when a stronger than he shall come upon him, and overcome him, he taketh from him all his armour wherein he trusted, and divideth his **spoils**.

23 He that is not with me is against me: and he **that** gathereth not with me scattereth.

24 When the unclean spirit is gone out of a man, **he** walketh through dry
(continued in column 3)

---

15 And he was casting a devil **out of a man**, and he was dumb. And it came to pass, when the devil was gone out, the dumb spake; and the people wondered.

17 And others tempting, sought of him a sign from heaven.

18 But he, knowing their thoughts, said unto them, Every kingdom divided against itself is brought to desolation; and a house divided **cannot stand, but** falleth.

19 If Satan also be divided against himself, how **can** his kingdom stand? **I say this**, because **you** say I cast out devils through Beelzebub.

20 And if I, by Beelzebub, cast out devils, by whom do your sons cast out **devils**? Therefore shall they be your judges.

21 But if I, with the finger of God cast out devils, no doubt the kingdom of God **has** come upon you.

23 But when a stronger than he shall come upon him, and overcome him, he taketh from him all his armor wherein he trusted and divideth his **goods**.

24 He that is not with me, is against me: and he **who** gathereth not with me, scattereth.

25 When the unclean spirit is gone out of a man, **it** walketh through dry
(continued in column 4)

---

places, seeking rest; and finding none, **he** saith, I will return unto **my** house whence I came out.

25 And when **he** cometh, **he** findeth **it** swept and garnished.

26 Then goeth **he**, and taketh **to him** seven other spirits more wicked than himself; and they enter in, and dwell there: and the last **state** of that man is worse than the first.

27 ¶ And it came to pass, as he spake these things, a certain woman of the company lifted up her voice, and said unto him, Blessed is the womb **that** bare thee, and the paps which thou hast sucked.

28 **But** he said, Yea **rather**, blessed are they **that** hear the word of God, and keep it.

TPJS-- As a Church and a people it behooves us to be wise, and to seek to know the will of God, and then be willing to do it; for "blessed is he that heareth the word of the Lord, and keepeth it," say the Scriptures. (p. 253)

29 ¶ **And** when the people were gathered thick together, he began to say, This is an evil generation: they seek a sign; and there shall no sign be given **it**, but the sign of Jonas the prophet.

30 For as Jonas was a sign unto the Ninevites, so shall also the Son of man be to this generation.

31 The queen of the south shall rise up in the judgment with the men of this generation, and condemn them: for she came from the utmost parts of the earth to hear the wisdom of Solomon; and, behold, a

---

places, seeking rest; and finding none, **it** saith, I will return unto **mine** house whence I came out.

26 And when **it** cometh, **it** findeth **the house** swept and garnished.

27 Then goeth **the evil spirit**, and taketh seven other spirits more wicked than himself, and they enter in, and dwell there; and the last **end** of that man is worse than the first.

28 And it came to pass, as he spake these things, a certain woman of the company, lifted up her voice, and said unto him, Blessed is the womb **which** bare thee, and the paps which thou hast sucked.

29 **And** he said, Yea, **and** blessed are **all** they **who** hear the word of God, and keep it.

30 When the people were gathered thick together, he began to say, This is an evil generation; they seek a sign, and there shall no sign be given **them**, but the sign of Jonas the prophet.

32 The queen of the south shall rise up in the **day of** judgment with the men of this generation, and condemn them; for she came from the utmost parts of the earth, to hear the wisdom of Solomon; and,

Luke 11	JST Luke 11	D&C	
greater than Solomon is here. 32 The men of Nineve shall rise up in the judgment with this generation, and shall condemn it: for they repented at the preaching of Jonas; and, behold, a greater than Jonas is here. 33 No man, when he hath lighted a candle, putteth it in a secret place, neither under a bushel, but on a candlestick, that they **which** come in may see the light. 34 The light of the body is the eye: therefore when thine eye is single, thy whole body also is full of light; but when thine eye is evil, thy body also is full of darkness. 35 Take heed therefore that the light which is in thee be not darkness. 36 If thy whole body therefore **be** full of light, having no part dark, the whole shall be full of light, as when the bright shining of a candle doth give **thee** light.	behold, a greater than Solomon is here. 33 The men of Nineveh shall rise up in the **day of** judgment with this generation; and shall condemn it; for they repented at the preaching of Jonas; and, behold, a greater than Jonas is here. 34 No man when he hath lighted a candle, putteth it in a secret place, neither under a bushel, but on a candlestick, that they **who** come in may see the light. 37 If thy whole body therefore **is** full of light, having no part dark, the whole shall be full of light, as when the bright shining of a candle **lighteth a room and** doth give **the** light **in all the room.**	88:67 And if your eye be single to my glory, your whole bodies shall be filled with light, and there shall be no darkness in you; and that body which is filled with light comprehendeth all things.	

96. Pharisees, Lawyers, Scribes Rebuked

Luke 11	JST Luke 11	D&C	
37 ¶ And as he spake, a certain Pharisee besought him to dine with him: and he went in, and sat down to meat. 38 And when the Pharisee saw **it**, he marvelled that he had not first washed before dinner. 39 And the Lord said unto him, Now do **ye** Pharisees make clean the outside of the cup and the platter; but your inward part is full of ravening and wickedness.	39 And when the Pharisee saw **him**, he marvelled that he had not first washed before dinner.		

Luke 11	JST Luke 11	Luke 11	JST Luke 11
40 Ye fools, did not he that made that which is without make that which is within also?	41 O fools, did not he who made that which is without, make that which is within also?	send them prophets and apostles, and some of them they shall slay and persecute:	
41 But rather give alms of such things as ye have; and, behold, all things are clean unto you.	42 But if ye would rather give alms of such things as ye have; and observe to do all things which I have commanded you, then would your inward parts be clean also.	50 That the blood of all the prophets, which was shed from the foundation of the world, may be required of this generation;	
		51 From the blood of Abel unto the blood of Zacharias, which perished between the altar and the temple: verily I say unto you, It shall be required of this generation.	51 ... from the blood of Abel unto the blood of Zacharias, who perished between the altar and the temple:
42 But woe unto you, Pharisees! for ye tithe mint and rue and all manner of herbs, and pass over judgment and the love of God: these ought ye to have done, and not to leave the other undone.	43 But I say unto you, Woe be unto you, Pharisees! For ye tithe mint, and rue, and all manner of herbs, and pass over judgment, and the love of God; these ought ye to have done, and not to leave the other undone.		52 Verily I say unto you, It shall be required of this generation.
43 Woe unto you, Pharisees! for ye love the uppermost seats in the synagogues, and greetings in the markets.		TPJS-- When Herod's edict went forth to destroy the young children, John was about six months older than Jesus, and came under this hellish edict, and Zacharias caused his mother to take him into the mountains, where he was raised on locusts and wild honey. When his father refused to disclose his hiding place, and being the officiating high priest at the Temple that year, was slain by Herod's order, between the porch and the altar, as Jesus said. (p. 261)	
44 Woe unto you, scribes and Pharisees, hypocrites! for ye are as graves which appear not, and the men that walk over them are not aware of them.			
45 ¶ Then answered one of the lawyers, and said unto him, Master, thus saying thou reproachest us also.			
46 And he said, Woe unto you also, ye lawyers! for ye lade men with burdens grievous to be borne, and ye yourselves touch not the burdens with one of your fingers.	47 And he said, Woe unto you, lawyers, also! For ye lade men with burdens grievous to be borne, and ye yourselves touch not the burdens with one of your fingers.	52 Woe unto you, lawyers! for ye have taken away the key of knowledge: ye entered not in yourselves, and them that were entering in ye hindered.	53 Woe unto you, lawyers! For ye have taken away the key of knowledge, the fulness of the scriptures; ye enter not in yourselves into the kingdom; and those who were entering in, ye hindered.
47 Woe unto you! for ye build the sepulchres of prophets, and your fathers killed them.		53 And as he said these things unto them, the scribes and the Pharisees began to urge him vehemently, and to provoke him to speak of many things:	54 And as he said these things unto them, the scribes and Pharisees began to be angry, and to urge vehemently, endeavoring to provoke him to speak of many things;
48 Truly ye bear witness that ye allow the deeds of your fathers: for they indeed killed them, and ye build their sepulchres.		54 Laying wait for him, and seeking to catch something out of his mouth, that they might accuse him.	
49 Therefore also said the wisdom of God, I will (continued in column 3)	(continued in column 4)		

97. The Leaven of the Pharisees

In the mean time, when there were gathered together an innumerable multitude of people, insomuch that they trode one upon another, he began to say to his disciples first of all, Beware ye of the leaven of the Pharisees, which is hypocrisy.

2 For there is nothing covered, **that shall not be** revealed; neither hid, **that** shall not be known.

3 Therefore whatsoever ye have spoken in darkness shall be heard in the light; and that which ye have spoken in the ear in closets shall be proclaimed upon the housetops.

4 And I say unto you my friends, Be not afraid of them **that** kill the body, and after that have no more that they can do.

5 But I will forewarn you whom ye shall fear: Fear him, **which** after he hath killed hath power to cast into hell; yea, I say unto you, Fear him.

6 Are not five sparrows sold for two farthings, and not one of them is forgotten before God?

7 But even the very hairs of your head are all numbered. Fear not therefore: ye are of more value than many sparrows.

8 Also I say unto you, Whosoever shall confess me before men, him shall the Son of man also confess before the angels of God:

9 But he **that** denieth me before men shall be denied before the angels of God:

(continued in column 3)

---

2 For there is nothing covered **which** shall not be revealed; neither hid **which** shall not be known.

4 And I say unto you my friends, Be not afraid of them **who** kill the body, and after that have no more that they can do;

5 But I will forewarn you whom ye shall fear; fear him, **who** after he hath killed, hath power to cast into hell; yea, I say unto you, Fear him.

9 But he **who** denieth me before men, shall be denied before the angels of

(continued in column 4)

---

10 **And** whosoever shall speak a word against the Son of man, it shall be forgiven him: but unto him **that** blasphemeth against the Holy Ghost it shall not be forgiven.

11 And **when** they bring you unto the synagogues, **and unto** magistrates, and powers,

take ye no thought how or what thing ye shall answer, or what ye shall say:

12 For the Holy Ghost shall teach you in the same hour what ye ought to say.

13 ¶ And one of the company said unto him, Master, speak to my brother, that he divide the inheritance with me.

14 And he said unto him, Man, who made me a judge or a divider over you?

15 And he said unto them, Take heed, and beware of covetousness: for a man's life consisteth not in the abundance of the things which he possesseth.

God:

10 **Now his disciples knew that he said this, because they had spoken evil against him before the people; for they were afraid to confess him before men.**

11 **And they reasoned among themselves, saying, He knoweth our hearts, and he speaketh to our condemnation, and we shall not be forgiven. But he answered them, and said unto them,**

12 Whosoever shall speak a word against the Son of Man, **and repenteth,** it shall be forgiven him; but unto him **who** blasphemeth against the Holy Ghost, it shall not be forgiven **him.**

13 And **again I say unto you,** They **shall** bring you unto the synagogues, and **before** magistrates, and powers. **When they do this,** take ye no thought how, or what thing ye shall answer, or what ye shall say;

Luke 12	JST Luke 12	Luke 12	JST Luke 12
16 And he spake a parable unto them, saying, The ground of a certain rich man brought forth plentifully: 17 And he thought within himself, saying, What shall I do, because I have **no** room where to bestow my fruits? 18 And he said, This will I do: I will pull down my barns, and build greater; and there will I bestow all my fruits and my goods. 19 And I will say to my soul, Soul, thou hast much goods laid up for many years; take thine ease, eat, drink, and be merry. 20 But God said unto him, Thou fool, this night thy soul shall be required of thee: then whose shall those things be, which thou hast provided? 21 So **is he that** layeth up treasure for himself, and is not rich toward God.	23 So **shall it be with him who** layeth up treasure for himself, and is not rich toward God.		

98. Disciples-- Seek the Kingdom of God

Luke 12	JST Luke 12	Luke 12	JST Luke 12
22 ¶ And he said unto his disciples, Therefore I say unto you, Take no thought for your life, what ye shall eat; neither for the body, what ye shall put on. 23 The life is more than meat, and the body **is more** than raiment. 24 Consider the ravens: for they neither sow nor reap; which neither have storehouse nor barn; **and** God feedeth them: **how much more** are ye better than the fowls? 25 And **which** of you **with** taking thought can add to his stature one cubit? 26 If ye then be not able to do that thing which is (continued in column 3)	25 **For** the life is more than meat, and the body than raiment. 26 Consider the ravens; for they neither sow nor reap; which neither have storehouse nor barn; **nevertheless** God feedeth them. Are ye **not** better than the fowls? 27 And **who** of you **by** taking thought, can add to his stature one cubit? (continued in column 4)	least, why take ye thought for the rest? 27 Consider the lilies how they grow: they toil not, they spin not; and yet I say unto you, that Solomon in all his glory was not arrayed like one of these. 28 If then God so clothe the grass, which is to day in the field, and to morrow is cast into the oven; how much more will he **clothe** you, **O** ye of little faith? 29 **And** seek not what ye shall eat, or what ye shall drink, neither be ye of doubtful mind. 30 For all these things do the nations of the world seek after: and your Father	30 If then God so clothe the grass, which is today in the field, and tomorrow is cast in the oven; how much more will he **provide for** you, **if ye are not** of little faith? 31 **Therefore,** seek not what ye shall eat, or what ye shall drink, neither be ye of doubtful mind; 32 For all these things do the nations of the world seek after; and your Father

Luke 12	JST Luke 12	Luke 12	JST Luke 12
knoweth that ye have need of these things.	who is in heaven knoweth that ye have need of these things. 33 And ye are sent unto them to be their ministers, and the laborer is worthy of his hire; for the law saith, That a man shall not muzzle the ox that treadeth out the corn. 34 Therefore seek ye to bring forth the kingdom of God, and all these things shall be added unto you.		the night, and he shall also come in the second watch, and again he shall come in the third watch. 42 And verily I say unto you, He hath already come, as it is written of him; and again when he shall come in the second watch, or come in the third watch, blessed are those servants when he cometh, that he shall find so doing;
31 ¶ But rather seek ye the kingdom of God; and all these things shall be added unto you. 32 Fear not, little flock; for it is your Father's good pleasure to give you the kingdom.		38 And if he shall come in the second watch, or come in the third watch, and find them so, blessed are those servants.	43 For the Lord of those servants shall gird himself, and make them to sit down to meat, and will come forth and serve them.
33 Sell that ye have, and give alms; provide yourselves bags which wax not old, a treasure in the heavens that faileth not, where no thief approacheth, neither moth corrupt.	36 This he spake unto his disciples, saying, Sell that ye have and give alms; provide not for yourselves bags which wax old, but rather provide a treasure in the heavens, that faileth not; where no thief approacheth, neither moth corrupteth.		44 And now, verily I say these things unto you, that ye may know this, that the coming of the Lord is as a thief in the night. 45 And it is like unto a man who is an householder, who, if he watcheth not his goods, the thief cometh in an hour of which he is not aware, and taketh his goods, and divideth them among his fellows.
34 For where your treasure is, there will your heart be also. 35 Let your loins be girded about, and your lights burning;	38 Let your loins be girded about and have your lights burning;	39 And this know, that if the goodman of the house had known in what hour the thief would come, he would have watched, and not have suffered his house to be broken through.	46 And they said among themselves, If the good man of the house had known in what hour the thief would come, he would have watched, and not have suffered his house to be broken through and the loss of his goods.
36 And ye yourselves like unto men that wait for their lord, when he will return from the wedding; that when he cometh and knocketh, they may open unto him immediately.	39 That ye yourselves may be like unto men who wait for their Lord, when he will return from the wedding; that, when he cometh and knocketh, they may open unto him immediately.		
37 Blessed are those servants, whom the lord when he cometh shall find watching: verily I say unto you, that he shall gird himself, and make them to sit down to meat, and will come forth and serve them.	40 Verily I say unto you, Blessed are those servants, whom the Lord when he cometh shall find watching; for he shall gird himself, and make them sit down to meat, and will come forth and serve them. 41 For, behold, he cometh in the first watch of	40 Be ye therefore ready also: for the Son of man cometh at an hour when ye think not. 41 ¶ Then Peter said unto him, Lord, speakest thou this parable unto us, or even to all?	47 And he said unto them, Verily I say unto you, be ye therefore ready also; for the Son of Man cometh at an hour when ye think not. 48 Then Peter said unto him, Lord, speakest thou this parable unto us, or unto all?
	(continued in column 4)		

218

Luke 12	JST Luke 12	D & C	
42 And the Lord said, **Who then is that faithful and wise steward,** whom **his** lord shall make ruler over his household, to give **them** their portion of meat in due season?	49 And the Lord said, **I speak unto those** whom **the** Lord shall make rulers over his household, to give **his children** their portion of meat in due season. 50 **And they said, Who then is that faithful and wise servant?** 51 **And the Lord said unto them, It is that servant who watcheth, to impart his portion of meat in due season.**		
43 Blessed **is** that servant, whom his lord when he cometh **shall find** so doing.	52 Blessed **be** that servant whom his Lord **shall find,** when he cometh, so doing.		
44 Of a truth I say unto you, that he will make him ruler over all that he hath.			
45 But and if that servant say in his heart, My lord delayeth his coming; and shall begin to beat the menservants and the maidens, and to eat and drink, and to be drunken;	54 But **the evil servant is he who is not found watching.** And if that servant **is not found watching, he will** say in his heart, My Lord delayeth his coming; and shall begin to beta the menservants, and **the** maidens, and to eat, and drink, and to be drunken.	106:4 And again, verily I say unto you, the coming of the Lord draweth nigh, and it overtaketh the world as a thief in the night— 5 Therefore, gird up your loins, that you may be the children of light, and that day shall not overtake you as a thief.	
46 The lord of that servant will come in a day **when** he looketh not for **him**, and at an hour when he is not aware, and will cut him **in sunder**, and will appoint him his portion with the unbelievers.	55 The Lord of that servant will come in a day he looketh not for, and at an hour when he is not aware, and will cut him **down**, and will appoint him his portion with the unbelievers.		
47 And that servant, **which** knew his **lord's** will, and prepared not **himself,** neither did according to his will, shall be beaten with many stripes.	56 And that servant **who** knew his Lord's will, and prepared not **for his Lord's coming,** neither did according to his will, shall be beaten with many stripes.		
48 But he that knew not, and did commit things worthy of stripes, shall be beaten with few **stripes**. For unto whomsoever much is given, of him shall **be** much required: and to	57 But he that knew not **his Lord's will,** and did commit things worthy of stripes, shall be beaten with few. For unto whomsoever much is given, of him shall much **be**	82:3 for of him unto whom much is given much is required; and he who sins against the greater light shall receive the greater condemnation.	

219

Luke 12	JST Luke 12	Luke 12	JST Luke 12
whom **men have** committed much, of him **they** will ask the more.	required; and to whom **the Lord has** committed much, of him will **men** ask the more. 58 **For they are not well pleased with the Lord's doings; therefore** I am come to send fire on the earth; and **what is it to you, if I will that** it be already kindled?	the way, give diligence that thou mayest be delivered from him; lest he hale thee to the judge, and the judge deliver thee to the officer, and the officer cast thee into prison. 59 I tell thee, thou shalt not depart thence, till thou hast paid the very last mite.	the way **with thine enemy? Why not** give diligence that thou mayest be delivered from him; lest he hale thee to the judge, and the judge deliver thee to the officer, and the officer cast thee into prison?
49 ¶ I am come to send fire on the earth; and **what will I, if** it be already kindled?	59 But I have a baptism to be baptized with; and how am I straitened **until** it be accomplished!		
50 But I have a baptism to be baptized with; and how am I straitened **till** it be accomplished!			
51 Suppose ye that I am come to give peace on earth? I tell you, Nay; but rather division:			
52 For from henceforth there shall be five in one house divided, three against two, and two against three.			
53 The father shall be divided against the son, and the son against the father; the mother against the daughter, and the daughter against the mother; the mother in law against her daughter in law, and the daughter in law against her mother in law.			
54 ¶ And he said also to the people, When ye see a cloud rise out of the west, **straightway** ye say, There cometh a shower; and so it is.	63 And he said also **unto** the people, When ye see a cloud rise out of the west, ye say **straightway**, There cometh a shower; and so it is.		
55 And when ye **see** the south wind blow, ye say, There will be heat; and it cometh to pass.	64 And when the south wind blows, ye say, There will be heat; and it cometh to pass.		
56 **Ye** hypocrites, ye can discern the face of the sky and of the earth; but how is it that ye do not discern this time?	65 **O** hypocrites! Ye can discern the face of the sky, and of the earth; but how is it that ye do not discern this time?		
57 Yea, and why even of yourselves judge ye not what is right?			
58 ¶ **When thou goest with** thine adversary **to the magistrate, as** thou art in (continued in column 3)	67 **Why goest thou to** thine adversary **for a mag**istrate, **when** thou art in (continued in column 4)		

Luke 13	JST Luke 13		

99. Galileans Sacrificed-- Tower of Siloam

There were present at that **season** some **that told** him of the Galilæans, whose blood Pilate had mingled with their sacrifices.

2 And Jesus **answering** said unto them, Suppose ye that these Galilæans were sinners above all the Galilæans, because they suffered such things?

3 I tell you, Nay: but, except ye repent, ye shall all likewise perish.

4 Or those eighteen, upon whom the tower in Siloam fell, and slew them, think ye that they were sinners above all men **that** dwelt in Jerusalem?

5 I Tell you, Nay: but, except ye repent, ye shall all likewise perish.

And there were present at that **time**, some **who spake unto** him of the Galilæans, whose blood Pilate had mingled with their sacrifices.

2 And Jesus said unto them; Suppose ye that these Galilæans were sinners above all the Galilæans, because they suffered such things?

4 Or those eighteen, on whom the tower in Siloam fell, and slew them; think ye that they were sinners above all men **who** dwelt in Jerusalem?

100. Parable of the Barren Fig Tree

6 ¶ He spake also this parable; A certain man had a fig tree planted in **his** vineyard; **and** he came and sought fruit thereon, and found none.

7 Then said he unto the dresser of his vineyard, Behold, these three years I come seeking fruit on this fig tree, and find none: cut it down; why cumbereth it the ground?

8 And he answering said unto him, Lord, let it alone this year also, till I shall dig about **it**, and dung it:

9 And if it bear fruit, **well**: and if not, **then** after that thou shalt cut it down.

6 He spake also this parable; A certain **husbandman** had a fig tree planted in **the** vineyard. He came and sought fruit thereon and found none.

8 And he, answering, said unto him, Lord, let it alone this year also, till I shall dig about and dung it.

9 And if it bear fruit, **the tree is saved,** and if not, after that thou shalt cut it down. **And many other parables spake he unto the people.**

101. Woman Healed on the Sabbath

Luke 13	JST Luke 13
10 And he was teaching in one of the synagogues on the sabbath.	10 And **after this, as** he was teaching in one of the synagogues on the Sabbath;
11 ¶ **And**, behold, there was a woman **which** had a spirit of infirmity eighteen years, and was bowed together, and could in no wise **lift** up **herself**.	11 Behold, there was a woman **who** had a spirit of infirmity eighteen years, and was bowed together, and could in no wise **straighten** up.
12 And when Jesus saw her, he called **her to him**, and said unto her, Woman, thou art loosed from thine infirmity.	12 And when Jesus saw her, he called and said unto her, Woman, thou art loosed from thine infirm-ities.
13 And he laid **his** hands on her: and immediately she was made straight, and glorified God.	13 And he laid hands on her; and immediately she was made straight, and glorified God.
14 And the ruler of the synagogue **answered** with indignation, because that Jesus had healed on the sabbath day, and said unto the people, There are six days in which men ought to work: in them therefore come and be healed, and not on the sabbath day.	14 And the ruler of the synagogue **was filled** with indignation, because that Jesus had healed on the Sabbath day, and said unto the people, There are six days in which men ought to work; in them therefore come and be healed, and not on the Sabbath day.
15 The Lord then **an-swered** him, **and said, Thou** hypocrite, doth not each one of you on the sabbath loose his ox or his ass from the stall, and lead him away to watering?	15 The Lord then **said unto** him, **O** hypocrite! Doth not each one of you on the Sabbath loose his ox or his ass from the stall, and lead him away to watering?
16 And ought not this woman, being a daughter of Abraham, whom Satan hath bound, lo, these eigh-teen years, be loosed from this bond on the sabbath day?	
17 And when he had said these things, all his adver-saries were ashamed: and all **the people** rejoiced for all the glorious things **that** were done by him.	17 And when he had said these things, all his adver-saries were ashamed; and all **his disciples** rejoiced for all the glorious things **which** were done by him.

Matt. 11	JST Matt. 11	Luke 10	JST Luke 10

102. The Seventy's Return

Matt. 11	JST Matt. 11	Luke 10	JST Luke 10
		17 ¶ And the seventy returned again with joy, saying, Lord, even the devils are subject **unto** us through thy name. 18 And he said unto them, **I beheld Satan** as lightening fall from heaven.	19 And he said unto them, As lightening **falleth** from heaven, **I beheld Satan also falling.**
		19 Behold, I give unto you power **to tread on** serpents and scorpions, and over all the power of the enemy: and nothing shall by any means hurt you. 20 Notwithstanding in this rejoice not, that the spirits are subject unto you; but rather rejoice, because your names are written in heaven.	20 Behold, I **will** give unto you power **over** serpents and scorpions, and over all the power of the enemy; and nothing shall by any means hurt you.
25 ¶ At that time Jesus answered and said, I thank thee, O Father, Lord of heaven and earth, because thou hast hid these things from the wise and prudent, and hast revealed them unto babes.	27 **And** at that time, **there came a voice out of heaven, and** Jesus answered and said, I thank thee, O Father, Lord of heaven and earth, because thou hast hid these things from the wise and prudent, and hast revealed them unto babes. Even so, Father, for so it seemed good in thy sight!	21 ¶ In that hour Jesus rejoiced in spirit, and said, I thank thee, O Father, Lord of heaven and earth, that thou hast hid these things from **the** wise and prudent, and hast revealed them unto babes: even so, Father; for so it seemed good in thy sight.	22 In that hour Jesus rejoiced in spirit, and said, I thank thee, O Father, Lord of heaven and earth, that thou hast hid these things from **them who think they are** wise and prudent, and hast revealed them unto babes; even so, Father; for so it seemed good in thy sight.
26 Even so, Father: for so it seemed good in thy sight.			
27 All things are delivered unto me of my Father: and no man knoweth the Son, but the Father; neither knoweth any man the Father, save the Son, and **he** to whom**so**ever the Son will reveal him.	28 All things are delivered unto me of my Father; and no man knoweth the Son, but the Father; neither knoweth any man the Father, save the Son, and **they** to whom the Son will reveal himself; **they shall see the Father also.**	22 All things are delivered to me of my Father: and no man knoweth **who** the Son is, **but** the Father; and **who** the Father is, **but** the Son, **and he** to whom the Son will reveal **him.**	23 All things are delivered to me of my Father; and no man knoweth **that** the Son is the Father, and the Father is the Son, **but him** to whom the Son will reveal **it.**
		23 ¶ And he turned him unto **his** disciples, and said privately, Blessed are the eyes which see the things that ye see: 24 For I tell you, that many prophets and kings have desired to see those things which ye see, and have not seen them; and to	24 And he turned him unto **the** disciples, and said privately, Blessed are the eyes which see the things that ye see.

Matt. 11	JST Matt. 11	Luke 10	John 10
		hear those things which ye hear, and have not heard them.	
28 ¶ Come unto me, all ye that labour and are heavy laden, and I will give you rest. 29 Take my yoke upon you, and learn of me; for I am meek and lowly in heart: and ye shall find rest unto your souls. 30 For my yoke is easy, and my burden is light.	29 Then spake Jesus, saying, Come unto me, all ye that labor and are heavy laden, and I will give you rest.		

TPJS-- Some of the company thought I was not a very meek Prophet; so I told them: "I am meek and lowly in heart," and will personify Jesus for a moment, to illustrate the principle, and cried out with a loud voice, " Woe unto you, ye doctors; woe unto you, ye lawyers; woe unto you, ye scribes, Pharisees, and hypocrites!" But you cannot find the place where I ever went that I found fault with their food, their drink, their house, their lodgings; no, never; and this is what is meant by the meekness and lowliness of Jesus. (p. 270)

103. The Feast of Dedication

			John 10
			22 ¶ And it was at Jerusalem the feast of dedication, and it was winter. 23 And Jesus walked in the temple in Solomon's porch. 24 Then came the Jews round about him, and said unto him, How long dost thou make us to doubt? If thou be the Christ, tell us plainly. 25 Jesus answered them, I told you, and ye believed not: the works that I do in my Father's name, they bear witness of me. 26 But ye believe not, because ye are not of my sheep, as I said unto you. 27 My sheep hear my voice, and I know them, and they follow me: 28 And I give unto them eternal life; and they shall never perish, neither shall any man pluck them out of my hand.

	D & C	John 10	Psalms
	50:43 And the Father and I are one. I am in the Father and the Father in me; and inasmuch as ye have received me, ye are in me and I in you.	29 My Father, which gave them me, is greater than all; and no man is able to pluck them out of my Father's hand. 30 I and my Father are one. 31 Then the Jews took up stones again to stone him. 32 Jesus answered them, Many good works have I shewed you from my Father; for which of those works do ye stone me? 33 The Jews answered him, saying, For a good work we stone thee not; but for blasphemy; and because that thou, being a man, makest thyself God. 34 Jesus answered them, Is it not written in your law, I said, Ye are gods? 35 If he called them gods, unto whom the word of God came, and the scripture cannot be broken; 36 Say ye of him, whom the Father hath sanctified, and sent into the world, Thou blasphemest; because I said, I am the Son of God?	82:6 I have said, Ye are gods; and all of you are children of the most High.

TPJS-- I want to stick to my text, to show that when men open their lips against these truths they do not injure me, but injure themselves. To the law and to the testimony, for these principles are poured out all over the Scriptures. When things that are of the greatest importance are passed over by the weakminded men without even a thought, I want to see truth in all its bearings and hug it to my bosom. I believe all that God ever revealed, and I never hear of a man being damned for believing too much; but they are damned for unbelief.

They found fault with Jesus Christ because He said He was the Son of God, and made Himself equal with God. They say of me, like they did of the Apostles of old, that I must be put down. What did Jesus say? [John 10:34-36] (p. 373-374)

		John 10	
		37 If I do not the works of my Father, believe me not. 38 But if I do, though ye believe me not, believe the works: that ye may know, and believe, that the Father is in me, and I in him. 39 Therefore they sought again to take him: but he escaped out of their hand,	

Luke 13	JST Luke 13	John 10	Book of Mormon

The Perean Ministry

104. Cities and Villages—Jesus Teaching

Luke 13	JST Luke 13	John 10	Book of Mormon
		40 And went away again beyond Jordan into the place where John at first baptized; and there he abode.	1 Nephi 10:9 And my father said he should baptize in Bethabara, beyond Jordan; and he also said he should baptize with water; even that he should baptize the Messiah with water.
		41 And many resorted unto him, and said, John did no miracle: but all things that John spake of this man were true.	
22 And he went through the cities and villages, teaching, and journeying toward Jerusalem.		42 And many believed on him there.	
23 **Then** said one unto him, Lord, are there few that be saved? And he said **unto them,**	23 **And there** said one unto him, Lord, are there few **only** that be saved? and he **answered him, and** said,		
24 ¶ Strive to enter in at the strait gate: for **many,** I say unto you, **will** seek to enter in, and shall not be able.	24 Strive to enter in at the strait gate; for I say unto you, **Many shall** seek to enter in, and shall not be able; **for the Lord shall not always strive with man.**		
25 When once the **master** of the **house** is risen up, and hath shut to the door, **and** ye **begin to** stand without, and **to** knock at the door, saying, Lord, Lord, open unto us; **and he** shall answer and say unto you, I know **you** not whence ye are:	25 **Therefore,** when once the **Lord** of the **kingdom** is risen up, and hath shut the door **of the kingdom then** ye **shall** stand without, and knock at the door, saying, Lord, Lord, open unto us. **But the Lord** shall answer and say unto you, I **will not receive you, for ye** know not **from** whence ye are.		
26 Then shall ye being to say, We have eaten and drunk in thy presence, and thou hast taught in our streets.			
27 But he shall say, I tell you, **I** know not from whence ye are; depart from me, all **ye** workers of iniquity.	27 But he shall say, I tell you, **ye** know not **from** whence ye are; depart form me, all workers of iniquity.		
28 There shall be weeping and gnashing of teeth, when ye shall see Abraham, and Isaac, and Jacob, and all the prophets, in the	28 There shall be weeping and gnashing of teeth **among you,** when ye shall see Abraham, and Isaac, and Jacob, and all the		

Luke 13	JST Luke 13	TPJS
kingdom of God, and you **yourselves** thrust out.	prophets, in the kingdom of God, and you **are** thrust out.	
29 And they shall come from the east, and **from** the west, and from the north, and **from** the south, and shall sit down in the kingdom of God.	29 And **verily I say unto you,** They shall come from the east, and the west; and from the north, and the south, and shall sit down in the kingdom of God.	
30 And, behold, there are last which shall be first, and there are first which shall be last.	30 And, behold, there are last which shall be first, and there are first which shall be last, **and shall be saved therein.**	
31 ¶ **The same day** there came certain of the Pharisees, saying unto him, Get thee out, and depart hence: for Herod will kill thee.	31 **And as he was thus teaching,** there came **to him** certain of the Pharisees, saying unto him, Get thee out, and depart hence; for Herod will kill thee.	My feelings at the present time are that, inasmuch as the Lord Almighty has preserved me until today, He will continue to preserve me, by the united faith and prayers of the Saints, until I have fully accomplished my mission in this life, and so firmly established the dispensation of the fullness of the priesthood in the last days, that all the powers of earth and hell can never prevail against it.
32 And he said unto them, Go ye, and tell **that fox,** Behold, I cast out devils, and I do cures to day and to morrow, and the third day I shall be perfected.	32 And he said unto them, Go ye, and tell **Herod,** Behold, I cast out devils, and do cures to-day and to-morrow, and the third day I shall be perfected.	This constant persecution reminds me of the words of the Savior, when He said to the Pharisees, "Go ye, and tell that fox, Behold, I cast out devils, and I do cures today and tomorrow, and the third day I shall be perfected." I suspect that my Heavenly Father has decreed that the Missourians shall not get me into their power; if they do, it will be because I do not keep out of their way. (p. 258)
33 Nevertheless I must walk to day, and to morrow, and the day **following**: for it cannot be that a prophet perish out of Jerusalem.	33 Nevertheless I must walk to-day and to-morrow, and the **third** day; for it cannot be that a prophet perish out of Jerusalem.	
	34 **This he spake, signifying of his death. And in this very hour he began to weep over Jerusalem,**	
34 O Jerusalem, Jerusalem, **which** killest the prophets, and stonest them **that** are sent unto thee; how often would I have gathered thy children together, as a hen **doth gather** her brood under her wings, and ye would not!	35 **Saying,** O Jerusalem, Jerusalem, **thou who** killest the prophets, and stonest them **who** are sent unto thee; how often would I have gathered thy children together, as a hen her brood under her wings, and ye would not.	
35 Behold, your house is left unto you desolate: and verily I say unto you, Ye shall not **see** me,	36 Behold, your house is left unto you desolate. And verily I say unto you, Ye shall not **know** me, **until ye have received from the hand of the Lord a just recompense for all your sins;** until the time come	
until the time come when ye shall say, Blessed is he **that** cometh in the name of the Lord.	when ye shall say, Blessed is he **who** cometh in the name of the Lord.	

Luke 14	JST Luke 14		

105. House of One of the Chief Pharisees-- Man with Dropsy Healed

And it came to pass, as he went into the house of one of the chief Pharisees to eat bread on the sabbath day, that they watched him.			
2 And, behold, there was a certain man before him **which** had the dropsy.	2 And, behold, there was a certain man before him, **who** had the dropsy.		
3 And Jesus **answering** spake unto the lawyers and Pharisees, saying, Is it lawful to heal on the sabbath day?	3 And Jesus spake unto the lawyers, and Pharisees, saying, Is it lawful to heal on the Sabbath day?		
4 And they held their peace. And he took **him**, and healed him, and let him go;	4 And they held their peace. And he took **the man,** and healed him, and let him go;		
5 And **answered** them, saying, Which of you shall have an ass or an ox fallen into a pit, and will not straightway pull him out on the sabbath day?	5 And **spake unto** them **again,** saying, Which of you shall have an ass or an ox fallen into a pit, and will not straightway pull him out on the Sabbath day?		
6 And they could not answer him **again** to these things.	6 And they could not answer him to these things.		

106. Parable of the Wedding Feast

7 ¶ And he put forth a parable to those **which** were bidden, **when he marked** how they chose out the chief rooms; **saying** unto them,	7 And he put forth a parable **unto them concerning** those **who** were bidden **to a wedding; for** h e **knew** how they chose out the chief rooms, **a n d exalted themselves one above another; wherefore he spake** unto them, **saying,**		
8 When thou art bidden of any man to a wedding, sit not down in the highest room; lest a more honourable man than thou be bidden of him;			
9 And he **that** bade thee **and** him come and say to thee, Give this man place; and thou begin with shame to take the lowest room.	9 And he **who** bade thee, **with** him **who is more honorable,** come, and say to thee; Give this man place; and thou begin with shame to take the lowest room.		

228

Luke 14	JST Luke 14	D & C	
10 But when thou art bidden, go and sit down in the lowest room; that when he **that** bade thee cometh, he may say unto thee, Friend, go up higher: then shalt thou have **worship** in the presence of them **that** sit at meat with thee.	10 But when thou art bidden, go and sit down in the lowest room; that when he **who** bade thee, cometh, he may say unto thee, Friend, go up higher; then shalt thou have **honor of God,** in the presence of them **who** sit at meat with thee.		
11 For whosoever exalteth himself shall be abased; and he **that** humbleth himself shall be exalted.	11 For whosoever exalteth himself shall be abased; and he **who** humbleth himself shall be exalted.		

107. Parable of the Great Supper

12 ¶ Then said he also **to** him **that** bade **him,** When thou makest a dinner or a supper, call not thy friends, nor thy brethren, neither thy kinsmen, nor **thy** rich neighbours; lest they also bid thee again, and a recompence be made thee.	12 Then said he also **concerning** him **who** bade **to the wedding,** When thou makest a dinner, or a supper, call not thy friends, nor thy brethren, neither thy kinsmen, nor rich neighbors; lest they also bid thee again, and a recompense be made thee.		
13 But when thou makest a feast, call the poor, the maimed, the lame, the blind:			
14 And thou shalt be blessed; for they cannot recompense thee: for thou shalt be recompensed at the resurrection of the just.			
15 ¶ And when one of them **that** sat at meat with him heard these things, he said unto him, Blessed is he **that** shall eat bread in the kingdom of God.	15 And when one of them **who** sat at meat with him, heard these things, he said unto him, Blessed is he **who** shall eat bread in the kingdom of God.		
16 Then said he unto him, A certain man made a great supper, and bade many:		58:9 Yea, a supper of the house of the Lord, well prepared, unto which all nations shall be invited.	
17 And sent his **servant** at supper time to say to them **that** were bidden, Come; for all things are now ready.	17 And sent his **servants** at supper time, to say to them **who** were bidden, Come, for all things are now ready.	10 First, the rich and the learned, the wise and the noble;	
18 And they all with one consent began to make excuse. The first said unto him, I have bought a piece of ground, and I must			

Luke 14	JST Luke 14	D & C	
needs go and see it: I pray thee have me excused.			
19 And another said, I have bought five yoke of oxen, and I go to prove them: I pray thee have me excused.			
20 And another said, I have married a wife, **and** therefore I cannot come.	20 And another said, I have married a wife, therefore I cannot come.		
21 So that servant came, and shewed his lord these things. Then the master of the house being angry said to his **servant**, Go out quickly into the streets and lanes of the city, and bring **in** hither the poor, and the maimed, **and** the halt, and the blind.	21 So that servant came and showed his lord these things. Then the master of the house, being angry, said to his **servants**, Go out quickly into the streets and lanes of the city, and bring hither the poor, and the maimed, the halt and the blind.	58:11 And after that cometh the day of my power; then shall the poor, the lame, and the blind, and the deaf, come in unto the marriage of the Lamb, and partake of the supper of the Lord, prepared for the great day to come.	
22 And the servant said, Lord, it is done as thou hast commanded, and yet there is room.			
23 **And** the lord said unto **the** servant, Go out into the highways and hedges, and compel **them** to come in, that my house may be filled.	23 The Lord said unto **his** servant, Go out into the highways, and hedges, and compel **men** to come in, that my house may be filled;		
24 For I say unto you, That none of those men **which** were bidden shall taste of my supper.	24 For I say unto you, That none of those men **who** were bidden, shall taste of my supper.		

108. Perea-- Multitudes Follow Jesus-- Cost of Discipleship

	25 **And when he had finished these sayings, he departed thence**, and there went great multitudes with him, and he turned and said unto them,		
25 ¶ And there went great multitudes with him: and he turned, and said unto them,			
26 If any man come to me, and hate not his father, and mother, and wife, and children, and brethren, and sisters, yea, and his own life also,	26 If any man come to me, and hate not his father, and mother, and wife, and children, and brethren, and sisters, **or husband**, yea and his own life also; **or in other words, is afraid to lay down his life for my sake**, cannot be my disciple.		
he cannot be my disciple.			
27 And whosoever doth not bear his cross, and			

Luke 14	JST Luke 14	Luke 14	JST Luke 14
come after me, cannot be my disciple.			to this intent they were written. For I am sent that ye might have life. Therefore I will liken it unto salt which is good;
	28 Wherefore, settle this in your hearts, that ye will do the things which I shall teach, and command you.	34 ¶ Salt is good: but if the salt have lost his savour, wherewith shall it be seasoned?	37 But if the salt has lost its savor, wherewith shall it be seasoned?
28 For which of you, intending to build a tower, sitteth not down first, and counteth the cost, whether he have sufficient to finish it?	29 For which of you intending to build a tower, sitteth not down first, and counteth the cost, whether he have money to finish his work?	35 It is neither fit for the land nor yet for the dunghill; but men cast it out. He that hath ears to hear, let him hear.	38 It is neither fit for the land, nor yet for the dunghill; men cast it out. He who hath ears to hear, let him hear. These things he said, signifying that which was written, verily must all be fulfilled.
29 Lest haply, after he hath laid the foundation, and is not able to finish it, all that behold it begin to mock him,	30 Lest, unhappily, after he has laid the foundation and is not able to finish his work, all who behold, begin to mock him,		
30 Saying, This man began to build, and was not able to finish.	31 Saying, This man began to build, and was not able to finish. And this he said, signifying there should not any man follow him, unless he was able to continue; saying,		
31 Or what king, going to make war against another king, sitteth not down first, and consulteth whether he be able with ten thousand to meet him that cometh against him with twenty thousand?			
32 Or else, while the other is yet a great way off, he sendeth an ambassage, and desireth conditions of peace.			
33 So likewise, whosoever he be of you that forsaketh not all that he hath, he cannot be my disciple.	34 So likewise, whosoever of you forsaketh not all that he hath he cannot be my disciple.		
	35 Then certain of them came to him, saying, Good Master, we have Moses and the prophets, and whosoever shall live by them, shall he not have life?		
	36 And Jesus answered, saying, Ye know not Moses, neither the prophets; for if ye had known them, ye would have believed on me; for		
(continued in column 3)	(continued in column 4)		

231

109. Parables of the Lost

Then drew near unto him **all** the publicans and sinners **for** to hear him.

2 And the Pharisees and scribes murmured, saying, This man receiveth sinners, and eateth with them.

3 ¶ And he spake this parable unto them, saying,

4 What man of you, having **an** hundred sheep, if he lose one of them, doth not leave the ninety and nine in the wilderness, **and** go after that which is lost, until he find it?

5 And when he hath found it, he layeth it on his shoulders, rejoicing.

6 And when he cometh home, he calleth together his friends and neighbours, **saying** unto them, Rejoice with me; for I have found my sheep which was lost.

7 I say unto you, that likewise joy shall be in heaven over one sinner that repenteth, more than over ninety and nine just persons, **which** need no repentance.

Then drew near unto him, **many of** the publicans, and sinners, to hear him.

4 What man of you having **a** hundred sheep, if he lose one of them, doth not leave the ninety and nine, **and** go into the wilderness after that which is lost, until he find it?

6 And when he cometh home, he calleth together his friends and neighbors, **and saith** unto them, Rejoice with me; for I found my sheep which was lost.

7 I say unto you, that likewise joy shall be in heaven over one sinner that repenteth, more than over ninety and nine just persons, **who** need no repentance.

TPJS-- The hundred sheep represent one hundred Sadducees and Pharisees, as though Jesus had said, "If you Sadducees and Pharisees are in the sheepfold, I have no mission for you; I am sent to look up sheep that are lost; and when I have found them, I will back them up and make joy in heaven." This represents hunting after a few individuals, or one poor publican, which the Pharisees and Sadducees despised (p. 277).

8 ¶ Either what woman having ten pieces of silver, if she lose one piece, doth not light a candle, and sweep the house, and seek diligently till she find it?

9 And when she hath found it, she calleth her
(continued in column 3)

---

9 And when she hath found it, she calleth her
(continued in column 4)

---

friends and **her** neighbours together, saying, Rejoice with me; for I have found the piece which I had lost.

10 Likewise, I say unto you, there is joy in the presence of the angels of God over one sinner **that** repenteth.

TPJS-- He also gave them the parable of the woman and her ten pieces of silver, and how she lost one, and searching diligently, found it again, which gave more joy among the friends and neighbors than the nine which were not lost; like I say unto you, there is joy in the presence of the angels of God over one sinner that repenteth, more than over the ninety-and-nine just persons that are so righteous; they will be damned anyhow; you cannot save them. (pp. 277-278)

11 ¶ And he said, A certain man had two sons:

12 And the younger of them said to his father, Father, give me the portion of goods **that** falleth to me. And he divided unto them his living.

13 And not many days after the younger son gathered all together, and took his journey into a far country, and there wasted his substance with riotous living.

14 And when he had spent all, there arose a mighty famine in that land; and he began to be in want.

15 And he went and joined himself to a citizen of that country; and he sent him into his fields to feed swine.

16 And he would fain have filled his belly with the husks **that** the swine did eat: and no man gave unto him.

17 And when he came to himself, he said, How many hired servants of my

---

friends and neighbors together, saying, Rejoice with me, for I have found the piece which I had lost.

10 Likewise I say unto you, there is joy in the presence of the angels of God over one sinner **who** repenteth.

12 And the younger of them said unto his father, Father, give me the portion of goods **which** falleth to me. And he divided unto them his living.

16 And he would fain have filled his belly with the husks **which** the swine did eat; and no man gave unto him.

Luke 15	JST Luke 15	Luke 15	JST Luke 15
father's have bread enough and to spare, and I perish with hunger! 18 I will arise and go to my father, and will say unto him, Father, I have sinned against heaven, and before thee, 19 And am no more worthy to be called thy son: make me as one of thy hired servants. 20 And he arose, and came to his father. But when he was yet a great way off, his father saw him, and had compassion, and ran, and fell on his neck, and kissed him. 21 And the son said unto him, Father, I have sinned against heaven, and in thy sight, and am no more worthy to be called thy son. 22 But the father said to his servants, Bring forth the best robe, and put it on him; and put a ring on his **hand**, and shoes on his feet: 23 And bring hither the fatted calf, and kill it; and let us eat, and be merry: 24 For this my son was dead, and is alive again; he was lost, and is found. And they began to be merry. 25 Now his elder son was in the field: and as he came and drew nigh to the house, he heard musick and dancing. 26 And he called one of the servants, and asked what these things meant. 27 And he said unto him, Thy brother is come; and thy father hath killed the (continued in column 3)	22 But the father said **un**to his servants, Bring forth the best robe, and put it on him; and put a ring on his **finger**, and shoes on his feet;	fatted calf, because he hath received him safe and sound. 28 And he was angry, and would not go in: therefore came his father out, and in-treated him. 29 And he answering said to his father, Lo, these many years do I serve thee, neither transgressed I at any time thy command-ment: and **yet** thou never gavest me a kid, that I might make merry with my friends: 30 But as soon as this thy son was come, **which** hath devoured thy living with harlots, thou hast killed for him the fatted calf. 31 And he said unto him, Son, thou art ever with me, and all that I have is thine. 32 It was meet that we should make merry, and be glad: for this thy brother was dead, and is alive again; **and** was lost, and is found.	29 And he answering, said to his father, Lo, these many years do I serve thee, neither transgressed I at any time thy command-ment; and thou never gav-est me a kid, that I might make merry with my friends; 30 But as soon as this thy son was come, **who** hath devoured thy living with harlots, thou hast killed for him the fatted calf. 32 It was meet that we should make merry, and be glad; for this thy brother was dead, and is alive again; was lost, and is found.

TPJS-- In reference to the prodigal son, I said it was a subject I had never dwelt upon; that it was understood by many to be one of the intricate subjects of the scriptures; and even the Elders of this Church have preached largely upon it, without having any rule of interpretation. What is the rule of interpretation? Just no interpretation at all. Understand it precisely as it reads. I have a key by which I understand the scriptures. I enquire, what was the question which drew out the answer, or caused Jesus to utter the parable? It is not national; it does not refer to Abraham, Israel or the Gentiles, in a national capacity, as some suppose. To ascertain its meaning, we must dig up the root and ascertain what it was that drew the saying out of Jesus.

While Jesus was teaching the people, all the publicans and sinners drew near to Him; "and the Pharisees and scribes murmured, saying: This man receiveth sinners, and eateth with them." This is the keyword which unlocks the parable of the prodigal son. It was given to answer the murmurings and questions of the Sadducees and Pharisees, who were querying, finding fault, and saying, "How is it that this man as great as He pretends to be, eats with publicans and sinners?" Jesus was not put to it so, but He could have found something to illustrate His subject, if He had designed it for a nation or nations; but He did not. It was for men in an individual capacity; and all straining on this point is a bubble. "This man receiveth sinners and eateth with them." (pp. 276-277)

233

Luke 16	JST Luke 16 D&C	Luke 16	JST Luke 16 D&C

110. Parable of the Unjust Steward

And he said also unto his disciples, There was a certain rich man, which had a steward; and the same was accused unto him that he had wasted his goods.

2 And he called him, and said unto him, How is it that I hear this of thee? give an account of thy stewardship; for thou mayest be no longer steward.

3 Then the steward said within himself, What shall I do? for my lord taketh away from me the stewardship: I cannot dig; to beg I am ashamed.

4 I am resolved what to do, that, when I am put out of the stewardship, they may receive me into their houses.

5 So he called every one of his lord's debtors **unto him**, and said unto the first, How much owest thou unto my lord?

6 And he said, An hundred measures of oil. And he said unto him, Take thy bill, and sit down quickly, and write fifty.

7 Then said he to another, And how much owest thou? And he said, **An** hundred measures of wheat. And he said unto him, Take thy bill, and write fourscore.

8 And the lord commended the unjust steward, because he had done wisely: for the children of this world are in their generation **wiser** than the children of light.

9 And I say unto you, Make to yourselves friends of the mammon of unrighteousness; that, when ye
(continued in column 3)

---

5 So he called every one of his lord's debtors, and said unto the first, How much owest thou unto my lord?

8 And the lord commended the unjust steward, because he had done wisely; for the children of this world are **wiser** in their generation, than the children of light.

D&C 82:22 And now, verily I say unto you, and this is wisdom, make unto yourselves friends with
(continued in column 4)

---

fail, they may receive you into everlasting habitations.

10 He **that** is faithful in that which is least is faithful also in much: and he **that** is unjust in the least is unjust also in much.

11 If therefore ye have not been faithful in the unrighteous mammon, who will commit to your trust the true riches?

12 And if ye have not been faithful in that which is another man's, who shall give you that which is your own?

13 ¶ No servant can serve two masters: for either he will hate the one, and love the other; or else he will hold to the one, and despise the other. Ye cannot serve God and mammon.

14 And the Pharisees also, who were covetous, heard all these things: and they derided him.

15 And he said unto them, Ye are they **which** justify yourselves before men; but God knoweth your hearts: for that which is highly esteemed among men is abomination in the sight of God.

16 The law and the prophets **were** until John:

---

the mammon of unrighteousness, and they will not destroy you.

10 He **who** is faithful in that which is least, is faithful also in much; and he **who** is unjust in the least, is also unjust in much.

12 And if ye have not been faithful in that which is another man's, who shall give **unto** you that which is your own?

15 And he said unto them, Ye are they **who** justify yourselves before men; but God knoweth your hearts; for that which is highly esteemed among men, is **an** abomination in the sight of God.

16 **And they said unto him, We have the law, and the prophets; but as for this man we will not receive him to be our ruler; for he maketh himself to be a judge over us.**

17 **Then said Jesus unto them**, The law and the prophets **testify of me; yea, and all the prophets who have written, even until John, have foretold of these days.**

234

Luke 16	JST Luke 16		
since that time the kingdom of God is preached, and every man presseth into it. 17 And it is easier for heaven and earth to pass, than one tittle of the law to fail.	18 Since that time, the kingdom of God is preached, and every man **who seeketh truth** presseth into it. 19 And it is easier for heaven and earth to pass, than **for** one tittle of the law to fail. 20 **And why teach ye the law, and deny that which is written; and condemn him whom the Father hath sent to fulfill the law, that ye might all be redeemed?** 21 **O fools! for you have said in your hearts, There is no God. And you pervert the right way; and the kingdom of heaven suffereth violence of you; and you persecute the meek; and in your violence you seek to destroy the kingdom; and ye take the children of the kingdom by force. Woe unto you, ye adulterers!** 22 **And they reviled him again, being angry for the saying, that they were adulterers.** 23 **But he continued, saying,** Whosoever putteth		
18 Whosoever putteth away his wife, and marrieth another, committeth adultery: and whosoever marrieth her that is put away from her husband committeth adultery.	away his wife, and marrieth another, committeth adultery; and whosoever marrieth her who is put away from her husband, committeth adultery. **Verily I say unto you, I will liken you unto the rich man.**		

Luke 16	JST Luke 16	Luke 16	JST Luke 16 B of M

111. Parable of the Rich Man and Lazarus

Luke 16	JST Luke 16	Luke 16	JST Luke 16 B of M
19 ¶ There was a certain rich man, **which** was clothed in purple and fine linen, and fared sumptuously every day:	24 **For** there was a certain rich man, **who** was clothed in purple, and fine linen, and fared sumptuously every day.	26 And beside all this, between us and you there is a great gulf fixed: so that they **which** would pass from hence to you cannot; neither can they pass to us, that would come from thence.	31 And besides all this, between us and you, there is a great gulf fixed; so that they **who** would pass from hence to you cannot; neither can they pass to us that would come from thence.
20 And there was a certain beggar named Lazarus, **which** was laid at his gate, full of sores.	25 And there was a certain beggar named Lazarus, **who** was laid at his gate, full of sores,	27 Then he said, I pray thee therefore, father, that thou wouldest send him to my father's house:	1 Nephi 15:28 And I said unto them that it was an awful gulf, which separated the wicked from the tree of life, and also from the saints of God.
21 And desiring to be fed with the crumbs which fell from the rich man's table: moreover the dogs came and licked his sores.		28 For I have five brethren; that he may testify unto them, lest they also come into this place of torment.	
22 And it came to pass, that the beggar died, and was carried **by** the angels into Abraham's bosom: the rich man also died, and was buried;	27 And it came to pass, that the beggar died, and was carried **of** the angels into Abraham's bosom. The rich man also died, and was buried.	29 Abraham saith unto him, They have Moses and the prophets: let them hear them.	29 And I said unto them that it was a representation of that awful hell, which the angel said unto me was prepared for the wicked.
23 And in hell he lift up his eyes, being in torments, and **seeth** Abraham afar off, and Lazarus in his bosom.	28 and in hell he lif**ted** up his eyes, being in torments, and **saw** Abraham afar off, and Lazarus in his bosom.	30 And he said, Nay, father Abraham: but if one went unto them from the dead, they will repent.	30 And I said unto them that our father also saw that the justice of God did also divide the wicked from the righteous. . .
D&C 104:18 therefore, if any man shall take of the abundance which I have made, and impart not his portion, according to the law of my gospel, unto the poor and the needy, he shall with the wicked, lift up his eyes in hell, being in torment.		31 And he said unto him, If they hear not Moses and the prophets, neither will they be persuaded, though one **rose** from the dead.	(See also Alma 40:9-14) JST Luke 16:36 And he said unto him, If they hear not Moses and the prophets, neither will they be persuaded, though one **should rise** from the dead.
24 And he cried and said, Father Abraham, have mercy on me, and send Lazarus, that he may dip the tip of his finger in water, and cool my tongue; for I am tormented in this flame.			
25 But Abraham said, Son, remember that thou in thy lifetime receivedst thy good tings, and likewise Lazarus evil things: but now he is comforted, and thou art tormented.			
(continued in column 3)	(continued in column 4)		

236

Luke 17	JST Luke 17		

112. Disciples Warned of Offences

Then said he unto the disciples, It is impossible but that offences will come: but woe **unto** him, through whom they come!

2 It were better for him that a millstone were hanged about his neck, and he cast into the sea, than that he should offend one of these little ones.

3 ¶ Take heed to yourselves: If **thy** brother trespass against **thee**, rebuke him; and if he repent, forgive him.

4 And if he trespass against **thee** seven times in a day, and seven times in a day turn again to **thee**, saying, I repent; **thou** shalt forgive him.

5 And the apostles said unto **the** Lord, Increase our faith.

6 And the Lord said, If **ye** had faith as a grain of mustard seed, **ye** might say unto this **sycamine** tree, Be thou plucked up by the root, and be thou planted in the sea; and it should obey you.

7 But **which** of you, having a servant plowing or feeding cattle, will say unto him **by and by**, when he is come from the field, Go and sit down to meat?

8 **And** will not rather say unto him, Make ready wherewith I may sup, and gird **thyself**, and serve me, till I have eaten and drunken; and afterward **thou** shalt eat and drink?

9 Doth he thank that servant because he **did the** things **that** were commanded him? I **trow not**.

3 Take heed to yourselves. If **your** brother trespass against you, rebuke him; and if he repent, forgive him.

4 And if he trespass against **you** seven times in a day, and seven times in a day turn to **you** again, saying, I repent; **you** shall forgive him.

5 And **the** apostles said unto **him**, Lord, increase our faith.

6 And the Lord said, If **you** had faith as a grain of mustard seed, **you** might say unto this **sycamore** tree, Be thou plucked up by the roots, and be thou planted in the sea; and it should obey you.

7 But **who** of you, having a servant plowing, or feeding cattle, will say unto him when he is come from the field, Go and sit down to meat?

8 **Will** **he** not rather say unto him, Make ready wherewith I may sup, and gird **yourself** and serve me till I have eaten and drunken; and afterward, **by and by, you** shall eat and drink?

9 Doth he thank that servant because he **doeth** the things **which** were commanded him? I **say unto you, Nay.**

Luke 17	JST Luke 17		
10 So likewise ye, when ye shall have done all those things which are commanded of you, say, We are unprofitable servants: we have done that which was our duty to do.	10 So likewise ye, when ye shall have done all those things which are commanded you, say, We are unprofitable servants. We have done that which was **no more than** our duty to do.		

113. Village (Galilee and Samaria)-- Ten Lepers Cleansed

11 ¶ **And** it came to pass, as he went to Jerusalem, that he passed through the midst of **Samaria and Galilee.**	11 It came to pass, as he went to Jerusalem, that he passed through the midst of Galilee **and Samaria.**		
12 And as he entered into a certain village, there met him ten men **that** were lepers, **which** stood afar off:	12 And as he entered into a certain village, there met him ten men **who** were lepers, **who** stood afar off;		
13 And they lifted up their voices, and said, Jesus, Master, have mercy on us.			
14 And **when he saw them,** he said unto them, Go shew yourselves unto the priests. And it came to pass, **that,** as they went, they were cleansed.	14 And he said unto them, Go show yourselves unto the priests. And it came to pass, as they went, they were cleansed.		
15 **And** one of them, when he saw **that** he was healed, turned back, and with a loud voice glorified God,	15 One of them, when he saw he was healed, turned back, and with a loud voice glorified God,		
16 And fell down on his face at **his** feet, giving him thanks: and he was a Samaritan.	16 And fell down on his face at **Jesus'** feet, giving him thanks; and he was a Samaritan.		
17 And Jesus answering said, Were there not ten cleansed? but where are the nine?			
18 There are not found that returned to give glory to God, save this stranger.			
19 And he said unto him, Arise, go thy way: thy faith hath made thee whole.			

John 11	JST John 11	John 11	JST John 11

114. Bethany-- Lazarus Raised from the Dead

Now a certain man was sick, **named** Lazarus, of Bethany, **the town of Mary and her sister Martha.**
2 **(It was that** Mary **which** anointed the Lord with ointment, and wiped his feet with her hair, whose brother Lazarus was sick.)

3 Therefore his sisters sent unto him, saying, Lord, behold, he whom thou lovest is sick.
4 When Jesus heard **that,** he said, This sickness is not unto death, but for the glory of God, that the Son of God might be glorified thereby.
5 Now Jesus loved Martha, and her sister, and Lazarus.
6 **When** he **had** heard **therefore** that **he** was sick, **he abode two days still in** the same place where he was.
7 **Then** after that **saith** he to his disciples, Let us go into Judæa again.
8 His disciples **say** unto him, Master, the Jews of late sought to stone thee; and goest thou thither again?
9 Jesus answered, Are there not twelve hours in the day? If any man walk in the day, he stumbleth not, because he seeth the light of this world.
10 But if a man walk in the night, he stumbleth, because there is no light in him.
11 These things said he: and after that he saith unto them, Our friend Lazarus sleepeth; but I go, that I
(continued in column 3)

Now a certain man was sick, **whose name was** Lazarus, of **the town of** Bethany;
2 **And** Mary, **his sister, who** anointed the Lord with ointment and wiped his feet with her hair, **lived with her sister Martha, in** whose **house her** brother Lazarus was sick.

4 **And** when Jesus heard **he was sick,** he said, This sickness is not unto death, but for the glory of God, that the Son of God might be glorified thereby.

6 **And Jesus tarried two days,** after he heard that **Lazarus** was sick, in the same place where he was.
7 After that he **said unto** his disciples, Let us go into Judea again.
8 **But** his disciples **said** unto him, Master, the Jews of late sought to stone thee; and goest thou thither again?

(continued in column 4)

may awake him out of sleep.
12 Then said his disciples, Lord, if he sleep, he shall do well.
13 Howbeit Jesus spake of his death: but they thought that he had spoken of taking of rest in sleep.
14 Then said Jesus unto them plainly, Lazarus is dead.
15 And I am glad for your sakes that I was not there, to the intent ye may believe; nevertheless let us go unto him.
16 Then said Thomas, which is called Didymus, unto his fellow disciples, Let us also go, that we may die with him.

17 **Then** when Jesus came, **he found that he** had **lain** in the grave four days **already.**
18 Now Bethany was nigh unto Jerusalem, about fifteen furlongs off:
19 And many of the Jews came to Martha and Mary, to comfort them concerning their brother.
20 Then Martha, as soon as she heard that Jesus was coming, went and met him: but Mary sat still in the house.
21 Then said Martha unto Jesus, Lord, if thou hadst been here, my brother had not died.
22 But I know, that even now, whatsoever thou wilt ask of God, God will give it thee.

16 Then said Thomas, which is called Didymus, unto his fellow disciples, Let us also go, that we may die with him; **for they feared lest the Jews should take Jesus and put him to death, for as yet they did not understand the power of God.**
17 **And** when Jesus came **to Bethany, to Martha's house, Lazarus** had **already been** in the grave four days.

John 11	JST John 11	John 11	John 11
23 Jesus saith unto her, Thy brother shall rise again. 24 Martha saith unto him, I know that he shall rise again in the resurrection at the last day. 25 Jesus said unto her, I am the resurrection, and the life: he that believeth in me, though he were dead, yet shall he live: 26 And whosoever liveth and believeth in me shall never die. Believest thou this? 27 She saith unto him, Yea, Lord: I believe that thou art the Christ, the Son of God, which should come into the world. 28 And when she had so said, she went her way, and called Mary her sister secretly, saying, The Master is come, and calleth for thee. 29 As soon as **she** heard that, she arose quickly, and came unto him. 30 Now Jesus was not yet come into the town, but was in **that** place where Martha met him. 31 The Jews then which were with her in the house, and comforted her, when they saw Mary, that she rose up hastily and went out, followed her, saying, She goeth unto the grave to weep there. 32 Then when Mary was come where Jesus was, and saw him, she fell down at his feet, saying unto him, Lord, if thou hadst been here, my brother had not died. 33 When Jesus therefore saw her weeping, and the Jews also weeping which came with her, he groaned in the spirit, and was (continued in column 3)	29 As soon as **Mary** heard that **Jesus was come,** she arose quickly, and came unto him. 30 Now Jesus was not yet come into the town, but was in **the** place where Martha met him.	troubled, 34 And said, Where have ye laid him? They said unto him, Lord, come and see. 35 Jesus wept. 36 Then said the Jews, Behold how he loved him! 37 And some of them said, Could not this man, which opened the eyes of the blind, have caused that even this man should not have died? 38 Jesus therefore again groaning in himself cometh to the grave. It was a cave, and a stone lay upon it. 39 Jesus said, Take ye away the stone. Martha, the sister of him that was dead, saith unto him, Lord, by this time he stinketh: for he hath been dead four days. 40 Jesus saith unto her, Said I not unto thee, that, if thou wouldest believe, thou shouldest see the glory of God? 41 Then they took away the stone from the place where the dead was laid. And Jesus lifted up his eyes, and said, Father, I thank thee that thou hast heard me. 42 And I knew that thou hearest me always: but because of the people which stand by I said it, that they may believe that thou hast sent me. 43 And when he thus had spoken, he cried with a loud voice, Lazarus, come forth. 44 And he that was dead came forth, bound hand and foot with graveclothes: and his face was bound about with a napkin. Jesus saith unto them, Loose (continued in column 4)	him, and let him go. 45 Then many of the Jews which came to Mary, and had seen the things which Jesus did, believed on him. 46 But some of them went their ways to the Pharisees, and told them what things Jesus had done.

Luke 17		John 11	JST John 11

115. Chief Priests and Pharisees Plot to Kill Jesus

		47 ¶ Then gathered the chief priests and the Pharisees a council, and said, What do **we**? for this man doeth many miracles. 48 If we let him thus alone, all men will believe on him: and the Romans shall come and take away both our place and nation. 49 And one of them, named Caiaphas, being the high priest that same year, said unto them, Ye know nothing at all, 50 Nor consider that it is expedient for us, that one man should die for the people, and that the whole nation perish not. 51 And this spake he not of himself: but being high priest that year, he prophesied that Jesus should die for that nation; 52 And not for that nation only, but that also he should gather together in one the children of God that were scattered abroad. 53 Then from that day forth they took counsel together for to put him to death. 54 Jesus therefore walked no more openly among the Jews; but went thence unto a country near to the wilderness, into a city called Ephraim, and there continued with his disciples.	47 Then gathered the chief priests and the Pharisees a council, and said, What **shall we** do? for this man doeth many miracles.

116. Discourse on the Kingdom of God

20 ¶ And when he was demanded of the Pharisees, when the kingdom of God should come, he answered them and said, The kingdom of God cometh not with observation:			

Luke 17	JST Luke 17	Luke 17	JST Luke 17
21 Neither shall they say, Lo here! or, lo there! for, behold, the kingdom of God **is within** you.	21 Neither shall they say, Lo, here! or, Lo, there! For, behold, the kingdom of God **has already come unto** you.	him likewise not return back.	field, let him likewise not return back.
22 And he said unto **the** disciples, The days will come, when ye **shall** desire to see one of the days of the Son of **man**, and **ye** shall not see it.	22 And he said unto **his** disciples, The days will come, when **they will** desire to see one of the days of the Son of M an, and **they** shall not see it.	32 Remember Lot's wife. 33 Whosoever shall seek to save his life shall lose it; and whosoever shall lose his life shall preserve it.	
23 And they shall say to you, See here; or, see there: go not after them, nor follow them.	23 And **if** they shall say to you, See here! or, See there! Go not after them, nor follow them.	34 I tell you, in that night there shall be two **men** in one bed; the one shall be taken, and the other shall be left.	34 I tell you, in that night there shall be two in one bed; the one shall be taken, and the other shall be left.
24 For as the **lightning,** that **lighteneth** out of the one part under heaven, **shineth unto** the other part under heaven; so shall also the Son of **man** be in his day.	24 For as the **light of the morning,** that **shineth** out of the one part under heaven, **and lighteneth** to the other part under heaven; so shall also the Son of Man be in his day.	35 Two **women** shall be grinding together; the one shall be taken, and the other left.	Two shall be grinding together; the one shall be taken, and the other left.
25 But first must **he** suffer many things, and be rejected of this generation.	25 But first **he** must suffer many things, and be rejected of this generation.	36 Two **men** shall be in the field; the one shall be taken, and the other left.	35 Two shall be in the field; the one shall be taken, and the other left.
26 And as it was in the days of Noe, so shall it also be in the days of the Son of **man**.	26 And as it was in the days of Noe; so shall it be also in the days of the Son of Man.	37 And they answered and said unto him, Where, Lord? And he said unto them, Wheresoever the body is,	36 And they answered and said unto him, Where, Lord, **shall they be taken.**
27 They did eat, they drank, they married wives, they were given in marriage, until the day that Noe entered into the ark, and the flood came, and destroyed them all.		thither will the eagles be gathered together.	37 And he said unto them, Wheresoever the body is **gathered; or, in other words, whithersoever the saints are gathered,** thither will the eagles be gathered together; **or, thither will the remainder be gathered together.**
28 Likewise also as it was in the days of Lot; they did eat, they drank, they bought, they sold, they planted, they builded;			38 **This he spake, signifying the gathering of his saints; and of angels descending and gathering the remainder unto them; the one from the bed, the other from the grinding, and the other from the field, whithersoever he listeth.**
29 But the same day that Lot went out of Sodom it rained fire and brimstone from heaven, and destroyed them all.			39 **For verily there shall be new heavens, and a new earth, wherein dwelleth righteousness.**
30 Even thus shall it be in the day when the Son of man is revealed.	30 Even thus shall it be in the day when the Son of Man is revealed.		40 **And there shall be no unclean thing; for the earth becoming old, even as a garment, having waxed in corruption, wherefore it vanisheth away, and the footstool remaineth sanctified, cleansed from all sin.**
31 In that day, **he which** shall be **upon** the housetop, and his stuff in the house, let him not come down to take it away: and he **that** is in the field, let (continued in column 3)	31 In that day, **the disciple who** shall be on the housetop, and his stuff in the house, let him not come down to take it away; and he **who** is in the (continued in column 4)		

Luke 18	JST Luke 18	D & C	D & C

117. Two Parables

Luke 18	JST Luke 18	D & C	D & C
And he spake a parable unto them **to this end**, that men ought always to pray, and not **to** faint;	And he spake a parable unto them, **saying**, that men ought always to pray and not faint.	101:81 Now, unto what shall I liken the children of Zion? I will liken them unto the parable of the woman and the unjust judge, for men ought always to pray and not to faint, which saith--	91 Even in outer darkness, where there is weeping, and wailing, and gnashing of teeth.
2 Saying, There was in a city a judge, **which** feared not God, **neither** regarded man:	2 Saying, There was in a city a judge, **who** feared not God, **nor** regarded man.	(vss. 82-84 = Lk 18:2-5.)	92 Pray ye, therefore, that their ears may be opened unto your cries, that I may be merciful unto them, that these things may not come upon them.
3 And there was a widow in that city; and she came unto him, saying, Avenge me of mine adversary.		85 Thus will I liken the children of Zion.	93 What I have said unto you must needs be, that all men may be left without excuse;
4 And he would not for a while: but afterward he said within himself, Though I fear not God, nor regard man;		86 Let them importune at the feet of the judge;	94 That wise men and rulers may hear and know that which they have never considered;
5 Yet because this widow troubleth me, I will avenge her, lest by her continual coming she weary me.		87 And if he heed them not, let them importune at the feet of the governor;	
6 And the Lord said, Hear what the unjust judge saith.		88 And if the governor heed them not, let them importune at the feet of the president;	
7 And shall not God avenge his own elect, **which** cry day and night unto him, though he bear long with **them**?	7 And shall not God avenge his own elect, **who** cry day and night unto him, though he bear long with **men**?	89 And if the president heed them not, then will the Lord arise and come forth out of his hiding place, and in his fury vex the nation;	
8 I tell you that he will avenge **them** speedily. Nevertheless when the Son of man cometh, shall he find faith on the earth?	8 I tell you that he will **come, and when he does come, he** will avenge his **saints** speedily. Nevertheless, when the Son of Man cometh, shall he find faith on the earth?	90 And in his hot displeasure, and in his fierce anger, in his time, will cut off those wicked, unfaithful, and unjust stewards, and appoint them their portion among hypocrites, and unbelievers;	
9 **And** he spake this parable unto certain **which** trusted in themselves that they were righteous, and despised others:	9 He spake this parable unto certain **men, who** trusted in themselves that they were righteous, and despised others.		
10 Two men went up into the temple to pray; the one a Pharisee, and the other a publican.			
11 The Pharisee stood and prayed thus with himself, God, I thank thee, that I am not as other men **are**, extortioners, unjust, adulterers, or even as this publican.	11 The Pharisee stood and prayed thus with himself; God, I thank thee that I am not as other men, extortioners, unjust, adulterers; or even as this publican.		

Luke 18	JST Luke 18		D & C
12 I fast twice in the week, I give tithes of all that I possess. 13 **And** the publican, standing afar off, would not lift up so much as his eyes unto heaven, but smote upon his breast, saying, God be merciful to me a sinner. 14 I tell you, this man went down to his house justified rather than the other: for every one **that** exalteth himself shall be abased; and he **that** humbleth himself shall be exalted.	13 **But** the publican, standing afar off, would not lift up so much as his eyes unto heaven, but smote upon his breast, saying, God, be merciful to me a sinner. 14 I tell you, this man went down to his house justified, rather than the other; for every one **who** exalteth himself, shall be abased; and he **who** humbleth himself, shall be exalted.		101:95 That I may proceed to bring to pass my act, my strange act, and perform my work, my strange work, that men may discern between the righteous and the wicked, saith your God.

Matt.19	JST Matt. 19	Mark 10	JST Mark 10

118. Galilee to Judea-- Marriage and Divorce

And it came to pass, **that** when Jesus had finished these sayings, he departed from Galilee, and came into the coasts of Judæa beyond Jordan; 2 And great multitudes followed him; and he healed them there. 3 ¶ The Pharisees **also** came unto him, tempting him, and saying unto him, Is it lawful for a man to put away his wife for every cause?	And it came to pass, when Jesus had finished these sayings, he departed from Galilee, and came into the coasts of Judea beyond Jordan. 2 And great multitudes followed him; **and many believed on him,** and he healed them there. 3 The Pharisees came **also** unto him, tempting him, and saying unto him, Is it lawful for a man to put away his wife for every cause?	And he arose from thence, and cometh into the coasts of Judæa by the farther side of Jordan: and the people resort unto him again; and, as he was **wont,** he taught them again. 2 ¶ And the Pharisees came to him, and asked him, Is it lawful for a man to put away his wife? tempting him. 3 And he answered and said unto them, What did Moses command you? 4 And they said, Moses suffered to write a bill of divorcement, and to put her away.	And he arose from thence and cometh into the coasts of Judea by the farther side of Jordan; and the people resort unto him again; and as he was **accustomed to teach,** he also taught them again. 2 And the Pharisees came to him and asked him, Is it lawful for a man to put away his wife? **This they said, thinking to** tempt him.
4 And he answered and said unto them, Have ye not read, that he **which** made **them** at the beginning made **them** male and female,	4 And he answered and said unto them, Have ye not read, that he **who made man** at the beginning, made **him,** male and female,	6 But from the beginning of the creation God made them male and female.	

Matt. 19	JST Matt. 19	Mark 10	JST Mark 10
5 And said, For this cause shall a man leave father and mother, and shall cleave to his wife: and they twain shall be one flesh? 6 Wherefore they are no more twain, but one flesh. What therefore God hath joined together, let not man put asunder. 7 They say unto him, Why did Moses then command to give a writing of divorcement, and to put her away? 8 He **saith** unto them, Moses because of the hardness of your hearts suffered you to put away your wives: but from the beginning it was not so.		7 For this cause shall a man leave his father and mother, and cleave to his wife; 8 And they twain shall be one flesh: so then they are no more twain, but one flesh. 9 What therefore God hath joined together, let not man put asunder. 5 **And** Jesus answered and said unto them, For the hardness of your heart he wrote you this precept. 10 And in the house his disciples asked him again of the same matter.	 5 Jesus answered and said unto them, For the hardness of your hearts he wrote you this precept;
9 And I say unto you, Whosoever shall put away his wife, except **it be** for fornication, and shall marry another, committeth adultery: and whoso marrieth her **which** is put away doth commit adultery.	9 And I say unto you, Whosoever shall put away his wife, except for fornication, and shall marry another, committeth adultery; and whoso marrieth her **that** is put away, doth commit adultery.	11 And he saith unto them, Whosoever shall put away his wife, and marry another, committeth adultery against her. 12 And if a woman shall put away her husband, and be married to another, she committeth adultery.	
10 ¶ His disciples say unto him, If the case of the man be so with **his** wife, it is not good to marry. 11 But he said unto them, All **men** cannot receive this saying, save **they** to whom it is given. 12 For their are some eunuchs, which were so born from their mother's womb: and there are some eunuchs, which were made eunuchs of men: and there be eunuchs, which have made themselves eunuchs for the kingdom of heaven's sake. He that is able to receive **it**, let him receive **it**.	10 His disciples say unto him, If the case of the man be so with **a** wife, it is not good to marry. 11 But he said unto them, All cannot receive this saying; **it is not for them** save to whom it is given. 12 For their are some eunuchs, which so were born from their mother's womb; and there are some eunuchs which were made eunuchs of men; and there be eunuchs, which have made themselves eunuchs for the kingdom of heaven's sake. He that is able to receive, let him receive **my sayings.**		

245

Matt. 19	JST Matt. 19	Mark 10	JST Mark 10

119. Blesses Little Children

13 ¶ Then were there brought unto him little children, that he should put his hands on them, and pray: and the disciples rebuked them.	13 Then were there brought unto him little children, that he should put his hands on them, and pray. And the disciples rebuked them, **saying, There is no need, for Jesus hath said, Such shall be saved.**	13 ¶ And they brought young children to him, that he should touch them: and **his** disciples rebuked those that brought them.	11 And they brought young children to him, that he should touch them; and **the** disciples rebuked those that brought them.
		14 But when Jesus saw it, he was much displeased, and said unto them, Suffer the little children to come unto me, and forbid them not: for of such is the kingdom of God.	12 But when Jesus saw **and heard them,** he was much displeased, and said unto them, Suffer the little children to come unto me, and forbid them not; for of such is the kingdom of God.
14 But Jesus said, Suffer little children, and forbid them not, **to come unto me:** for of such is the kingdom of heaven.	14 But Jesus said, Suffer little children **to come unto me,** and forbid them not, for of such is the kingdom of heaven.	15 Verily I say unto you, Whosoever shall not receive the kingdom of God as a little child, he shall not enter therein.	
15 And he laid **his** hands on them, and departed thence.	15 And he laid hands on them, and departed thence.	16 And he took them up in his arms, put his hands upon them, and blessed them.	

120. The Rich Young Ruler

		17 ¶ And when he was gone forth into the way, there came one running, and kneeled to him, and asked him, Good Master, what shall I do that I may inherit eternal life?	
16 ¶ And, behold, one came and said **unto him,** Good Master, what good thing shall I do, that I may have eternal life?	16 And, behold, one came and said, Good master, what good thing shall I do, that I may have eternal life?		
17 And he said unto him, Why callest thou me good? there is none good but one, that is, God: but if thou wilt enter into life, keep the commandments.		18 And Jesus said unto him, Why callest thou me good? **there is** none good but one, that is, God.	16 And Jesus said unto him, Why callest thou me good? None **is** good but one, that is God.
18 He saith unto him, Which? Jesus said, Thou shalt **do no murder,** Thou shalt not commit adultery, Thou shalt not steal, Thou shalt not bear false witness,	18 He saith unto him, Which? Jesus said, Thou shalt **not kill.** Thou shalt not commit adultery. Thou shalt not steal. Thou shalt not bear false witness.	19 Thou knowest the commandments, Do not commit adultery, Do not kill, Do not steal, Do not bear false witness, Defraud not, Honour thy father and mother.	
19 Honour thy father and **thy** mother: and, Thou shalt love thy neighbour as thyself.	19 Honor thy father and mother. And, Thou shalt love thy neighbor as thyself.		

Luke 18	JST Luke 18		

15 And they brought unto him also infants, that he **would** touch them: but when his disciples saw it, they rebuked them.

15 And they brought unto him also, infants, that he **might** touch them; but when his disciples saw it, they rebuked them.

16 But Jesus called them **unto him**, and said, Suffer little children to come unto me, and forbid them not: for of such is the kingdom of God.
17 Verily I say unto you, Whosoever **shall** not receive the kingdom of God as a little child shall in no wise enter therein.

16 But Jesus called them, and said, Suffer little children to come unto me, and forbid them not; for of such is the kingdom of God.
17 Verily I say unto you, Whosoever **will** not receive the kingdom of God as a little child, shall in no wise enter therein.

18 And a certain ruler asked him, saying, Good Master, what shall I do to inherit eternal life?
19 And Jesus said unto him, Why callest thou me good? none is good, save one, that is, God.

20 Thou knowest the commandments, Do not commit adultery, Do not kill, Do not steal, Do not bear false witness, Honour thy father and thy mother.

Matt. 19	JST Matt. 19	Mark 10	JST Mark 10
20 The young man saith unto him, All these things have I kept from my youth up: what lack I yet?		20 And **he** answered and said unto him, Master, all these have I observed from my youth.	18 And **the man** answered and said unto him, Master, all these have I observed from my youth.
21 Jesus said unto him, If thou wilt be perfect, go **and** sell that thou hast, and give to the poor, and thou shalt have treasure in heaven: and come and follow me.	21 Jesus said unto him, If thou wilt be perfect, go sell that thou hast, and give to the poor and thou shalt have treasure in heaven, and come and follow me.	21 Then Jesus beholding him love him, and said unto him, One thing thou lackest: go thy way, sell whatsoever thou hast, and give to the poor, and thou shalt have treasure in heaven: and come, take up the cross, and follow me.	
22 But when the young man heard that saying, he went away sorrowful: for he had great possessions.		22 And **he** was sad at that saying, and went away grieved: for he had great possessions.	21 And **the man** was sad at that saying, and went away grieved; for he had great possessions.
23 ¶ Then said Jesus unto his disciples, Verily I say unto you, That a rich man shall hardly enter the kingdom of heaven.		23 ¶ And Jesus looked round about, and sai**th** unto his disciples, How hardly shall they that have riches enter into the kingdom of **God!**	22 And Jesus looked round about, and said unto his disciples, How hardly shall they that have riches enter into the kingdom of **my Father!**
		24 And the disciples were astonished at his words. But Jesus **answereth** again, and sai**th** unto them, Children, how hard is it for them **that** trust in riches to enter the kingdom of God!	23 and the disciples were astonished at his words. But Jesus **spake** again and said unto them, Children, how hard is it for them **who** trust in riches to enter into the kingdom of God!
24 And again I say unto you, It is easier for a camel to go through the eye of a needle, than for a rich man to enter **into** the kingdom of God.	24 and again I say unto you, It is easier for a camel to go through the eye of a needle, than for a rich man to enter the kingdom of God.	25 It is easier for a camel to go through the eye of a needle, than for a rich man to enter into the kingdom of God.	
25 When his disciples heard **it**, they were exceedingly amazed, saying, Who then can be saved?	25 When his disciples heard **this**, they were exceedingly amazed, saying, who then can be saved?	26 And they were astonished out of measure, saying among themselves, Who then can be saved?	
26 But Jesus beheld **them**, and said unto them, With men this is impossible;	26 But Jesus beheld **their thoughts**, and said unto them, With men this is impossible; **but if they will forsake all things for my sake,** with God **whatsoever** things I **speak** are possible.	27 And Jesus looking upon them sai**th**, With men I it is impossible, but not with God:	26 And Jesus, looking upon them said, With men **that trust in riches,** it is impossible; but not **impossible** with **men who trust in** God **and leave all for my sake,** for with **such** all **these** things are possible.
but with God **all** things are possible.		for with **God** all things are possible.	
27 ¶ Then answered Peter and said unto him, Behold, we have forsaken all, and followed thee; what shall we have therefore?		28 ¶ Then Peter began to say unto him, Lo, we have left all, and have followed thee.	

Luke 18	JST Luke 18	JST James 2	TPJS
21 And he said, All these have I kept from my youth up.			Happiness if the object and design of our existence; and will be the end thereof, if we pursue the path that leads to it; and this path is virtue, uprightness, faithfulness, holiness, and keeping all the commandments of God. But we cannot keep all the commandments without first knowing them, and we cannot expect to know all, or more than we now know unless we comply with or keep those we have already received. That which is wrong under one circumstance may be, and often is, right under another (p. 255-56).
22 Now when Jesus heard these things, he said unto him, yet **lackest thou** one thing: sell all that thou hast, and distribute unto the poor, and thou shalt have treasure in heaven: and come, follow me.	22 Now when Jesus heard these things, he said unto him, Yet **thou lackest** one thing: sell all that thou hast, and distribute unto the poor, and thou shalt have treasure in heaven, and come, follow me.	10 For whosoever shall, **save** in one point, keep the whole law, he is guilty of all.	
23 And when he heard this, he was very sorrowful: for he was very rich.			
24 And when Jesus saw that he was very sorrowful, he said, How hardly shall they **that** have riches enter into the kingdom of God!	24 And when Jesus saw that he was very sorrowful, he said, How hardly shall they **who** have riches enter into the kingdom of God!		. . .any person who is exalted to the highest mansion has to abide a celestial law, and the whole law too (p. 331).
25 For it is easier for a camel to go through a needle's eye, than for a rich man to enter into the kingdom of God.			
26 And they **that** heard it said, Who then can be saved?	26 And they **who** heard said unto him, Who then can be saved?		
27 And he said, **The things which are** impossible with **men** are possible with God.	27 And he said **unto them, It is** impossible **for them who trust in riches, to enter into the kingdom of God; but he who forsaketh the things which are of this world, it is** possible with God, **that he should enter in.**		
28 Then Peters said, Lo, we have left all, and followed thee.			

Matt. 19	JST Matt. 19	Mark 10	JST Mark 10 Joseph Smith
28 And Jesus said unto them, Verily I say unto you, That ye **which** have followed me, in the **regeneration** when the Son of man shall **sit in** the throne of his glory, ye **also** shall sit upon twelve thrones, judging the twelve tribes of Israel.	28 And Jesus said unto them, Verily I say unto .you, that ye **w h o** have followed me, **shall**, in the **resurrection**, when the Son of M an shall **come sitting on** the throne of his glory, ye shall **also** sit upon twelve thrones, judging the twelve tribes of Israel.		...in the day of judgment (God) designs to make us the Judges of the generation in which we live. (Personal Writings of Joseph Smith p. 287).
29 And every one that **hath** forsaken houses, or brethren, or sisters, or father, or mother, or wife, or children, or lands, for my name's sake, shall receive an hundredfold, and shall inherit everlasting life.	29 And every one that **has** forsaken houses, or brethren, or sisters, or father, or mother, or wife, or children, or lands, for my name's sake, shall receive an hundred-fold, and shall inherit everlasting life.	29 And Jesus answered and said, Verily I say unto you, There is no man that hath left house, or brethren, or sisters, or father, or mother, or wife, or children, or lands, for my sake, and the gospel's, 30 But he shall receive an hundred fold now in this time, houses, and brethren, and sisters, and mothers, and children, and lands, with persecutions; and in the world to come eternal life.	
30 But many **that are** first shall be last; and the last **shall be** first.	30 But many **of the** first shall be last, and the last first.	31 But many **that are** first shall be last; and the last first.	30 But **there are** many **who make themselves** first, **that** shall be last, and the last first. 31 **This he said, rebuking Peter** . . .

Luke 18	JST Luke 18	B of M	D & C
		1 Ne 12:9 And he said unto me: Thou rememberest the twelve apostles of the Lamb? Behold they are they who shall judge the twelve tribes of Israel; wherefore, the twelve ministers of thy seed shall be judged of them; for ye are of the house of Israel.	29:12 And again, verily, verily, I say unto you, and it hath gone forth in a firm decree, by the will of the Father, that mine apostles, the Twelve which were with me in my ministry at Jerusalem, shall stand at my right hand at the day of my coming in a pillar of fire, being clothed with robes of righteousness, with crowns upon their heads, in glory even as I am, to judge the whole house of Israel, even as many as have loved me and kept my commandments, and none else.
29 And he said unto them, Verily I say unto you, There is no man **that hath** left house, or parents, or brethren, or wife, or children, for the kingdom of God's sake,	29 And he said unto them, Verily I say unto you, There is no man **who has** left house, or parents, or brethren, or wife, or children, for the kingdom of God's sake,	10 And these twelve ministers whom thou beholdest shall judge thy seed. And, behold, they are righteous forever; for because of their faith in the Lamb of God their garments are made white in his blood. (See also Morm. 3:18-19.)	
30 Who shall not receive manifold more in this present time, and in the world to come life everlasting.			90:9 That through your administration they may receive the word, and through their administration the word may go forth unto the ends of the earth, unto the Gentile first, and then, behold, and lo, they shall turn unto the Jews.

Matt. 20	JST Matt. 20		

121. Parable of the Laborers in the Vineyard

For the kingdom of heaven is like unto a man **that is** an householder, **which** went out early in the morning to hire labourers into his vineyard.	For the kingdom of heaven is like unto a man, an householder, **who** went out early in the morning to hire laborers into his vineyard.		
2 And when he had agreed with the labourers for a penny a day, he sent them into his vineyard.			
3 And he went out about the third hour, and **saw** others standing idle in the marketplace,	3 And he went out about the third hour, and **found** others standing idle in the market place.		
4 And said unto them; Go ye also into the vineyard, and whatsoever is right I will give you. And they went their way.			
5 Again he went out about the sixth and ninth hour, and did likewise.	5 **And** again he went out about the sixth and ninth hour and did likewise.		
6 And about the eleventh hour he went out, and found others standing idle, and saith unto them, Why stand ye here all the day idle?			
7 They **say** unto him, Because no man hath hired us. He **saith** unto them, Go ye also into the vineyard; and whatsoever is right, **that shall** ye receive.	8 Go ye also into the vineyard; and whatsoever is right **ye shall** receive.		
8 So when even was come, the lord of the vineyard **saith** unto his steward, Call the labourers, and give them their hire, beginning from the last unto the first.			
9 And when they came that **were hired** about the eleventh hour, they received every man a penny.	10 And when they came that **began** about the eleventh hour, they received every man a penny.		
10 But when the first came, they supposed that they should have received more; and they likewise received every man a penny.	11 But when the first came, they supposed that they should have received more; and they likewise received every man a penny.		

Matt. 20	JST Matt. 20		
11 And when they had received **it**, they murmured against the goodman of the house,	And when they had received **a penny**, they murmured against the good man of the house, saying, These last have wrought one hour **only** and thou hast made them equal unto us, **who** have borne the burden and the heat of the day.		
12 Saying, These last have wrought **but** one hour, and thou hast made them equal unto us, **which** have borne the burden and heat of the day.			
13 But he answered one of them, and said, Friend, I do thee no wrong: didst thou not agree with me for a penny?			
14 Take **that** thine **is**, and go thy way: I will give unto this last, even as unto thee.	13 Take thine and go thy way; I will give unto this last even as unto thee.		
15 Is it not lawful for me to do what I will with mine own? Is thine eye evil, because I am good?	Is it not lawful for me to do what I will with mine own?		
16 So the last shall be first, and the first last: for many **be** called, but few chosen.	15 So the last shall be first, and the first last, for many **are** called, but few chosen.		

Matt. 20	JST Matt. 20	Mark 10	JST Mark 10

122. Going to Jerusalem-- Twelve Told of Jesus' Death and Resurrection

Matt. 20	JST Matt. 20	Mark 10	JST Mark 10
		32 ¶ And they were in the way going up to Jerusalem; and Jesus went before **them**: and they were amazed; and as they followed, they were afraid. And he took again the twelve, and began to tell them what things should happen unto him,	31 . . . and they were in the way going up to Jerusalem; and Jesus went before, and they were amazed; and as they followed, they were afraid.
17 ¶ And Jesus going up to Jerusalem took the twelve disciples apart in the way, and said unto them,			
18 Behold, we go up to Jerusalem;	17 Behold, we go up to Jerusalem,	33 **Saying**, Behold, we go up to Jerusalem;	33 **And Jesus said**, Behold, we go up to Jerusalem;
and the Son of man shall be betrayed unto the chief priests and unto the scribes, and they shall condemn him to death,	and the Son of Man shall be betrayed unto the chief priests, and unto the Scribes, and they shall condemn him to death;	and the Son of man shall be delivered unto the chief priests, and unto the scribes; and they shall condemn him to death, and shall deliver him to the Gentiles:	and the Son of Man shall be delivered unto the chief priests, and unto the scribes; and they shall condemn him to death; and shall deliver him to the Gentiles.
19 And shall deliver him to the Gentiles to mock,	19 And shall deliver him to the Gentiles to mock,	34 And they shall mock him,	
and to scourge, and to crucify **him**: and the third day he shall rise again.	and to scourge, and to crucify. And the third day he shall rise again.	and shall scourge him, and shall spit upon him, and shall kill him: and the third day he shall rise again.	

254

Luke 18	JST Luke 18		
31 ¶ Then he took **unto him** the twelve, and said unto them,	31 Then he took the twelve, and said unto them,		
Behold, we go up to Jerusalem, and all things **that** are written by the prophets concerning the Son of **man** shall be accomplished.	Behold, we go up to Jerusalem, and all things **which** are written by the prophets concerning the Son of Man, shall be accomplished.		
32 For he shall be delivered unto the Gentiles, and shall be mocked, and spitefully entreated, and spitted on:			
33 And they shall scourge **him**, and put him to death: and the third day he shall rise again.	33 And they shall scourge and put him to death; and the third day he shall rise again.		
34 And they understood none of these things: and this saying was hid from them, neither **knew** they the things which were spoken.	34 And they understood none of these things; and this saying was hid from them; neither **remembered** they the things which were spoken.		

Matt. 20	JST Matt. 20	Mark 10	JST Mark 10

123. Jericho-- Mother of James and John Requests Favor for Her Sons

Matt. 20	JST Matt. 20	Mark 10	JST Mark 10
20 ¶ Then came to him the mother of Zebedee's children with her sons, worshipping **him**, and desiring a certain thing of him.	18 Then came to him the mother of Zebedee's children with her sons, worshipping **Jesus**, and desiring a certain thing of him.	35 ¶ And James and John, the sons of Zebedee, **come** unto him, saying, Master, we would that thou shouldest do for us whatsoever we shall desire.	35 And James, and John, the sons of Zebedee, **came** unto him, saying, Master, we would that thou shouldst do for us whatsoever we shall desire.
21 And he said unto her, What wilt thou?	19 And he said unto her, What wilt thou **that I should do?**	36 And he said unto them, What **would** ye that I should do for you?	36 And he said unto them, What **will** ye that I should do **unto** you?
She **saith** unto him, Grant that these my two sons may sit, the one on thy right hand, and the other on the left, in thy kingdom.	20 **And** she **said** unto him, Grant that these my two sons may sit, the one on thy right hand, and the other on thy left, in thy kingdom.	37 They said unto him, Grant unto us that we may sit, one on thy right hand, and the other on thy left hand, in thy glory.	
22 But Jesus answered and said, Ye know not what ye ask. Are ye able to drink of the cup that I shall drink of, and to be baptized with the baptism that I am baptized with? They say unto him, We are able.		38 But Jesus said unto them, Ye know not what ye ask: can ye drink of the cup that I drink of? and be baptized with the baptism that I am baptized with? 39 And they said unto him, We can. And Jesus	
23 And he **saith** unto them, Ye shall drink indeed of my cup, and be baptized with the baptism that I am baptized with:	23 And he **said** unto them, Ye shall drink indeed of my cup, and be baptized with the baptism that I am baptized with;	said unto them, Ye shall indeed drink of the cup that I drink of; and **with the baptism** that I am baptized **withal shall ye be baptized:**	40 And Jesus said unto them, Ye shall indeed drink of the cup that I drink of; and **be baptized with the baptism** that I am baptized **with;**
but to sit on my right hand, and on my left, is **n o t mine to give, but it shall be given to them** for whom it is prepared of my Father.	but to sit on my right hand, and on my left, is for whom it is prepared of my Father, **but not mine to give.**	40 But to sit on my right hand and on my left hand is not mine to give; but **it** shall **be given to them** for whom it is prepared.	but to sit on my right hand, and on my left hand, is not mine to give; but **they** shall **receive it** for whom it is prepared.
24 And when the ten heard **it**, they were moved with indignation against the two brethren.	24 And when the ten heard **this**, they were moved with indignation against the two brethren.	41 And when the ten heard **it**, they began to be much displeased with James and John.	41 And when the ten heard, they began to be much displeased with James and John.
25 But Jesus called them **unto him**, and said, Ye know that the princes of the Gentiles exercise dominion over them, and they that are great exercise authority upon them.	25 But Jesus called them, and said, Ye know that the princes of the Gentiles exercise dominion over them, and they that are great exercise authority upon them;	42 But Jesus called them **to him**, and **saith** unto them, Ye know that they **which** are **accounted** to rule over the Gentiles exercise lordship over them; and their great ones exercise authority upon them.	42 But Jesus called them, and **said** unto them, Ye know that they **who** are **appointed** to rule over the Gentiles exercise lordship over them; and their great ones exercise authority upon them.

Matt. 20	JST Matt. 20	Mark 10	JST Mark 10
26 But it shall not be so among you: but whosoever will be great among you, let him be your minister;	but it shall not be so among you.	43 But so shall it not be among you: but whosoever will be great among you, shall be your minister:	43 But it shall not be so among you; but whosoever will be great among you, shall be your minister.
27 And whosoever will be chief among you, let him be your servant:		44 And whosoever of you will be the chiefest, shall be servant of all.	
28 Even as the Son of man came not to be ministered unto, but to minister, and to give his life a ransom for many.	28 Even as the Son of Man came, not to be ministered unto, but to minister; and to give his life a ransom for many.	45 For even the Son of man came not to be ministered unto, but to minister, and to give his life a ransom for many.	45 For even the Son of Man came, not to be ministered unto, but to minister, and to give his life a ransom for many.

Matt. 20	JST Matt. 20	Mark 10	JST Mark 10

124. Bartaemus Healed of Blindness

Matt. 20	JST Matt. 20	Mark 10	JST Mark 10
29 And as they departed from Jericho, a great multitude followed him.		46 ¶ And they came to Jericho: and as he went out of Jericho with his disciples and a great number of people, blind Bartimaeus, the son of Timæus, sat by the highway side begging.	
30 ¶ And, behold, two blind men sitting by the way side,	30 And, behold, two blind men sitting by the wayside,		
when they heard that Jesus passed by, cried out, saying, Have mercy on us, O Lord, **thou** Son of David.	when they heard that Jesus passed by, cried out, saying, Have mercy on us, O Lord, Son of David.	47 And when he heard that it was Jesus of Nazareth, he began to cry out, and say, Jesus, **thou** Son of David, have mercy on me.	47 And when he heard that it was Jesus of Nazareth, he began to cry out, and say, Jesus, son of David, have mercy on me.
31 And the multitude rebuked them, **because** they should hold their peace: but they cried the more, saying, Have mercy on us, O Lord, **thou** Son of David.	31 And the multitude rebuked them, **saying,** they should hold their peace; but they cried the more, saying, Have mercy on us, O Lord, Son of David.	48 And many charged him that he should hold his peace: but he cried the more **a great deal, Thou** Son of David, have mercy on me.	48 And many charged him that he should hold his peace; but he cried the more **exceedingly, saying,** Son of David, have mercy on me.
		49 And Jesus stood still, and commanded him to be called. And they call the blind man, saying unto him, Be of good comfort, rise; he calleth thee.	
		50 And he, casting away his garment, rose, and came to Jesus.	50 And he, casting away his garment, arose and came to Jesus.
32 And Jesus stood still, and called them, and said, What will ye that I shall do unto you?		51 And Jesus **answered and** said unto him, What wilt thou that I should do unto thee? The blind man said unto him, Lord, that I might receive my sight.	51 And Jesus said unto him, What wilt thou that I should do unto thee?
33 They say unto him, Lord, that our eyes may be opened.			52 **And** the blind man said unto him, Lord, that I might receive my sight.
34 So Jesus had compassion **on them**, and touched their eyes: and immediately their eyes received sight, and they followed him.	34 So Jesus had compassion, and touched their eyes; and immediately their eyes received sight, and they followed him.	52 And Jesus said unto him, Go thy way; thy faith hath made thee whole. And immediately he received his sight, and followed Jesus in the way.	

Luke 18	JST Luke 18		

35 ¶ And it came to pass, **that** as he was come nigh unto Jericho, a certain blind man sat by the way side begging:

36 And hearing the multitude pass by, he asked what it meant.

37 And they told him, that Jesus of Nazareth **passeth** by.

38 And he cried, saying, Jesus, **thou** Son of David, have mercy on me.

39 And they **which** went before rebuked him, that he should hold his peace: but he cried so much the more, **Thou** Son of David, have mercy on me.

40 And Jesus stood, and commanded him to be brought unto him: and when he was come near, he asked him,

41 Saying, What wilt thou that I shall do unto thee? And he said, Lord, that I may receive my sight.

42 And Jesus said unto him, Receive thy sight: thy faith hath saved thee.

43 And immediately he received his sight, and followed him, glorifying God: and all the **people**, when they saw **it**, gave praise unto God.

---

35 And it came to pass, as he was come nigh unto Jericho, a certain blind man sat by the wayside begging.

38 And he cried, saying, Jesus, Son of David, have mercy on me.

39 And they **who** went before, rebuked him, **telling him** that he should hold his peace; but he cried so much the more, **saying,** Son of David, have mercy on me.

43 And immediately he received his sight; and **he** followed him, glorifying God. And all the **disciples** when they saw **this,** gave praise unto God.

259

Luke 19	JST Luke 19	Luke 19	JST Luke 19

125. Zachaeus Promised Salvation

And Jesus entered and passed through Jericho.

2 And, behold, there was a man named Zacchæus, **which** was the chief among the publicans, and he was rich.

3 And he sought to see Jesus who he was; and could not for the press, because he was little of stature.

4 And he ran before, and climbed up into a sycomore tree to see him: for he was to pass that way.

5 And when Jesus came to the place, he looked up, and saw him, and said unto him, Zacchæus, make haste, and come down; for to day I must abide at thy house.

6 And he made haste, and (continued in column 3)

2 And behold, there was a man named Zaccheus, **who** was chief among the publicans; and he was rich.

(continued in column 4)

came down, and received him joyfully.

7 And when **they** saw it, they all murmured, saying, That he was gone to be guest with a man **that** is a sinner.

8 And Zacchæus stood, and said unto the Lord; Behold, Lord, the half of my goods I give to the poor; and if I have taken any thing from any man by **false accusation**, I restore him fourfold.

9 And Jesus said unto him, This day is salvation come to this house, forsomuch as he also is a son of Abraham.

10 For the Son of man is come to seek and to save that which was lost.

7 And when **the disciples** saw it, they all murmured, saying, That he was gone to be a guest with a man **who** is a sinner.

8 And Zaccheus stood, and said unto the Lord, Behold, Lord, the half of my goods I give to the poor; and if I have taken any thing from any man by **unjust means**, I restore fourfold.

10 For the Son of Man is come to seek and to save that which was lost.

126. Parable of the Ten Pounds

11 And as they heard these things, he added and spake a parable, because he was nigh to Jerusalem, and because **they thought** that the kingdom of God should immediately appear.

12 He said therefore, A certain nobleman went into a far country to receive for himself a kingdom, and to return.

13 And he called his ten servants, and delivered them ten pounds, and said unto them, Occupy till I come.

14 But his citizens hated him, and sent a **message** after him, saying, We will not have this man to reign over us.

(continued in column 3)

11 And as they heard these things, he added and spake a parable, because he was nigh to Jerusalem, and because **the Jews taught** that the kingdom of God should immediately appear.

14 But his citizens hated him, and sent a **messenger** after him, saying, We will not have this man to reign over us.

(continued in column 4)

15 And it came to pass, that when he was returned, having received the kingdom, then he commanded these servants to be called unto him, to whom he had given the money, that he might know how much every man had gained by trading.

16 Then came the first, saying, Lord, thy pound hath gained ten pounds.

17 And he said unto him, Well, thou good servant: because thou hast been faithful in a very little, have thou authority over ten cities.

18 And the second came, saying, Lord, thy pound hath gained five pounds.

17 And he said unto him, Well **done**, thou good servant; because thou hast been faithful in a very little, have thou authority over ten cities.

Luke 19	JST Luke 19	Luke 19	JST Luke 19 D&C
19 And he said likewise unto him, Be thou also over five cities. 20 And another came, saying, Lord, behold, **here is** thy pound, which I have kept laid up in a napkin: 21 For I feared thee, because thou art an austere man: thou takest up that thou layedst not down, and reapest that thou didst not sow. 22 And he **saith** unto him, Out of thine own mouth will I judge thee, **thou** wicked servant. Thou knewest that I was an austere man, taking up that I laid not down, and reaping that I did not sow: 23 Wherefore then gavest not thou my money into the bank, that at my coming I might have **required** mine own with usury? 24 And he said unto them **that** stood by, Take from (continued in column 3)	20 And another came, saying, Lord, behold thy pound which I have kept laid up in a napkin; 21 For I feared thee, because thou art an austere man; thou takest up that thou layedst not down, and reapest that **which** thou didst not sow. 22 And he **said** unto him, Out of thine own mouth will I judge thee, **O** wicked servant. Thou knewest that I was an austere man, taking up that I laid not down, and reaping that I did not sow. 23 Wherefore then, gavest not thou my money into the bank, that at my coming I might have **received** mine own with usury? 24 And he said unto them **who** stood by, Take from (continued in column 4)	him the pound, and give it to him **that** hath ten pounds. 25 **(And they said unto him, Lord, he hath ten pounds.)** 26 For I say unto you, That unto everyone **which hath** shall be given; and from him **that hath** not, even he that hath shall be taken away from him. 27 But those mine enemies, **which** would not that I should reign over them, bring hither, and slay them before me. 28 ¶ And when he had thus spoken, he went before, ascending up to Jerusalem.	him the pound, and give it to him **who** hath ten pounds. (Luke 19: 25 omitted in JST.) 25 For I say unto you, That unto every one **who occupieth,** shall be given; and from him **who occupieth** not, even he that hath **received** shall be taken away from him. 26 But those mine enemies, **who** would not that I should reign over them, bring **them** hither, and slay them before me. D&C 60:2 But with some I am not well pleased, for they will not open their mouths, but they hide the talent which I have given unto them, because of the fear of man. Wo unto such, for mine anger is kindled against them. 3 And it shall come to pass, if they are not more faithful unto me, it shall be taken away, even that which they have.
John 11	JST John 11		

127. Passover Of Jesus Ministry

55 ¶ And the Jews' passover was nigh at hand: and many went out of the country up to Jerusalem before the passover, **to** purify themselves. 56 Then sought they for Jesus, and spake among themselves, as they stood in the temple, What think ye, **that he will** not come to the feast? 57 Now both the chief priests and the Pharisees had given a commandment, that, if any man knew where he **were,** he should shew **it,** that they might take him.	56 Then sought they for Jesus, and spake among themselves, as they stood in the temple, What think ye **of Jesus.? Will he** not come to the feast? 57 Now both the chief priests and the Pharisees had given a commandment, that, if any man knew where he **was,** he should show **them,** that they might take him.		

Matt. 26	JST Matt. 26	Mark 14	JST Mark 14

128. Bethany, House of Simon the Leper-- Mary Anoints Jesus

Matt. 26	JST Matt. 26	Mark 14	JST Mark 14
6 ¶ Now when Jesus was in Bethany, in the house of Simon the leper,	5 Now when Jesus was in Bethany, in the house of Simon the leper,	3 ¶ And being in Bethany in the house of Simon the leper,	4 And **Jesus** being in Bethany, in the house of Simon the leper,
7 There came unto him a woman having an alabaster box of very precious ointment, and poured it on his head, as he sat **at meat**.	There came unto him a woman having an alabaster box of very precious ointment, and poured it on his head as he sat **in the house.**	as he sat at meat, there came a woman having an alabaster box of ointment of spikenard very precious; and she brake the box, and poured it on his head.	as he sat at meat, there came a woman having an alabaster box of ointment of spikenard, very precious, and she brake the box, and poured **the ointment** on his head.
8 But when **his disciples** saw **it**, they had indignation, saying, To what purpose is this waste?	6 But when **some saw this,** they had indignation, saying, Unto what purpose is this waste?	4 **And** there were some **that** had indignation within themselves, and said, Why was this waste of the ointment made?	5 There were some **among the disciples who** had indignation within themselves, and said, Why was this waste of the ointment made? for it might
9 For this ointment might have been sold for much, and given to the poor.	For this ointment might have been sold for much, and given to the poor.	5 For it might have been sold for more than three hundred pence, and have been given to the poor.	have been sold for more than three hundred pence, and have been given to the poor.
10 When Jesus understood **it**, he said unto them, Why trouble ye the woman? for she hath wrought a good work upon me.	7 When **they had said thus,** Jesus understood **them, and** he said unto them, Why trouble ye the woman? For she hath wrought a good work upon me.	And they murmured against her. 6 And Jesus said, Let her alone; why trouble ye her? she hath wrought a good work on me.	And they murmured against her. 6 And Jesus said **unto them,** Let her alone; why trouble ye her? **For she** hath wrought a good work on me.
11 For ye have the poor always with you; but me ye have not always.		7 **For** ye have the poor with you always, and whensoever ye will ye may do them good: but me ye have not always.	7 Ye have the poor with you always, and whensoever ye will, ye may do them good; but me ye have not always.
12 For **in that** she hath poured this ointment on my body, **she did it** for my burial.	9 For she hath poured this ointment on my body, for my burial. 10 **And in this thing that she hath done, she shall be blessed;**	8 She **hath** done what she could:	8 She **has** done what she could, **and this which she has done unto me, shall be had in remembrance in generations to come, wheresoever my gospel shall be preached; for**
		she **is** come aforehand to	verily she **has** come

262

		John 12	JST John 12
		Then Jesus six days before the passover came to Bethany, where Lazarus was which had been dead, whom he raised from the dead. 2 There they made him a supper; and Martha served: but Lazarus was one of them that sat at the table with him. 3 Then took Mary a pound of ointment of spikenard, very costly, and anointed the feet of Jesus, and wiped his feet with her hair: and the house was filled with the odour of the ointment. 4 Then saith one of his disciples, Judas Iscariot, Simon's son, which should betray him, 5 Why was not this ointment sold for three hundred pence, and given to the poor? 6 This he said, not that he cared for the poor; but because he was a thief, and had the bag, and bare what was put therein.	
		7 Then said Jesus, Let her alone: **against the day of** my **burying hath she kept this.**	7 Then said Jesus, Let her alone; **for she hath preserved this ointment until now, that she might anoint me in token** of my **burial.**
		8 For the poor always ye have with you; but me ye have not always.	

Matt. 26	JST Matt. 26	Mark 14	JST Mark 14
		anoint my body to the burying.	beforehand to anoint my body to the burying.
13 Verily I say unto you, Wheresoever this gospel shall be preached in the whole world, **there shall also** this, that this woman hath done, be told for a memorial of her.	**for** verily I say unto you, Wheresoever this gospel shall be preached in the whole world, this **thing** that this woman hath done, **shall also** be told for a memorial of her.	9 Verily I say unto you, Wheresoever this gospel shall be preached through-out the whole world, **this also that** she hath done shall be spoken of for a memorial of her.	9 Verily I say unto you, Wheresoever this gospel shall be preached through-out the whole world, **what** she hath done shall be spoken of **also** for a memorial of her.

Matt. 21	JST Matt. 21	Mark 11	JST Mark 11

The Week of the Atonement
Sunday

129. Mount of Olives, Bethphage-- The Triumphal Entry

And when **they** drew nigh unto Jerusalem, and were come to Bethphage, unto the mount of Olives, then sent Jesus two disciples,	And when **Jesus** drew nigh unto Jerusalem, and **they** were come to Bethphage, unto the mount of Olives, then sent Jesus two disciples,	And when they came nigh to Jerusalem, unto Beth-phage and Bethany, at the mount of Olives, he sendeth forth two of his disciples,	
2 Saying unto them, Go into the village over against you, and straight-way ye shall find **an ass** tied, **and a colt with her:** loose **them**, and bring **them** unto me.	2 Saying unto them, Go into the village over against you, and straight-way ye shall find **a colt** tied; loose **it**, and bring **it** unto me;	2 And **saith** unto them, Go your way into the vil-lage over against you: and as soon as ye be entered into it, ye shall find a colt tied, whereon **never** man sat; loose him, and bring him.	2 Go your way into the village over against you; and as soon as ye **have** entered into it, ye shall find a colt tied, whereon **no man ever** sat; loose him and bring him **to me.**
3 And if any **man** say ought unto you, ye shall say, The Lord hath need of **them**; and straightway he will send **them**.	and if any **shall** say aught unto you, ye shall say, The Lord hath need of **it**; and straightway he will send **it**.	3 And if any man say unto you, Why do ye do this? say ye that the Lord hath need of him; and straight-way he will send him hither.	
6 And the disciples went, and did as Jesus com-manded them,	5 And the disciples went, and did as Jesus com-manded them;	4 And they went their way, and found the colt tied by the door without in	

264

Luke 19	JST Luke 19	John 12	
		9 Much people of the Jews therefore knew that he was there: and they came not for Jesus' sake only, but that they might see Lazarus also, whom he had raised from the dead. 10 ¶ But the chief priests consulted that they might put Lazarus also to death; 11 Because that by reason of him many of the Jews went away, and believed on Jesus.	
29 And it came to pass, when he was come nigh to Bethphage and Bethany, at the mount called the mount of Olives, he sent two of his disciples, 30 Saying, Go ye into the village over against you; in the which at your entering ye shall find a colt tied, whereon yet never man sat: loose him, and bring him **hither**.	29 Saying, Go ye into the village over against you, in the which at your entering ye shall find a colt tied, whereon yet never man sat; loose him, and bring him **to me.**		
31 And if any man ask you, Why do ye loose **him**? thus shall ye say unto him, Because the Lord hath need of him.	30 And if any man ask you, Why do ye loose **the colt**? Thus shall ye say unto him, Because the Lord hath need of him.		
32 And they **that** were sent went their way, and found even as he had said	31 And they **who** were sent, went their way, and found even as he had said		

Matt. 21	JST Matt. 21	Mark 11	JST Mark 11
		a place where two ways met; and they loose him. 5 And certain of them **that** stood **there** said unto **them, What do ye, loosing** the colt? 6 And they said unto them even as Jesus had commanded: and they let them go.	5 And certain of them **who** stood **by,** said unto **the disciples, Why loose** ye the colt?
7 And brought the **ass, and the** colt, and put on **them** their clothes, and **they set him** thereon.	and brought the colt, and put on **it** their clothes; and **Jesus took the colt and sat thereon; and they followed him.**	7 And they brought the colt to Jesus, and cast their garments on **him;** and he sat upon **him.**	7 And they brought the colt to Jesus, and cast their garments on **it;** and **Jesus** sat upon **it.**
4 All this was done, that it might be fulfilled which was spoken by the prophet, saying,			
5 Tell ye the daughter of **Sion,** Behold, thy King cometh unto thee, meek, and sitting upon an ass, and a colt the foal of an ass.	4 Tell ye the daughter of **Zion,** Behold, thy king cometh unto thee, **and he is meek, and he is** sitting upon an ass, and a colt, the foal of an ass.		
8 And a very great multitude spread their garments in the way; others cut down branches from the trees, and strawed **them** in the way.	7 And a very great multitude spread their garments in the way; others cut down branches from the trees, and strewed in the way.	8 And many spread their garments in the way: and others cut down branches **off the** trees, and strawed them in the way.	8 And many spread their garments in the way; and others cut down branches **of** trees and strewed them in the way.
9 And the multitudes that went before, and that followed, cried, saying,	8 And the multitudes that went before, **and also** that followed **after,** cried, saying,	9 And they that went before, and they that followed, cried, saying,	9 And they that went before **him,** and they that followed **after,** cried, saying,

Luke 19	Old Testament	John 12	JST John 12
unto them. 33 And as they were loosing the colt, the owners thereof said unto them, Why loose ye the colt? 34 And they said, The Lord hath need of him. 35 And they brought him to Jesus: and they cast their garments upon the colt, and they set Jesus thereon.		14 And Jesus, when he had **found** a young ass, sat thereon, as it is written,	14 And Jesus, when he had **sent two of his disciples and** got a young ass, sat thereon; as it is written,
	Zechariah 9:9 Rejoice greatly, O daughter of Zion; shout, O daughter of Jerusalem: behold, thy King cometh unto thee: he is just, and having salvation; lowly, and riding upon an ass, and upon a colt the foal of an ass.	15 Fear not, daughter of Sion: behold, thy King cometh, sitting on an ass's colt. 16 These things understood not his disciples at the first: but when Jesus was glorified, then remembered they that these things were written of him, and that they had done these things unto him. 12 ¶ On the next day much people that were come to the feast, when they heard that Jesus was coming to Jerusalem, 13 Took branches of palm trees, and went forth to meet him . . .	
36 And as he went, they spread their clothes in the way. 37 And when he was come nigh, even now at the descent of the mount of Olives, the whole multitude of the disciples began to rejoice and praise God with a loud voice for all the mighty works that they had seen;		17 The people therefore that was with him when he called Lazarus out of his grave, and raised him from the dead, bare record. 18 For this cause the people also met him, for that they heard that he had done this miracle.	

Matt. 21	JST Matt. 21	Mark 11	JST Mark 11
Hosanna to the Son of David: Blessed is he **that** cometh in the name of the Lord; Hosanna in the highest.	Hosanna to the Son of David; blessed is he **who** cometh in the name of the Lord! Hosanna in the highest!	Hosanna; Blessed is he that cometh in the name of the Lord: 10 **Blessed be** the kingdom of our father David, that cometh in the name of the Lord: Hosanna in the highest.	11 **That bringeth** the kingdom of our father David; 12 **Blessed is he** that cometh in the name of the Lord; Hosanna in the highest.
10 And when he was come into Jerusalem, all the city was moved, saying, Who is this? 11 And the multitude said, This is Jesus the prophet **of Nazareth** of Galilee.	9 And the multitude said, This is Jesus **of Nazareth,** the prophet of Galilee.	11 And Jesus entered into Jerusalem, and into the temple: and when he had looked round about upon all things, and **now** the eventide was come, he went out unto Bethany with the twelve.	13 And Jesus entered into Jerusalem, and into the temple. And when he had looked round about upon all things, and **blessed the disciples,** the eventide was come; **and** he went out unto Bethany with the twelve.

Luke 19	JST Luke 19	John 12	
38 Saying, blessed **be the** King **that** cometh in the name of the Lord: peace in heaven, and glory in the highest.	37 Saying, Blessed **is the** King **who** cometh in the name of the Lord, peace in heaven, and glory in the highest!	13 . . . and cried, Hosanna: Blessed is the King of Israel that cometh in the name of the Lord.	
39 And some of the Pharisees from among the multitude said unto him, Master, rebuke thy disciples. 40 And he answered and said unto them, **I tell you that**, if these should hold their peace, the stones would immediately cry out. 41 ¶ And when he was come near, he beheld the city, and wept over it, 42 Saying, If thou hadst known, even thou, at least in this thy day, the things which belong unto thy peace! but now they are hid from thine eyes. 43 For the days shall come upon thee, that thine enemies shall cast a trench about thee, and compass thee round, and keep thee in on every side, 44 And shall lay thee even with the ground, and thy children within thee; and they shall not leave in thee one stone upon another; because thou knewest not the time of thy visitation.	39 And he answered and said unto them. If these should hold their peace, the stones would immediately cry out.	19 The Pharisees therefore said among themselves, Perceive ye how ye prevail nothing? behold, the world is gone after him.	

John 12	JST John 12	John 12	JST John 12

130. Jerusalem-- Greeks Hear the Voice of the Father

John 12	JST John 12	John 12	JST John 12
20 ¶ And there were certain Greeks among them that came up to worship at the feast: 21 The same came therefore to Philip, which was of Bethsaida of Galilee, and desired him, saying, Sir, we would see Jesus. 22 Philip cometh and telleth Andrew: and again Andrew and Philip tell Jesus. 23 ¶ And Jesus answered them, saying, The hour is come, that the Son of man should be glorified. 24 Verily, verily, I say unto you, Except a corn of wheat fall into the ground and die, it abideth alone: but if it die, it bringeth forth much fruit. 25 He that loveth his life shall lose it; and he that hateth his life in this world shall keep it unto life eternal. 26 If any man serve me, let him follow me; and where I am, there shall also my servant be: if any man serve me, him will my Father honour. 27 Now is my soul troubled; and what shall I say? Father, save me from this hour: but for this cause came I unto this hour. 28 Father, glorify thy name. Then came there a voice from heaven, saying, I have both glorified it, and will glorify it again. 29 The people therefore, that stood by, and heard it, said that it thundered: others said, An angel spake to him. 30 Jesus answered and said, This voice came not (continued in column 3)	23 And Jesus answered them, saying, The hour is come, that the Son of Man should be glorified. (continued in column 4)	because of me, but for your sakes. 31 Now is the judgment of this world: now shall the prince of this world be cast out. 32 And I, if I be lifted up from the earth, will draw all men unto me. 33 This he said, signifying what death he should die. 34 The people answered him, We have heard out of the law that Christ abideth for ever: and how sayest thou, The Son of man must be lifted up? who is this Son of man? 35 Then Jesus said unto them, Yet a little while is the light with you. Walk while ye have the light, lest darkness come upon you: for he that walketh in darkness knoweth not whither he goeth. 36 While ye have light, believe in the light, that ye may be the children of light. These things spake Jesus, and departed, and did hide himself from them.	34 The people answered him, We have heard out of the law that Christ abideth for ever; and how sayest thou, The Son of Man must be lifted up? who is this Son of Man?

Matt. 21	JST Matt. 21	Mark 11	JST Mark 11

2nd Day-- Monday

131. Bethany to Jerusalem-- Fig Tree Cursed

Matt. 21	JST Matt. 21	Mark 11	JST Mark 11
18 Now in the morning as he returned into the city, he hungered.		12 ¶ And on the morrow, when they **were come** from Bethany, he was hungry:	14 And on the morrow, when they **came** from Bethany he was hungry;
19 And when he saw a fig tree in the way, he came to it,	17 And when he saw a fig tree in the way, he came to it,	13 And seeing a fig tree afar off having leaves, he came, if **haply** he might find any thing thereon:	and seeing a fig tree afar off having leaves, he came **to it with his disciples; and as they supposed, he came to it to see** if he might find anything thereon.
and **found nothing there-on**, but leaves only,	and **there was not any fruit on it**, but leaves only.	and when he came to it, **he found** nothing but leaves; for the **time of figs was** not **yet**.	15 And when he came to it, **there was** nothing but leaves; for **as yet the figs were** not **ripe**.
and said unto it, Let no fruit grow on thee hence-forward for ever.	And **he** said unto it, Let no fruit grow on thee hence-forward, for ever.	14 And Jesus **answered** and said unto it, No man eat fruit of thee hereafter for ever. And **his** disciples heard **it**.	16 And Jesus **spake** and said unto it, No man eat fruit of thee hereafter, for-ever. And **the** disciples heard **him**.
And presently the fig tree withered away.	And presently the fig tree withered away.		

Matt. 21	JST Matt. 21	Mark 11	JST Mark 11

132. Jerusalem-- Temple Cleansed Again

Matt. 21	JST Matt. 21	Mark 11	JST Mark 11
12 ¶ And Jesus went into the temple of God, and cast out all them that sold and bought in the temple, and overthrew the tables of the moneychangers, and the seats of them that sold doves,		15 ¶ And they **come** to Jerusalem: and Jesus went into the temple, and began to cast out them that sold and bought in the temple, and overthrew the tables of the moneychangers, and the seats of them **that** sold doves; 16 And would not suffer that any man should carry **any** vessel through the temple. 17 And he taught, saying unto them, Is it not written, My house shall be called of all nations the house of prayer? but ye have made it a den of thieves.	17 And they **came** to Jerusalem. And Jesus went into the temple, and began to cast out them that sold and bought in the temple, and overthrew the tables of the money-changers, and the seats of them **who** sold doves; 18 And would not suffer that any man should carry a vessel through the temple.
13 And said unto them, It is written, My house shall be called the house of prayer; but ye have made it a den of thieves.			
14 And the blind and the lame came to him in the temple; and he healed them.			
15 And when the chief priests and scribes saw the wonderful things that he did, and the children crying in the temple, and saying, Hosanna to the Son of David; they were sore displeased, 16 And said unto him, Hearest thou what these say? And Jesus **saith** unto them, Yea; have ye never read, Out of the mouth of babes and sucklings thou hast perfected praise?	13 And when the chief priests and Scribes saw the wonderful things that he did, and the children **of the kingdom** crying in the temple, and saying, Hosanna to the Son of David they were sore displeased; and said unto him, Hearest thou what these say? 14 And Jesus **said** unto them, Yea; have ye never read **the scriptures which saith,** Out of the mouths of babes and sucklings, **O Lord,** thou hast perfected praise?	18 And the scribes and chief priests heard **it,** and sought how they might destroy him: for they feared him, because all the people **was** astonished at his doctrine.	20 And the scribes and chief priests heard **him,** and sought how they might destroy him; for they feared him because all the people **were** astonished at his doctrine.

TPJS-- That which hath been hid from before the foundation of the world is revealed to babes and sucklings in the last days. (p. 321)

Matt. 21	JST Matt. 21	Mark 11	JST Mark 11
17 ¶ And he left them, and went out of the city into Bethany; and he lodged there.		19 And when even was come, he went out of the city.	

Luke 19	JST Luke 19	Old Testament	
45 And he went into the temple, and began to cast out them **that** sold therein, and them **that** bought;	44 And he went into the temple, and began to cast out them **who** sold therein, and them **who** bought,		
46 Saying unto them, It is written, My house is **the** house of prayer: but ye have made it a den of thieves.	45 Saying unto them, It is written, My house is **a** house of prayer; but ye have made it a den of thieves.	Isaiah 56:7 Even them will I bring to my holy mountain, and make them joyful in my house of prayer: their burnt offerings and their sacrifices shall be accepted upon mine altar; for mine house shall be called an house of prayer for all people.	
47 And he taught daily in the temple. But the chief priests and the scribes and the chief of the people sought to destroy him, 48 And could not find what they might do: for all the people were very attentive to hear him.			
		Psalm 8:2 Out of the mouth of babes and sucklings hast thou ordained strength because of thine enemies, that thou mightest still the enemy and the avenger.	
Luke 21	JST Luke 21		
37 And in the day time he was teaching in the temple; and at night he went out, and abode in the mount that is called **the mount of** Olives.	37 And in the day time, he was teaching in the temple; and at night, he went out and abode in the mount that is called Olives.		

273

Matt. 21	JST Matt. 21	Mark 11	JST Mark 11

3rd Day-- Tuesday

133. Bethany to Jerusalem-- Withered Fig Tree-- Discourse on Faith

Matt. 21	JST Matt. 21	Mark 11	JST Mark 11
		20 ¶ And in the morning, as they passed by, they saw the fig tree dried up from the roots.	
20 And when the disciples saw **it**, they marvelled, **saying**, How soon is the fig tree withered away!	18 And when the disciples saw **this**, they marvelled **and said**, How soon is the fig tree withered away!	21 And Peter calling to remembrance saith unto him, Master, behold, the fig tree which thou cursedst is withered away.	
21 Jesus answered and said unto them, Verily I say unto you, If ye have faith, and doubt not, ye shall not only do this **which is done** to the fig tree, but also if ye shall say unto this mountain, Be thou removed, and be thou cast into the sea; it shall be done.	19 Jesus answered and said unto them, Verily I say unto you, if ye have faith, and doubt not, ye shall not only do this to the fig tree, but also, if ye shall say unto this mountain, Be thou removed, and be thou cast into the sea, it shall be done.	22 And Jesus **answering saith** unto **them**, Have faith in God.	24 And Jesus **spake and said** unto **him**, Have faith in God.
		23 For verily I say unto you, That whosoever shall say unto this mountain, Be thou removed, and be thou cast into the sea; and shall not doubt in his heart, but shall believe that those things which he saith shall come to pass; he shall have whatsoever he saith.	25 For verily I say unto you, That whosoever shall say unto this mountain, Be thou removed, and be thou cast into the sea; and shall not doubt in his heart, but shall believe that those things which he saith shall come to pass; he shall have whatsoever he saith **fulfilled**.
22 And all things, whatsoever ye shall ask in prayer, believing, ye shall receive.	20 And all things, whatsoever ye shall ask in prayer, **in faith** believing, ye shall receive.	24 Therefore I say unto you, **What** things **soever** ye desire, when ye pray, believe that ye receive **them**, and ye shall have **them**.	26 Therefore I say unto you, **Whatsoever** things ye desire, when ye pray, believe that ye receive, and ye shall have **whatsoever ye ask**.
		25 And when ye stand praying, forgive, if ye have ought against any: that your Father also **which** is in heaven may forgive you your trespasses.	27 And when ye stand praying, forgive if ye have aught against any; that your Father also **who** is in heaven, may forgive you your trespasses.
		26 But if ye do not forgive, neither will your Father **which** is in heaven forgive your trespasses.	28 But if **you** do not forgive, neither will your Father **who** is in heaven forgive your trespasses.

Luke 21	JST Luke 21		D & C
			29:6 And, as it is written-- Whatsoever ye shall ask in faith, being united in prayer according to my command, ye shall receive.
38 And **all** the people came early in the morning to him in the temple, **for** to hear him.	38 And the people came early in the morning to him in the temple, to hear him.		

Matt. 21	JST Matt. 21	Mark 11	JST Mark 11

134. Jerusalem-- Question on Authority

Matt. 21	JST Matt. 21	Mark 11	JST Mark 11
		27 ¶ And they **come** again to Jerusalem: and as he was walking in the temple, there **come** to him the chief priests, and the scribes, and the elders,	
23 ¶ And when he was come into the temple, the chief priests and the elders of the people came unto him as he was teaching, and said, By what authority doest thou these things? and who gave thee this authority?		28 And **say** unto him, By what authority doest thou these things? and who gave thee this authority to do these things?	
24 And Jesus answered and said unto them, I also will ask you one thing, which if ye tell me, I **in** like wise will tell you by what authority I do these things.	22 And Jesus answered and said unto them, I also will ask you one thing, which if ye tell me, I, likewise, will tell you by what authority I do these things.	29 And Jesus answered and said unto them, I will also ask of you one question, **and** answer me, and I will tell you by what authority I do these things.	31 And Jesus answered and said unto them, I will also ask of you one question, answer me, and **then** I will tell you by what authority I do these things.
25 The baptism of John, whence was it? from heaven, or of men? And they reasoned with themselves, saying, If we shall say, From heaven; he will say unto us, Why did ye not then believe him?		30 The baptism of John, **was it** from heaven, or of **men**? answer me. 31 And they reasoned with themselves, saying, If we shall say, From heaven; he will say, Why then did ye not believe him?	30 **Was** the baptism of John from heaven, or of **man**? Answer me.
26 But if we shall say, Of men; we fear the people; for all **hold** John as a prophet.	24 . . . But if we shall say, Of men; we fear the people. For all **people held** John as a prophet.	32 But if we shall say, Of men; they feared the people: for all **men counted** John, that he was a prophet indeed.	32 But if we shall say, Of men; **we shall offend the people. Therefore** they feared the people; for all **people believed** John, that he was a prophet indeed.
27 And they answered Jesus, and said, We cannot tell. And he said **unto them**, Neither tell I you by what authority I do these things.	And they answered Jesus and said, We cannot tell. 25 And he said, Neither tell I you by what authority I do these things.	33 And they answered and said unto Jesus, We cannot tell. And Jesus answering saith unto them, Neither do I tell you by what authority I do these things.	

135. Parable of the Two Sons

Matt. 21	JST Matt. 21	Mark 11	JST Mark 11
28 ¶ But what think ye? A **certain** man had two sons; and he came to the first, **and said**, Son, go work to day in my vineyard.	26 But what think ye? A man had two sons; and he came to the first, **saying**, Son, go work to-day in my vineyard.		
29 He answered and said, I will not: but afterward he repented, and went.			

276

Luke 20	JST Luke 20		

And it came to pass, that on one of those days, as he taught the people in the temple, and preached the gospel, the chief priests and the scribes came upon him with the elders,

2 And spake unto him, saying, Tell us, by what authority doest thou these things? or who is he **that** gave thee this authority?

3 And he answered and said unto them, I will also ask you one thing; **and** answer me:

    2 And spake unto him, saying, Tell us, by what authority doest thou these things? Or, who is he **who** gave thee this authority?

3 And he answered, and said unto them, I will also ask you one thing; answer me.

4 The baptism of John, was it from heaven, or of men?

5 And they reasoned with themselves, saying, If we shall say, From heaven; he will say, Why then believed ye him not?

6 **But** and if we say, Of men; all the people will stone us: for they **b e** persuaded that John was a prophet.

    6 **And** if we say, Of men, all the people will stone us; for they **are** persuaded that John was a prophet.

7 And they answered, that they could not tell whence it was.

8 **And** Jesus said unto them, Neither tell I you by what authority I do these things.

    8 Jesus said unto them, Neither tell I you, by what authority I do these things.

Matt. 21	JST Matt. 21	Mark 12	JST Mark 12
30 And he came to the second, and said likewise. And he answered and said, I **go, sir**: and went not. 31 Whether of **them** twain did the will of his father? They say unto him, The first. Jesus **saith** unto them, Verily I say unto you, That the publicans and **the** harlots go into the kingdom of God before you. 32 For John came unto you in the way of righteousness, and ye believed him not: but the publicans and the harlots believed him: and ye, when ye had seen **it**, repented not **afterward**, that ye might believe him.	28 And he came to the second, and said likewise. And he answered and said, I **will serve**; and went not. 29 Whether of **these** twain did the will of their father? 31 Jesus **said** unto them, Verily I say unto you, That the publicans and harlots **shall** go into the kingdom of God before you. 32 For John came unto you in the way of righteousness, **and bore record of me,** and ye believed him not; but the publicans and the harlots believed him; and ye, **afterward**, when ye had seen **me**, repented not, that ye might believe him. 33 **For he that believed not John concerning me, cannot believe me, except he first repent.** 34 **And except ye repent, the preaching of John shall condemn you in the day of judgment.**		

136. Parable of the Wicked Husbandmen

Matt. 21	JST Matt. 21	Mark 12	JST Mark 12
33 ¶ Hear another parable: There was a certain householder, **which** planted a vineyard, and hedged it round about, and digged a winepress in it, and built a tower, and let it out to husbandmen, and went into a far country: 34 And when the time of the fruit drew near, he sent his servants to the husbandmen, that they might receive the fruits of it.	**And, again**, hear another parable; **for unto you that believe not, I speak in parables; that your unrighteousness may be rewarded unto you.** 35 **Behold**, there was a certain householder, **who** planted a vineyard, and hedged it round about, and digged a wine-press in it; and built a tower, and let it out to husbandmen, and went into a far country.	And he began to speak unto them by parables. A **certain** man planted a vineyard, and set an hedge about it, and digged **a place for the winefat,** and built a tower, and let it out to husbandmen, and went into a far country. 2 And at the season he sent to the husbandmen a servant, that he might receive from the husbandmen of the fruit of the vineyard.	And **Jesus** began to speak unto them by parables, **saying,** 2 A man planted a vineyard, and set a hedge about it, and digged **the wine vat,** and built a tower, and let it out to husbandmen, and went into a far country.

Luke 20	JST Luke 20		
9 Then began he to speak to the people this parable;	9 Then began he to speak to the people, this parable.		
A certain man planted a vineyard,	A certain man planted a vineyard,		
and let it **forth** to husbandmen, and went into a far country for a long time.	and let it **out** to husbandmen, and went into a far country for a long time.		
10 And at the season he sent **a** servant to the husbandmen, that they should give him of the fruit of the vineyard:	10 And at the season **of the harvest,** he sent **his** servant to the husbandmen, that they should give him of the fruit of the vineyard;		

Matt. 21	JST Matt. 21	Mark 12	JST Mark 12
35 And the husbandmen took his servants, and beat one, and killed another, and stoned another.		3 And they caught **him**, and beat him, and sent him away empty.	4 And they caught **the servant** and beat him, and sent him away empty.
36 Again, he sent other servants more than the first: and they did unto them likewise.		4 And again he sent unto them another servant; and at him they cast stones, and wounded him in the head, and sent him away shamefully handled.	
		5 And again he sent another; and him they killed, and many others; beating some, and killing some.	
37 But last of all he sent unto them his son, saying, They will reverence my son.		6 Having yet therefore one son, his wellbeloved, he sent him also last unto them, saying, They will reverence my son.	
38 But when the husbandmen saw the son, they said among themselves, This is the heir; come, let us kill him, and let us seize on his inheritance.		7 But those husbandmen said among themselves, This is the heir; come, let us kill him, and the inheritance shall be ours.	
39 And they caught him, and cast him out of the vineyard, and slew him.		8 And they took him, **and killed him**, and cast him out of the vineyard.	9 And they took him and cast him out of the vineyard, **and killed him**.
40 When the lord therefore of the vineyard cometh, what will he do unto those husbandmen?	42 **And Jesus said unto them,** When the Lord therefore of the vineyard cometh, what will he do unto those husbandmen?	9 What shall therefore the lord of the vineyard do?	9 What shall therefore the lord of the vineyard do?
41 They say unto him, He will **miserably** destroy those wicked men, and will let out **his** vineyard unto other husbandmen, **which** shall render him the fruits in their seasons.	43 They say unto him, He will destroy those **miserable,** wicked men, and will let out **the** vineyard unto other husbandmen, **who** shall render him the fruits in their seasons.	he will come and destroy the husbandmen, and will give the vineyard unto others.	**Lo,** he will come and destroy the husbandmen, and will give the vineyard unto others.
42 Jesus saith unto them, Did ye never read in the scriptures, The stone which the builders rejected, the same is become the head of the corner: this is the Lord's doing, and it is marvellous in our eyes?		10 **And** have ye not read this scripture; The stone which the builders rejected is become the head of the corner:	11 **Again,** have ye not read this Scripture; The stone which the builders rejected, is become the head of the corner; this was the Lord's doing, and it is marvellous in our eyes.
43 Therefore say I unto you, The kingdom of God shall be taken from you, and given to a nation bringing forth the fruits thereof.		11 This was the Lord's doing, and it is marvellous in our eyes?	

280

Luke 20	JST Luke 20	B of M	Psalms
but the husbandmen beat him, and sent him away empty. 11 And again he sent another servant: and they beat him also, and entreated him shamefully, and sent him away empty. 12 And again he sent a third: and they wounded him also, and cast him out. 13 Then said the lord of the vineyard, What shall I do? I will send my beloved son: it may be they will reverence him when they see him. 14 But when the husbandmen saw him, they reasoned among themselves, saying, This is the heir: come, let us kill him, that the inheritance may be ours. 15 So they cast him out of the vineyard, and killed him. What therefore shall the lord of the vineyard do unto them?			
16 He shall come and destroy these husbandmen, and shall give the vineyard to others. And when they heard it, they said, God forbid. 17 And he beheld them, and said, What is this then **that** is written, The stone which the builders rejected, the same is become the head of the corner?	16 He shall come and destroy these husbandmen, and shall give the vineyard to others. And when they heard **this**, they said, God forbid! 17 And he beheld them, and said, What is this then **which** is written, The stone which the builders rejected, the same is become the head of the corner?	Jac. 4:15 And now I, Jacob, am led on by the Spirit unto prophesying; for I perceive by the workings of the Spirit which is in me, that by the stumbling of the Jews they will reject the stone upon which they might build and have safe foundation. 16 But behold, according to the scriptures, this stone shall become the great, and the last, and the only sure foundation, upon which the Jews can build.	Psalm 118:22 The stone, which the builders refused is become the head stone of the corner.

Matt. 21	JST Matt. 21	Mark 12	JST Mark 12
44 **And** whosoever shall fall on this stone shall be broken: but on whomsoever it shall fall, it will grind him to powder. 45 And when the chief priests and Pharisees had heard his parables, they perceived that he spake of them.	46 **For** whosoever shall fall on this stone, shall be broken; but on whomsoever it shall fall, it will grind him to powder. **48 And they said among themselves, Shall this man think that he alone can spoil this great kingdom? And they were angry with him.**		
46 But when they sought to lay hands on him, they feared the multitude, because they took him for a prophet.	49 But when they sought to lay hands on him, they feared the multitude, because they **learned that the multitude** took him for a prophet.	12 And they sought to lay hold on him, but feared the people: for they knew that he had spoken the parable against them: and they left him, and went their way.	12 And **now they were angry when they heard these words;** and they sought to lay hold on him, but feared the people.

Matt. 22	JST Matt. 22	Matt. 22	JST Matt. 22

137. Parable of the Royal Marriage Feast

Matt. 22	JST Matt. 22	Matt. 22	JST Matt. 22
And Jesus answered and spake unto them **again by** parables, and said,	And Jesus answered **the people again,** and spake unto them **in** parables, and said,	5 But they made light of **it,** and went their ways, one to his farm, another to his merchandise:	5 But they made light of **the servants,** and went their ways; one to his farm, another to his merchandise;
2 The kingdom of heaven is like unto a certain king, **which** made a marriage for his son, 3 And sent forth his servants to call them that were bidden to the wedding: and they would not come.	2 The kingdom of heaven is like unto a certain king, **who** made a marriage for his son. 3 And **when the marriage was ready, he** sent forth his servants to call them that were bidden to the wedding; and they would not come.	6 And the remnant took his servants, and entreated them spitefully, and slew them. 7 But when the king heard **thereof,** he was wroth: and he sent forth his **armies,** and destroyed those murderers, and burned up their city.	7 But when the king heard **that his servants were dead,** he was wroth; and he sent forth his armies, and destroyed those murderers, and burned up their city.
4 Again, he sent forth other servants, saying, Tell them **which** are bidden, Behold, I have prepared **my dinner:** my oxen and my fatlings **are** killed, and all things are **ready:** come unto the marriage.	4 Again he sent forth other servants, saying, Tell them **that** are bidden, Behold, I have prepared my oxen, and my fatlings **have been** killed, and **my dinner is ready,** and all things are **prepared; therefore** come unto the marriage.	8 Then **saith** he to his servants, The wedding is ready, but they **which** were bidden were not worthy. 9 Go ye therefore into the highways, and as many as ye shall find, bid to the marriage.	8 Then **said** he to his servants, The wedding is ready; but they **who** were bidden were not worthy.
(continued in column 3)	(continued in column 4)		

Luke 20	JST Luke 20		
18 Whosoever shall fall upon that stone shall be broken; but on whomsoever it shall fall, it **will** grind him to powder.	18 Whosoever shall fall upon that stone, shall be broken; but on whomsoever it shall fall, it **shall** grind him to powder.		
19 ¶ And the chief priests and the scribes the same hour sought to lay hands on him; **and** they feared the people: for they perceived that he had spoken this parable against them.	19 And the chief priests, and the scribes, the same hour, sought to lay hands on him; **but** they feared the people; for they perceived that he had spoken this parable against them.		

Matt. 22	JST Matt. 22	Mark 12	D & C
10 So those servants went out into the highways, and gathered together all as many as they found, both good and bad: and the wedding was furnished with guests.			
11 ¶ **And** when the king came in to see the guests, he saw there a man **which** had not **on** a wedding garment:	11 **But** when the king came in to see the guests, he saw there a man **who** had not a wedding garment.		
12 And he sai**th** unto him, Friend, how camest thou in hither not having a wedding garment? And he was speechless.			
13 Then said the king to **the** servants, Bind him hand and foot, and take **him away**, and cast him into outer darkness; there shall be weeping and gnashing of teeth.	13 Then said the king **un**to **his** servants, Bind him hand and foot, and take and cast him **away** into outer darkness; there shall be weeping and gnashing of teeth.		95:5 But behold, verily I say unto you, that there are many who have been ordained among you, whom I have called but few of them are chosen. (See also D&C 121:34-40.)
14 For many are called, but few **are** chosen.	14 For many are called, but few chosen; **wherefore all do not have on the wedding garment.**		

TPJS-- I have tried for a number of years to get the minds of the Saints prepared to receive the things of God; but we frequently see some of them, after suffering all they have for the work of God, will fly to pieces like glass as soon as anything comes that is contrary to their traditions: they cannot stand the fire at all. How many will be able to abide a celestial law, and go through and receive their exaltation, I am unable to say, as many are called, but few are chosen. (p. 331)

138. Pharisees Question on Tribute to Caesar

Matt. 22	JST Matt. 22	Mark 12	D & C
15 ¶ Then went the Pharisees, and took counsel how they might entangle him in his talk.			
		13 ¶ And they send unto him certain of the Pharisees and of the Herodians, to catch him in his words.	
16 And they sent out unto him their disciples with the Herodians, saying, Master, we know that thou art true, and teachest the way of God in truth, neither carest thou for any **man**: for thou regardest not the person of men.	16 And they sent out unto him their disciples with the Herodians, saying, Master, we know that thou art true, and teachest the way of God in truth, neither carest thou for any: for thou regardest not the person of men.	14 And when they were come, they say unto him, Master, we know that thou art true, and carest for no man: for thou regardest not the person of men, but teachest the way of God in truth:	

284

Luke 20	JST Luke 20	TPJS
		In the 22nd chapter of [Matthew's] account of the Messiah, we find the kingdom of heaven likened unto a king who made a marriage for his son. That this sone was the Messiah will not be disputed, since it was the kingdom of heaven that was represented in the parable; and that the Saints, or those who are found faithful to the Lord, are the individuals who will be found worthy to inherit a seat at the marriage supper, is evident from the sayings of John in the Revelation where he represents the sound which he heard in heaven to be like a great multitude, or like the voice of mighty thunderings, saying, the Lord God Omnipotent reigneth. Let us be glad and rejoice and give honor to Him; for the marriage of the Lamb is come, and His wife hath made herself ready. And to her was granted that she should be arrayed in fine linen, clean and white: for the fine linen is the righteousness of Saints (Rev. 19:7-8) (p. 63).
20 And they watched him, and sent forth spies, **which** should feign themselves just men, that they might take hold of his words, that so they might deliver him unto the power and authority of the governor.	20 And they watched him, and sent forth spies, **who** should feign themselves just men, that they might take hold of his words, that so **doing**, they might deliver him unto the power and authority of the governor.	
21 And they asked him, saying, Master, we know that thou sayest and teaches rightly, neither **acceptest** thou the person of any, but teaches the way of God truly:	21 And they asked him, saying, Master, we know that thou sayest and teaches rightly; neither **regardest** thou the person of any, but teaches the way of God truly.	

Matt. 22	JST Matt. 22	Mark 12	JST Mark 12
17 Tell us therefore, What thinkest thou? Is it lawful to give tribute unto Cæsar, or not?		Is it lawful to give tribute to Cæsar, or not?	
18 But Jesus perceived their wickedness, and said, Why tempt ye me, ye **hypocrites**?	18 But Jesus perceived their wickedness, and said, **Ye hypocrites**! why tempt ye me?	15 Shall we give, or shall we not give? But he, knowing their hypocrisy, said unto them, Why tempt ye me? bring me a penny, that I may see it.	
19 Shew me the tribute money. And they brought unto him a penny.		16 And they brought **it**. And he saith unto them, Whose **is this** image and superscription? And they said unto him, Cæsar's.	18 And they brought **the penny**; and he said unto them; Whose image and superscription **is this**?
20 **And he saith** unto them, Whose **is this** image and superscription?	20 He said unto them, Whose image **is this**, and superscription?		
21 They say unto him, Cæsar's. Then **saith** he unto them, Render therefore unto Cæsar the things which are Cæsar's; and unto God the things **that** are God's.	21 They said unto him, Cæsar's. Then said he unto them, Render therefore unto Cæsar, the things which are Cæsar's; and unto God the things **which** are God's.	17 And Jesus answering said unto them, Render to Cæsar the things **that** are Cæsar's, and to God the things that are God's.	19 And Jesus answering said unto them, Render to Cæsar the things **which** are Cæsar's; and to God the things that are God's.
22 When they had heard these words, they marvelled, and left him, and went their way.	22 **And** when they had heard **him say** these words, they marvelled, and left him, and went their way.	And they marvelled at **him**.	21 And they marvelled at **it**.

139. Sadducees Question on Marriage and the Resurrection

Matt. 22	JST Matt. 22	Mark 12	JST Mark 12
23 ¶ The same day came **to him** the Sadducees, **which** say that there is no resurrection, and asked him,	23 The same day came the Sadducees **to him, who** say that there is no resurrection, and asked him,	18 ¶ Then **come** unto him the Sadducees, **which** say there is no resurrection; and they asked him, saying,	22 Then **came** unto him the Sadducees, **who** say there is no resurrection; and they asked him saying,
24 Saying, Master, Moses said, If a man die, having no children, his brother shall marry his wife, and raise up seed unto his brother.		19 Master, Moses wrote unto us, If a man's brother die, and leave **his** wife be**hind him**, and leave no children, that his brother should take his wife, and raise up seed unto his brother.	23 Master, Moses wrote unto us **in his law**, If a man's brother die, and leave **a** wife, and leave no children, that his brother should take his wife, and raise up seed unto his brother.
25 Now there were with us seven brethren: and the first, when he had married a wife, deceased, and, having no issue, left his wife unto his brother:		20 Now there were seven brethren: **and the first took a wife, and dying left no seed**.	24 Now there were seven brethren; the first took a wife, and dying left no seed.
26 Likewise the second also, and the third, unto the seventh.	25 Likewise the second also, and the third, **and even** unto the seventh.	21 And the second took her, and died, neither left he any seed: and the third likewise.	
		22 And the seven had her, and left no seed:	

Luke 20	JST Luke 20		D & C
22 Is it lawful for us to give tribute unto Cæsar, or no? 23 But he perceived their craftiness, and said unto them, Why tempt ye me? 24 Shew me a penny. Whose image and superscription hath it? They answered and said, Cæsar's. 25 And he said unto them, Render therefore unto Cæsar the things which be Cæsar's, and unto God the things which be God's. 26 And they could not take hold of his words before the people: and they marvelled at his answer, and held their peace.			63:25 Behold, the land of Zion-- I, the Lord, hold it in mine own hands; 26 Nevertheless, I, the Lord, render unto Cæsar the things which are Cæsar's. 27 Wherefore, I the Lord will that you should purchase the lands, that you may have advantage of the world, that you may have claim on the world, that they may not be stirred up unto anger.
27 ¶ Then came to him certain of the Sadducees, **which** deny **that** there is any resurrection; and they asked him, 28 Saying, Master, Moses wrote unto us, If any man's brother die, having a wife, and he die without children, that his brother should take his wife, and raise up seed unto his brother. 29 There were therefore seven brethren: and the first took a wife, and died without children. 30 And the second took her to wife, and he died childless. 31 And the third took her; **and** in like manner the seven also: and they left no children, and died.	27 Then came to him certain of the Sadducees, **who** deny there is any resurrection; and they asked him, 31 And the third took her in like manner; **and** the seven also; and they left no children, and died.		132:15 Therefore, if a man marry him a wife in the world, and he marry her not by me nor by my word, and he covenant with her so long as he is in the world and she with him, their covenant and and marriage are not of force when they are dead, and when they are out of the world; therefore, they are not bound by any law when they are out of the world. 16 Therefore, when they are out of the world they neither marry nor are given in marriage; but are appointed angels in heaven, which angels are ministering servants, to minister for those who are worthy of a far more, and an exceeding, and an eternal weight of glory.

287

Matt. 22	JST Matt. 22	Mark 12	JST Mark 12
27 And last of all the woman died also. 28 Therefore in the resurrection whose wife shall she be of the seven? for they all had her. 29 Jesus answered and said unto them, Ye do err, not knowing the scriptures, nor the power of God.		last of all the woman died also. 23 In the resurrection therefore, when they shall rise, whose wife shall she be of them? for the seven had her to wife. 24 And Jesus answering said unto them, **Do ye not** therefore **err**, because ye know not the scriptures, neither the power of God?	 28 And Jesus answering said unto them, **Ye do err** therefore, because ye know not, **and understand not** the Scriptures, neither the power of God.
30 For in the resurrection they neither marry, nor are given in marriage, but are as the angels of God in heaven.		25 For when they shall rise from the dead, they neither marry, nor are given in marriage; but are as the angels **which** are in heaven.	29 For when they shall rise from the dead, they neither marry, nor are given in marriage; but are as the angels **of God who** are in heaven.
31 But as touching the resurrection of the dead, have ye not yet read that which was spoken unto you **by** God, saying, 32 I am the God of Abraham, and the God of Isaac, and the God of Jacob? God is not the God of the dead, but of the living.	30 But as touching the resurrection of the dead, have ye not yet read that which was spoken unto you **of** God, saying,	26 And as touching the dead, that they rise: have ye not read in the book of Moses, how in the bush God spake unto him, saying, I am the God of Abraham, and the God of Isaac, and the God of Jacob? 27 He is not the God of the dead, but the God of the living: ye therefore do greatly err.	32 He is not **therefore** the God of the dead, but the God of the living; **for he raiseth them up out of their graves.** Ye therefore do greatly err.
33 And when the multitude heard **this**, they were astonished at his doctrine.	32 And when the multitude heard **him**, they were astonished at his doctrine.		

Luke 20	JST Luke 20	D & C	Joseph Smith
32 Last of all the woman died also. 33 Therefore in the resurrection whose wife of them is she? for seven had her to wife.	32 **And** last of all, the woman died also.	132:17 For these angels did not abide my law; therefore, they cannot be enlarged, but remain separately and singly, without exaltation, in their saved condition, to all eternity; and from henceforth are not gods, but are angels of God forever and ever. (See also vv. 18-19.)	
34 And Jesus answering said unto them, The children of this world marry, and are given in marriage: 35 But they **which** shall be accounted worthy to obtain that world, **and the** resurrection from the dead, neither marry, nor are given in marriage: 36 Neither can they die any more: for they are equal unto the angels; and are the children of God, being the children of the resurrection. 37 Now that the dead are raised, even Moses shewed at the bush, when he calleth the Lord the God of Abraham, and the God of Isaac, and the God of Jacob. 38 For he is not a God of the dead, but of the living: for all live unto him.	35 But they **who** shall be accounted worthy to obtain that world, **through** resurrection from the dead, neither marry nor are given in marriage.		WJS-- ...all contracts in view of this life only terminate with this life. (Such is the) case of the woman and seven husbands (p. 232).

Matt. 22	JST Matt. 22	Mark 12	JST Mark 12

140. A Pharisee Questions-- The First Commandment of the Law

Matt. 22	JST Matt. 22	Mark 12	JST Mark 12
34 ¶ But when the Pharisees had heard that he had put the Sadducees to silence, they were gathered together.			
35 Then one of them, **which was a lawyer, asked him a question,** tempting him, **and** saying,	34 Then one of them, a lawyer, tempting him, **asked**, saying,	28 ¶ And one of the scribes came, and having heard them reasoning together, and perceiving that he had answered them well, asked him, Which is the first commandment of all?	
36 Master, which is the great commandment in the law?			
37 Jesus said unto him,		29 And Jesus answered him, The first of all the commandments is, Hear, O Israel; The Lord our God is one Lord:	34 And Jesus answered him, The first of all the commandments is: **Hearken, and** hear, O Israel; The Lord our God is one Lord;
Thou shalt love the Lord thy God with all thy heart, and with all thy soul, and with all thy mind.		30 And thou shalt love the Lord thy God with all thy heart, and with all thy soul, and with all thy mind, and with all thy strength: this is the first commandment.	
38 This is the first and great commandment.			36 This is the first commandment.
39 And the second is like unto it, Thou shalt love thy neighbour as thyself.		31 And the second is like, **namely** this, Thou shalt love thy neighbour as thyself. There is none other commandment greater than these.	And the second is like this, Thou shalt love thy neighbor as thyself. There is none other commandment greater than these.
40 On these two commandments hang all the law and the prophets.			
		32 And the scribe said unto him, Well, Master, thou hast said the truth: for there is one God; and there is none other but **he**:	37 And the scribe said unto him, Well, Master, thou hast said the truth; for there is one God, and there is none other but **him**.
		33 And to love him with all the heart, and with all the understanding, and with all the soul, and with all the strength, and to love his neighbour as himself, is more than all whole burnt offerings and sacrifices.	
		34 And when Jesus saw that he answered discreetly, he said unto him, Thou art not far from the kingdom of God. And no man after that durst ask him **any question**.	40 And no man after that durst ask him, **saying, Who art thou?**

290

Luke 20		D & C	
		59:5 Wherefore, I give unto them a commandment, saying thus: Thou shalt love the Lord thy God with all thy heart, with all thy might, mind, and strength; and in the name of Jesus Christ thou shalt serve him. 6 Thou shalt love thy neighbor as thyself. Thou shalt not steal; neither commit adultery, nor kill, nor do anything like unto it.	
39 ¶ Then certain of the scribes answering said, Master, thou hast well said.			
40 And after that they durst not ask him any question at all.			

Matt. 22		Mark 12	JST Mark 12

141. Jesus Questions the Pharisees—What Think Ye of Christ?

Matt. 22		Mark 12	JST Mark 12
41 ¶ While the Pharisees were gathered together, Jesus asked them,			
42 Saying, What think ye of Christ? whose son is he? They say unto him, The Son of David.			
43 He saith unto them,		35 ¶ And Jesus **answered** and said, while he taught in the temple, How say the scribes that Christ is the Son of David?	41 And Jesus **spake** and said, while he taught in the temple, How way the scribes that Christ is the Son of David?
How then doth David in spirit call him Lord, saying, 44 The Lord said unto my Lord, Sit thou on my right hand, till I make thine enemies thy footstool?		36 For David himself said by the Holy Ghost, The Lord said to my Lord, Sit thou on my right hand, **till** I make thine enemies thy footstool.	
45 If David then call him Lord, how is he his son?		37 David therefore himself calleth him Lord; and whence is he **then** his son? And the common people heard him gladly.	43 David therefore himself calleth him Lord; and whence is he his son? 44 And the common people heard him gladly; **but the high priest and the elders were offended at him.**
46 And no man was able to answer him a word, neither durst any man from that day forth ask him any more question.			

Luke 20		Psalms	

41 And he said unto them, How say they that Christ is David's son?

42 And David himself saith in the book of Psalms, The LORD said unto my Lord, Sit thou on my right hand,
43 Till I make thine enemies thy footstool.
44 David therefore calleth him Lord, how is he then his son?

110:1 A Psalm of David. The LORD said unto my Lord, Sit thou at my right hand, until I make thine enemies thy footstool.

Matt. 23	JST Matt. 23	Mark 12	JST Mark 12

142. Jesus Chastizes the Scribes and Pharisees

Matt. 23	JST Matt. 23	Mark 12	JST Mark 12
Then spake Jesus to the multitude, and to his disciples, 2 Saying, The scribes and the Pharisees sit in Moses' seat:		38 ¶ And he said unto them in his doctrine, Beware of the scribes,	45 And he said unto them in his doctrine, Beware of the scribes
3 All therefore whatsoever they bid you observe, **that** observe and do;	2 All, therefore, whatsoever they bid you observe, **they will make you** observe and do; **for they are ministers of the law, and they make themselves your judges.** But do not ye after their works; for they say, and do not.		
but do not ye after their works: for they say, and do not.			
4 For they bind heavy burdens and grievous to be borne, **and lay them on men's shoulders;** but they **themselves** will not move them with one of their fingers.	3 For they bind heavy burdens **and lay on men's shoulders, and they are** grievous to be borne; but they will not move them with one of their fingers.		
5 **But** all their works they do **for** to be seen of men: they make broad their phylacteries, and enlarge the borders of their garments,	4 **And** all their works they do to be seen of men. They make broad their phylacteries, and enlarge the borders of their garments, and love the uppermost rooms at feasts, and the chief seats in the synagogues, and greetings in the markets, and to be called of men, Rabbi, Rabbi, **(which is master.)**	which love to go in long clothing, **and love** salutations in the marketplaces, 39 And the chief seats in the synagogues, and the uppermost rooms at feasts:	which love to go in long clothing, and **have** salutations in the marketplaces, and the chief seats in the synagogues, and the uppermost rooms at feasts;
6 And love the uppermost rooms at feasts, and the chief seats in the synagogues,			
7 And greetings in the markets, and to be called of men, Rabbi, Rabbi.			
8 But be not ye called Rabbi: for one is your Master, **even** Christ; and all ye are brethren.	5 But be not ye called Rabbi; for one is your master, **which is** Christ; and all ye are brethren.		
9 And call no **man** your **father** upon the earth:	6 And call no **one** your **creator** upon the earth, **or your heavenly Father**; for one is your **creator and heavenly** Father, **even he who** is in heaven.		
for one is your			
Father, **which** is in heaven.			
10 Neither be ye called masters: for one is your Master, even Christ.	7 Neither be ye called masters; for one is your master, even **he whom your heavenly Father sent, which is** Christ;		

Luke 20	JST Luke 20		

45 ¶ Then in the audience of all the people he said unto his disciples,
46 Beware of the scribes,

46 Beware of the scribes,

which desire to walk in long robes, and love greetings in the markets,

who desire to walk in long robes, and love greetings in the markets,

and the highest seats in the synagogues, and the chief rooms at feasts;

and the highest seats in the synagogues, and the chief rooms at feasts;

Matt. 23	JST Matt. 23	Mark 12	D & C Luke 20
	for he hath sent him among you that ye might have life.		
11 But he that is greatest among you shall be your servant.			
12 And whosoever shall exalt himself shall be abased; and he that shall humble himself shall be exalted.	9 And whosoever shall exalt himself shall be abased of him; and he that shall humble himself shall be exalted of him.		D&C 101:42 He that exalteth himself shall be abased, and he that abaseth himself shall be exalted. (See also 112:3, 124:114.)
13 ¶ But woe unto you, scribes and Pharisees, hypocrites! for ye shut up the kingdom of heaven against men: for ye neither go in yourselves, neither suffer ye them that are entering to go in.			
14 Woe unto you, scribes and Pharisees, hypocrites! for ye devour widows' houses, and for pretence make long prayer: therefore ye shall receive the greater damnation.	11 Woe unto you, Scribes and Pharisees! for ye are hypocrites! Ye devour widows' houses, and for pretence ye make long prayers; therefore ye shall receive the greater punishment.	40 Which devour widows' houses, and for a pretence make long prayers: these shall receive greater damnation.	Luke 20:47 Which devour widows' houses, and for a shew make long prayers: the same shall receive greater damnation.
15 Woe unto you, scribes and Pharisees, hypocrites! for ye compass sea and land to make one proselyte, and when he is made, ye make him twofold more the child of hell than yourselves.	12 Woe unto you, Scribes and Pharisees, hypocrites! For ye compass sea and land to make one proselyte; and when he is made, ye make him two-fold more the child of hell than he was before, like unto yourselves.		
16 Woe unto you, ye blind guides, which say, Whosoever shall swear by the temple, it is nothing; but whosoever shall swear by the gold of the temple, he is a debtor!	13 Woe unto you, blind guides, who say, Whosoever shall swear by the temple, it is nothing; but whosoever shall swear by the gold of the temple, he committeth sin, and is a debtor.		
17 Ye fools and blind: for whether is greater, the gold, or the temple that sanctifieth the gold?	14 You are fools and blind; for which is the greater, the gold, or the temple that sanctifieth the gold?		
18 And, Whosoever shall swear by the altar, it is nothing; but whosoever sweareth by the gift that is upon it, he is guilty.	15 And ye say, Whosoever sweareth by the altar, it is nothing; but whosoever sweareth by the gift that is upon it, he is guilty.		

Matt. 23	JST Matt. 23		TPJS
19 **Ye** fools and blind: for **whether** is greater, the gift, or the altar that sanctifieth the gift?	16 **O** fools, and blind! For **which** is **the** greater, the gift, or the altar that sanctifieth the gift?		
20 Whoso therefore **shall** swear by the altar, **sweareth by it**, and by all things thereon.	17 **Verily I say unto you**, Whoso, therefore, **sweareth by it**, sweareth by the altar, and by all things thereon.		We may tithe mint and rue, and all manner of herbs, and still not obey the commandments of God. The object with me is to obey and teach others to obey God in just what He tells us to do. It mattereth not whether the principle is popular or unpopular, I will always maintain a true principle, even if I stand alone in it (p. 332).
21 And whoso shall swear by the temple, sweareth by it, and by him **that** dwelleth therein.	18 And whoso shall swear by the temple, sweareth by it, and by him **who** dwelleth therein.		
22 And he that shall swear by heaven, sweareth by the throne of God, and by him **that** sitteth thereon.	19 And he that shall swear by heaven, sweareth by the throne of God, and by him **who** sitteth thereon.		
23 Woe unto you, scribes and Pharisees, hypocrites! for ye pay tithe of mint and anise and cummin, and have omitted the weightier **matters** of the law, judgment, mercy, and faith: these ought ye to have done, and not to leave the other undone.	20 Woe unto you, Scribes and Pharisees, hypocrites! For ye pay tithe of mint, and anise, and cummin; and have omitted the weightier **things** of the law; judgment, mercy, and faith; these ought ye to have done, and not to leave the other undone.		
24 Ye blind guides, **which** strain at a gnat, and swallow a camel.	21 Ye blind guides, **who** strain at a gnat, and swallow a camel; **who make yourselves appear unto men that ye would not commit the least sin, and yet ye yourselves, transgress the whole law.**		
25 Woe unto you, scribes and Pharisees, hypocrites! for ye make clean the outside of the cup and of the platter, but within they are full of extortion and excess.			
26 **Thou** blind Pharisee, cleanse first **that which is within** the cup and platter, that the outside of them may be clean also.	23 Ye blind Pharisees! Cleanse first the cup and platter **within**, that the outside of them may be clean also.		
27 Woe unto you, scribes and Pharisees, hypocrites! for ye are like unto whited sepulchres, which indeed appear beautiful outward, but are within full of **dead men's** bones, and of all uncleanness.	24 Woe unto you, Scribes and Pharisees, hypocrites! For ye are like unto whited sepulchers, which indeed appear beautiful outwardly, but are within full of **the** bones **of the dead**, and of all uncleanness.		

Matt. 23	JST Matt. 23	JST Matt. 23	

Matt. 23

28 Even so ye also outwardly appear righteous unto men, but within ye are full of hypocrisy and iniquity.

29 Woe unto you, scribes and Pharisees, hypocrites! because ye build the tombs of the prophets, and garnish the sepulchres of the righteous,

30 And say, If we had been in the days of our fathers, we would not have been partakers with them in the blood of the prophets.

31 Wherefore ye **be** witnesses unto yourselves,

that ye are the children of them **which** killed the prophets.

32 Fill **ye** up **then** the measure of your fathers.

33 Ye serpents, ye generation of vipers, how can ye escape the damnation of hell?

34 ¶ Wherefore, behold, I send unto you prophets, and wise men, and scribes: and **some** of them ye shall kill and crucify; and **some** of them shall ye scourge in your synagogues, and persecute **them** from city to city:

35 That upon you may come all the righteous blood shed upon the earth, from the blood of righteous Abel unto the blood of Zacharias son of Barachias, whom ye slew between the temple and the altar.

36 Verily I say unto you, All these things shall come upon this generation.

JST Matt. 23

28 Wherefore, ye **are** witnesses unto yourselves **of your own wickedness, and** ye are the children of them **who** killed the prophets;

29 **And will** fill up the measure **then** of your fathers; **for ye, yourselves, kill the prophets like unto your fathers.**

30 Ye serpents, **and** generation of vipers! How can ye escape the damnation of hell?

31 Wherefore, behold, I send unto you prophets, and wise men, and scribes; and of them ye shall kill and crucify; and of them ye shall scourge in your synagogues, and persecute from city to city;

(continued in column 3)

JST Matt. 23

34 **Ye bear testimony against your fathers, when ye, yourselves, are partakers of the same wickedness.**

35 **Behold your fathers did it through ignorance, but ye do not; wherefore, their sins shall be upon your heads.**

TPJS-- Hence as they [Jesus' generation] possessed greater privileges than any other generation, not only pertaining to themselves, but to their dead, their sin was greater, as they not only neglected their own salvation but that of their progenitors, and hence their blood was required at their hands. (pp. 222-23)

TPJS-- When Herod's edict went forth to destroy the young children, John was about six months older than Jesus, and came under this hellish edict, and Zacharias caused his mother to take him into the mountains, where he was raised on locusts and wild honey. When his father refused to disclose his hiding place, and being officiating high priest at the Temple that year, was slain by Herod's order, between the porch and the altar, as Jesus said. (p. 261)

Matt. 23	JST Matt. 23	B of M	D & C / TPJS

143. Jesus Weeps Over Jerusalem

Matt. 23	JST Matt. 23	B of M	D & C / TPJS
	36 Then Jesus began to weep over Jerusalem, saying,		
37 O Jerusalem, Jerusalem, **thou that** killest the prophets, and stonest them **which** are sent unto **thee,** how often would I have gathered **thy** children together, even as a hen gather**eth** her chickens under her wings, and ye would not! 38 Behold, your house is left unto you desolate. 39 For I say unto you, Ye shall not see me henceforth,	37 O Jerusalem! Jerusalem! **Ye who will** kill the prophets, and **will** stone them **who** are sent unto **you**; how often would I have gathered **your** children together, even as a hen gathers her chickens under her wings, and ye would not. 39 For I say unto you, **that** ye shall not see me henceforth, **and know that I am he of whom it is written by the prophets, until** ye shall say,	3 Ne 10:4 O ye people of these great cities which have fallen, who are descendents of Jacob, yea, who are of the house of Israel, how oft have I gathered you as a hen gathereth her chickens under her wings, and have nourished you. 5 And again, how oft would I have gathered you as a hen gathereth her chickens under her wings, yea, O ye people of the house of Israel, who have fallen; yea, O ye people of the house of Israel, ye that dwelt at Jerusalem, as ye that have fallen; yea, how oft would I have gathered you as a hen gathereth her chickens, and ye would not.	10:65 For, behold, I will gather them as a hen gathereth her chickens under her wings, if they will not harden their hearts; (See also 29:1-2; 43:24-25.) TPJS-- The doctrine of baptism for the dead is clearly shown in the New Testament; and if the doctrine is not good, then throw the New Testament away; but if it is the word of God, then let the doctrine be acknowledged; and it was the reason why
till ye shall say, Blessed is he **that** cometh in the name of the Lord.	40 Blessed is he **who** cometh in the name of the Lord, **in the clouds of heaven, and all the holy angels with him.** 41 **Then understood his disciples that he should come again on the earth, after that he was glorified and crowned on the right hand of God.**	6 O ye house of Israel whom I have spared, how oft will I gather you as a hen gathereth her chickens under her wings, if ye will repent and return unto me with full purpose of heart. 7 But if not, O house of Israel, the places of your dwellings shall become desolate until the time of the fulfilling of the covenant to your fathers.	Jesus said unto the Jews, [Matt. 23:37]-- that they might attend to the ordinances of baptism for the dead as well as other ordinances of the priesthood, and receive revelations from heaven, and be perfected in the things of the kingdom of God--but they would not. This was the case on the day of Pentecost: those blessings were poured out on the disciples on that occasion. God ordained that He would save the dead, and would do it by gathering His people together. (p. 310)

TPJS-- This subject was presented to me since I came to the stand. What was the object of gathering the Jews, or the people of God in any age of the world? I can never find much to say in expounding a text. A man never has half so much fuss to unlock a door, if he has key, as though he had not, and had to cut it open with his jack-knife.

The main object was to build unto the Lord a house whereby He could reveal unto His people the ordinances of His house and the glories of His kingdom, and teach the people the way of salvation; for there are certain ordinances and principles that, when they are taught and practiced, must be done in a place or house built for that purpose. (pp. 307-308)

Why gather the people together in this place? For the same pupose that Jesus wanted to gather the Jews-- to receive the ordinances, the blessings, and glories that God has in store for His Saints. (p. 312)

Mark 12	JST Mark 12	Luke 21	

144. The Widow's Mite

41 ¶ And Jesus sat over against the treasury, and beheld how the people cast money into the treasury: and many that were rich cast in much.

42 And there came a certain poor widow, and she **threw** in two mites, which make a farthing.

43 And **he** called **unto him** his disciples, and **saith** unto them, Verily I say unto you, That this poor widow hath cast more in, than all they **which** have cast into the treasury:

44 For all **they** did cast in of their abundance; but she **of** her want did cast in all that she had, even all her living.

47 And **after this**, Jesus sat over against the treasury, and beheld how the people cast money into the treasury; and many that were rich cast in much.

48 And there came a certain poor widow, and she **cast** in two mites, which make a farthing.

49 And **Jesus** called his disciples, and **said** unto them, Verily I say unto you, that this poor widow hath cast more in, than all they **who** have cast into the treasury;

44 For all **the rich** did cast in of their abundance; but she, **notwithstanding** her want, did cast in all that she had; **yea**, even all her living.

And he looked up, and saw the rich men casting their gifts into the treasury.

2 And he also saw a certain poor widow casting in thither two mites.

3 And he said, Of a truth I say unto you, that this poor widow hath cast in more than they all:

4 For all these have of their abundance cast in unto the offerings of God: but she of her penury hath cast in all the living that she had.

145. The People and Chief Rulers Reject Christ

37 ¶ But though he had done so many miracles before them, yet they believed not on him:

38 That the saying of Esaias the prophet might be fulfilled, which he spake, Lord, who hath believed our report? and to whom hath the arm of the Lord been revealed?

39 Therefore they could not believe, because that Esaias said again,

40 He hath blinded their eyes, and hardened their heart; that they should not see with their eyes, nor understand with their heart, and be converted, and I should heal them.

41 These things said Esaias, when he saw his glory, and spake of him.

42 ¶ Nevertheless among the chief rulers also many believed on him; but because of the Pharisees they did not confess him, lest they should be put out of the synagogue:

43 For they loved the praise of men more than the praise of God.

44 ¶ Jesus cried and said, He that believeth on me, believeth not on me, but on him that sent me.

45 And he that seeth me seeth him that sent me.

46 I am come a light into the world, that whosoever believeth on me should not abide in darkness.

47 And if any man hear my words, and believe not, I judge him not: for I came not to judge the world, but to save the world.

48 He that rejecteth me, and receiveth not my
(continued in column 3)

words, hath one that judgeth him: the word that I have spoken, the same shall judge him in the last day.

49 For I have not spoken of myself; but the Father which sent me, he gave me a commandment, what I should say, and what I should speak.

50 And I know that his commandment is life everlasting: whatsoever I speak therefore, even as the Father said unto me, so I speak.

Matt. 24	JS-Matt.	Mark 13	JST Mark 13

146. Signs of My Coming

			(The text of JST Mark 13 is essentially that of JS-Matt. The text is given here *only* when it differs from that of JS-Matt.)
And Jesus went out, and departed from the temple: and his disciples came to him for to shew him the buildings of the temple.	2 And Jesus went out, and departed from the temple; and his disciples came to him, for to **hear him, saying: Master, show us concerning** the buildings of the temple, **as thou hast said--**	And as **he** went out of the temple, **one of his** disciples **saith unto him;** Master, **see what manner of stones and what** buildings **are here!**	And as **Jesus** went out of the temple, his disciples **came to him for to hear him, saying,** Master, **show us concerning** the build-ings **of the Temple.**
			2 And **he** said unto **them, Behold ye** these **stones of the temple, and all this great work, and** buildings **of the temple?**
		2 And **Jesus answering** said unto **him, Seest thou** these great buildings? **there shall** not **be left one** stone upon another, that **shall** not **be thrown down.**	3 **Verily I say unto you,** they shall be thrown down **and left unto the Jews desolate.**
	They shall be thrown down, and left unto you desolate.		
2 And Jesus said unto them, See ye not all these things?	3 And Jesus said unto them: See ye not all these things, **and do ye not understand them?**		
verily I say unto you, There shall not be left here one stone upon another, that shall not be thrown down.	Verily I say unto you, there shall not be left here, **upon this temple,** one stone upon another that shall not be thrown down.		
	4 **And Jesus left them, and went upon the Mount of Olives.** And as he sat upon the Mount of Olives, the disciples came unto him privately, saying:	3 And as he sat upon the mount of Olives over against the temple, Peter and James and John and Andrew asked him privat-ely,	
3 ¶ And as he sat upon the mount of Olives, the disciples came unto him privately, saying,			

Luke 21	JST Luke 21	D & C 45	
		16 . . . As ye have asked of me concerning the signs of my coming, in the day when I shall come in my glory in the clouds of heaven, to fulfil the promises that I have made unto your fathers,	
		17 For as ye have looked upon the long absence of your spirits from your bodies to be a bondage, I will show unto you how the day of redemption shall come, and also the restoration of the scattered Israel.	
		18 And now ye behold this temple which is in Jerusalem, which ye call the house of God, and your enemies say that this house shall never fall.	
5 ¶ And as some spake of the temple, how it was adorned with goodly stones and gifts, he said,		19 But verily I say unto you, that desolation shall come upon this generation as a thief in the night, and this people shall be destroyed and scattered among all nations.	
6 As for these things which ye behold, the days will come, in the which there shall not be left one stone upon another, that shall not be thrown down.	6 These things which ye behold, the days will come, in the which there shall not be left one stone upon another, which shall not be thrown down.	20 And this temple which ye now see shall be thrown down that there shall not be left one stone upon another.	
7 And they asked him,	7 And the disciples asked		

303

Matt. 24	JS-Matt.	Mark 13	TPJS
Tell us, when shall these things be?	Tell us when shall these things be **which thou hast said concerning the destruction of the temple, and the Jews;** and what is the sign of thy coming, and of the end of the world, **or the destruction of the wicked, which is the end of the world?**	4 Tell us, when shall these things be?	
and what **shall be the** sign of thy coming, and of the end of the world?		and what shall be the sign when all these things shall be fulfilled?	
4 And Jesus answered and said unto them, Take heed that no man deceive you.	JST verse 5	5 And Jesus answering them began to say, Take heed lest any man deceive you:	Woe, woe be to that man or set of men who lift up their hands against God and His witness in these last days: for they shall deceive almost the very chosen ones! (p. 365)
5 For many shall come in my name, saying, I am Christ; and shall deceive many.	JST verse 6	6 For many shall come in my name, saying, I am Christ; and shall deceive many.	
9 Then shall they deliver you up to be afflicted, and shall kill you:	JST verse 7	9 ¶ But take heed to yourselves: for they shall deliver you up to councils; and in the synagogues ye shall be beaten: and ye shall be brought before rulers and kings for my sake, for a testimony against them. 11 But when they shall lead you, and deliver you up, take no thought beforehand what ye shall speak, neither do ye premeditate: but whatsoever shall be given you in that hour, that speak ye: for it is not ye that speak, but the Holy Ghost. 12 Now the brother shall betray the brother to death, and the father the son; and children shall rise up against their parents, and shall cause them to be put to death.	
and ye shall be hated of all nations for my name's sake.		13 And ye shall be hated of all men for my name's sake:	
10 And then shall many be offended, and shall betray one another, and shall hate one another.	JST verse 8		

Luke 21	JST Luke 21		
saying, Master, **but** when shall these things be?	him, saying, Master, when shall these things be?		
and what sign **will there be** when these things shall come to pass?	And what sign **wilt thou show**, when these things shall come to pass?		
8 And he said, Take heed that ye be not deceived: for many shall come in my name, saying, I am Christ; **and the time draweth near:** go ye not therefore after them.	8 And he said, **The time draweth near, and therefore** take heed that ye be not deceived; for many shall come in my name, saying, I am Christ; go ye not therefore after them.		
12 But before all these, they shall lay their hands on you, and persecute you, delivering you up to the synagogues, and into prisons, being brought before kings and rulers for my name's sake.	11 But before all these **things shall come,** they shall lay their hands on you, and persecute you; delivering you up to the synagogues, and into prisons; being brought before kings and rulers for my name's sake.		
13 And it shall turn to you for a testimony.	JST verse 14		
14 Settle **it** therefore in your hearts, not to meditate before what ye shall answer:	12 Settle **this** therefore in your hearts, not to meditate before what ye shall answer;		
15 For I will give you a mouth and wisdom, which all your adversaries shall not be able to gainsay nor resist.	JST verse 13		
16 And ye shall be betrayed both by parents, and brethren, and kinsfolks, and friends; and some of you shall they cause to be put to death.			
17 And ye shall be hated of all **men** for my name's sake.	16 And ye shall be hated of all **the world** for my name's sake.		
18 But there shall not an hair of your head perish.			

Matt. 24	JS-Matt.	Mark 13	JST Mark 13
11 And many false prophets shall rise, and shall deceive many.	JST verse 9		
12 And because iniquity shall abound, the love of many shall wax cold.	JST verse 10		13 **And because iniquity shall abound, the love of many shall wax cold;** but he that shall endure unto the end, the same shall be saved.
13 But he that **shall endure unto the end,** the same shall be saved.	11 But he that **remaineth steadfast and is not overcome,** the same shall be saved.	but he that shall endure unto the end, the same shall be saved.	
15 When ye therefore shall see the abomination of desolation, spoken of by Daniel the prophet,	12 When **you,** therefore, shall see the abomination of desolation spoken of by Daniel the prophet, **concerning the destruction of Jerusalem, then you shall** stand in the holy place; whoso readeth let him understand.	14 ¶ But when ye shall see the abomination of desolation, spoken of by Daniel the prophet, standing where it ought not,	
stand in the holy place, (whoso readeth, let him understand:)		(let him that readeth understand,)	
16 Then let them **which be** in Judæa flee into the mountains:	13 Then let them **who are** in Judea flee into the mountains;	then let them **that** be in Judæa flee to the mountains:	15 Then let them **who** be in Judea flee **into** the mountains;
17 Let him **which** is on the housetop not **come down** to take any thing out of his house:	14 Let him **who** is on the housetop **flee, and** not **return** to take anything out of his house;	15 And let him **that** is on the housetop **not go down into the house, neither enter therein,** to take any thing out of his house:	16 And let him **who** is on the housetop **flee, and not return** to take anything out of his house;
18 Neither let him **which** is in the field return back to take his clothes.	15 Neither let him **who** is in the field return back to take his clothes;	16 And let him that is in the field not turn back again for to take up his garment.	

Luke 21	JST Luke 21	D & C	Daniel
			12:11 And from the time that the daily sacrifices should be taken away, and the abomination that maketh desolate set up, there shall be a thousand two hundred and ninety days. (See also 8:8-11, 23-25; 11:31)
19 In your patience possess ye your souls.			
20 And when ye shall see Jerusalem compassed with armies, then know that the desolation thereof is nigh.			
21 Then let them **which** are in Judæa flee to the mountains; and let them **which** are in the midst of it depart out; and let not them **that** are in the countries enter **thereinto**.	20 Then let them **who** are in Judea flee to the mountains; and let them **who** are in the midst of it, depart out; and let not them **who** are in the countries, **return to** enter into **the cities**.		
22 For these be the days of vengeance, that all things which are written may be fulfilled.			

Matt. 24	JS-Matt.	Mark 13	JST Mark 13
19 And woe unto them that are with child, and to them that give suck in those days!	JST verse 16	17 But woe to them that are with child, and to them that give suck in those days!	
20 **But** pray ye that your flight be not in the winter, neither on the sabbath day:	17 **Therefore,** pray ye **the Lord** that your flight be not in the winter, neither on the Sabbath day;	18 And pray ye that your flight be not in the winter.	
21 For then shall be great tribulation,	18 For then, **in those days,** shall be great tribulation **on the Jews, and upon the inhabitants of Jerusalem,** such as was not **before sent upon Israel, of God,** since the beginning of **their kingdom**	19 For in those days shall be **affliction,**	20 For then, in those days, shall be great tribulation on the Jews, and upon the inhabitants of Jerusalem; such as was not before sent upon Israel, of God, since the beginning of their kingdom, (for it is written their enemies shall scatter them,) until this time; no, nor ever shall be sent again upon Israel.
such as was not since the beginning of **the world to**		such as was not **from** the beginning of **the creation which God created unto**	
this time, no, nor ever shall be.	until this time; no, nor ever shall be **sent again upon Israel.**	this time, **neither shall be.**	
8 All **these** are the beginning of sorrows.	19 All **things which have befallen them are only the** beginning of the sorrows **which shall come upon them.**		21 **All these things are the beginnings of sorrows.**
22 And except those days should be shortened, there should **no flesh** be saved: but for the elect's sake those days shall be shortened.	20 And except those days should be shortened, there should **none of their flesh** be saved; but for the elect's sake, **according to the covenant,** those days shall be shortened.	20 And except that the Lord had shortened those days, no flesh should be saved: but for the elect's sake, whom he hath chosen, he hath shortened the days.	
	21 **Behold, these things I have spoken unto you concerning the Jews; and again, after the tribulation of those days which shall come upon Jerusalem,** if any man shall say unto you, Lo, here is Christ, or there, believe **him not;**		24 And **then immediately after the tribulation of those days which shall come upon Jerusalem,** if any man shall say unto you, Lo, here is Christ; or there; believe him not.
23 **Then** if any man shall say unto you, Lo, here is Christ, or there; believe **it not.**		21 And then if any man shall say to you, Lo, here is Christ; or, **lo, he is there;** believe him not:	
24 For there shall arise false Christs, and false prophets, and shall shew great signs and wonders; insomuch that, if it **were** possible, they shall deceive the very elect.	22 For **in those days** there shall **also** arise false Christs, and false prophets, and shall show great signs and wonders, insomuch, that, if possible, they shall deceive the very elect, **who are the elect according to the covenant.**	22 For false Christs and false prophets shall rise, and shall shew signs and wonders, to seduce, if it were possible, even the elect.	
	23 **Behold, I speak these things unto you for the elect's sake; and you also**		

Luke 21	JST Luke 21	D & C	B of M
23 But woe unto them **that** are with child, and to them **that** give suck, in those days!	22 But woe unto them **who** are with child, and to them **who** give suck, in those days!		1 Nephi 19:13 And as for those who are at Jerusalem, saith the prophet, they shall be scourged by all people, because they crucify the God of Israel, and turn their hearts aside, rejecting signs and wonders, and the power and glory of the God of Israel.
for there shall be great distress in the land, and wrath upon this people. 24 And they shall fall by the edge of the sword, and shall be led away captive into all nations: and Jerusalem shall be trodden down of the Gentiles, until the times of the Gentiles be fulfilled.		45:21 And it shall come to pass, that this generation of Jews shall not pass away until every desolation which I have told you concerning them shall come to pass. 22 Ye say that ye know that the end of the world cometh; ye say also that ye know that the heavens and the earth shall pass away; 23 And in this ye say truly, for so it is; but these things which I have told you shall not pass away until all shall be fulfilled.	14 And because they turn their hearts aside, saith the prophet, and have despised the Holy One of Israel, they shall wander in the flesh, and perish, and become a hiss and a byword, and be hated among all nations. 15 Nevertheless, when that day cometh, saith the prophet, that they no more turn aside their hearts against the Holy One of Israel, then will he remember the covenants which he made to their fathers.
		24 And this I have told you concerning Jerusalem; and when that day shall come, shall a remnant be scattered among all nations; 25 But they shall be gathered again; but they shall remain until the times of the Gentiles be fulfilled.	2 Nephi 25:14 And behold it shall come to pass that after the Messiah hath risen from the dead, and hath manifested himself unto his people, unto as many as will believe on his name, behold, Jerusalem shall be destroyed again: for wo unto them that fight against God and the people of his church.
	24 Now **these things he spake unto them, concerning the destruction of Jerusalem** ...		15 Wherefore, the Jews shall be scattered among all nations: yea, and also Babylon shall be destroyed; wherefore, the Jews shall be scattered by other nations.

Matt. 24	JS-Matt.	Mark 13	
6 And ye shall hear of wars, and rumours of wars: see that ye be not troubled: for all these things must come to pass, but the end is not yet.	shall hear of wars, and rumors of wars; see that ye be not troubled, for all I have told you must come to pass; but the end is not yet.	7 And when ye shall hear of wars and rumours of wars, be ye not troubled: for such things must needs be; but the end shall not be yet.	
25 Behold, I have told you before.	JST verse 24		
26 Wherefore if they shall say unto you, Behold, he is in the desert; go not forth: behold, he is in the secret chambers; believe it not.	JST verse 25		
27 For as the lightning cometh out of the east, and shineth even unto the west;	26 For as the light of the morning cometh out of the east, and shineth even unto the west, and covereth the whole earth, so shall also the coming of the Son of Man be.		
so shall also the coming of the Son of man be.			
	27 And now I show unto you a parable. Behold, wheresoever the carcass is, there will the eagles be gathered together; so likewise shall mine elect be gathered from the four quarters of the earth.		
28 For wheresoever the carcase is, there will the eagles be gathered togeth-·er.			
	28 And they shall hear of wars, and rumors of wars.		
	29 Behold I speak for mine elect's sake; for nation shall rise against nation, and kingdom against kingdom; there shall be famines, and pestilences, and earthquakes, in divers places.		
7 For nation shall rise against nation, and kingdom against kingdom: and there shall be famines, and pestilences, and earthquakes, in divers places.		8 For nation shall rise against nation, and kingdom against kingdom: there shall be earthquakes in divers places, and there shall be famines and troubles: these are the beginnings of sorrows.	
	30 And again, because iniquity shall abound, the love of men shall wax cold; but he that shall not be overcome, the same shall be saved.		

TPJS-- Judah must return, Jerusalem must be rebuilt, and the temple, and water come out from under the temple, and the waters of the Dead Sea be healed. It will take some time to rebuild the walls of the city and the temple, &c.; and all this must be done before the Son of Man will make His appearance. There will be wars and rumors of wars, signs in the heavens above and on the earth beneath, the sun turned into darkness and the moon to blood, earthquakes in divers places, the seas heaving beyond their bounds; then will appear one grand sign of the Son of Man in heaven. But what will the world do? They will say it is a planet, a comet, etc. But the Son of man will come as the sign of the coming of the Son of Man, which will be as the light of the morning cometh out of the east. (pp. 286-87)

Luke 21	JST Luke 21	D & C	
9 **But** when ye shall hear of wars and commotions, be not terrified: for these things must first come to pass; but the end **is not by and by**.	9 **And** when ye shall hear of wars and commotions, be not terrified; for these things must first come to pass; but **this is not** the end.	45:26 And in that day shall be heard of wars and rumors of wars, and the whole earth shall be in commotion, and men's hearts shall fail them, and they shall say that Christ delayeth his coming until the end of the earth.	
10 Then said he unto them, Nation shall rise against nation, and kingdom against kingdom: 11 And great earthquakes shall be in divers places, and famines, and pestilences; and fearful sights and great signs shall there be from heaven.		33 And there shall be earthquakes also in divers places, and many desolations; yet men will harden their hearts against me, and they will take up the sword, one against another, and they will kill one another. 27 And the love of men shall wax cold, and iniquity shall abound.	

Matt. 24	JS-Matt.	TPJS Mark 13	
14 And this gospel of the kingdom shall be preached in all the world for a witness unto all nations; and then shall the end come.	31 And **again**, this Gospel of the Kingdom shall be preached in all the world, for a witness unto all nations, and then shall the end come, **or the destruction of the wicked;**	TPJS-- I shall read the 24th chapter of Matthew, and give it a literal rendering and reading; and when it is rightly understood, it will be edifying. I thought the very oddity of its rendering would be edifying anyhow--- "And it will be preached, the Gospel of the kingdom, in the whole world, to a witness over all people: and then will the end come." I will now read it in German [which he did, and many Germans who were present said he translated it correctly]. The Savior said when these tribulations should take place, it should be committed to a man who should be a witness over the whole world: the keys of knowledge, power and revelations should be revealed to a witness who should hold the testimony to the world. It has always been my province to dig up hidden mysteries-- new things-- for my hearers. Just at the time when some men think that I have no right to the keys of the Priesthood-- just at that time I have the greatest right. The Germans are an exalted people. The old German translators are the most nearly correct-- most honest of any of the translators; and therefore I get testimony to bear me out in the revelations that I have preached for the last fourteen years. The old German, Latin, Greek and Hebrew translations all say it is true: they cannot be impeached, and therefore I am in good company. (p. 364).	
	32 **And again shall the abomination of desolation, spoken of by Daniel the prophet, be fulfilled.**		
29 ¶ Immediately after the tribulation of those days **shall** the sun be darkened, and the moon shall not give her light, and the stars shall fall from heaven,	33 **And** immediately after the tribulation of those days, the sun **shall** be darkened, and the moon shall not give her light, and the stars shall fall from heaven,	24 ¶ But in those days, after that tribulation, the sun shall be darkened, and the moon shall not give her light, 25 And the stars of heaven shall fall,	
and the powers of **the** heavens shall be shaken: 34 Verily I say unto you, This generation	and the powers of heaven shall be shaken. 34 Verily, I say unto you, this generation,**in which these things shall be shown forth,** shall not	and the powers that are in heaven shall be shaken. 30 Verily I say unto you, that this generation	

Luke 21	JST Luke 21	D & C	D & C
		45:28 And when the times of the Gentiles is come in, a light shall break forth among them that sit in darkness, and it shall be the fulness of my gospel;	
		29 But they receive it not; for they perceive not the light, and they turn their hearts from me because of the precepts of men.	
		30 And in that generation shall the times of the Gentiles be fulfilled.	
		31 And there shall be men standing in that generation, that shall not pass until they shall see an overflowing scourge; for a desolating sickness shall cover the land.	
	24 . . . And then his disciples asked him, saying, Master, tell us concerning thy coming?	32 But my disciples shall stand in holy places, and shall not be moved; but among the wicked, men shall lift up their voices and curse God and die.	49:23 Wherefore, be not deceived, but continue in steadfastness, looking forth for the heavens to be shaken, and the earth to tremble and to reel to and fro as a drunken man, and for the valleys to be exalted, and for the mountains to be made low, and for the rough places to become smooth-- and all this when the angel shall sound his trumpet.
25 ¶ And there shall be signs in the sun, and in the moon, and in the stars; and upon the earth distress of nations, with perplexity; the sea and the waves roaring;	25 And he answered them, and said, In the generation in which the times of the Gentiles shall be fulfilled, there shall be signs in the sun, and in the moon, and in the stars; and upon the earth distress of nations with perplexity, like the sea and the waves roaring. The earth also shall be troubled, and the waters of the great deep;	40 And they shall see signs and wonders, for they shall be shown forth in the heavens above, and in the earth beneath. 41 And they shall behold blood, and fire, and vapors of smoke.	

TPJS-- All, all, speak with a voice of thunder, that man is not able to govern himself, to legislate for himself, to protect himself, to promote his own good, nor the good of the world. (p. 250)

To bring about this state of things, there must of necessity be great confusion among the nations of the earth; "distress of nations with perplexity." Am I asked what is the cause of the present distress? I would answer, "Shall there be evil in a city and the Lord hath not done it?" (pp. 252-53)

Luke 21	JST Luke 21	D & C	D & C
26 Men's hearts failing them for fear, and for looking after those things which are coming on the earth: for the powers of heaven shall be shaken.		42 And before the day of the Lord shall come, the sun shall be darkened, and the moon be turned into blood, and the stars fall from heaven.	88:91 And all things shall be in commotion; and surely, men's hearts shall fail them; for fear shall come upon all people.
32 Verily I say unto you, This generation	32 Verily I say unto you, this generation, the generation when the times of the Gentiles be fulfilled,		

Matt. 24	JS-Matt.	Mark 13	JST Mark 13
shall not pass, till all **these things** be fulfilled.	**pass away until all I have told you shall be fulfilled.**	shall not pass, till all these things be done.	
35 Heaven and earth shall pass away,	35 **Although, the days will come, that** heaven and earth shall pass away;	31 Heaven and earth shall pass away:	
but my words shall not pass away.	yet my words shall not pass away, **but all shall be fulfilled.** 36 **And, as I said before, after the tribulation of those days, and the powers of the heavens shall be shaken, then shall ap-**pear the sign of the Son of Man in heaven, and then	but my words shall not pass away.	
30 And then shall appear the sign of the Son of man in heaven: and then shall all the tribes of the earth mourn, and they shall see the Son of man coming in the clouds of heaven with power and great glory.	shall all the tribes of the earth mourn; and they shall see the Son of Man com-ing in the clouds of hea-ven, with power and great glory; 37 **And whoso treasur-eth up my word, shall not be deceived, for the Son of Man shall come**, and he	26 And then shall they see the Son of man com-ing in the clouds with great power and glory.	44 **For the Son of Man shall come; and he shall** send his angels **before him with the great sound of a**
31 And he shall send his angels with **a great sound of a trumpet, and they shall gather together his elect from the four winds**, from one end of heaven to the other.	shall send his angels be-**fore him with the great sound of a trumpet, and** they shall gather together **the remainder of his elect** from the four winds, from one end of heaven to the other.	27 And then shall he send his angels, and shall gather together his elect from the four winds, from **the ut-termost part of the earth to the uttermost part of** heaven.	**trumpet, and they shall** gather together his elect from the four winds, from **one end of heaven to the other.**
32 Now learn a parable of the fig tree;	38 Now learn a parable of the figtree--	28 Now learn a parable of the fig tree;	45 Now learn a parable of the fig tree.

314

Luke 21	JST Luke 21	D & C	B of M
shall not pass away, till all be fulfilled.	Shall not pass away till all be fulfilled.	56:11 And though the heaven and the earth pass away, these words shall not pass away, but shall be fulfilled.	2 Nephi 25:16 And after they have been scattered and the Lord God hath scourged them by other nations for the space of
33 Heaven and earth shall pass away:		45:43 And the remnant shall be gathered unto this place;	many generations, yea, even down from generation to generation
but my words shall not pass away.		44 And then they shall look for me, and, behold, I will come; and they shall see me in the clouds of heaven, clothed with power and great glory; with all the holy angels; and he that watches not for me shall be cut off.	Until they shall be persuaded to believe in Christ, the Son of God, and the atonement, which is infinite for all mankind—and when that day shall come that they shall believe in Christ, and worship the Father in
27 And then shall they see the Son of man coming in a cloud with power and great glory.	(Vs. 27-28 reversed in JST.)		His name, with pure hearts and clean hands, and look not forward any more for another
		88:93 And immediately there shall appear a great sign in heaven, and all people shall see it together.	Messiah, then, at that time, the day will come that it must needs be expedient that they should believe these things.
		76:63 These are they whom he shall bring with him, when he shall come in the clouds of heaven to reign on the earth over his people.	17 And the Lord will set his hand again the second time to restore his people from their lost and fallen state. Wherefore, he will proceed to do a marvelous work and a wonder among the children of men.
		45:34 And now, when I the Lord had spoken these words unto my disciples, they were troubled.	18 Wherefore, he shall bring forth his words unto them, which words shall judge them at the last day, for they shall be
28 And when these things begin to come to pass, then look up, and lift up your heads: for your redemption draweth nigh.	27 And when these things begin to come to pass, then look up and lift up your heads, for **the day of** your redemption draweth nigh.	35 And I said unto them: Be not troubled, for, when all these things shall come to pass, ye may know that the promises which have been made unto you shall be fulfilled.	given them for the purpose of convincing them of the true Messiah, who was rejected by them:. . . (see rest of verse 18, and also 2 Nephi 30:7).
		36 And when the light shall begin to break forth, it shall be with them like unto a parable which I will show you—	
29 And he spake to them a parable; Behold the fig tree, and all the trees:	29 And he spake to them a parable, **saying,** Behold the fig tree, and all the trees.	37 Ye look and behold the fig trees, and ye see them	

Matt. 24	JS-Matt.	Mark 13	JST Mark 13
When **his branch is** yet tender, and **putteth** forth leaves, ye know that summer is nigh:	When **its branches are** yet tender, and **it begins to put forth** leaves, you know that summer is nigh **at hand**;	When **her branch is** yet tender, and putteth forth leaves, ye know that summer is **near**:	When **his branches are** yet tender, and putteth forth leaves, ye know that summer is **nigh at hand.**
33 So likewise ye, when ye shall see all these things, know that it is near, even at the doors.	39 So likewise, **mine elect,** when they shall see all these things, **they shall** know that he is near, even at the doors;	29 So ye in like manner, when ye shall see these things come to pass, know that it is nigh, even at the doors.	
36 ¶ But of that day and hour knoweth **no man**, no, not the angels of heaven, but my Father only.	40 But of that day, and hour, **no one** knoweth; no, not the angels of **God in** heaven, but my Father only.	32 ¶ But of that day and **that hour knoweth no man**, no, not the angels **which are in** heaven, **neither the Son, but the Father.**	47 But of that day and hour **no one** knoweth; no, not the angels **of God in** heaven, but **my Father** only.
37 But as the days of **Noe were**, so shall also the coming of the Son of **man be.**	41 But as it **was in the** days of **Noah**, so it shall **be also** at the coming of the Son of Man;		
38 For as in the days **that** were before the flood they were eating and drinking, marrying and giving in marriage, **until the day that Noe entered into the ark,**	42 For **it shall be with them**, as it **was** in the days **which** were before the flood; for **until the day that Noah entered into the ark** they were eating and drinking, marrying and giving in marriage;		49 **Until the day that Noah entered into the ark, they** were eating and drinking, marrying and giving in marriage, and **knew** not until the flood came and took them all away; so shall also the coming of the Son of Man be.
39 And knew not until the flood came, and took them all away; so shall also the coming of the Son of man be.	43 And knew not until the flood came, and took them all away; so shall also the coming of the Son of Man be.		
40 Then shall two be in the field; the one shall be taken, and the other left.	44 Then shall **be fulfilled that which is written, that in the last days,** two **shall** be in the field, the one shall be taken, and the other left;		
41 Two **women** shall be grinding at the mill; the one shall be taken, and the other left.	45 Two shall be grinding at the mill, the one shall be taken, and the other left;		
	46 **And what I say unto one, I say unto all men;** watch, therefore, for **you** know not at what hour your Lord doth come.	37 And what I say unto you I say unto all, Watch.	
42 ¶ Watch therefore: for ye know not what hour your Lord doth come.			

Luke 21	JST Luke 21	D & C	D & C
30 When they now shoot forth, ye see and know of your own selves that summer is now nigh at hand.		with your eyes, and ye say when they begin to shoot forth, and their leaves are yet tender, that summer is now nigh at hand;	35:15 and the poor and the meek shall have the gospel preached unto them, and they shall be looking forth for the time of my coming, for it is nigh at hand—
31 So likewise ye, when ye see these things come to pass, know ye that the kingdom of God is nigh at hand.		45:38 Even so it shall be in that day when they shall see all these things, then shall they know that the hour is nigh.

39 And it shall come to pass that he that feareth me shall be looking forth for the great day of the Lord to come, even for the signs of the coming of the Son of Man. | 16 And they shall learn the parable of the fig tree, for even now already summer is nigh. |
| Did Christ speak this as a general principle throughout all generations? Oh no, he spoke in the present tense. No man that was then living upon the footstool of God knew the day or the hour. But he did not say that there was no man throughout all generations that should not know the day or the hour. No, for this would be in flat contradiction with other scripture. For the prophet says that God will do nothing but what he reveals unto his servants the prophets. Consequently, if it is not made known to the prophets, it will not come to pass;

WJS pp. 180-181 | | | 39:21 For the time is at hand; the day or the hour no man knoweth; but it surely shall come. (See also D&C 49:7) |
| 36 Watch ye therefore, and pray always,

that ye may be accounted | 36 **And what I say unto one, I say unto all**, Watch ye therefore, and pray always, **and keep my commandments,** that ye may be counted worthy | | |

Matt. 24	JS-Matt.	Mark 13	
43 But know this, **that** if the goodman of the house had known in what watch the thief would come, he would have watched, and would not have suffered his house to **be** broken up.	47 But know this, if the good man of the house had known in what watch the thief would come, he would have watched, and would not have suffered his house to **have been** broken up, **but would have been ready**.		
44 Therefore be ye also ready: for in such an hour as ye think not the Son of man cometh.	48 Therefore be ye also ready, for in such an hour as ye think not, the Son of Man cometh.	33 Take ye heed, watch and pray: for ye know not when the time is. 34 For the Son of man is a man taking a far journey, who left his house, and gave authority to his servants, and to every man his work, and commanded the porter to watch.	
45 Who then is a faithful and wise servant, whom his lord hath made ruler over his household, to give them meat in due season?	JST verse 49		
46 Blessed is that servant, whom his lord when he cometh shall find so doing.	50 Blessed is that servant whom his lord, when he cometh, shall find so doing; **and** verily I say unto you, he shall make him ruler over all his goods.		
47 Verily I say unto you, **That** he shall make him ruler over all his goods.			
48 But **and** if that evil servant shall say in his heart, My lord delayeth his coming;	51 But if that evil servant shall say in his heart: My lord delayeth his coming,		
49 And shall begin to smite his fellowservants, and to eat and drink with the drunken;	JST verse 52		
50 The lord of that servant shall come in a day when he looketh not for him, and in an hour that he is not aware of,	JST verse 53		
		35 Watch ye therefore: for ye know not when the master of the house cometh, at even, or at midnight, or at the cockcrowing, or in the morning:	

Luke 21	JST Luke 21		D & C
worthy to escape all these things **that** shall come to pass, and to stand before the Son of man.	to escape all these things **which** shall come to pass, and to stand before the Son of Man **when he shall come clothed in the glory of his Father**.		
			61:38 Gird up your loins and be watchful and be sober, looking forth for the coming of the Son of Man, for he cometh in an hour you think not.

124:10 For the day of my visitation cometh speedily, in an hour when ye think not of; and where shall be the safety of my people, and refuge for those who shall be left of them? |
| 34 ¶ **And** take heed to **your**selves, lest at any time **your** hearts be overcharged with surfeiting, and drunkeness, and cares | 34 **Let my disciples therefore** take heed to **them**selves, lest at any time **their** hearts be overcharged with surfeiting, and drunkeness, and cares | | |

Matt. 24	JS-Matt.	Mark 13	JST Mark 13
51 And shall cut him asunder, and appoint him his portion with the hypocrites: there shall be weeping and gnashing of teeth.	JST verse 54 55 And thus cometh the end of the wicked, according to the prophecy of Moses, saying: They shall be cut off from among the people; but the end of the earth is not yet, but by and by.	36 Lest coming suddenly he find you sleeping. 37 And what I say unto you I say unto all, Watch.	61 There shall be weeping and gnashing of teeth; and thus cometh the end.

Matt. 25	JST Matt. 25		D & C

147. Parable of the Ten Virgins

Then **shall** the kingdom of heaven be likened unto ten virgins, **which** took their lamps, and went forth to meet the bridegroom. 2 And five of them were wise, and five were foolish. 3 They that were foolish took their lamps, and took no oil with them: 4 But the wise took oil in their vessels with their lamps. 5 While the bridegroom tarried, they all slumbered and slept. 6 And at midnight there was a cry made, Behold, the bridegroom cometh; go ye out to meet him. 7 Then all those virgins arose, and trimmed their lamps. 8 And the foolish said unto the wise, Give us of your oil; for our lamps are gone out. 9 But the wise answered,	**And** then, **at that day, before the Son of Man comes,** the kingdom of heaven **shall** be likened unto ten virgins, **who** took their lamps, and went forth to meet the bridegroom. 8 But the wise answered,		33:17 Wherefore, be faithful, praying always, having your lamps trimmed and burning, and oil with you, that you may be ready at the coming of the Bridegroom— 18 For behold, verily, verily, I say unto you, that I come quickly. Even so. Amen. 63:54 And until that hour there will be foolish virgins among the wise; and at that hour cometh an

(continued on page 321)

Luke 21	JST Luke 21		
of this life, and **so** that day come upon **you** unawares. 35 For as a snare **shall it** come on all them **that** dwell on the face of the whole earth.	of this life, and that day come upon **them** unawares. 35 For as a snare **it shall** come on all them **who** dwell on the face of the whole earth.		

Matt. 25	JST Matt. 25		D & C
saying, **Not so**: lest their be not enough for us and you: **but** go ye rather to them that sell, and buy for yourselves.	saying, Lest their be not enough for us and you, go ye rather to them that sell, and buy for yourselves.		entire separation of the righteous and the wicked; and in that day will I send mine angels to pluck out the wicked and cast them into unquenchable fire.
10 And while they went to buy, the bridegroom came; and they that were ready went in with him to the marriage: and the door was shut.			45:56 And at that day, when I shall come in my glory, shall the parable be fulfilled which I spake concerning the ten virgins.
11 Afterward came also the other virgins, saying, Lord, Lord, open to us.	10 Afterward came also the other virgins, saying, Lord, Lord, upon **un**to us.		57 For they that are wise and have received the truth, and have taken the Holy Spirit for their guide, and have not been deceived—verily I say unto you, they shall not be hewn down and cast into the fire, but shall abide the day.
12 But he answered and said, Verily I say unto you, **I** know **you** not.	11 But he answered and said, Verily I say unto you, **Ye** know **me** not.		
13 Watch therefore, for ye know neither the day nor the hour wherein the Son of **man** cometh.	12 Watch therefore, for ye know neither the day nor the hour wherein the Son of **Man** cometh.		

TPJS—Behold, He will not fail you! He will come with ten thousand of His Saints, and all His adversaries shall be destroyed with the breath of His lips! All those who keep their inheritances, notwithstanding they should be beaten and driven, shall be likened unto the wise virgins who took oil in their lamps. But all those who are unbelieving and fearful, will be likened unto the foolish virgins, who took no oil in their lamps: and when they shall return and say unto the Saints, Give us of your lands—behold, there will be no room found for them. (p. 36).

Matt. 25	JST Matt. 25		

148. Parable of the Talents

13 Now I will liken these things unto a parable.

14 ¶ For **the kingdom of heaven** is as a man travelling into a far country, who called his own servants, and delivered unto them his goods.

14 For **it** is **like** as a man travelling into a far country, who called his own servants, and delivered unto them his goods.

15 And unto one he gave five talents, to another two, and to another one; to every man according to his several ability; and straightway **took** his journey.

15 And unto one he gave five talents, to another two, and to another one; to every man according to his several ability; and straightway **went on** his journey.

16 Then he that had received the five talents went and traded with the same, and **made them** other five talents.

16 Then he that had received the five talents, went and traded with the same; and **gained** other five talents.

17 And likewise he **that had** received two, he also gained other two.

17 And likewise he **who** received two **talents**, he also gained other two.

18 But he **that** had received one went and digged in the earth, and hid his lord's money.

18 But he **who** had received one, went and digged in the earth and hid his lord's money.

19 After a long time the lord of those servants cometh, and reckoneth with them.

20 And so he that had received five talents came and brought other five talents, saying, Lord, thou deliveredst unto me five talents: behold, I have gained beside them five talents more.

20 And so he that had received **the** five talents came, and brought other five talents, saying, Lord, thou deliveredst unto me five talents; behold, I have gained besides them, five talents more.

21 His lord said unto him, Well done, **thou** good and faithful servant: thou hast been faithful over a few things, I will make thee ruler over many things: enter thou into the joy of thy lord.

21 His lord said unto him, Well done, good and faithful servant; thou hast been faithful over a few things, I will make thee ruler over many things; enter thou into the joy of thy lord.

22 He also that had received two talents came and said, Lord, thou deliveredst unto me two talents:

22 He also that had received two talents came and said, Lord, thou deliveredst unto me two talents;

Matt. 25	JST Matt. 25		D & C
behold, I have gained two **other** talents beside them.	behold, I have gained two talents besides them.		
23 His lord said unto him, Well done, good and faithful servant; thou hast been faithful over a few things, I will make thee ruler over many things: enter thou into the joy of thy lord.			132:53 For I am the Lord thy God, and ye shall obey my voice; and I give unto my servant Joseph that he shall be made ruler over many things; for he hath been faithful over a few things, and from henceforth I will strengthen him. (See also 52:13; 78:15; 82:18; 101:61; 177:10; 124:13.)
24 Then he **which** had received the one talent came and said, Lord, I knew thee that thou art **an** hard man, reaping where thou hast not sown, and gathering where thou hast not **strawed**:	24 Then he **who** had received the one talent came, and said, Lord, I knew thee that thou art **a** hard man, reaping where thou hast not sown, and gathering where thou hast not **scattered**.		
25 And I was afraid, and went and hid thy talent in the earth: lo,

there thou hast **that** is thine. | 25 And I was afraid, and went and hid thy talent in the earth; **and** lo, **here is thy talent; take it from me as** thou hast **from thine other servants, for it** is thine. | | |
26 His lord answered and said unto him, **Thou** wicked and slothful servant, thou knewest that I reap where I sowed not, and gather where I have not **strawed**:	26 His lord answered and said unto him, **O** wicked and slothful servant, thou knewest that I reap where I sowed not, and gather where I have not **scattered**.		
	27 **Having known this, therefore,** thou oughtest to have put my money to the exchangers, and at my coming I should have received mine own with usury.		
27 Thou oughtest **therefore** to have put my money to the exchangers, and **then** at my coming I should have received mine own with usury.			
28 Take therefore the talent from **him**, and give it unto him **which** hath ten talents.	28 **I will** take, therefore, the talent from **you**, and give it unto him **who** hath ten talents.		
29 For unto every one **that** hath shall be given, and he shall have abundance:

but from him that hath not

shall be taken away even that which he hath. | 29 For unto every one **who** hath **obtained other talents**, shall be given, and he shall have **in** abundance.
30 But from him that hath not **obtained other talents**, shall be taken away even that which he hath **received**. | | 60:3 And it shall come to pass, if they are not more faithful unto me, it shall be taken away, even that which they have. |
| 30 And cast ye the unprofitable servant into outer | 31 And **his lord shall say unto his servants,** Cast ye the unprofitable servant | | |

Matt. 25	JST Matt. 25		D & C
darkness: there shall be weeping and gnashing of teeth.	into outer darkness; there shall be weeping and gnashing of teeth.		

TPJS-- Blessings offered, but rejected, are no longer blessings, but become like the talent hid in the earth by the wicked and slothful servant; the proffered good returns to the giver; the blessing is bestowed on those who will receive and occupy; for unto him that hath shall be given, and he shall have abundantly, but unto him that hath not or will not receive, shall be taken away that which he hath, or might have had. (p. 257)

. . . when the Master in the Savior's parable of the stewards called his servants before him he gave them several talents to improve on while he should tarry abroad for a little season, and when he returned he called for an accounting. So it is now. Our Master is absent only for a little season and at the end of it He will call each to render an account; and where the five talents were bestowed, ten will be required; and he that has made no improvement will be cast out as an unprofitable servant, while the faithful will enjoy everlasting honors. Therefore we earnestly implore the grace of our Father to rest upon you, through Jesus Christ His Son, that you may not faint in the hour of temptation, nor be overcome in the time of persecution. (p. 68)

149. The Final Judgment

Matt. 25	JST Matt. 25		D & C
31 ¶ When the Son of man shall come in his glory, and all the holy angels with him, then **shall** he sit upon the throne of his glory:	32 When the Son of Man shall come in his glory, and all the holy angels with him, then he **shall** sit upon the throne of his glory;		
32 And before him shall be gathered all nations: and he shall separate them one from another, as a shepherd divideth **his** sheep from the goats:	33 And before him shall be gathered all nations; and he shall separate them one from another, as a shepherd divideth sheep from the goats;		
33 **And he shall set** the sheep on his right hand, but the goats on **the** left.	the sheep on his right hand, but the goats on **his** left.		29:27 And the righteous shall be gathered on my right hand unto eternal life; and the wicked on my left hand will I be ashamed to own before the Father;
	34 **And he shall sit upon his throne, and the twelve apostles with him.**		
34 Then shall the King say unto them on his right hand, Come, ye blessed of my Father, inherit the kingdom prepared for you from the foundation of the world:			
35 For I was an hungred, and ye gave me meat: I was thirsty, and ye gave me drink: I was a stranger, and ye took me in:			
36 Naked, and ye clothed me: I was sick, and ye visited me: I was in prison, and ye came unto me.			
37 Then shall the righteous answer him, saying,			

Matt. 25	JST Matt. 25		D & C
Lord, when saw we thee an hungred, and fed thee? or thirsty, and gave thee drink?			
38 When saw we thee a stranger, and took thee in? or naked, and clothed thee?			
39 Or when saw we thee sick, or in prison, and came unto thee?			
40 And the King shall answer and say unto them, Verily I say unto you, Inasmuch as ye have done it unto one of the least of these my brethren, ye have done it unto me.			42:38 For inasmuch as ye do it unto the least of these, ye do it unto me.
41 Then shall he say also unto them on the left hand, Depart from me, ye cursed, into everlasting fire, prepared for the devil and his angels:			
42 For I was an hungred, and ye gave me no meat: I was thirsty, and ye gave me no drink:			
43 I was a stranger, and ye took me not in: naked, and ye clothed me not: sick, and in prison, and ye visited me not.			
44 Then shall they also answer him, saying, Lord, when saw we thee an hungred, or athirst, or a stranger, or naked, or sick, or in prison, and did not minister unto thee?			
45 Then shall he answer them, saying, Verily I say unto you, Inasmuch as ye did it not to one of the least of these, ye did it not to me.	46 Then shall he answer them, saying, Verily I say unto you, Inasmuch as ye did it not to one of the least of these **my brethren**, ye did it not **unto** me.		
46 And these shall go away into everlasting punishment: but the righteous into life eternal.			

Matt. 26	JST Matt. 26	Mark 14	JST Mark 14

150. Jesus to be Betrayed

Matt. 26	JST Matt. 26	Mark 14	JST Mark 14
And it came to pass, when Jesus had finished all these sayings, he said unto his disciples,			
2 Ye know that after two days is **the feast of** the passover, and the Son of **man** is betrayed to be crucified.	2 Ye know that after two days is the passover, and **then** the Son of **Man** is betrayed to be crucified.	After two days was the **feast of the** passover, and of unleavened bread:	After two days was the passover, and **the feast** of unleavened bread.
3 Then assembled together the chief priests, and the scribes, and the elders of the people, unto the palace of the high priest, who was called Caiaphas,			
4 And consulted that they might take Jesus by subtilty, and kill him.		and the chief priests and the scribes sought how they might take **him** by craft, and put him to death.	2 And the chief priests, and the scribes, sought how they might take **Jesus** by craft, and put him to death.
5 But they said, No on the feast day, lest there be an uproar among the people.		2 But they said, Not on the feast day, lest there be an uproar **of** the people.	3 But they said **among themselves, Let us** not **take him** on the feast day, lest there be an uproar **among** the people.
14 ¶ Then one of the twelve, called Judas Iscariot, went unto the chief priests,	11 Then one of the twelve, called Judas Iscariot, went unto the chief priests,	10 ¶ **And** Judas Iscariot, one of the twelve, went unto the chief priests, to betray **him** unto them.	31 **Nevertheless,** Judas Iscariot, **even** one of the twelve, went unto the chief priests to betray **Jesus** unto them; **for he turned away from him, and was offended because of his words.**
15 And said **unto them,** What will ye give me, and I will deliver him unto you? And they covenanted with him for thirty pieces of silver.	And said, What will ye give me, and I will deliver him unto you? And they covenanted with him for thirty pieces of silver.	11 And when **they** heard **it,** they were glad, and promised to give him money.	32 And when **the chief priests** heard **of him** they were glad, and promised to
16 And from that time he sought opportunity to betray **him.**	12 And from that time he sought opportunity to betray **Jesus.**	And he sought how he might conveniently betray **him.**	give him money; and he sought how he might conveniently betray **Jesus.**

4th Day—Wednesday (Please see explanation on 7th Day—Saturday—No Record p. 391)

151. The Passover Meal

Matt. 26	JST Matt. 26	Mark 14	JST Mark 14
17 ¶ Now the first day of the feast of unleavened bread	13 Now **on** the first day of the feast of unleavened bread. . .	12 ¶ And the first day of unleavened bread, when they killed the passover,	10 And **now** the first day of unleavened bread, when they killed the passover. . .

Luke 22	JST Luke 22 Old Testament	Note
Now the feast of unleavened bread drew nigh, which is called the Passover.		Most harmonies and commentaries list Wednesday as a day of "no record." This listing probably comes because of the traditional "Good Friday" as the day of Christs crucifixion. However, in this harmony, the traditional events of Thursday of the last week of the Savior's life are listed under Wednesday, and the traditional even s of Friday are listed on Thursday. Some Bible scholars consider this listing because of there being a double Sabbath in certain years of the Jewish calendar. They consider John 19:31 as a reference to such a day, "for that Sabbath day was an high day." Elder James E. Talmage suggests this as a possibility in his great work, *Jesus the Christ*. (See his quote on page 391 of this work.)
2 And the chief priests and scribes sought how they might kill him; **for** they feared the people.	2 And the chief priests, and **the** scribes, sought how they might kill him; **but** they feared the people.	Another consideration was the prophecy of Christ concerning the prophet Jonah being "three days and three nights in the whale" as a sign of Christ being "three days and three nights in the heart of the earth." (Matt. 12:39-40, see also JST Mark 8:12, the Prophet Joseph's addition to the text). The Book of Mormon also strongly implies three full days of his being in the spirit world (see 1 Nephi 19:10; 2 Nephi 25:13; 3 Nephi 8:19-23; 10:9). The crucifixion on Friday evening and the resurrection on Sunday does not fulfill the prophecies of the Savior or of the Book of Mormon. While the time period is not as significant as the events themselves, an explanation for the departure from the usual time table is given.
3 ¶ Then entered Satan into Judas surnamed Iscariot, being of the number of the twelve.		
4 And he went his way, and communed with the chief priests and captains, how he might betray him unto them.	Zechariah 11:12 And I said unto them, If ye think good, give me my price; and if not, forbear. So they weighed for my price thirty pieces of silver. (quoted later in Matt. 27:9)	
5 And they were glad, and covenanted to give him money.		
6 And he promised, and sought opportunity to betray him unto them in the absence of the multitude.	6 And he promised **them**, and sought opportunity to betray him unto them in the absence of the multitude.	
7 ¶ Then came the day of unleavened bread, when the passover must be killed.		

Matt. 26	JST Matt. 26	Mark 14	JST Mark 14
the disciples came to Jesus, saying unto him, Where wilt thou that we prepare for thee to eat the passover?		his disciples said unto him, Where wilt thou that we go and prepare that thou mayest eat the passover? 13 And he sendeth forth two of his disciples, and saith unto them, Go ye into the city, and there shall meet you a man bearing a pitcher of water: follow him.	
18 And he said, Go into the city to such a man, and say unto him, The Master saith, My time is at hand; I will keep the passover at thy house with my disciples.		14 And wheresoever he shall go in, say ye to the goodman of the house, The Master saith, Where is the guestchamber, where I shall eat the passover with my disciples? 15 And he will shew you a large upper room furnished and prepared: there make ready for us.	
19 And the disciples did as Jesus **had** appointed them; and they made ready the passover.	15 And the disciples did as Jesus appointed them; and they made ready the passover.	16 And his disciples went forth, and came into the city, and found as he had said unto them: and they made ready the passover.	
20 Now when the **even** was come, he sat down with the twelve.	(JST says eveni**ng**.)	17 And in the evening he cometh with the twelve.	
29 But I say unto you, I will not drink henceforth of this fruit of the vine, until that day when I drink it new with you in my Father's kingdom.	26 But I say unto you, I will not drink henceforth of this fruit of the vine, until that day when I **shall come and** drink it new with you in my Father's kingdom.	25 Verily I say unto you, I will **drink** no more of the fruit of the vine, until that day that I drink it new in the kingdom of God.	25 Verily I say unto you, **Of this ye shall bear record; for** I will no more **drink** of the fruit of the vine **with you**, until that day that I drink it new in the kingdom of God.

Luke 22	JST Luke 22		D & C
8 And he sent Peter and John, saying, Go and prepare us the passover, that we may eat. 9 And they said unto him, Where wilt thou that we prepare?			
10 And he said unto them, Behold, when ye **are** entered into the city, there shall a man meet you, bearing a pitcher of water; follow him into the house where he entereth in. 11 And ye shall say unto the goodman of the house, The Master saith unto **thee,** Where is the guestchamber, where I shall eat the passover with my disciples? 12 And he shall shew you a large upper room furnished: there make ready.	10 And he said unto them, Behold, when ye **have** entered into the city, there shall a man meet you bearing a pitcher of water; follow him into the house where he entereth in. 11 And ye shall say unto the good man of the house, The Master saith unto **you,** Where is the guestchamber, where I shall eat the passover with my disciples?		
13 And they went, and found as he had said unto them: and they made ready the passover. 14 And when the hour was come, he sat down, and the twelve apostles with him. 15 And he said unto them, With desire I have desired to eat this passover with you before I suffer:			
16 For I say unto you, I will not any more eat thereof, until it be fulfilled in the kingdom of God.	16 For I say unto you, I will not any more eat thereof, until it be fulfilled **which is written in the prophets concerning me. Then I will partake with you,** in the kingdom of God.		27:5 Behold, this is wisdom in me; wherefore, marvel not, for the hour cometh that I will drink of the fruit of the vine with you on the earth, and with Moroni, whom I have sent unto you to reveal the Book of Mormon, containing the fulness of my everlasting gospel, to whom I have committed the keys of the record of the stick of Ephraim;
17 And he took the cup, and gave thanks, and said, Take this, and divide **it** among yourselves: 18 For I say unto you, I will not drink of the fruit of the vine, until the king-	17 And he took the cup, and gave thanks, and said, Take this and divide among yourselves; 18 For I say unto you, **that** I will not drink of the fruit of the vine, until the		

Luke 22	JST Luke 22	Isaiah	
dom of God shall come.	kingdom of God shall come.		
24 ¶ And there was also a strife among them, **which** of them should be accounted the greatest.	24 There was also a strife among them, **who of them** should be accounted the greatest.		
25 And he said unto them, The kings of the Gentiles exercise lordship over them; and they **that** exercise authority upon them are called benefactors.	25 And he said unto them, The kings of the Gentiles exercise lordship over them, and they **who** exercise authority upon them, are called benefactors.		
26 But **ye shall** not be so: but he **that is** greatest among you, let him be as the younger; and **he that is** chief, as **he that** doth serve.	26 But **it ought** not **to** be so **with you**; but he **who is** greatest among you, let him be as the younger; and **he who** is chief, as **he who** doth serve.		
27 For whether is greater, **he that** sitteth at meat, or he **that** serveth? is not he **that** sitteth at meat? but I am among you as **he that** serveth.	27 For whether is **he** greater, **who** sitteth at meat, or he **who** serveth? I **am** not **as** he **who** sitteth at meat, but I am among you as **he who** serveth.		
28 Ye are they **which** have continued with me in my temptations.	28 Ye are they **who have** continued with me in my temptations;	53:12 Therefore will I divide him a portion with the great, and he shall divide the spoil with the strong; because he hath poured out his soul unto death: and he was numbered with the transgressors; and he bare the sin of many, and made intercession for the transgressors.	
29 And I appoint unto you a kingdom, as my Father hath appointed unto me;			
30 That ye may eat and drink at my table in my kingdom, and sit on thrones judging the twelve tribes of Israel.	30 That ye may eat and drink at my table in my kingdom; and sit on **twelve** thrones, judging the twelve tribes of Israel.		

Matt. 26	JST Matt. 26	Mark 14	JST Mark 14

152. The Sacrament Introduced

Matt. 26	JST Matt. 26	Mark 14	JST Mark 14
26 ¶ And as they were eating, Jesus took bread, and blessed it, **and brake it**, and gave **it** to **the** disciples, and said, Take, eat; this is my body.	22 And as they were eating, Jesus took bread **and brake it**, and blessed it, and gave to **his** disciples, and said, Take, eat; this is **in remembrance of** my body **which I give a ransom for you.**	22 ¶ And as they did eat, Jesus took bread, and blessed, and brake it, and gave to them, and said, Take, eat: this is my body.	20 And as they did eat, Jesus took bread and blessed it, and brake, and gave to them, and said, Take it, **and** eat. 21 **Behold, this is for you to do in remembrance of my body; for as oft as ye do this ye will remember this hour that I was with you.**
27 And he took the cup, and gave thanks, and gave		23 And he took the cup, and when he had given	

330

Luke 22	JST Luke 22		
19 ¶ And he took bread, and gave thanks, and brake it, and gave unto them, saying, This is my body which is given for you: this do in remembrance of me.	19 And he took bread, and gave thanks, and brake, and gave unto them, saying, This is my body which is given for you; this do in remembrance of me.		
20 Likewise also the cup after supper,			

Matt. 26	JST Matt. 26	Mark 14	JST Mark 14
it to them, saying, Drink ye all of it; 28 For this is my blood of the new testament, which is shed for many for the remission of sins.	24 For this is **in remembrance of** my blood of the new testament, which is shed for **as many as shall believe on my name,** for the remission of **their** sins. 25 **And I give unto you a commandment, that ye shall observe to do the things which ye have seen me do, and bear record of me even unto the end.**	thanks, he gave it to them: and they all drank of it. 24 And he said unto them, This is my blood **of** the new testament, which **is** shed **for many.**	23 And he said unto them, This is **in remembrance of my blood which is shed for many, and** the new testament which I **give unto you;** **for of me ye shall bear record unto all the world.** 24 **And as oft as ye do this ordinance, ye will remember me in this hour that I was with you and drank with you of this cup, even the last time in my ministry.**

John 13	JST John 13	John 13	JST John 13

153. Jesus Washes Apostles' Feet

John 13	JST John 13	John 13	JST John 13
Now before the feast of the passover, when Jesus knew that his hour was come that he should depart out of this world unto the Father, having loved his own which were in the world, he loved them unto the end. 2 And supper being ended, the devil having now put into the heart of Judas Iscariot, Simon's son, to betray him; 3 Jesus knowing that the Father had given all things into his hands, and that he was come from God, and went to God; 4 He riseth from supper, and laid aside his garments; and took a towel, and girded himself. 5 After that he poureth (continued in column 3)	5 After that he poureth (continued in column 4)	water into a bason, and began to wash the disciples' feet, and to wipe them with the towel wherewith he was girded. 6 Then cometh he to Simon Peter: and Peter saith unto him, Lord, dost thou wash my feet? 7 Jesus answered and said unto him, What I do thou knowest not now; but thou shalt know hereafter. 8 Peter saith unto him, Thou **shalt never** wash my feet. Jesus answered him, If I wash thee not, thou hast no part with me. 9 Simon Peter saith unto him, Lord, not my feet only, but also my hands and my head. 10 Jesus saith to him, He that is washed needeth not (continued on page 333)	water into a basin, and **he** began to wash the disciples' feet, and to wipe them with the towel wherewith he was girded. 8 Peter saith unto him, Thou **needest not to** wash my feet. Jesus answered him, If I wash thee not, thou hast no part with me. 10 Jesus saith to him, He that **has** washed **his hands**

Luke 22		D & C
saying, This cup is the new testament in my blood, which is shed for you.		27:2 For, behold, I say unto you, that it mattereth not what ye shall eat or what ye shall drink when ye partake of the sacrament, if it so be that ye do it with an eye single to my glory-- remembering unto the Father my body which was laid down for you, and my blood which was shed for the remission of your sins. 3 Wherefore, a commandment I give unto you, that you shall not purchase wine neither strong drink of your enemies; 4 Wherefore, you shall partake of none except it is made new among you; yea, in this my Father's kingdom which shall be built up on the earth.

John 13	JST John 13 D & C	John 13	D & C
save to wash his feet, but is clean every whit: and ye are clean, but not all. 11 For he knew who should betray him; therefore said he, Ye are not all clean. 12 So after he had washed their feet, and had taken his garments, and was set down again, he said unto them, Know ye what I have done to you? 13 Ye call me Master and Lord: and ye say well; for so I am. (continued in column 3)	**and his head**, needeth not save to wash his feet, but is clean every whit; and ye are clean, but not all. **Now this was the custom of the Jews under their law; wherefore, Jesus did this that the law might be fulfilled.** D&C 88:138 And ye shall not receive any among you into this school save he is clean from the blood of this generation; 139 And he shall be received by the ordinance of the washing of feet, for unto this end was the ordinance of the washing of feet instituted.	14 If I then, your Lord and Master, have washed your feet; ye also ought to wash one another's feet. 15 For I have given you an example, that ye should do as I have done to you. 16 Verily, verily, I say unto you, The servant is not greater than his lord; neither he that is sent greater than he that sent him. 17 If ye know these things, happy are ye if ye do them.	88:140 And again, the ordinance of washing feet is to be administered by the president, or presiding elder of the church. 141 It is to be commenced with prayer; and after partaking of bread and wine, he is to gird himself according to the pattern given in the thirteenth chapter of John's testimony concerning me. Amen.

TPJS-- . . . in order to make the foundation of this church complete and permanent, we must . . . attend to certain duties that we have not as yet attended to. . . . The item to which I wish the more particularly to call your attention tonight, is the ordinance of washing of feet. This we have not done as yet, but it is necessary now, as much as it was in the days of the Savior; . . . The house of the Lord must be prepared, and the solemn assembly called and organized in it, according to the order of the house of God; and in it we must attend to the ordinance of washing of feet. It was never intended for any but official members. It is calculated to unite our hearts, that we may be one in feeling and sentiment, and that our faith may be strong, so that Satan cannot overthrow us, nor have any power over us here. (pp. 90-91)

At an early hour on Thursday, the 6th of April, the official members assembled in the House of the Lord, when the time for the first two or three hours was spent by the different quorums in washing of feet, singing, praying, and preparing to receive instructions from the Presidency. (pp. 110-11)

Matt. 26	JST Matt. 26	Mark 14	JST Mark 14

154. Upper Room-- Jesus Indicates the Betrayer

Matt. 26	JST Matt. 26	Mark 14	JST Mark 14
		18 And as they sat and did eat, Jesus said, Verily I say unto you, One of you **which** eateth with me shall betray me.	16 And as they sat and did eat, Jesus said, Verily I say unto you, One of you **who** eateth with me shall betray me.
21 And as they did eat, he said, Verily I say unto you, that one of you shall betray me.			
22 And they were exceedingly sorrowful, and began every one of them to say unto him, Lord, is it I?		19 And they began to be sorrowful, and to say unto him one by one, Is it I? and another said, Is it I?	17 And they **all** began to be **very** sorrowful, and **began** to say unto him one by one, Is it I? and another said, Is it I?
23 And he answered and said, He that dippeth his hand with me in the dish, the same shall betray me.		20 And he answered and said unto them, It is one of the twelve, **that** dippeth with me in the dish.	18 And he answered and said unto them, It is one of the twelve **who** dippeth with me in the dish.
24 The Son of man goeth as it is written of him: but woe unto that man by whom the Son of man is betrayed! it had been good for that man if he had not been born.	20 **But** the Son of Man goeth as it is written of him; but woe unto that man by whom the Son of Man is betrayed! It had been good for that man if he had not been born.	21 The Son of man indeed goeth, as it is written of him: but woe to that man by whom the Son of man is betrayed! good were it for that man if he had never been born.	19 The Son of Man indeed goeth as it is written of him; but woe to that man by whom the Son of Man is betrayed! Good were it for that man if he had never been born.
25 Then Judas, **which** betrayed him, answered and said, Master, is it I? He said unto him, Thou hast said.	21 Then Judas, **who** betrayed him, answered and said, Master, is it I? He said unto him, Thou hast said.		

Luke 22	Psalms D & C	John 13	JST John 13
		18 ¶ I speak not of you all: I know whom I have chosen: but that the scripture may be fulfilled, He that eateth bread with me hath lifted up his heel against me.	
	Psalm 41:9 Yea, mine own familiar friend, in whom I trusted, which did eat of my bread, hath lifted up his heel against me.		
		19 Now I tell you before it come, that, when it is come to pass, ye may believe that I am he.	19 Now I tell you before it come, that, when it is come to pass, ye may believe that I am **the Christ.**
		20 Verily, verily, I say unto you, He that receiveth whomsoever I send receiveth me; and he that receiveth me receiveth him that sent me.	
21 ¶ But, behold, the hand of him that betrayeth me is with me on the table.		21 When Jesus had thus said, he was troubled in spirit, and testified, and said, Verily, verily, I say unto you, that one of you shall betray me.	
		22 Then the disciples looked one on another, doubting of whom he spake.	
23 And they began to enquire among themselves, which of them it was that should do this thing.			
22 And truly the Son of man goeth, as it was determined: but woe unto that man by whom he is betrayed!	D&C 76:32 They are they who are the sons of perdition, of whom I say that it had been better for them never to have been born;		

Matt. 26	JST Matt. 26	Mark 14	JST Mark 14 Zechariah
			30 **And he said unto Judas Iscariot, What thou doest, do quickly; but beware of innocent blood.**

155. Peter's Denial Prophesied

Matt. 26	JST Matt. 26	Mark 14	JST Mark 14 Zechariah
31 Then saith Jesus unto them, All ye shall be offended because of me this night: for it is written, I will smite the shepherd, and the sheep of the flock shall be scattered abroad.		27 And Jesus saith unto them, All ye shall be offended because of me this night: for it is written, I will smite the shepherd, and the sheep shall be scattered.	Zech. 13:7 Awake, O sword, against my shepherd, and against the man that is my fellow, saith the Lord of hosts; smite the shepherd, and the sheep will be scattered: and I will turn mine hand upon the little ones.
32 But after I am risen again, I will go before you into Galilee.		28 But after that I am risen, I will go before you into Galilee.	
33 Peter answered and said unto him, Though all men shall be offended because of thee, **yet will I** never be offended.	30 Peter answered and said unto him, Though all men shall be offended because of thee, **I will** never be offended.	29 But Peter said unto **him**, Although all shall be offended, yet will **not** I.	33 But Peter said unto **Jesus**, Although all **men** shall be offended **with thee**, yet I will **never be offended.**

23 Now there was leaning on Jesus' bosom one of his disciples, whom Jesus loved.

24 Simon Peter therefore beckoned to him, that he should ask who it should be of whom he spake.

25 He then lying on Jesus' breast saith unto him, Lord, who is it?

26 Jesus answered, He it is, to whom I shall give a sop, when I have dipped it. And when he had dipped the sop, he gave it to Judas Iscariot, the son of Simon.

27 And after the sop Satan entered into him. Then said Jesus unto him, That thou doest, do quickly.

28 Now no man at the table knew for what intent he spake this unto him.

29 For some of them thought, because Judas had the bag, that Jesus had said unto him, Buy those things that we have need of against the feast; or, that he should give something to the poor.

(continued in column 4)

30 He then having received the sop went immediately out: and it was night.

31 ¶ Therefore, when he was gone out, Jesus said, Now is the Son of man glorified, and God is glorified in him.

32 If God be glorified in him, God shall also glorify him in himself, and shall straightway glorify him.

33 Little children, yet a little while I am with you. Ye shall seek me: and as I said unto the Jews, Whither I go, ye cannot come; so now I say to you.

34 A new commandment I give unto you, That ye love one another; as I have loved you, that ye also love one another.

35 By this shall all men know that ye are my disciples, if ye have love one to another.

Matt. 26		Mark 14	JST Mark 14
34 Jesus said unto him, Verily I say unto thee, That this night, before the cock crow, thou shalt deny me thrice.		30 And Jesus saith unto him, Verily I say unto thee, That this day, even in this night, before the cock crow twice, thou shalt deny me thrice.	
35 Peter said unto him, Though I should die with thee, yet will I not deny thee. Likewise also said all the disciples.		31 But he spake the more vehemently, If I should die with thee, I will not deny thee in any wise. Likewise also said they all.	35 But he spake the more vehemently. If I should die with thee, yet will I not deny thee in any wise. Likewise also said they all.

Luke 22	JST Luke 22	John 13	TPJS D&C
31 ¶ And the Lord said, Simon, Simon, behold, Satan hath desired **to have** you, that he may sift **you** as wheat:	31 And the Lord said, Simon, Simon, behold Satan hath desired you, that he may sift **the children of the kingdom** as wheat.		
32 But I have prayed for **thee**, that **thy** faith fail not: and when **thou art** converted, strengthen **thy** brethren.	32 But I have prayed for **you**, that **your** faith fail not; and when **you are** converted strengthen **your** brethren.		How mild the Savior dealt with Peter, saying, "When thou art converted, strengthen thy brethren." (p.241)
		36 ¶ Simon Peter said unto him, Lord, whither goest thou? Jesus answered him, Whither I go, thou canst not follow me now; but thou shalt follow me afterwards.	
33 And he said unto him, Lord, I am ready to go with **thee**, both into prison, and to death.	33 And he said unto him, **being aggrieved**, Lord, I am ready to go with **you**, both into prison, and **unto** death.	37 Peter said unto him, Lord, why cannot I follow thee now? I will lay down my life for thy sake.	
34 And **he** said, I tell **thee**, Peter, the cock shall not crow this day, before that **thou shalt** thrice deny that **thou** knowest me.	34 And **the Lord** said, I tell **you**, Peter, **that the** cock shall not crow this day, before that **you will** thrice deny that **you know** me.	38 Jesus answered him, Wilt thou lay down thy life for my sake? Verily, verily, I say unto thee, The cock shall not crow, till thou hast denied me thrice.	
35 And he said unto them, When I sent you without purse, and scrip, **and** shoes, lacked ye any thing? And they said, Nothing.	35 And he said unto them, When I sent you without purse and scrip, **or shoes**, lacked ye any thing? And they said, Nothing.		24:18 And thou shalt take no purse nor scrip, neither staves, neither two coats, for the church shall give unto thee in the very hour what thou needest for food and for raiment, and for shoes and for money, and for scrip.
36 Then said he unto them, **But now**, he **that** hath a purse, let him take it, and likewise his scrip: and he **that** hath no sword, let him sell his garment, and buy one.	36 Then said he unto them, **I say unto you again**, He **who** hath a purse, let him take it, and likewise his scrip; and he **who** hath no sword, let him sell his garment and buy one.		84:86 Therefore, let no man among you, for this commandment is unto all the faithful who are called of God in the church unto the ministry, from this hour take purse or scrip, that goeth forth to proclaim this gospel of the kingdom.
37 For I say unto you, **that** this that is written must yet be accomplished in me, And he was reckoned among the transgressors: for the things concerning me have an end.	37 For I say unto you, This that is written must yet be accomplished in me, And he was reckoned among the transgressors; for the things concerning me have an end.		
38 And they said, Lord, behold, here are two swords. And he said unto them, It is enough.			

B of M	D & C	John 14	JST John 14 TPJS

156. Discourse on the Comforter

B of M	D & C	John 14	JST John 14 TPJS
Enos 1:27 And I soon go to the place of my rest, which is with my Redeemer; for I know that in him I shall rest. And I rejoice in the day when my mortal shall put on immortality, and shall stand before him; then shall I see his face with pleasure, and he will say unto me: Come unto me, ye blessed, there is a place prepared for you in the mansions of my Father. Amen. (See also Ether 12:34, 37.)	98:18 Let not your hearts be troubled; for in my Father's house there are many mansions, and I have prepared a place for you; and where my Father and I am, there ye shall be also.	Let not your heart be troubled: ye believe in God, believe also in me. 2 In my Father's house are many mansions: if it were not so, I would have told you. I go to prepare a place for you. 3 And **if** I go **and** prepare a place for you, **I will** come again, and receive you unto myself; that where I am, **there** ye may be also. 4 And whither I go ye know, and the way ye know.	 3 And **when** I go, **I will** prepare a place for you, **and** come again, and receive you unto myself; that where I am, ye may be also.

TPJS—Jesus said there are many mansion in my Father's house, and I will go and prepare a place for you. *House* here named should have been translated kingdom; and any person who is exalted to the highest mansion has to abide a celestial law, and the whole law too. (p. 331; see also p. 311)

B of M	D & C	John 14	JST John 14 TPJS
	132:12 I am the Lord thy God; and I give unto you this commandment—that no man shall come unto the Father but by me or by my word, which is my law, saith the Lord.	5 Thomas saith unto him, Lord, we know not wither thou goest; and how can we know the way? 6 Jesus saith unto him, I am the way, the truth, and the life: not man cometh unto the Father, but by me. 7 If ye had known me, ye should have known my Father also: and form henceforth ye know him, and have seen him. 8 Philip saith unto him, Lord, shew us the Father, and it sufficeth us. 9 Jesus saith unto him, Have I been so long time with you, and yet has thou not known me, Philip? he that hath seen me hath seen the Father; and how sayest thou then, Shew us the Father?	TPJS—It should be—"In my father's kingdom are many kingdoms," in order that ye may be heirs of God and joint-heirs with me. . . There are mansions for those who obey a celestial law, and there are other mansions for those who come short of the law, every man in his own order. (p. 366)
	93:3 And that I am in the Father, and the Father in me, and the Father and I are one—	10 Believest thou not that I am in the Father, and the Father in me? the words	

340

John 14	D & C	John 14	D & C B of M
that I speak unto you I speak not of myself: but the Father that dwelleth in me, he doeth the works. 11 Believe me that I am in the Father, and the Father in me: or else believe me for the very works' sake. 12 Verily, verily, I say unto you, He that believeth on me, the works that I do shall he do also; and greater works than these shall he do; because I go unto my Father. 13 And whatsoever ye shall ask in my name, that will I do, that the Father may be glorified in the Son. 14 If ye shall ask any thing in my name, I will do it. 15 ¶ If ye love me, keep my commandments. 16 And I will pray the Father, and he shall give you another Comforter, that he may abide with you for ever; 17 Even the Spirit of truth; whom the world cannot receive, because it seeth him not, neither knoweth him: but ye know him; for he dwelleth with you, and shall be in you. 18 I will not leave you comfortless: I will come to you. 19 Yet a little while, and the world seeth me no more; but ye see me: because I live, ye shall live also. (continued in column 3)	88:3 Wherefore, I now send upon you another Comforter, even upon you my friends, that it may abide in your hearts, even the Holy Spirit of promise; which other Comforter is the same that I promised unto my disciples, as is recorded in the testimony of John.	20 At that day ye shall know that I am in my Father, and ye in me, and I in you. 21 He that hath my commandments, and keepeth them, he it is that loveth me: and he that loveth me shall be loved of my Father, and I will love him, and will manifest myself to him. 22 Judas saith unto him, not Iscariot, Lord, how is it that thou wilt manifest thyself unto us, and not unto the world? 23 Jesus answered and said unto him, If a man love me, he will keep my words: and my Father will love him, and we will come unto him, and make our abode with him. 24 He that loveth me not keepeth not my sayings: and the word which ye hear is not mine, but the Father's which sent me. 25 These things have I spoken unto you, being yet present with you. 26 But the Comforter, which is the Holy Ghost, whom the Father will send in my name, he shall teach you all things, and bring all things to your remembrance, whatsoever I have said unto you. 27 Peace I leave with you, my peace I give unto you: not as the world giveth, give I unto you. Let not your heart be troubled, neither let it be afraid. (continued on page 342)	130:3 John 14:23-- The appearing of the Father and the Son, in that verse, is a personal appearance; and the idea that the Father and the Son dwell in a man's heart is an old sectarian notion, and is false. 2 Ne. 32:3 Angels speak by the power of the Holy Ghost; wherefore, they speak the words of Christ. Wherefore, I said unto you, feast upon the words of Christ; for behold, the words of Christ will tell you all things what ye should do. 5 For behold, again I say unto you that if ye will enter in by the way, and receive the Holy Ghost, it will show unto you all things what ye should do.

TPJS-- The other Comforter spoken of is a subject of great interest, and perhaps understood by few of this generation. After a person has faith in Christ, repents of his sins, and is baptized for the remission of his sins and receives the Holy Ghost, (by the laying on of hands), which is the first Comforter, then let him continue to humble himself before God, hungering and thirsting after righteousness, and living by every word of God, and the Lord will soon say unto him, Son, thou shalt be exalted. When the Lord has thoroughly proved him, and finds that the man is determined to serve Him at all hazards, then the man will find his calling and his election made sure, then it

	D & C	John 14	JST John 14

will be his privilege to receive the other Comforter, which the Lord hath promised the Saints, as is recorded in the testimony of St. John, in the 14th chapter, from the 12th to the 27th verses...

Now what is this other Comforter? It is no more nor less than the Lord Jesus Christ Himself; and this is the sum and substance of the whole matter; that when any man obtains this last Comforter, he will have the personage of Jesus Christ to attend him, or appear unto him from time to time, and even He will manifest the Father unto him, and they will take up their abode with him, and the visions of the heavens will be opened unto him, and the Lord will teach him face to face, and he may have a perfect knowledge of the mysteries of the Kingdom of God; and this is the state and place the ancient Saints arrived at when they had such glorious visions---Isaiah, Ezekiel, John upon the Isle of Patmos, St. Paul in the three heavens, and all the Saints who held communion with the general assembly and Church of the Firstborn. (pp. 150-51)

D & C	John 14	JST John 14
	28 Ye have heard how I said unto you, I go away, and come again unto you. If ye loved me, ye would rejoice, because I said, I go unto the Father: for my Father is greater than I.	
	29 And now I have told you before it come to pass, that, when it is come to pass, ye might believe.	
127:11 I now close my letter for the present, for the want of more time; for the enemy is on the alert, and as the Savior said, the prince of this world cometh, but he hath nothing in me.	30 Hereafter I will not talk much with you: for the prince of this world cometh, **and** hath **nothing in** me.	30 Hereafter I will not talk much with you; for the prince **of darkness, who is** of this world, cometh, **but** hath **no power over me, but he hath power over you.**
	31 **But** that **the world** may know that I love the Father; and as the Father gave me commandment, even so I do. Arise, let us go hence.	31 **And I tell you these things,** that ye may know that I love the Father; and as the Father gave me commandment, even so I do. Arise, let us go hence.

TPJS-- We believe in the gift of the Holy Ghost being enjoyed now, as much as it was in the Apostles' days; we believe that it [the gift of the Holy Ghost] is necessary to make and to organize the Priesthood, that no man can be called to fill any office in the ministry without it; we also believe in prophecy, in tongues, in visions, and in revelations, in gifts, and in healings; and that these things cannot be enjoyed without the gift of the Holy Ghost. We believe that the holy men of old spake as they were moved by the Holy Ghost, and that holy men in these days speak by the same principle; we believe in its being a comforter and a witness bearer, that it brings things past to our remembrance, leads us into all truth, and shows us of things to come; we believe that "no man can know that Jesus is the Christ, but by the Holy Ghost." We believe in it [this gift of the Holy Ghost] in all its fullness, and power, and greatness, and glory; but whilst we do this, we believe in it rationally, consistently, and scripturally, and not according to the wild vagaries, foolish notions and traditions of men. (p. 243)

Matt. 26	Mark 14	Luke 22	JST Luke 22

157. Enroute to the Mount of Olives

30 And when they had sung an hymn, they went out into the mount of Olives.	26 ¶ And when they had sung an hymn, they went out into the mount of Olives.	39 ¶ And he came out, and went, as he was **wont**, to the mount of Olives; and his disciples **also** followed him.	39 And he came out, and went, as he was **accustomed**, to the mount of Olives; and his disciples followed him.

John 15	B of M TPJS	John 15	TPJS B of M

158. Mount of Olives-- Jesus, the True Vine

John 15	B of M / TPJS	John 15	TPJS / B of M
I am the true vine, and my Father is the husbandman. 2 Every branch in me that beareth not fruit he taketh away: and every branch that beareth fruit, he purgeth it, that it may bring forth more fruit. 3 Now ye are clean through the word which I have spoken unto you. 4 Abide in me, and I in you. As the branch cannot bear fruit of itself, except it abide in the vine; no more can ye, except ye abide in me.	1 Ne. 15:15 And then at that day will they not rejoice and give praise unto their everlasting God, their rock and their salvation? Yea, at that day, will they not receive the strength and nourishment from the true vine? Yea, will they not come unto the true fold of God?	you: continue ye in my love. 10 If ye keep my commandments, ye shall abide in my love; even as I have kept my Father's commandments, and abide in his love. 11 These things have I spoken unto you, that my joy might remain in you, and that your joy might be full. 12 This is my commandment, That ye love one another, as I have loved you.	
	TPJS-- President Joseph arose and said: "Brother Kimball has given you a true explanation of the parable," and then read the parable of the vine and its branches, and explained it, and said, "If we keep the commandments of God, we should bring forth fruit and be the friends of God, and know what our Lord did." (p.194)	13 Greater love hath no man than this, that a man lay down his life for his friends. 14 Ye are my friends, if ye do whatsoever I command you. 15 Henceforth I call you not servants; for the servant knoweth not what his lord doeth: but I have called you friends; for all things that I have heard of my Father I have made known unto you. 16 Ye have not chosen me, but I have chosen you, and ordained you, that ye should go and bring forth fruit, and that your fruit should remain: that whatsoever ye shall ask of the	TPJS-- What greater love hath any man than that he lay down his life for his friend; then why not fight for our friend until we die? (p. 195) There is no greater love than this, that a man lay down his life for his friends. I discover hundreds and thousands of my brethren ready to sacrifice their lives for me. (p. 315)
6 If a man abide not in me, he is cast forth as a branch, and is withered; and men gather them, and cast them into the fire, and they are burned. 7 If ye abide in me, and my words abide in you, ye shall ask what ye will, and it shall be done unto you. 8 Herein is my Father glorified, that ye bear much fruit; so shall ye be my disciples. 9 As the Father hath loved me, so have I loved (continued in column 3)			3 Ne. 27:28 And now I go unto the Father. And verily I say unto you, whatsoever things ye shall ask the Father in my name shall be given unto you.

John 15		John 15	Psalms
Father in my name, he may give it you. 17 These things I command you, that ye love one another. 18 If the world hate you, ye know that it hated me before it hated you. 19 If ye were of the world, the world would love his own: but because ye are not of the world, but I have chosen you out of the world, therefore the world hateth you. 20 Remember the word that I said unto you, The servant is not greater than his lord. If they have persecuted me, they will also persecute you; if they have kept my saying, they will keep yours also. 21 But all these things will they do unto you for my name's sake, because they know not him that sent me. (continued in column 3)		22 If I had not come and spoken unto them, they had not had sin: but now they have no cloke for their sin. 23 He that hateth me hateth my Father also. 24 If I had not done among them the works which none other man did, they had not had sin: but now have they both seen and hated both me and my Father. 25 But this cometh to pass, that the word might be fulfilled that is written in their law, They hated me without a cause. 26 But when the Comforter is come, whom I will send unto you from the Father, even the Spirit of truth, which proceedeth from the Father, he shall testify of me: 27 And ye also shall bear witness, because ye have been with me from the beginning.	Psalm 35:19 Let not them that are mine enemies wrongfully rejoice over me: neither let them wink with the eye that hate me without a cause. (See also Psalm 69:4)
John 16		John 16	

159. Jesus Has Overcome the World

These things have I spoken unto you, that ye should not be offended.

2 They shall put you out of the synagogues: yea, the time cometh, that whosoever killeth you will think that he doeth God service.

3 And these things will they do unto you, because they have not known the Father, nor me.

4 But these things have I told you, that when the time shall come, ye may remember that I told you

(continued in column 3)

of them. And these things I said not unto you at the beginning, because I was with you.

5 But now I go my way to him that sent me; and none of you asketh me, Whither goest thou?

6 But because I have said these things unto you, sorrow hath filled your heart.

7 Nevertheless I tell you the truth; It is expedient for you that I go away: for if I go not away, the Comforter will not come unto

344

John 16	JST John 16 B of M	John 16	JST John 16
you; but if I depart, I will send him unto you. 8 And when he is come, he will reprove the world of sin, and of righteousness, and of judgment: 9 Of sin, because they believe not on me; 10 Of righteousness, because I go to my Father, and ye see me no more; 11 Of judgment, because the prince of this world is judged. 12 I have yet many things to say unto you, but ye cannot bear them now. 13 Howbeit when he, the Spirit of truth, is come, he will guide you into all truth: for he shall not speak of himself; but whatsoever he shall hear, that shall he speak: and he will shew you things to come. 14 He shall glorify me: for he shall receive of mine, and shall shew it unto you. 15 All things that the Father hath are mine: therefore said I, that he shall take of mine, and shall shew it unto you. 16 A little while, and ye shall not see me: and again, a little while, and ye shall see me, because I go to the Father. 17 Then said some of his disciples among themselves, What is this that he saith unto us, A little while, and ye shall not see me: and again, a little while, and ye shall see me: and, Because I go to the Father? 18 They said therefore, What is this that he saith, A little while? we cannot tell what he saith. 19 Now Jesus knew that they were desirous to ask him, and said unto them, Do ye enquire among (continued in column 3)	10 Of righteousness, because I go to my Father, and **they** see me no more; 2 Ne. 32:5 For behold, again I say unto you that if ye will enter in by the way, and receive the Holy Ghost, it will show unto you all things what ye should do. D&C 38:8 But the day soon cometh that ye shall see me, and know that I am; for the veil of darkness shall soon be rent, and he that is not purified shall not abide the day.	yourselves of that I said, A little while, and ye shall not see me: and again, a little while, and ye shall see me? 20 Verily, verily, I say unto you, That ye shall weep and lament, but the world shall rejoice: and ye shall be sorrowful, but your sorrow shall be turned into joy. 21 A woman when she is in travail hath sorrow, because her hour is come: but as soon as she is delivered of the child, she remembereth no more the anguish, for joy that a man is born into the world. 22 And ye now therefore have sorrow: but I will see you again, and your heart shall rejoice, and your joy no man taketh from you. 23 And in that day ye shall ask me nothing. Verily, verily, I say unto you, Whatsoever ye shall ask the Father in my name, he will give it you. 24 Hitherto have ye asked nothing in my name: ask, and ye shall receive, that your joy may be full. 25 These things have I spoken unto you in proverbs: but the time cometh, when I shall no more speak unto you in proverbs, but I shall shew you plainly of the Father. 26 At that day ye shall ask in my name: and I say not unto you, that I will pray the Father for you: 27 For the Father himself loveth you, because ye have loved me, and have believed that I came out from God. 28 I came forth from the Father, and am come into the world: again, I leave	23 And in that day ye shall ask me nothing **but it shall be done unto you.** Verily, verily, I say unto you, Whatsoever ye shall ask the Father in my name, he will give it you.

John 16		John 16	D & C
the world, and go to the Father. 29 His disciples said unto him, Lo, now speakest thou plainly, and speakest no proverb. 30 Now are we sure that thou knowest all things, and needest not that any man should ask thee: by this we believe that thou camest forth from God. 31 Jesus answered them, Do ye now believe? (continued in column 3)		32 Behold, the hour cometh, yea, is now come, that ye shall be scattered, every man to his own, and shall leave me alone: and yet I am not alone, because the Father is with me. 33 These things I have spoken unto you, that in me ye might have peace. In the world ye shall have tribulation: but be of good cheer; I have overcome the world.	64:2 For verily I say unto you, I will that ye should overcome the world; wherefore I will have compassion upon you.

John 17	D & C	TPJS

160. The Intercessory Prayer

John 17	D & C	TPJS
These words spake Jesus, and lifted up his eyes to heaven, and said, Father, the hour is come; glorify thy Son, that thy Son also may glorify thee: 2 As thou hast given him power over all flesh, that he should give eternal life to as many as thou hast given him. 3 And this is life eternal, that they might know thee the only true God, and Jesus Christ, whom thou hast sent.	132:24 This is eternal lives-- to know the only wise and true God, and Jesus Christ, whom he hath sent. I am he. Receive ye, therefore, my law.	I will go back to the beginning before the world was, to show what kind of being God is. What sort of a being was God in the beginning? Open your ears and hear, all ye ends of the earth, for I am going to prove it to you by the Bible, and to tell you the designs of God in relation to the human race, and why he interferes with the affairs of man. *God himself was once as we are now, and is an exalted man, and sits enthroned in yonder heavens! That is the great secret. If the veil were rent today, and the great God who holds this world in its orbit, and who upholds all worlds and all things by his power, was to make himself visible, -- I say, if you were to see him today, you would see him like a man in form -- like yourselves in all the person, image, and very form as a man . . .* (p. 345)

TPJS-- Here, then, is eternal life -- to know the only wise and true God; and you have got to learn how to be Gods yourselves, and to be kings and priests to God, the same as all Gods have done before you, namely, by going from one small degree to another, and from a small capacity to a great one; from grace to grace, from exaltation to exaltation, until you attain to the resurrection of the dead, and are able to dwell in everlasting burnings, and to sit in glory, as do those who sit enthroned in everlasting power. And I want you to know that God, in the last days, while certain individuals are proclaiming his name, is not trifling with you or me. (pp. 346-47)

John 17	D & C	TPJS
4 I have glorified thee on the earth: I have finished the work which thou gavest me to do. 5 And now, O Father, glorify thou me with thine own self with the glory which I had with thee before the world was.		

John 17	John 17	John 17	D & C
6 I have manifested thy name unto the men which thou gavest me out of the world: thine they were, and thou gavest them me; and they have kept thy word. 7 Now they have known that all things whatsoever thou hast given me are of thee. 8 For I have given unto them the words which thou gavest me; and they have received them, and have known surely that I came out from thee, and they have believed that thou didst send me. 9 I pray for them: I pray not for the world, but for them which thou hast given me; for they are thine. 10 And all mine are thine, and thine are mine; and I am glorified in them. 11 And now I am no more in the world, but these are in the world, and I come to thee. Holy Father, keep through thine own name those whom thou hast given me, that they may be one, as we are.	the son of perdition; that the scripture might be fulfilled. 13 And now I come to thee; and these things I speak in the world, that they might have my joy fulfilled in themselves. 14 I have given them thy word; and the world hath hated them, because they are not of the world, even as I am not of the world. 15 I pray not that thou shouldest take them out of the world, but that thou shouldest keep them from the evil. 16 They are not of the world, even as I am not of the world. 17 Sanctify them through thy truth: thy word is truth. 18 As thou hast sent me into the world, even so have I also sent them into the world. 19 And for their sakes I sanctify myself, that they also might be sanctified through the truth. 20 Neither pray I for these alone, but for them also which shall believe on me (continued in column 3)	through their word; 21 That they all may be one; as thou, Father, art in me, and I in thee, that they also may be one in us: that the world may believe that thou hast sent me. 22 And the glory which thou gavest me I have given them; that they may be one, even as we are one. 23 I in them, and thou in me, that they may be made perfect in one; and that the world may know that thou hast sent me, and hast loved them, as thou hast loved me. 24 Father, I will that they also, whom thou hast given me, be with me where I am; that they may behold my glory, which thou hast given me: for thou lovedst me before the foundation of the world. 25 O righteous Father, the world hath not known thee: but I have known thee, and these have known that thou hast sent me. 26 And I have declared unto them thy name, and will declare it: that the	35:2 I am Jesus Christ, the Son of God, who was crucified for the sins of the world, even as many as will believe on my name, that they may become the sons of God, even one in me as I am one in the Father, as the Father is one in me, that we may be one.

TPJS-- Jesus prayed that those that the Father had given him out of the world might be made one in them, as they were one [one in spirit, in mind, in purpose]. If I were to testify that the Christian world were wrong on this point, my testimony would be true. (p. 311)

All are to be crammed into one God, according to sectarianism. It would make the biggest God in all the world. He would be a wonderfully big God--- he would be a giant or a monster. I want to read the text to you myself--- "I am agreed with the Father and the Father is agreed with me, and we are agreed as one." The Greek shows that it should be agreed. "Father, I pray for them which Thou hast given me out of the world, and not for those alone, but for them also which shall believe on me through their word, that they all may be agreed, as Thou, Father, are with me, and I with Thee, that they also may be agreed with us," and all come to dwell in unity, and in all the glory and everlasting burnings of the Gods; and then we shall see as we are seen, and be as our God and He as His Father. I want to reason a little on this subject. I learned it by translating the papyrus which is now in my house. (pp. 372-373)

12 While I was with them in the world, I kept them in thy name: those that thou gavest me I have kept, and none of them is lost, but (continued in column 2)		love wherewith thou hast loved me may be in them, and I in them.	

Matt. 26	JST Matt 26	Mark 14	JST Mark 14

161. Gethsemane-- The Bitter Cup of the Atonement

Matt. 26	JST Matt 26	Mark 14	JST Mark 14
36 ¶ Then cometh Jesus with them unto a place called Gethsemane,	33 Then cometh Jesus with them unto a place called Gethsemane,	32 And they came to a place which was named Gethsemane:	36 And they came to a place which was named Gethsemane, **which was a garden; and the disciples began to be sore amazed, and to be very heavy, and to complain in their hearts, wondering if this be the Messiah.**
and saith unto the disciples, Sit ye here, while I go and pray **yonder.**	and said unto the disciples, Sit ye here, while I go **yonder** and pray.	and **he saith** to his disciples, Sit ye here, while I pray.	37 And **Jesus knowing their hearts,** said to his disciples, Sit ye here, while I pray.
37 And he took with him Peter and the two sons of Zebedee, and began to be sorrowful and very heavy.		33 And he taketh with him Peter and James and John, and **began to be sore amazed, and to be very heavy;**	38 And he taketh with him, Peter, and James, and John, and **rebuked them,**
38 Then saith he unto them, My soul is exceeding sorrowful, even unto death: tarry ye here, and watch with me.		34 And saith unto them, My soul is exceeding sorrowful unto death: tarry ye here and watch.	and said unto them, My soul is exceedingly sorrowful **even** unto death; tarry ye here and watch.
39 And he went a little further, and fell on his face, and prayed,		35 And he went forward a little, and fell on the ground, and prayed that, if it were possible, the hour might pass from him.	
saying, O my Father, if it be possible, let this cup pass from me: nevertheless not as I will, but as thou wilt.		36 And he said, Abba, Father, all things are possible unto thee; take away this cup from me: nevertheless not **what I** will, but **what thou wilt.**	40 And he said, Abba, Father, all things are possible unto thee; take away this cup from me; nevertheless, not **my** will, but **thine be done.**
40 And he cometh unto the disciples, and findeth them asleep, and saith unto Peter, What, could ye not watch with me one hour?		37 And he cometh, and findeth them sleeping, and saith unto Peter, Simon, sleepest thou? couldest not thou watch one hour?	
41 Watch and pray, that ye enter not into temptation:		38 Watch and pray, lest ye enter not into temptation.	

Luke 22	JST Luke 22	John 18 D & C	B of M
		John 18:1 When Jesus had spoken these words, he went forth with his disciples over the brook Cedron, where was a garden, into the which he entered, and his disciples.	Alma 34:9 For it is expedient that an atonement should be made; for according to the great plan of the Eternal God there must be an atonement made, or else all mankind must unavoidably perish; yea, all are hardened; yea, all are fallen and are lost, and must perish except it be through the atonement which it is expedient should be made.
40 And when he was at the place, he said unto them, Pray that ye enter not into temptation.			10 For it is expedient that there should be a great and last sacrifice; yea, not a sacrifice of man, neither of beast, neither of any manner of fowl; for it shall not be a human sacrifice; but it must be an infinite and eternal sacrifice.
41 And he was withdrawn from them about a stone's cast, and kneeled down, and prayed, 42 Saying, Father, if thou be willing, remove this cup from me: nevertheless not my will, but thine, be done. 43 And there appeared an angel unto him from heaven, strengthening him.			3 Ne. 11:11 And behold, I am the light and the life of the world; and I have drunk out of that bitter cup which the Father hath given me, and have glorified the Father in taking upon me the sins of the world, in the which I have suffered the will of the Father in all things from the beginning.
44 And being in agony he prayed more earnestly: and **his** sweat **was** as it were great drops of blood falling down to the ground. 45 And when he rose up from prayer, and was come to his disciples, he found them sleeping for sorrow,	44 And being in an agony, he prayed more earnestly; and he sweat as it **were** great drops of blood falling down to the ground. 45 And when he rose up from prayer, and was come to his disciples, he found them sleeping; for **they were filled with** sorrow;	D&C 19:18 Which suffering caused myself, even God, the greatest of all, to tremble because of pain, and to bleed at every pore, and to suffer both body and spirit—and would that I might not drink the bitter cup, and shrink—	Mosiah 3:7 And lo, he shall suffer temptations, and pain of body, hunger, thirst, and fatigue, even more than man can suffer, except it be unto death; for behold, blood cometh from every pore, so great shall be his anguish for the wickedness and the abominations of his people.
46 And said unto them, Why sleep ye? rise and pray, lest ye enter into temptation.	46 And **he** said unto them, Why sleep ye? rise and pray, lest ye enter into temptation.		

Matt. 26	JST Matt. 26	Mark 14	JST Mark 14
the spirit indeed is willing, but the flesh is weak.		The spirit truly is ready, but the flesh is weak.	43 **And they said unto him,** The spirit truly is ready, but the flesh is weak.
42 He went away again the second time, and prayed, saying, O my Father, if this cup may not pass away from me, except I drink it, thy will be done.		39 And again he went away, and prayed, and spake the same words.	
43 And he came and found them asleep again: for their eyes were heavy.		40 And when he returned, he found them asleep again, (for their eyes were heavy,) neither **wist** they what to answer him.	45 And when he returned, he found them asleep again, for their eyes were heavy; neither **knew** they what to answer him.
44 And he left them, and went away again, and prayed the third time, saying the same words.			
45 Then cometh he to his disciples, and saith unto them, Sleep on now, and take **your** rest: behold, the hour is at hand, and the Son of man is betrayed into the hands of sinners.	42 Then cometh he to his disciples, and saith unto them, Sleep on now, and take rest. Behold, the hour is at hand, and the Son of Man is betrayed into the hands of sinners.	41 And he cometh the third time, and saith unto them, Sleep on now, and take **your** rest: it is enough, the hour is come; behold, the Son of man is betrayed into the hands of sinners.	46 And he cometh **to them** the third time, and said unto them, Sleep on now and· take rest; it is enough, the hour is come; behold, the Son of Man is betrayed into the hands of sinners.
	43 **And after they had slept, he said unto them, Arise, and** let us be going. Behold, he is at hand that doth betray me.		47 **And after they had finished their sleep, he said,** Rise up, let us go; lo, he **who** betrayeth me is at hand.
46 **Rise,** let us be going: behold, he is at hand that doth betray me.		42 Rise up, let us go; lo, he **that** betrayeth me is at hand.	

5th Day-- Thursday

162. Jerusalem-- Judas Betrays the Christ

Matt. 26	JST Matt. 26	Mark 14	JST Mark 14
47 ¶ And while he yet spake, lo, Judas, one of the twelve, came, and with him a great multitude with swords and staves, from the chief priests and elders of the people.		43 ¶ And immediately, while he yet spake, cometh Judas, one of the twelve, and with him a great multitude with swords and staves, from the chief priests and the scribes and the elders.	
48 Now he that betrayed him gave them a sign, saying, Whomsoever I shall kiss, that same is he: hold him fast.		44 And he **that** betrayed him had given them a token, saying, Whomsoever I shall kiss, that same is he; take him, and lead him away safely.	49 And he **who** betrayed him, had given them a token, saying, Whomsoever I shall kiss, that same is he; take him, and lead him away safely.

Isaiah 53 Luke 22	JST Luke 22	Book of Mormon John 18	Book of Mormon
			2 Nephi 9:10 O how great the goodness of our God, who prepareth a way for our escape from the grasp of this awful monster; yea, that monster, death and hell, which I call the death of the body, and also the death of the spirit.
			2 Nephi 9:12 And this death of which I have spoken, which is the spiritual death, shall deliver up its dead; which spiritual death is hell; wherefore, death and hell must deliver up their dead, and hell must deliver up its captive spirits, and the grave must deliver up its captive bodies, and the bodies and the spirits of men will be restored one to the other; and it is by the power of the resurrections of the Holy One of Israel.
Isaiah 53: 10 Yet it pleased the Lord to bruise him; he hath put *him* to grief: when thou shalt make his soul an offering for sin, he shall see *his* seed, he shall prolong *his* days, and the pleasure of the Lord shall prosper in his hand.		Alma 7:13 Now the spirit knoweth all things; nevertheless the Son of God suffereth according to the flesh that he might take upon him the sins of his people, that he might blot out their transgressions according to the power of his deliverance; and now behold, this is the testimony which is in me.	2 Nephi 9:20 O how great the holiness of our God! For he knoweth all things, and there is not anything save he knows it.
11 He shall see of the travail of his soul, *and* shall be satisfied: by his knowledge shall my righteous servant justify many; for he shall bear their iniquities.			21 And he cometh into the world that he may save all men if they will hearken unto his voice; for behold, he suffereth the pains of all men, yea, the pains of every living creature, both me, women, and children, who belong to the family of Adam.
		2 And Judas also, which betrayed him, knew the place: for Jesus oftimes resorted thither with his disciples.	
47 ¶ And while he yet spake, behold a multitude, and he **that** was called Judas, one of the twelve, went before them, and drew near unto Jesus to kiss him.	47 And while he yet spake, behold, a multitude, and he **who** was called Judas, one of the twelve, went before them, and drew near unto Jesus to kiss him.	3 Judas then, having received a band of men and officers from the chief priests and Pharisees, cometh thither with lanterns and torches and weapons.	

351

Matt. 26	JST Matt. 26	Mark 14	JST Mark 14
		45 And as soon as he was come, he goeth straight-way to him, and saith, Master, master; and kissed him.	
49 And forthwith he came to Jesus, and said, Hail, master; and kissed him. 50 And Jesus said unto him, Friend, wherefore art thou come? . . .	47 And Jesus said unto him, **Judas,** wherefore art thou come **to betray me with a kiss?**		
51 And, behold, one of them which were with Jesus stretched out his hand, and drew his sword, and struck a servant of the high priest's, and smote off his ear.		47 And one of them **that** stood by drew **a** sword, and smote a servant of the high priest, and cut off his ear.	52 And one of them, **who** stood by, drew **his** sword, and smote a servant of the high priest, and cut off his ear.
52 Then said Jesus unto him, Put up again thy sword into **his** place: for all they that take the sword shall perish with the sword.	50 Then said Jesus unto him, Put up again thy sword into **its** place; for all they that take the sword shall perish with the sword.		53 **But Jesus com-manded him to return his sword, saying, He who taketh the sword shall perish with the sword.**
53 Thinkest thou that I cannot now pray to my			

Luke 22	JST Luke 22	John 18	
48 But Jesus said unto him, Judas, betrayest thou the Son of man with a kiss?			
		4 Jesus therefore, knowing all things that should come upon him, went forth, and said unto them, Whom seek ye?	
		5 They answered him, Jesus of Nazareth. Jesus saith unto them, I am he. And Judas also, which betrayed him, stood with them.	
		6 As soon then as he had said unto them, I am he, they went backward, and fell to the ground.	
		7 Then asked he them again, Whom seek ye? And they said, Jesus of Nazareth.	
		8 Jesus answered, I have told you that I am he: if therefore ye seek me, let these go their way:	
		9 That the saying might be fulfilled, which he spake, Of them which thou gavest me have I lost none.	
49 When they **which** were about him saw what would follow, they said unto him, Lord, shall we smite with **the** sword?	49 When they **who** were about him, saw what would follow, they said unto him, Lord, shall we smite with **a** sword?		
50 ¶ And one of them smote the servant of the high priest, and cut off his right ear.		10 Then Simon Peter having a sword drew it, and smote the high priest's servant, and cut off his right ear. The servant's name was Malchus.	
		11 Then said Jesus unto Peter, Put up thy sword into the sheath:	

Matt. 26	JST Matt. 26	Mark 14	JST Mark 14
Father, and he shall presently give me more than twelve legions of angels? 54 But how then shall the scriptures be fulfilled, that thus it must be?			
55 In that same hour said Jesus to the multitudes, Are ye come out as against a thief with swords and staves for to take me?	53 In that same hour said Jesus unto the multitudes, Are ye come out as against a thief with swords and staves for to take me?	48 And Jesus answered and said unto them, Are ye come out, as against a thief, with swords and with staves to take me?	And he put forth his finger and healed the servant of the high priest. 54 And Jesus answered and said unto them, Are ye come out as against a thief, with swords and staves to take me?
I sat daily with you teaching in the temple, and ye laid no hold on me.	I sat daily with you in the temple, teaching, and ye laid no hold on me.	49 I was daily with you in the temple teaching, and ye took me not: but the scriptures must be fulfilled.	

163. Gethsemane-- The Arrest

Matt. 26	JST Matt. 26	Mark 14	JST Mark 14
50 . . . Then came they, and laid hands on Jesus, and took him. 56 But all this was done, that the scriptures of the prophets might be fulfilled. Then all the disciples forsook him, and fled.		46 ¶ And they laid their hands on him, and took him.	
		50 And they all forsook him, and fled.	56 And the disciples, when they heard this saying, all forsook him and fled.
		51 And there followed him a certain young man, having a linen cloth cast about his naked body; and the young men laid hold on him: 52 And he left the linen cloth, and fled from them naked.	57 And there followed him a certain young man, a disciple, having a linen cloth cast about his naked body; and the young men laid hold on him, and he left the linen cloth and fled from them naked, and saved himself out of their hands.

Luke 22	JST Luke 22	John 18	
		the cup which my Father hath given me, shall I not drink it?	
51 And Jesus answered and said, Suffer ye thus far. And he touched his ear, and healed him. 52 Then Jesus said unto the chief priests, and captains of the temple, and the elders, **which** were come to him, **Be** ye come out, as against a thief, with swords and staves? 53 When I was daily with you in the temple, ye stretched forth no hands against me: but this is your hour, and the power of darkness.	52 Then Jesus said unto the chief priests, and captains of the temple, and the elders, **who** were come to him, **Are** ye come out as against a thief, with swords and staves?		
		12 Then the band and the captain and officers of the Jews took Jesus, and bound him,	

Matt. 26	JST Matt. 26	Mark 14	JST Mark 14

164. Caiaphas' Palace-- Annas and Caiaphas Question Him

Matt. 26	JST Matt. 26	Mark 14	JST Mark 14
57 ¶ And they that had laid hold on Jesus led him away to Caiaphas the high priest, where the scribes and the elders were assembled.		53 ¶ And they led Jesus away to the high priest: and with him were assembled all the chief priests and the elders and the scribes.	
58 But Peter followed him afar off unto the high priest's palace,		54 And Peter followed him afar off, even into the palace of the high priest:	
and went in, and sat with the servants, to see the end.		and he sat with the servants, and warmed himself at the fire.	

Luke 22		John 18	John 18

54 ¶ Then took they him, and led him, and brought him into the high priest's house.

And Peter followed afar off.

55 And when they had kindled a fire in the midst of the hall, and were set down together, Peter sat down among them.

13 And led him away to Annas first; for he was father in law to Caiaphas, which was the high priest that same year.

14 Now Caiaphas was he, which gave counsel to the Jews, that it was expedient that one man should die for the people.

15 ¶ And Simon Peter followed Jesus, and so did another disciple: that disciple was known unto the high priest, and went in with Jesus into the palace of the high priest.

16 But Peter stood at the door without. Then went out that other disciple, which was known unto the high priest, and spake unto her that kept the door, and brought in Peter.

18 And the servants and officers stood there, who had made a fire of coals; for it was cold: and they warmed themselves: and Peter stood with them and (continued in column 4)

warmed himself.

19 ¶ The high priest then asked Jesus of his disciples, and of his doctrine.

20 Jesus answered him, I spake openly to the world; I ever taught in the synagogue, and in the temple, whither the Jews always resort; and in secret have I said nothing.

21 Why askest thou me? ask them which heard me, what I have said unto them: behold, they know what I said.

22 And when he had thus spoken, one of the officers which stood by struck Jesus with the palm of his hand, saying, Answerest thou the high priest so?

23 Jesus answered him, If I have spoken evil, bear witness of the evil: but if well, why smitest thou me?

24 Now Annas had sent him bound unto Caiaphas the high priest.

Matt. 26	JST Matt. 26	Mark 14	JST Mark 14

165. The Council Examines Jesus

Matt. 26	JST Matt. 26	Mark 14	JST Mark 14
59 Now the chief priests, and elders, and all the council, sought false witness against Jesus, to put him to death;		55 And the chief priests and all the council sought for witness against Jesus to put him to death; **and** found none.	60 And the chief priests and all the council sought for witness against Jesus, to put him to death, **but** found none;
60 **But found none:** yea, though many false witnesses came, **yet found** they none. At the last came two false witnesses,	59 Yea, though many false witnesses came, they **found** none **that could accuse him.**	56 **For** many bare false witness against him, **but** their witness agreed not together.	61 **Though** many bare false witness against him, **yet** their witness agreed not together.
61 And said,	60 . . . and said,	57 And there arose certain, and bare false witness against him, saying,	62 And there arose certain **men** and bare false witness against him, saying,
This **fellow** said, I am able to destroy the temple of God, and to build it in three days.	This **man** said, I am able to destroy the temple of God, and to build it in three days.	58 We heard him say, I will destroy this temple that is made with hands, and within three days I will build another made without hands.	
		59 But neither so did their witness agree together.	63 But neither did their witness agree together.
62 And the high priest arose, and said unto him, Answerest thou nothing? what **is it which** these witness against thee?	61 And the high priest arose and said unto him, Answerest thou nothing? **Knowest thou** what these witness against thee?	60 And the high priest stood up in the midst, and asked Jesus, saying, Answerest thou nothing? what **is it which** these witness against thee?	64 And the high priest stood up in the midst, and asked Jesus, saying,
63 But Jesus held his peace. And the high priest answered and said unto him, I adjure thee by the living God, that thou tell us whether thou be the Christ, the Son of God.		61 But he held his peace, and answered nothing. Again the high priest asked him, and said unto him, Art thou the Christ, the Son of the Blessed?	65 Answerest thou nothing? **Knowest thou not** what these witness against thee?
64 Jesus saith unto him, Thou hast said: nevertheless I say unto you, Hereafter shall ye see the Son of man sitting on the right hand of power, and coming in the clouds of heaven.		62 And Jesus said, I am: and ye shall see the Son of man sitting on the right hand of power, and coming in the clouds of heaven.	
65 Then the high priest rent his clothes, saying, He hath spoken blasphemy; what further need have we of witnesses? behold, now ye have heard his blasphemy.		63 Then the high priest rent his clothes, and saith, What need we any further witnesses?	
66 What think ye? They answered and said, He is guilty of death.	67 They answered and said, He is guilty, **and worthy** of death.	64 Ye have heard the blasphemy: what think ye? And they all condemned him to be guilty of death.	

Matt. 26	JST Matt. 26	Mark 14	Luke 22
67 Then did they spit in his face, and buffeted him; and others smote him with the palms of their hands, 68 Saying, Prophesy unto us, thou Christ, Who is **he** that smote thee?	68 Then did they spit in his face and buffet him; and others smote him with the palms of their hands, saying, Prophesy unto us, thou Christ, who is **it** that smote thee?	65 And some began to spit on him, and to cover his face, and to buffet him, and to say unto him, Prophesy: and the servants did strike him with the palms of their hands.	63 ¶ And the men **that** held Jesus mocked him, and smote him. 64 And when they had blindfolded him, they struck him on the face, and asked him, saying, Prophesy, who is it **that** smote thee? 65 And many other things blasphemously spake they against him. (JST Luke 22 changes "**that**" to "**who**" in vss. 63 and 64)

Matt. 26	JST Matt. 26	Mark 14	JST Mark 14

166. Peter's Denial Fulfilled

Matt. 26	JST Matt. 26	Mark 14	JST Mark 14
69 ¶ Now Peter sat without in the palace: and a damsel came unto him,		66 ¶ And as Peter was beneath in the palace, there cometh one of the maids of the high priest:	
		67 And when she saw Peter warming himself, she looked upon him, and said, **And** thou also wast with Jesus of Nazareth.	74 And when she saw Peter warming himself, she looked upon him and said, Thou also wast with Jesus of Nazareth.
saying, Thou also wast with Jesus of Galilee. 70 But he denied before them all, saying, I know not what thou sayest.		68 But he denied, saying, I know not, neither understand I what thou sayest. And he went out into the porch; and the cock crew.	
71 And when he was gone out into the porch, another **maid** saw him, and said unto them that were there, This **fellow** was also with Jesus of Nazareth.	71 And when he was gone out into the porch, another saw him, and said unto them that were there, This **man** was also with Jesus of Nazareth.	69 And a maid saw him again, and began to say to them **that** stood by, This is one of them.	77 And a maid saw him again, and began to say to them **who** stood by, This is one of them.
72 And again he denied with an oath, I do not know the man.	72 And again he denied with an oath, **saying,** I do not know the man.	70 And he denied it again. And a little after, they **that** stood by said again to Peter, Surely thou art one of them: for thou art a Galilæan, **and** thy speech agreeth thereto.	79 And a little after, they **who** stood by, said again to Peter, Surely thou art one of them; for thou art a Galilean, thy speech agreeth thereto.
73 And after a while came **unto him** they that stood by, and said to Peter, Surely thou also art one of them; for thy speech **bewrayeth.**	73 And after a while came they that stood by, and said to Peter, Surely thou also art one of them; for thy speech **betrayeth.**		
74 Then began he to curse and to swear, saying, I know not the man.		71 But he began to curse and to swear, saying, I know not this man of whom ye speak.	
And immediately the cock crew.		72 And the second time the cock crew.	
75 And Peter remembered the words of Jesus, which said unto him, Before the cock crow, thou shalt deny me thrice. And he went out, and wept bitterly.	76 And Peter remembered the words of Jesus, which **he** said unto him, Before the cock crow, thou shalt deny me thrice. And he went out and wept bitterly.	And Peter called to mind the word **that** Jesus said unto him, Before the cock crow twice, thou shalt deny me thrice. And **when he thought thereon,** he wept.	81 And Peter called to mind the words **which** Jesus said unto him, Before the cock crow twice, thou shalt deny me thrice. 82 And he **went out, and fell upon his face, and** wept **bitterly.**

Luke 22	JST Luke 22	John 18	JST John 18
56 But a certain maid beheld him as he sat by the fire, and earnestly looked upon him, and said, This man was also with him.		17 Then saith the damsel that kept the door unto Peter, Art not thou also one of this man's disciples?	
57 And he denied him, saying, Woman, I know him not.		He saith, I am not.	
58 And after a little while another saw him, and said, Thou art also of them. And Peter said, Man, I am not.		25 And Simon Peter stood and warmed himself. They said therefore unto him, Art not thou also one of his disciples? He denied it, and said, I am not.	
59 And about the space of one hour **after** another confidently affirmed, saying, Of a truth this **fellow also was** with him: for he is a Galilæan.	59 And about the space of one hour, another confidently affirmed, saying, Of a truth, this **man was also** with him; for he is a Galilean.	26 One of the servants of the high priest, being his kinsman whose ear Peter cut off, saith, Did **not** I see thee in the garden with him?	26 One of the servants of the high priest, being his kinsman whose ear Peter cut off, saith, Did **I not** see thee in the garden with him?
60 And Peter said, Man, I know not what thou sayest. And immediately, while he yet spake, the cock crew.		27 Peter then denied again: and immediately the cock crew.	
61 And the Lord turned, and looked upon Peter. And Peter remembered the word of the Lord, how he had said unto him, Before the cock crow, thou shalt deny me thrice.			
62 And Peter went out, and wept bitterly.			

Matt. 27	Mark 15	JST Mark 15	Luke 22

167. Formal Trial and Condemnation

Matt. 27	Mark 15	JST Mark 15	Luke 22
When the morning was come, all the chief priests and elders of the people took counsel against Jesus to put him to death:	And straightway in the morning the chief priests held a consultation with the elders and scribes and the whole council . . .	2 And the whole council **condemned him** . . .	66 ¶ And as soon as it was day, the elders of the people and the chief priests and the scribes came together, and led him into their council, saying, 67 Art thou the Christ? tell us. And he said unto them, If I tell you, ye will not believe: 68 And if I also ask you, ye will not answer me, nor let me go. 69 Hereafter shall the Son of man sit on the right hand of the power of God. 70 Then said they all, Art thou then the Son of God? And he said unto them, Ye say that I am. 71 And they said, What need we any further witness? for we ourselves have heard of his own mouth. (JST Luke 22 states "need we of any further...")

362

Matt. 27	JST Matt. 27		Old Testament

168. Judas Commits Suicide

Matt. 27	JST Matt. 27		Old Testament
3 ¶ Then Judas, which had betrayed him, when he saw that he was condemned, repented himself, and brought again the thirty pieces of silver to the chief priests and elders, 4 Saying, I have sinned in that I have betrayed the innocent blood. And they said, What is that to us? see thou to that. 5 And he cast down the pieces of silver in the temple, and departed, and went and hanged himself.			
	5 And they said **unto him,** What is that to us? See thou to **it; thy sins be upon thee.** 6 And he cast down the pieces of silver in the temple, and departed, and went, and hanged himself **on a tree. And straightway he fell down, and his bowels gushed out, and he died.**		Psalms 94:21 They gather themselves together against the soul of the righteous, and condemn the innocent blood.
6 And the chief priests took the silver pieces, and said, It is not lawful for to put them into the treasury, because it is the price of blood. 7 And they took counsel, and bought with them the potter's field, to bury strangers in. 8 Wherefore that field was called, The field of blood, unto this day. 9 Then was fulfilled that which was spoken by Jeremy the prophet, saying, And they took the thirty pieces of silver, the price of him that was valued, whom they of the children of Israel did value;			Zechariah 11:12 And I said unto them, If ye think good, give me my price; and if not, forbear. So they weighed for . my price thirty pieces of silver.
10 And gave them for the potter's field, as the Lord appointed **me.**	10 **And therefore they took the pieces of silver,** and gave them for the potter's field, as the Lord appointed **by the mouth of Jeremy.**		

Matt. 27		Mark 15	JST Mark 15

169. Pilate's Judgment Hall-- Before Pilate

Matt. 27		Mark 15	JST Mark 15
2 And when they had bound him, they led him away, and delivered him to Pontius Pilate the governor.		1 . . . and bound **Jesus**, and carried him away, and delivered him to Pilate.	2 . . . and bound **him**, and carried him away, and delivered him to Pilate.
11 And Jesus stood before the governor: and the governor asked him, saying, Art thou the King of the Jews? . . .		2 And Pilate asked him, Art thou the King of the Jews?	

Luke 23	JST Luke 23	John 18	B of M
And the whole multitude of them arose, and led him unto Pilate.		28 ¶ Then led they Jesus form Caiaphas unto the hall of judgment: and it was early; and they themselves went not into the judgment hall, lest they should be defiled; but that they might eat the passover.	1 Nephi 19:7 For the things which some men esteem to be of great worth, both to the body and soul, others set at naught and trample under their feet. Yea, even the very God of Israel do men trample under their feet. . . they set him at naught, and hearken not to the voice of his counsels.
		29 Pilate then went out unto them, and said, What accusation bring ye against this man?	8 And behold he cometh, according to the words of the angel, in six hundred years from the time my father left Jerusalem.
		30 They answered and said unto him, If he were not a malefactor, we would not have delivered him up unto thee. 31 Then said Pilate unto them, Take ye him, and judge him according to your law. The Jews therefore said unto him, It is not lawful for us to put any man to death:	9 And the wold, because of their iniquity, shall judge him to be a thing of naught: wherefore they scourge him. . . . . and they smite him. . . . . Yea, they spit upon him, and he suffereth it, because of his living kindness and his long suffering towards the children of men.
		32 That the saying of Jesus might be fulfilled, which he spake, signifying what death he should die.	10 And the God of our fathers, who were led out of Egypt, out of bondage, and also were preserved in the wilderness by him, yea, the God of Abraham, and of Isaac, and the God of Jacob, yieldeth himself, according to the words of the angel, as a man, into the hands of wicked men, to be lifted up, according to the words of Zenock, and to be crucified, according to the words of Neum, and to be buried in a sepulcher, according to the words of Zenos, which he spake concerning the three days of darkness, which should be a sign given of his death unto those who should inhabit the isles of the sea, more especially given unto those who are of the house of Israel.
2 And they began to accuse him, saying, We found this **fellow** perverting the nation, and forbidding to give tribute to Caesar, saying that he himself is Christ a King. 3 And Pilate asked him, saying, Art thou the King of the Jews?	2 And they began to accuse him, saying, We found this **man** perverting the nation, and forbidding to give tribute to Caesar, saying, that he himself is Christ, a king.	33 Then Pilate entered into the judgment hall again, and called Jesus, and said unto him, Art thou the king of the Jews? 34 Jesus answered him, Sayest thou this thing of thyself, or did others tell it thee of me? 35 Pilate answered, Am I a Jew? Thine own nation and chief priests have delivered thee unto me: what has thou done? 36 Jesus answered, My kingdom is not of this	

Matt. 27	JST Matt. 27	Mark 15	JST Mark 15
11 . . . And Jesus said unto him, Thou sayest.	12 And Jesus said unto him, Thou sayest **truly; for thus it is written of me.**	2 . . . And **he** answering said unto him, Thou sayest it.	4 And **Jesus** answering, said unto him, **I am,** even as thou sayest.
12 And when he was accused of the chief priests and elders, he answered nothing. 13 Then said Pilate unto him, Hearest thou not how many things they witness against thee? 14 And he answered him to never a word; insomuch that the governor marvelled greatly.	15 And he answered him **not to his questions; yea,** never a word, insomuch that the governor marvelled greatly.	3 And the chief priests accused him of many things: but he answered nothing. 4 And Pilate asked him again, saying, Answerest thou nothing? behold how many things they witness against thee. 5 But Jesus yet answered nothing; so that Pilate marvelled.	

Luke 23	JST Luke 23	John 18	JST John 18
		world: if my kingdom were of this world, then would my servants fight, that I should not be delivered to the Jews: but now is my kingdom not from hence.	
3 cont. And he answered him and said, Thou sayest it.	3 cont. And he answered him, and said, **Yea**, thou sayest it.	37 Pilate therefore said unto him, Art thou a king then? Jesus answered, Thou sayest that I am a king. To this end was I born, and for this cause came I into the world, that I should bear witness unto the truth. Every one that is of the truth heareth my voice.	
4 Then said Pilate to the chief priests and **to the** people, I find no fault in this man.	4 Then said Pilate to the chief priests and people, I find no fault in this man.	38 Pilate saith unto him, What is truth? And when he had said this, he went out again unto the Jews, and saith unto them, I find in him no fault **at all**.	38 Pilate saith unto him, What is truth? And when he had said this, he went out again unto the Jews, and saith unto them, I find in him no fault.
5 And they were the more fierce, saying, He stirreth up the people, teaching throughout all Jewry, beginning from Galilee to this place. 6 When Pilate heard of Galilee, he asked whether the man were a Galilæan. 7 And as soon as he knew that he belonged unto Herod's jurisdiction, he sent him to Herod, who himself also was at Jerusalem at that time.			

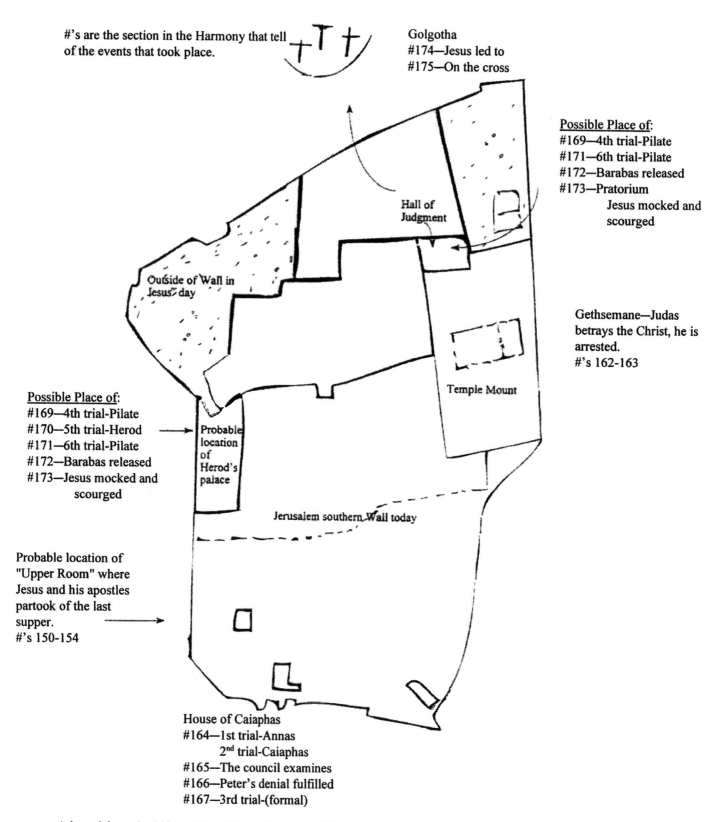

#'s are the section in the Harmony that tell of the events that took place.

Golgotha
#174—Jesus led to
#175—On the cross

Possible Place of:
#169—4th trial-Pilate
#171—6th trial-Pilate
#172—Barabas released
#173—Pratorium
   Jesus mocked and
   scourged

Hall of Judgment

Gethsemane—Judas betrays the Christ, he is arrested.
#'s 162-163

Outside of Wall in Jesus' day

Temple Mount

Possible Place of:
#169—4th trial-Pilate
#170—5th trial-Herod
#171—6th trial-Pilate
#172—Barabas released
#173—Jesus mocked and
   scourged

Probable location of Herod's palace

Jerusalem southern Wall today

Probable location of "Upper Room" where Jesus and his apostles partook of the last supper.
#'s 150-154

House of Caiaphas
#164—1st trial-Annas
   2nd trial-Caiaphas
#165—The council examines
#166—Peter's denial fulfilled
#167—3rd trial-(formal)

Adapted from the Life and Teachings of Jesus and His Apostles (Second Edition) Church Educational System, 1929.

Luke 23	JST Luke 23		Isaiah

170. Herod's Palace-- Jesus Before Herod

Luke 23	JST Luke 23		Isaiah
8 ¶ And when Herod saw Jesus, he was exceeding glad: for he was desirous to see him of a long **season**, because he had heard many things of him; and he hoped to have seen some miracle done by him. 9 Then he questioned with him in many words; but he answered him nothing. 10 And the chief priests and scribes stood and vehemently accused him. 11 And Herod with his men of war set him at nought, and mocked him, and arrayed him in a gorgeous robe, and sent him again to Pilate. 12 ¶ And the same day Pilate and Herod were made friends together: for before they were at enmity between themselves.	8 And when Herod saw Jesus, he was exceeding glad; for he was desirous to see him, of a long **time**, because he had heard many things of him; and hoped to have seen some miracle done by him. 12 And the same day Pilate and Herod were made friends together; for before **this** they were at enmity between themselves.		53:7 He was oppressed, and he was afflicted, yet he opened not his mouth: he is brought as a lamb to the slaughter, and as a sheep before her shearers is dumb, so he openeth not his mouth.

171. Pilate's Judgment Hall-- Again Before Pilate

Luke 23	JST Luke 23		Isaiah
13 ¶ And Pilate, when he had called together the chief priests and the rulers and the people, 14 Said unto them, Ye have brought this man unto me, as one **that** perverteth the people: and, behold, I, having examined him before you, have found no fault in this man touching those things whereof ye accuse him: 15 No, nor yet Herod: for I sent you to him; and, lo, nothing worthy of death is done unto him. 16 I will therefore chastise him, and release him.	14 Said unto them, **You** have brought this man unto me, as one **who** perverteth the people; and, behold, I, having examined him before you, have found no fault in this man, touching those things whereof ye accuse him.		

Matt. 27	JST Matt. 27	Mark 15	JST Mark 15
15 Now at **that** feast the governor was wont to release unto the people a prisoner, whom they would.	16 Now at **the** feast the governor was wont to release unto the people a prisoner, whom they would.	6 Now at **that** feast **he** released unto them one prisoner, whomsoever they desired.	8 Now **it was common** at **the** feast, **for Pilate to** release unto them one prisoner, whomsoever they desired.
16 And they had then a notable prisoner, called Barabbas.		7 And there was **one** named Barabbas, **which lay** bound with them **that** had made insurrection with him, who had committed murder in the insurrection.	9 And there was **a man** named Barabbas, bound with them **who** had made insurrection with him, who had committed murder in the insurrection.
		8 And the multitude crying aloud began to desire him to **do as he had ever done** unto them.	10 And the multitude, crying aloud, began to desire him to **deliver Jesus** unto them.
17 Therefore when they were gathered together, Pilate said unto them, Whom will ye that I release unto you? Barabbas, or Jesus which is called Christ?		9 But Pilate answered them, saying, Will ye that I release unto you the King of the Jews?	11 But Pilate answered **unto** them, saying, Will ye that I release unto you the King of the Jews?
18 For he knew that for envy they had delivered him.		10 For he knew that the chief priests had delivered him for envy.	
19 ¶ When he was set down on the judgment seat, his wife sent unto him, saying, Have thou nothing to do with that just man: for I have suffered many things this day in a **dream** because of him.	20 When he was set down on the judgment seat, his wife sent unto him, saying, Have thou nothing to do with that just man, for I have suffered many things this day in a **vision** because of him.		
20 But the chief priests and elders persuaded the multitude that they should ask for Barabbas, and destroy Jesus.		11 But the chief priests moved the people, that he should rather release Barabbas unto them.	13 But the chief priests moved the people, that he should rather release Barabbas unto them, **as he had before done unto them.**
21 The governor **answered and** said unto them, Whether of the twain will ye that I release unto you? They said, Barabbas.	22 **And** the governor said unto them, Whether of the twain will ye that I release unto you? They said, Barabbas.		
22 Pilate saith unto them, What shall I do **then** with	23 Pilate said unto them, What shall I do with Jesus,	12 And Pilate **answered** and said **again** unto them,	14 And Pilate **spake again** and said unto them,

370

Luke 23	JST Luke 23	John 18	
17 (For of necessity he must release one unto them at the feast.)		39 But ye have a custom, that I should release unto you one at the passover:	
		will ye therefore that I release unto you the King of the Jews?	
18 **And** they cried out all at once, saying, Away with this man, and release unto us Barabbas: 19 (Who for a certain sedition made in the city, and for murder, was cast into prison.) 20 Pilate therefore, will-ing to release Jesus, spake	18 **But** they cried out all at once, saying, Away with this man, and release unto us Barabbas;	40 Then cried they all again, saying, Not this man, but Barabbas. Now Barabbas was a robber.	

Matt. 27	JST Matt. 27	Mark 15	JST Mark 15
Jesus which is called Christ?	which is called Christ?	What will ye then that I shall do **unto** him whom ye call the King of the Jews?	What will ye then that I shall do **with** him whom ye call the King of the Jews?
They all **say** unto him, Let him be crucified.	**And** all **said** unto him, Let him be crucified.	13 And they cried out again,	15 And they cried out again, **Deliver him unto us to be crucified. Away with him.** Crucify him.
		Crucify him.	
23 And the governor said, Why, what evil hath he done? . . .		14 Then Pilate said unto them, Why, what evil hath he done? . . .	

172. Praetorium-- Jesus Mocked and Scourged

Matt. 27	JST Matt. 27	Mark 15	JST Mark 15
27 Then the soldiers of the governor took Jesus into the common hall, and gathered unto him the whole band **of soldiers.**	29 Then the soldiers of the governor took Jesus into the common hall, and gathered unto him the whole band.	16 And the soldiers led him away into the hall, called Prætorium; and they call together the whole band.	
28 And they stripped him, and put on him a **scarlet** robe.	30 And they stripped him, and put on him a **purple** robe.	17 And they clothed him with purple, and platted a crown of thorns, and put it **about** his head,	20 And they clothed him with purple, and platted a crown of thorns and put it **upon** his head;
29 ¶ And when they had platted a crown of thorns, they put it upon his head, and a reed in his right hand: and they bowed the knee before him, and mocked him, saying, Hail, King of the Jews!		18 And began to salute him, Hail, King of the Jews!	21 And began to salute him, **saying,** Hail, King of the Jews.
30 And they spit upon him, and took the reed, and smote him on the head.		19 And they smote him on the head with a reed, and did spit upon him, and bowing their knees worshipped him.	

Luke 23	John 19	John 19	JST John 19
again to them. 21 But they cried, saying, Crucify him, crucify him. 22 And he said unto them the third time, Why, what evil hath he done? I have found no cause of death in him: I will therefore chastise him, and let him go.			
	Then Pilate therefore took Jesus, and scourged him. 2 And the soldiers platted a crown of thorns, and put it on his head, and they put on him a purple robe, 3 And said, Hail, King of the Jews! and they smote him with their hands. 4 Pilate therefore went forth again, and saith unto them, Behold, I bring him forth to you, that ye may know that I find no fault in him. 5 Then came Jesus forth, wearing the crown of thorns, and the purple robe. And Pilate saith unto them, Behold the man! 6 When the chief priests therefore and officers saw him, they cried out, saying, Crucify him, crucify him. Pilate saith unto them, Take ye him, and crucify him: for I find no fault in him. (continued in column 3)	7 The Jews answered him, We have a law, and by our law he ought to die, because he made himself the Son of God. 8 ¶ When Pilate therefore heard that saying, he was the more afraid; 9 And went again into the judgment hall, and saith unto Jesus, Whence art thou? But Jesus gave him no answer. 10 Then saith Pilate unto him, Speakest thou not unto me? knowest thou not that I have power to crucify thee, and have power to release thee? 11 Jesus answered, Thou couldest have no power at all against me, except it were given thee from above: therefore he that delivered me unto thee hath the greater sin. 12 And from thenceforth Pilate sought to release him: but the Jews cried out, saying, If thou let this man go, thou art not Cæsar's friend: whosoever maketh himself a king speaketh against Cæsar. 13 ¶ When Pilate therefore heard that saying, he brought Jesus forth, and	11 Jesus answered, Thou couldest have no power against me, except it were given thee from above; therefore he that delivered me unto thee hath the greater sin.

Matt. 27	JST Matt. 27	Mark 15	JST Mark 15
23 . . . But they cried out the more, saying, Let him be crucified.		14 . . . **And** they cried out the more exceedingly, Crucify him.	17 **But** they cried out the more exceedingly, Crucify him.

173. Pilate Releases Barabbas

Matt. 27	JST Matt. 27	Mark 15	JST Mark 15
24 ¶ When Pilate saw that he could prevail nothing, but **that** rather a tumult was made, he took water, and washed his hands before the multitude, saying, I am innocent of the blood of this just person: see ye **to it.**	26 And when Pilate saw that he could prevail nothing, but rather **that** a tumult was made, he took water, and washed his hands before the multitude, saying, I am innocent of the blood of this person; see **that** ye **do nothing unto him.**		
25 Then answered all the people, and said, His blood **be** on us, and **on** our children.	27 Then answered all the people, and said, his blood **come upon** us, and our children.		
		15 ¶ And so Pilate, willing to content the people,	18 And **now** Pilate, willing to content the people,
26 ¶ Then released he Barabbas unto them: and when he had scourged Jesus, he delivered him to be crucified.		released Barabbas unto them, and delivered Jesus, when he had scourged him, to be crucified.	released Barabbas unto them, and delivered Jesus, when he had scourged him, to be crucified.
31 And after that they had mocked him, they took the robe off from him, and put his own raiment on him, and led him away to crucify him.		20 And when they had mocked him, they took off the purple from him, and put his own clothes on him, and led him out to crucify him.	

Luke 23	JST Luke 23	John 19	B of M
		sat down in the judgment seat in a place that is called the Pavement, but in Hebrew, Gabbatha.	2 Nephi 10:5 But because of priestcrafts and iniquities, they at Jerusalem will stiffen their necks against him, that he be crucified.
		14 And it was the preparation of the passover, and about the sixth hour: and he saith unto the Jews, Behold, your King!	6 Wherefore, because of their iniquities, destructions, famines, pestilence, and bloodshed shall come upon them; and they who shall not be destroyed shall be scattered among all nations.
23 And they were instant **with** loud voices, requiring that he might be crucified.	23 And they were instant **in** loud voiced, requiring that he might be crucified;	15 But they cried out, Away with him, away with him, crucify him. Pilate saith unto them, Shall I crucify your King? The chief priests answered, We have no king but Caesar.	
And the voices of them and of the chief priests prevailed.	and the voices of them, and of the chief priests, prevailed.		
24 And Pilate gave sentence that it should be as they required.			
25 And he released unto them him **that** for sedition and murder was cast into prison, whom they had desired; **but he** delivered Jesus to their will.	25 And he released unto them him **who** for sedition and murder was cast into prison, whom they had desired: **and** delivered Jesus to their will.	16 Then delivered he him therefore unto them to be crucified.	

Matt. 27		Mark 15	

174. Jerusalem-- Led to Golgotha

32 And as they came out, they found a man of Cyrene, Simon by name: him they compelled to bear his cross.

21 And they compel one Simon a Cyrenian, who passed by, coming out of the country, the father of Alexander and Rufus, to bear his cross.

Luke 23	JST Luke 23	John 19	

26 And as they led him away, they laid hold upon one Simon, a Cyrenian, coming out of the country, and on him they laid the cross, that he might bear it after Jesus.

27 ¶ And there followed him a great company of people, and of women, **which** also bewailed and lamented him.

28 But Jesus turning unto them said, Daughters of Jerusalem, weep not for me, but weep for your-selves, and for your child-ren.

29 For, behold, the days are coming, in the which they shall say, Blessed are the barren, and the wombs **that** never bare, and the paps which never gave suck.

30 Then shall they begin to say to the mountains, Fall on us; and to the hills, Cover us.

31 **For** if **they do** these things in **a** green tree, what shall be done in the dry?

32 And there were also two other, malefactors, led with him to be put to death.

---

27 And there followed him a great company of people, and of women, **who** also bewailed and lamented him.

28 But Jesus turned unto them **and** said, Daughters of Jerusalem, weep not for me, but weep for your-selves, and for your child-ren.

29 For behold, the days are coming, in the which they shall say, Blessed are the barren, and the wombs **which** never bare, and the paps which never gave suck.

31 **And** if these things **are done** in **the** green tree, what shall be done in the dry **tree**?

32 **This he spake, signi-fying the scattering of Israel, and the desolation of the heathen, or in other words, the Gen-tiles.**

(JST states others.)

---

16 cont. And they took Jesus, and led him away.

Matt. 27	JST Matt. 27	Mark 15	JST Mark 15

175. Golgotha—On the Cross

Matt. 27	JST Matt. 27	Mark 15	JST Mark 15
33 And when they were come unto a place called Golgotha, that is to say, a place of **a skull,**	35 And when they were come unto a place called Golgotha, (that is to say, a place of **burial,)**	22 And they bring him unto the place Golgotha, which is, being interpreted, The place of a **skull.**	25 And they bring him unto the place **called** Golgotha, which is, (being interpreted,) The place of a **burial.**
34 ¶ They gave him vinegar to drink mingled with gall: and when he had tasted **thereof,** he would not drink.	36 They gave him vinegar to drink mingled with gall; and when he had tasted **the vinegar,** he would not drink.	23 And they gave him to drink **wine** mingled with **myrrh: but he received it** not.	26 And they gave him to drink, **vinegar** mingled with **gall; and when he had tasted the vinegar,** he **would** not **drink.**
		25 And it was the third hour, **and** they crucified him.	28 And it was the third hour, **when** they crucified him.
38 Then were there two thieves crucified with him, one on the right hand, and another on the left.		27 And with him they **crucify** two thieves; the one on his right hand, **and the** other on his left.	32 And with him they **crucified** two thieves, the one on his right hand, the other on his left.
		28 And the scripture was fulfilled, which saith, And he was numbered with the transgressors.	
	39 **And Pilate wrote a title, and put it on the cross, and the writing was,**	26 And **the superscription of** his accusation **was written over,**	29 And **Pilate wrote** his accusation **and put it upon the cross,**
	40 **JESUS OF NAZARETH THE KING OF THE JEWS, in letters of Greek, and Latin, and Hebrew.**	THE KING OF THE JEWS.	THE KING OF THE JEWS.
37 And set up over his head his accusation written, THIS IS JESUS THE KING OF THE JEWS.	41 **And the chief priests said unto Pilate, It should be written** and set up over his head his accusation written, This is **he that said he was** Jesus, the King of the Jews.		30 **There were certain of the chief priests who stood by, that said unto Pilate, Write, that he said, I am the King of the Jews.**
	42 **But Pilate answered and said, What I have written, I have written; let it alone.**		31 **But Pilate said unto them, What I have written, I have written.**

176. Roman Soldiers—First Words

Luke 23	JST Luke 23	John 19	JST John 19
33 And when they were come to the place, which is called Calvary,		17 And he bearing his cross went forth into a place called the place of a **skull**, which is called in the Hebrew Golgotha:	17 And he bearing his cross went forth into a place called the place of a **burial**; which is called in the Hebrew Golgotha;
there they crucified him, and the malefactors, one on the right hand, and the other on the left.		18 Where they crucified him, and two other with him, on either side one, and Jesus in the midst.	
38 And a superscription also was written over him in letters of Greek, and Latin, and Hebrew, THIS IS THE KING OF THE JEWS.		19 ¶ And Pilate wrote a title, and put it on the cross. And the writing was, JESUS OF NAZARETH THE KING OF THE JEWS. 20 This title then read many of the Jews: for the place where Jesus was crucified was nigh to the city: and it was written in Hebrew, and Greek, and Latin. 21 Then said the chief priests of the Jews to Pilate, Write not, The King of the Jews; but that he said, I am the King of the Jews. 22 Pilate answered, What I have written I have written.	
34 ¶ Then said Jesus, Father, forgive them; for they know not what they do.	35 Then said Jesus, Father, forgive them; for they know not what they do. **(Meaning the soldiers who crucified him,)**	23 ¶ Then the soldiers, when they had crucified Jesus, took his garments, and made four parts, to every soldier a part; and	

379

Matt. 27	JST Matt. 27	Mark 15	JST Mark 15
35 And they crucified him, and parted his garments, casting lots: that it might be fulfilled which was spoken by the prophet, They parted my garments among them, and **upon** my vesture **did they** cast lots. 36 And sitting down they watched him there; 39 ¶ And they that passed by reviled him, wagging their heads, 40 And saying, Thou that destroyest the temple, and buildest it in three days, save thyself. If thou be the Son of God, come down from the cross. 41 Likewise also the chief priests mocking **him**, with the scribes and elders, said, 42 He saved others; himself he cannot save. If he be the King of Israel, let him now come down from the cross, and we will believe him. 43 He trusted in God; let him deliver him now, if he will **have** him: for he said, I am the Son of God.	37 And they crucified him, and parted his garments, casting lots: that it might be fulfilled which was spoken by the prophets, They parted my garments among them, and **for** my vesture **they did** cast lots. 44 And they that passed by reviled him, wagging their heads, and saying, Thou that destroyest the temple, and buildest it **again** in three days, save thyself. If thou be the Son of God, come down from the cross. 45 Likewise also the chief priests mocking with the scribes and elders, said, He saved others, himself he cannot save. If he be the King of Israel, let him now come down from the cross, and we will believe him. 46 He trusted in God; let him deliver him now, if he will **save** him: **let him save him** for he said, I am the Son of God.	24 And when they had crucified him, they parted his garments, casting lots upon them, what every man should take. 29 And they **that** passed by railed on him, wagging their heads, and saying, Ah, thou **that** destroyest the temple, and buildest it in three days, 30 Save thyself, and come down from the cross. 31 Likewise also the chief priests mocking said among themselves with the scribes, He saved others; himself he cannot save. 32 Let Christ the King of Israel descend now from the cross, that we may see and believe.	34 And they **who** passed by railed on him, wagging their heads, and saying, Ah, thou **who** destroyest the temple and buildest it in three days . . .

177. Thieves on the Cross-- 2nd Words

Matt. 27	JST Matt. 27	Mark 15	JST Mark 15
44 The thieves also, which were crucified with him, cast the same in his teeth.	47 **One of the thieves** also, which were crucified with him, cast the same in his teeth. **But the other rebuked him, saying, Dost thou not fear God, seeing thou art under the same condemnation; and this man is just, and hath not sinned;**	And **they that were** crucified with him reviled him.	37 And **one of them who** was crucified with him, reviled him also, **saying, If thou art the Christ, save thyself and us.**

Luke 23	JST Luke 23	John 19	Psalms
		also his coat: now the coat was without seam, woven from the top throughout.	
And they parted his raiment, and cast lots.		24 They said therefore among themselves, Let us not rend it, but cast lots for it, whose it shall be: that the scripture might be fulfilled, which saith, They parted my raiment among them, and for my vesture they did cast lots. These things therefore the soldiers did.	22:18 They part my garments among them, and cast lots upon my vesture.
35 And the people stood beholding. And the rulers also with them derided **him**, saying, He saved others; let him save himself, if he be Christ, the chosen of God. 36 And the soldiers also mocked him, coming to him, and offering him vinegar, 37 And saying, If thou be the king of the Jews, save thyself.	36 And the people stood, beholding, and the rulers also with them, derided, saying, He saved others; let him save himself, if he be **the** Christ, the chosen of God.		22:7 All they that see me laugh me to scorn: they shoot out the lip, they shake the head, saying, 8 He trusted on the LORD that he would deliver him: let him deliver him, seeing he delighted in him.
39 ¶ And one of the malefactors **which were hanged** railed on him, saying, If thou be Christ, save thyself and us. 40 But the other answering rebuked him, saying, Dost **not thou** fear God, seeing thou art in the same condemnation? 41 And we indeed justly; for we receive the due reward of our deeds: but this man hath done nothing amiss.	40 And one of the malefactors **who was crucified with him,** railed on him, saying, If thou be **the** Christ, save thyself and us. 41 But the other answering, rebuked him, saying, Dost **thou not** fear God, seeing thou art in the same condemnation?		

Matt. 27	JST Matt. 27	Mark 15	JST Mark 15
	and he cried unto the Lord that he would save him. 48 And the Lord said unto him, This day thou shalt be with me in Paradise.		

178. 3rd Words-- to His Mother

179. Darkness-- Sixth to Ninth Hour

Matt. 27	JST Matt. 27	Mark 15	JST Mark 15
45 Now from the sixth hour there was darkness over all the land unto the ninth hour.		33 And when the sixth hour was come, there was darkness over the whole land until the ninth hour.	

180. Final Words

Matt. 27	JST Matt. 27	Mark 15	JST Mark 15
46 And about the ninth hour Jesus cried with a loud voice, saying, Eli, Eli, lama sabachthani? that is to say, My God, my God, why hast thou forsaken me?		34 And at the ninth hour Jesus cried with a loud voice, saying, Eloi, Eloi, lama sabachthani? which is, being interpreted, My God, my God, why hast thou forsaken me?	
47 Some of them that stood there, when they heard **that**, said, This man calleth for Elias.	51 Some of them that stood there, when they heard **him**, said, This man calleth for Elias.	35 And some of them **that** stood by, when they heard **it**, said, Behold, he calleth Elias.	40 And some of them **who** stood by, when they heard **him**, said, Behold, he calleth Elias.

Luke 23	JST Luke 23	John 19	Psalms
42 And he said **unto** Jesus, Lord, remember me when thou comest into thy kingdom. 43 And Jesus said unto him, Verily I say unto thee, To day shalt thou be with me in paradise.			

TPJS-- King James' translators make [this] out to say paradise. But what is paradise? It is a modern word: it does not answer at all to the original word that Jesus made use of. . .There is nothing in the original word in Greek from which this was taken that signifies paradise; but it was---This day thou shalt be with me in the world of spirits. (p. 309)

Luke 23	JST Luke 23	John 19	Psalms
		25 ¶ Now there stood by the cross of Jesus his mother, and his mother's sister, Mary the wife of Cleophas, and Mary Magdalene. 26 When Jesus therefore saw his mother, and the disciple standing by, whom he loved, he saith unto his mother, Woman, behold thy son! 27 Then saith he to the disciple, Behold thy mother! And from that hour that disciple took her unto his own home.	
44 And it was about the sixth hour, and there was **a** darkness over all the earth until the ninth hour. 45 And the sun was darkened,. . .	45 And it was about the sixth hour, and there was darkness over all the earth until the ninth hour.		
			22:1 My God, my God, why hast thou forsaken me? why art thou so far from helping me, and from the words of my roaring?

Matt. 27	JST Matt. 27	Mark 15	JST Mark 15
48 And straightway one of them ran, and took a spunge, and filled it with vinegar, and put it on a reed, and gave him to drink. 49 The rest said, Let be, let us see whether Elias will come to save him.	53 The rest said, Let **him** be, let us see whether Elias will come to save him.	36 And one ran and filled a spunge full of vinegar, and put in on a reed, and gave him to drink, saying, Let alone; let us see whether Elias will come to take him down.	41 And one ran and filled a sponge full of vinegar, and put in on a reed and gave him to drink; **others spake**, saying, Let **him** alone; let us see whether Elias will come to take him down.
50 ¶ Jesus, when he had cried again with a loud voice, yielded up the ghost.	54 Jesus when he had cried again with a loud voice, **saying, Father, it is finished, thy will is done,** yielded up the ghost.	37 And Jesus cried with a loud voice, and gave up the ghost.	

181. Veil of Temple Rent

Matt. 27	JST Matt. 27	Mark 15	JST Mark 15
51 And, behold, the veil of the temple was rent in twain from the top to the bottom; and the earth did quake, and the rocks rent;		38 And the veil of the temple was rent in twain from the top to the bottom.	

182. Testimony of Witnesses

Matt. 27	JST Matt. 27	Mark 15	JST Mark 15
54 Now when the centurion, and they that were with him, watching Jesus, **saw** the earthquake, and those things **that** were done, they feared greatly, saying, Truly this was the Son of God.	58 Now when the centurion, and they that were with him, watching Jesus, **heard** the earth quake, and **saw** those things **which** were done, they feared greatly, saying, Truly this was the Son of God.	39 ¶ And when the centurion, **which** stood over against him, saw that he so cried out, and gave up the ghost, he said, Truly this man **was** the Son of God.	44 And when the centurion **who** stood over against him, saw that he so cried out and gave up the ghost, he said, Truly, this man **is** the Son of God.
55 And many women were there beholding afar off, which followed Jesus from Galilee, ministering unto him: 56 Among **which** was Mary Magdalene, and Mary	59 And many women were there beholding afar off, which followed Jesus from Galilee, ministering unto him **for his burial;** among **whom** was Mary Magdalene, and Mary. . .	40 There were also women looking on afar off: among whom was Mary Magdalene, and Mary the	45 There were also women looking on afar off, among whom was Mary Magdalene, and Mary the

Luke 23	Psalms JST Luke 23	John 19	JST John 19
		28 ¶ After this, Jesus knowing that all things were now accomplished, that the scripture might be fulfilled, saith, I thirst. 29 Now there was **set** a vessel full of vinegar: and they filled a spunge with **vinegar**, and put **it** upon hyssop, and put **it** to his mouth.	29 Now there was a vessel full of vinegar, **mingled with gall**, and they filled a sponge with **it**, and put upon hyssop, and put to his mouth.
46 ¶ And when Jesus had cried with a loud voice, he said, Father, into thy hands I commend my spirit: and having said thus, he gave up the ghost.	Psalm 31:5 Into thine hand I commit my spirit: thou hast redeemed me, O LORD God of truth.	30 When Jesus therefore had received the vinegar, he said, It is finished: and he bowed his head, and gave up the ghost.	
45. . . and the veil of the temple was rent in the midst.			
47 Now when the centurion saw what was done, he glorified God, saying, Certainly this was a righteous man.			
48 And all the people **that** came together to that sight, beholding the things which were done, smote their breasts, and returned. 49 And all his aquaintance, and **the women that** followed him from Galilee, stood afar off, beholding these things.	49 And all the people **who** came together to that sight, beholding the things which were done, smote their breasts, and returned. 50 And all his aquaintance, and women **who** followed him from Galilee, stood afar off, beholding these things.		

385

Matt. 27		Mark 15	JST Mark 15
the mother of James and Joses, and the mother of Zebedee's children.		mother of James the **less** and of Joses, and Salome; 41 (Who also, when he was in Galilee, followed him, and ministered unto him;) and many other women **which** came **up** with him unto Jerusalem.	mother of James the **younger,** and of Joses, and Salome; who also when he was in Galilee, followed him and ministered unto him; and many other women **who** came with him unto Jerusalem.

	Psalms	John 19	

183. Jesus' Side Pierced

	31 The Jews therefore, because it was the preparation, that the bodies should not remain upon the cross on the sabbath day, (for that sabbath day was an high day,) besought Pilate that their legs might be broken, and that they might be taken away.
	32 Then came the soldiers, and brake the legs of the first, and of the other which was crucified with him.
	33 But when they came to Jesus, and saw that he was dead already, they brake not his legs:
	34 But one of the soldiers with a spear pierced his side, and forthwith came there out blood and water.
	35 And he that saw it bare record, and his record is true: and he knoweth that he saith true, that ye might believe.
34:20 He keepeth all his bones: not one of them is broken.	36 For these things were done, that the scripture should be fulfilled, A bone of him shall not be broken.
	37 And again another scripture saith, They shall look on him whom they pierced.

Matt. 27		Mark 15	JST Mark 15

184. Garden Tomb-- Jesus' Burial

Matt. 27		Mark 15	JST Mark 15
57 When the even was come,		42 ¶ And now when the even was come, because it was the preparation, that is, the day before the sabbath,	46 And now, when the even was come; because it was the preparation **day**, that is the day before the Sabbath,
there came a rich man of Arimathæa, named Joseph, who also himself was Jesus' disciple:		43 Joseph of Arimathæa, an honourable counsellor,	47 Joseph of Arimathea, an honorable counsellor,
58 He went to Pilate, and begged the body of Jesus.		**which** also waited for the kingdom of God, came, and went in boldly unto Pilate, and craved the body of Jesus. 44 And Pilate marvelled if he were already dead: and calling **unto him** the centurion, he asked him **whether** he had been any while dead.	**who** also waited for the kingdom of God, came and went in boldly unto Pilate, and craved the body of Jesus. And Pilate marvelled, **and asked him** if he were already dead.
Then Pilate commanded the body to be delivered.		45 And when he knew it of the centurion, he gave the body to Joseph.	48 And calling the centurion, he asked him, **If** he had been any while dead?
59 And when Joseph had taken the body, he wrapped it in a clean linen cloth,		46 And **he** bought fine linen, and took him down, and wrapped him in the linen,	50 And **Joseph** bought fine linen, and took him down, and wrapped him in the linen,. . .
60 And laid it in his own new tomb, which he had hewn out in the rock: and he rolled a great stone to the door of the sepulchre, and departed.		and laid him in a sepulchre which was hewn out of a rock, and rolled a stone unto the door of the sepulchre.	

Luke 23	JST Luke 23	John 19	Psalms
50 ¶ And, behold, **there was** a man named Joseph, a counsellor; **and he was** a good man, and a just:	51 And, behold, a man named Joseph, a counsellor; a good man and a just **one;**	38 ¶ And after this Joseph of Arimathæa, being a disciple of Jesus, but secretly for fear of the Jews,	
51 (The same had not consented to the counsel and deed of them;) **he was** of Arimathæa, a city of the Jews: who also himself waited for the kingdom of God.	52 The same **day** had not consented to the counsel and deed of them; **a man** of Arimathea, a city of the Jews; who also himself waited for the kingdom of God.		
52 **This man** went unto Pilate, and begged the body of Jesus.	53 **He** went unto Pilate, and begged the body of Jesus.	besought Pilate that he might take away the body of Jesus:	
		and Pilate gave him leave. and He came therefore, and took the body of Jesus.	
		39 And there came also Nicodemus, which at the first came to Jesus by night, and brought a mixture of myrrh and aloes, about an hundred pound weight.	45:8 All thy garments smell of myrrh, and aloes, and cassia, out of the ivory palaces, whereby they have made thee glad.
53 And he took it down, and wrapped it in linen,	53 And he took it down and wrapped it in linen,	40 Then took they the body of Jesus, and wound it in linen clothes with the spices, as the manner of the Jews is to bury.	
		41 Now in the place where he was crucified there was a garden; and in the garden a new sepulchre, wherein was never yet man laid.	
and laid it in a sepulchre **that** was hewn in stone, wherein never man before was laid.	and laid it in a sepulcher, **which** was hewed in **a** stone, wherein never man before was laid.	42 There laid they Jesus therefore because of the Jews' preparation day; for the sepulchre was nigh at hand.	

Matt. 27	JST Matt. 27	Mark 15	
61 And there was Mary Magdalene, and the other Mary, sitting over against the sepulchre.		47 And Mary Magdalene and Mary the mother of Joses beheld where he was laid.	

6th Day-- Friday

185. Guards at the Tomb

Matt. 27	JST Matt. 27	Mark 15	
62 ¶ Now the next day, that followed the day of the preparation, the chief priests and Pharisees came together unto Pilate, 63 Saying, Sir, we remember that deceiver said, while he was yet alive, After three days I will rise again. 64 Command therefore that the sepulchre be made sure until the third day, lest his disciples come by night, and steal him away, and say unto the people, He is risen from the dead: so **the** last **error shall** be worse than the first. 65 Pilate said unto them, Ye have a watch: go your way, make it as sure as ye can. 66 So they went, and made the sepulchre sure, sealing the stone, and setting a watch.	65 Command therefore, that the sepulcher be made sure until the third day, lest his disciples come by night, and steal him away, and say unto the people, He is risen from the dead; so **this** last **imposture will** be worse than the first.		

390

Luke 23	JST Luke 23		
54 And that day was the preparation, and the sabbath drew on.			
55 And the women also, which came with him from Galilee, followed after, and beheld the sepulchre, and how his body was laid.	56 And the women also, who came with him from Galilee, followed after, and beheld the sepulcher, and how his body was laid.		
56 And they returned, and prepared spices and ointments; and rested the sabbath day according to the commandment.			

TPJS-- When our Savior was crucified his hasty burial obliged them only to wrap his body in linen with a hundred pounds of myrrh, aloes, and similar spices, (part of the ingredients of embalming) given by Nicodemus for that purpose; but Mary and other holy women had prepared ointment and spices for embalming it. (p. 232)

Most harmonies and commentaries list Wednesday as a day of "No record": this is probably because of the traditional "Good Friday" as the day of Christ's crucifixion. However, in this harmony, the traditional events of Thursday of the last week of the Savior's life are listed under Wednesday, and the traditional dates of Friday are listed on Thursday. Some Bible scholars consider this listing because of the double Sabbath in certain years of the Jewish calendar. They consider "for that sabbath day was an high day," in John 19:31 as a reference to this day. Elder James E. Talmage suggests this as a possibility in the quote below.

7th Day-- Saturday -- No Record

...Jesus and the Twelve may have partaken of the passover meal on the first of the two evenings, and the Jews who next day feared defilement may have deferred their observance until the second. Thirdly; the Lord's last paschal supper may have been eaten earlier than the time of general observance, He knowing that night to be His last in mortality. Supporters of this view explain the message to the man who provided the chamber for the last supper, "My time is at hand" (Matt. 26:18) as indicating a special urgency for the passover observance by Christ and the apostles, before the regularly appointed day. Some authorities assert that an error of one day had crept into the Jewish reckoning of time, and that Jesus ate the passover on the true date, while the Jews were a day behind. If "the preparation of the passover" (John 19:14) on Friday, the day of Christ's crucifixion, means the slaughtering of the paschal lambs, our Lord, the real sacrifice of which all earlier altar victims had been but prototypes, died on the cross while the passover lambs were being slain at the temple. (Talmage, Jesus the Christ, pp. 618-619)

Another reason for not following the traditional week days in this harmony is the prophecy of Christ concerning the Prophet Jonah being "three days and three nights in the whale's belly" as a sign of Christ being "three days and three nights in the heart of the earth" (Matt. 12:39–40; see also JST Mark 8:12, the Prophet Joseph's addition to the text). The Book of Mormon also strongly implies three full days of Christ being in the spirit world (see 1 Nephi 19:10; 2 Nephi 25:13; 3 Nephi 8:19–23; 10:9). The crucifixion on Friday and the resurrection on Sunday does not fulfill the prophecy of the Savior or of the Book of Mormon. While the time period is not as significant as the event, an explanation for the departure from the usual time frame is given.

Matt. 28	JST Matt. 28	Mark 16	JST Mark 16

8th Day-- Sunday

186. Sunday-- Woman at the Tomb

Matt. 28	JST Matt. 28	Mark 16	JST Mark 16
		And when the sabbath was **past**, Mary Magdalene, and Mary the mother of James, and Salome, **had** bought sweet spices, that they might come and anoint him.	And when the Sabbath was **passed**, Mary Magdalene, and Mary the mother of James and Salome, bought sweet spices, that they might come and anoint him.
2 And, behold, there **was** a great earthquake: for **the** angel of the Lord descended from heaven, and came and rolled back the stone from the door, and sat upon it.	2 And behold, there **had been** a great earthquake; for **two angels** of the Lord descended from heaven, and came and rolled back the stone from the door, and sat upon it.		
3 **His** countenance was like lightning, and **his** raiment white as snow:	3 **And their** countenance was like lightning, and **their** raiment white as snow;		
4 And for fear of **him** the keepers did shake, and became as dead **men**.	and for fear of **them** the keepers did shake, and became as **though they were** dead.		
1 In the end of the sabbath, as it began to dawn toward the first day of the week, came Mary Magdalene and the other Mary to see the sepulchre.	1 In the end of the Sabbath **day**, as it began to dawn towards the first day of the week, **early in the morning,** came Mary Magdalene, and the other Mary to see the sepulcher.	2 And very early in the morning the first day of the week, they came unto the sepulchre at the rising of the sun.	
		3 And they said among themselves, Who shall roll us away the stone from the door of the sepulchre?	
		4 **And** when they looked they saw that the stone was rolled away: for it was very great.	3 **But** when they looked, they saw that the stone was rolled away, (for it was very great,)

392

Luke 24	JST Luke 24	John 20	JST John 20
Now upon the first day of the week, very early in the morning, **they** came unto the sepulchre, bringing the spices which they had prepared, and certain others with them.	Now upon the first day of the week, very early in the morning, **the women** came unto the sepulcher, bringing the spices which they had prepared, and certain others with them.	The first day of the week cometh Mary Magdalene early, when it was yet dark, unto the sepulchre,	The first day of the week cometh Mary Magdalene early, when it was yet dark, unto the sepulcher,
2 And they found the stone rolled away from the sepulchre.	2 And they found the stone rolled away from the sepulcher, **and two angels standing by it in shining garments.**	and seeth the stone taken away from the sepulchre.	and seeth the stone taken away from the sepulcher, **and two angels sitting thereon.**
		2 Then she runneth, and cometh to Simon Peter, and to the other disciple, whom Jesus loved, and saith unto them, They have taken away the Lord out of the sepulchre, and we know not where they have laid him.	
3 And they entered in, and **found** not the body of the Lord Jesus.	3 And they entered into **the sepulcher,** and not **finding** the body of the Lord Jesus,		

Matt. 28	JST Matt. 28	Mark 16	JST Mark 16
		5 And **entering into the sepulchre, they saw a young man** sitting **on the right side,** clothed in **a** long white garment; and they were affrighted.	and **two angels** sitting **thereon,** clothed in long white garments; and they were affrighted.
5 And the angel answered and said unto the women, Fear not ye: for I know that ye seek Jesus, which was crucified. 6 He is not here: for he is risen, as he said. Come, see the place where the Lord lay.	4 And the angels answered and said unto the women, Fear not ye; for we know that ye seek Jesus who was crucified.	6 **And he saith unto** them, Be not affrighted: Ye seek Jesus of Nazareth, **which** was crucified: he is risen; he is not here: behold the place where they laid him.	4 **But the angels** said unto them, Be not affrighted; ye seek Jesus of Nazareth, **who** was crucified;
7 And go quickly, and tell his disciples that he is risen from the dead; and, behold, he goeth before you into Galilee; there shall ye see him: lo, I have told you.		7 **But** go your way, tell his disciples and Peter that he goeth before you into Galilee: there shall ye see him, as he said unto you.	5 **And** go your way, tell his disciples and Peter, that he goeth before you into Galilee; there shall ye see him as he said unto you. 6 **And they, entering into the sepulcher, saw the place where they laid Jesus.**
8 And they departed quickly from the sepulchre with fear and great joy; and did run to bring his disciples word.		8 And they went out quickly, and fled from the sepulchre; for they trembled and were amazed: neither said they any thing to any man; for they were afraid.	

Luke 24	JST Luke 24		
4 And it came to pass, as they were much perplexed thereabout, behold, two men stood by them in shining garments:	they were much perplexed thereabout;		
5 And as they were afraid, and bowed down their faces to the earth, they said unto them, Why seek ye the living among the dead?	4 And were **affrighted**, and bowed down their faces to the earth. **But behold the angels** said unto them, Why seek ye the living among the dead?		
6 He is not here, but is risen: remember how he spake unto you when he was yet in Galilee,			
7 Saying, The Son of man must be delivered into the hands of sinful men, and be crucified, and the third day rise again.			
8 And they remembered his words,			
9 And returned from the sepulchre, and told all these things unto the eleven, and to all the rest.			
10 It was Mary Magdalene, and Joanna, and Mary the mother of James, and other women **that** were with them, **which** told these things unto the apostles.	9 It was Mary Magdalene, and Joanna, and Mary the mother of James, and other women **who** were with them, **who** told these things unto the apostles.		
11 And their words seemed to them as idle tales, and they believed them not.			

Luke 24	JST Luke 24	John 20	

187. Peter and John at the Tomb

Luke 24	JST Luke 24	John 20
		3 Peter therefore went forth, and that other disciple, and came to the sepulchre.
		4 So they ran both together: and the other disciple did outrun Peter, and came first to the sepulchre.
		5 And he stooping down, and looking in, saw the linen clothes lying; yet went he not in.
12 Then arose Peter, and ran unto the sepulchre; and **stooping down**, he beheld the linen clothes laid by themselves,	11 Then arose Peter, and ran unto the sepulcher and **went in, and** he beheld the linen clothes laid by themselves;	6 Then cometh Simon Peter following him, and went into the sepulchre, and seeth the linen clothes lie,
		7 And the napkin, that was about his head, not lying with linen clothes, but wrapped together in a place by itself.
		8 Then went in also that other disciple, which came first to the sepulchre, and he saw, and believed.
		9 For as yet they knew not the scripture, that he must rise again from the dead.
and departed, wondering in himself at that which was come to pass.	and he departed, wondering in himself at that which was come to pass.	10 Then the disciples went away again unto their own home.

188. Jesus Appears to Mary

Luke 24	JST Luke 24	John 20
		11 ¶ But Mary stood without at the sepulchre weeping: and as she wept, she stooped down, and looked into the sepulchre,
		12 And seeth two angels in white sitting, the one at the head, and the other at the feet, where the body of Jesus had lain.
		13 And they say unto her, Woman, why weepest thou? She saith unto them, Because they have taken away my Lord, and I know

396

Mark 16	JST Mark 16 Luke 24	John 20	JST John 20 1 Corinthians
9 ¶ Now when Jesus was risen early the first day of the week, he appeared first to Mary Magdalene, out of whom he had cast seven devils.	8 Now when Jesus was risen, early on the first day of the week, he appeared first to Mary Magdalene, out of whom he had cast seven devils;	not where they have laid him. 14 And when she had thus said, she turned herself back, and saw Jesus standing, and knew not that it was Jesus. 15 Jesus saith unto her, Woman, why weepest thou? whom seekest thou? She, supposing him to be the gardener, saith unto him, Sir, if thou have borne him hence, tell me where thou hast laid him, and I will take him away. 16 Jesus saith unto her, Mary. She turned herself, and saith unto him, Rabboni; which is to say, Master.	
		17 Jesus saith unto her, **Touch** me not; for I am not yet ascended unto my Father: but go to my brethren, and say unto them, I ascend unto my Father, and your Father; and to my God, and your God.	17 Jesus saith unto her, **Hold** me not; for I am not yet ascended to my Father; but go to my brethren, and say unto them, I ascend unto my Father, and your Father; and to my God, and your God.
10 And she went and told them **that** had been with him, as they mourned and wept. 11 And they, when they had heard that he was alive, and had been seen of her, believed not.	9 And she went and told them **who** had been with him, as they mourned and wept.	18 Mary Magdalene came and told the disciples that she had seen the Lord, and that he had spoken these things unto her.	
	Luke 24:34 Saying, The Lord is risen indeed, and hath appeared to Simon.		1 Cor. 15:4 And that he was buried, and that he rose again the third day according to the scriptures: 5 And that he was seen of Cephas, then of the twelve: 6 After that, he was seen of above five hundred brethren at once; of whom the greater part remain unto this present, but some are fallen asleep. 7 After that, he was seen of James; then of all the apostles.

Matt. 28 - 27	JST Matt. 27	B of M	D & C

189. Appearance to Other Women

28:9 ¶ And as they went to tell his disciples, behold, Jesus met them, saying, All hail. And they came and held him by the feet, and worshipped him.

10 Then said Jesus unto them, Be not afraid: go tell my brethren that they go into Galilee, and there shall they see me.

190. Others Resurrected

Matt. 28 - 27	JST Matt. 27	B of M	D & C
27:52 And the graves were opened; and **many** bodies of the saints which slept arose, 53 And came out of the graves after his resurrection, **and** went into the holy city, and appeared unto many.	56 And the graves were opened; and **the** bodies of the saints which slept, arose, **who were many,** 57 And came out of the graves after his resurrection, went into the holy city, and appeared unto many.	3 Ne. 23:9 Verily I say unto you, I commanded my servant Samuel, the Lamanite, that he should testify unto this people, that at the day that the Father should glorify his name in me that there were many saints who should arise from the dead, and should appear unto many, and should minister unto them. And he said unto them: Was it not so? 10 And his disciples answered him and said: Yea, Lord, Samuel did prophesy according to thy words, and they were all fulfilled. 11 And Jesus said unto them: How be it that ye have not written this thing, that many saints did arise and appear unto many and did minister unto them? 12 And it came to pass that Nephi remembered that this thing had not been written. 13 And it came to pass that Jesus commanded that it should be written; therefore it was written according as he commanded.	133:54 Yea, and Enoch also, and they who were with him; the prophets who were before him; and Noah also, and they who were before him; and Moses also, and they who were before him; 55 And from Moses to Elijah, and from Elijah to John, who were with Christ in his resurrection, and the holy apostles, with Abraham, Isaac, and Jacob, shall be in the presence of the Lamb.

Matt. 28	JST Matt. 28		

191. Sanhedrin-- Chief Priests Bribe the Guards

11 ¶ Now when they were going, behold, some of the watch came into the city, and shewed unto the chief priests all the things that were done. 12 And when they were assembled with the elders, and had taken counsel, they gave large money unto the soldiers, 13 Saying, Say ye, His disciples came by night, and stole him **away** while we slept. 14 And if this come to the governor's ears, we will persuade him, and secure you. 15 So they took the money, and did as they were taught: and this saying is commonly reported among the Jews until this day.	12 Saying, Say ye, His disciples came by night, and stole him while we slept.		

Mark 16	Luke 24	JST Luke 2	

192. Road to Emmaus—Appears to Disciples

Mark 16	Luke 24	JST Luke 2
12 ¶ After that he appeared in another form unto two of them, as they walked, and went into the country.	13 ¶ And, behold, two of them went that same day to a village called Emmaus, which was from Jerusalem **about** three-score furlongs.	12 And behold, two of them went that same day to a village called Emmaus, which was from Jerusalem three-score furlongs.
	14 And they talked together of all these things which had happened.	
	15 And it came to pass, that, while they communed together and reasoned, Jesus himself drew near, and went with them.	
	16 But their eyes were holden that they **should** not know him.	15 But their eyes were holden, **or covered,** that they **could** not know him.
	17 And he said unto them, What manner of communications are these **that** ye have one **to** another, as ye walk, and are sad?	16 And he said unto them, What manner of communications are these **which** ye have one **with** another, as ye walk and are sad?
	18 And **the** one of them, whose name was Cleopas, answering said unto him, Art thou **only a** stranger in Jerusalem, and has not known the things which are come to pass there in these days?	17 And one of them, whose name was Cleopas, answering, said unto him, Art thou a stranger in Jerusalem, and has not known the things which are come to pass there in these days?
	19 And he said unto them, What things? And they said unto him, Concerning Jesus of Nazareth, **which** was a prophet might in deed and word before God and all the people:	18 And he said unto them, What things? And they said unto him, Concerning Jesus of Nazareth, **who** was a prophet mighty in deed and word before God and all the people;
	20 And now the chief priests and our rulers delivered him to be condemned to death, and have crucified him.	
	21 But we trusted that it had been he **which** should have redeemed Israel: and beside all this, to day is the third day since these things were done.	20 But we trusted that it had been he **who** should have redeemed Israel. And besides all this, today is the third day since these things were done;
	22 Yea, and certain women also of our company made us astonished, **which** were early at the	21 Yea, and certain women also of our company made us astonished, **who** were early at the

Luke 24	JST Luke 24	Luke 24 B of M	JST Luke 24 Mark 16
sepulchre:	sepulcher;	and while he opened us the scriptures?	
23 And when they found not his body, they came, saying, that they had also seen a vision of angels, **which** said that he was alive.	22 And when they found not his body, they came, saying, that they had also seen a vision of angels, **who** said that he was alive.	33 And they rose up to the same hour, and returned to Jerusalem, and found the eleven gathered together, and **them that** were with them,	32 And they rose up the same hour and returned to Jerusalem, and found the eleven gathered together, and **those who** were with them,
24 and certain of them **which** were with us went to the sepulcher, and	23 And certain of them **who** were with us, went to the sepulcher, and found it even so as the women had said; but him they saw not.	35 And they told what things **were done** in the way, and how he was	34 And they told what things **they saw and heard** in the way, and how he was known to them, in breaking of bread.
found it even so as the women had said: but him they saw not.		known **of** them in breaking of bread.	
25 Then he said unto them, O fools, and slow of heart to believe all that the prophets have spoken:			Mark 16:13 And they went and told it unto the residue: neither believed they them.
26 Ought not Christ to have suffered these things, and to enter into his glory?		Jacob 7:11 And I said unto him: then ye do not understand them; for they truly testify of Christ. Behold, I say unto you that none of the prophets have written, nor prophesied, save they have spoken concerning this Christ (see also Jacob 4:4; 1 Nephi 10:4-5).	
27 And beginning at Moses and all the prophets, he expounded unto them in all the scriptures the things concerning himself.			
28 And they drew nigh unto the village, whither they went: and he made as though he would have gone further.			
29 But they constrained him, saying, Abide with us: for it is toward evening, and the day is far spent. And he went in to tarry with them.			
30 And it came to pass, as he sat at meat with them, he took bread, and blessed it, and brake, and gave to them.	29 And it came to pass, as he sat at meat with them, he took bread, and blessed, and brake, and gave to them.		
31 And their eyes were opened, and they know him: and he **vanished** out of their sight.	30 And their eyes were opened, and they knew him; and he **was taken up** out of their sight.		
32 And they said one to another, Did not our heart burn within us, while he talked with us by the way, (continued in column 3)	(continued in column 4)		

401

Luke 24	Mark 16 / JST Luke 24	John 20	D & C

Later Appearances

193. Jerusalem-- Appearance to Peter and the Apostles

36 ¶ And as they thus spake, Jesus himself stood in the midst of them, and saith unto them, Peace be unto you.	Mark 16:14 ¶ Afterward he appeared unto the eleven as they sat at meat,	19 ¶ Then the same day at evening, being the first day of the week, when the doors were shut where the disciples were assembled for fear of the Jews, came Jesus and stood in the midst, and saith unto them, Peace be unto you.
37 But they were terrified and affrighted, and supposed that they had seen a spirit.		
38 And he said unto them, Why are ye troubled? and why do thoughts arise in your hearts?	and upbraided them with their unbelief and hardness of heart, because they believed not them **which** had seen him after he was risen. (JST changes "which" to "who" in vs. 14)	6:36 Look unto me in every thought; doubt not, fear not.
39 Behold my hands and my feet, that it is I myself: handle me, and see; for a spirit hath not flesh and bones, as **ye** see me have. (JST changes "ye" to "**you**" in vss. 38 & 39)		37 Behold the wounds which pierced my side, and also the prints of the nails in my hands and feet; be faithful, keep my commandments, and ye shall inherit the kingdom of heaven. Amen.

TPJS-- Jesus showed Himself to His disciples, and they thought it was His spirit, and they were afraid to approach His spirit. Angels have advanced higher in knowledge and power than spirits. (p. 325)

Luke 24	JST Luke 24	John 20	D & C
40 **And** when he had thus spoken, he shewed them his hands and his feet.	JST Luke 24:39 When he had thus spoken, he showed them his hands and his feet.	20 And when he had so said, he shewed unto them his hands and his side. Then were the disciples glad, when they saw the Lord.	129:1 There are two kinds of beings in heaven, namely: Angels, who are resurrected personages, having bodies of flesh and bones--
41 And while they yet believed not for joy, **and wondered**, he said unto them, Have ye here any meat?	40 And while they yet **wondered and** believed not for joy, he said unto them, Have ye here any meat?		2 For instance, Jesus said: *Handle me and see, for a spirit hath not flesh and bones, as ye see me have.*
42 And they gave him a piece of a broiled fish, and **of an** honeycomb.			3 Secondly: the spirits of just men made perfect, they who are not resurrected, but inherit the same glory.
43 And he took it, and did eat before them.			
44 And he said unto them, These are the words which I spake unto you, while I was yet with you, that all things must be fulfilled,			

402

Luke 24		John 20	D & C
which were written in the law of Moses, and in the prophets, and in the psalms, concerning me. 45 Then opened he their understanding, that they might understand the scriptures, 46 And said unto them, Thus it is written, and thus it behoved Christ to suffer, and to rise from the dead the third day: 47 And that repentance and remission of sins should be preached in his name among all nations, beginning at Jerusalem. 48 And ye are witnesses of these things.			

TPJS-- By this we learn that it behooved Christ to suffer, and to be crucified, and rise again on the third day for the express purpose that repentance and remission of sins should be preached to all nations. (p. 81)

		John 20	D & C
		21 Then said Jesus to them again, Peace be unto you: as my Father hath sent me, even so send I you. 22 And when he had said this, he breathed on them, and saith unto them, Receive ye the Holy Ghost: 23 Whose soever sins ye remit, they are remitted unto them; and whose soever sins ye retain, they are retained.	132:46 . . . and whosesoever sins you remit on earth shall be remitted eternally in the heavens; and whosesoever sins you retain on earth shall be retained in heaven.

194. Appearance to Thomas and the Apostles

20:24 ¶ But Thomas, one of the twelve, called Didymus, was not with them when Jesus came.

25 The other disciples therefore said unto him, We have seen the Lord. But he said unto them, Except I shall see in his hands the print of the nails, and put my finger into the print of the nails, and thrust my hand into his side, I will not believe.

26 ¶ And after eight days again his disciples were within, and Thomas with them: then came Je- (continued in column 3)

sus, the doors being shut, and stood in the midst, and said, Peace be unto you.

27 Then saith he to Thomas, Reach hither thy finger, and behold my hands; and reach hither thy hand, and thrust it into my side: and be not faithless, but believing.

28 And Thomas answered and said unto him, My Lord and my God.

29 Jesus saith unto him, Thomas, because thou hast seen me, thou hast believed: blessed are they that have not seen, and yet have believed.

195. Sea of Tiberias-- Appears to Seven Apostles

21:1 After these things Jesus shewed himself again to the disciples at the sea of Tiberias; and on this wise shewed he himself.

2 There were together Simon Peter, and Thomas called Didymus, and Nathanael of Cana in Galilee, and the sons of Zebedee, and two other of his disciples.

3 Simon Peter saith unto them, I go a fishing. They say unto him, We also go with thee. They went forth, and entered into a ship immediately; and that night they caught nothing.

4 But when the morning was now come, Jesus stood on the shore: but the disciples knew not that it was Jesus.

5 Then Jesus saith unto them, Children, have ye any meat? They answered him, No. (continued in column 3)

6 And he said unto them, Cast the net on the right side of the ship, and ye shall find. They cast therefore, and now they were not able to draw it for the multitude of fishes.

7 Therefore that disciple whom Jesus loved saith unto Peter, It is the Lord. Now when Simon Peter heard that it was the Lord, he girt his fisher's coat unto him, (for he was naked,) and did cast himself into the sea.

8 And the other disciples came in a little ship; (for they were not far from land, but as it were two hundred cubits,) dragging the net with fishes.

9 As soon as they were come to land, they saw a fire of coals there, and fish laid thereon, and bread.

10 Jesus saith unto them, Bring of the fish which ye have now caught.

		John 21	D & C
		11 Simon Peter went up, and drew the net to land full of great fishes, an hundred and fifty and three: and for all there were so many, yet was not the net broken. 12 Jesus saith unto them, Come and dine. And none of the disciples durst ask him, Who art thou? knowing that it was the Lord. 13 Jesus then cometh, and taketh bread, and giveth them, and fish likewise. 14 This is now the third time that Jesus shewed himself to his disciples, after that he was risen from the dead.	

196. Feed My Sheep

		John 21	D & C
		15 ¶ So when they had dined, Jesus saith to Simon Peter, Simon, son of Jonas, lovest thou me more than these? He saith unto him, Yea, Lord; thou knowest that I love thee. He saith unto him, Feed my lambs. 16 He saith to him again the second time, Simon, son of Jonas, lovest thou me? He saith unto him, Yea, Lord; thou knowest that I love thee. He saith unto him, Feed my sheep. 17 He saith unto him the third time, Simon, son of Jonas, lovest thou me? Peter was grieved because he said unto him the third time, Lovest thou me? And he said unto him, Lord, thou knowest all things; thou knowest that I love thee. Jesus saith unto him, Feed my sheep.	112:14 Now, I say unto you, and what I say unto you, I say unto all the Twelve: Arise and gird up your loins, take up your cross, follow me, and feed my sheep.

John 21	B of M Revelation	D & C	Joseph Smith D & C

197. Prophecies of Peter and John

18 Verily, verily, I say unto thee, When thou wast young, thou girdest thyself, and walkedst whither thou wouldest: but when thou shalt be old, thou shalt stretch forth thy hands, and another shall gird thee, and carry thee whither thou wouldest not.

19 This spake he, signifying by what death he should glorify God. And when he had spoken this, he saith unto him, Follow me.

20 Then Peter, turning about, seeth the disciple whom Jesus loved following; which also leaned on his breast at supper, and said, Lord, which is he that betrayeth thee?

21 Peter seeing him saith to Jesus, Lord, and what shall this man do?

22 Jesus saith unto him, If I will that he tarry till I come, what is that to thee? follow thou me.

23 Then went this saying abroad among the brethren, that that disciple should not die: yet Jesus said not unto him, He shall not die; but, If I will that he tarry till I come, what is that to thee?

B of M Revelation

3 Ne. 28:6 And he said unto them: Behold, I know your thoughts, and ye have desired the thing which John, my beloved, who was with me in my ministry, before that I was lifted up by the Jews, desired of me.

7 Therefore, more blessed are ye, for ye shall never taste of death; but ye shall live to behold all the doings of the Father unto the children of men, even until all things shall be fulfilled according to the will of the Father, when I shall come in my glory with the powers of heaven.

Rev. 10:11 And he said unto me, Thou must prophesy again before many peoples, and nations, and tongues, and kings

---

D & C

7:1 And the Lord said unto me: John, my beloved, what desirest thou? For if you shall ask what you will, it shall be granted unto you.

2 And I said unto him: Lord, give unto me power over death, that I may live and bring souls unto thee.

3 And the Lord said unto me: Verily, verily, I say unto thee, because thou desirest this thou shalt tarry until I come in my glory, and shalt prophesy before nations, kindreds, tongues and people.

4 And for this cause the Lord said unto Peter: If I will that he tarry till I come, what is that to thee? For he desired of me that he might bring souls unto me, but thou desiredst that thou mightest speedily come unto me in my kingdom.

5 I say unto thee, Peter, this was a good desire; but my beloved has desired that he might do more, or a greater work yet among men than what he has before done.

(continued in column 4)

Joseph Smith D & C

HC 1:176 fn   John the Revelator [is] among the ten tribes of Israel who had been led away by Shalmaneser, King of Assyria, to prepare them for their return from their long dispersion, to again posess the land of their fathers.

6 Yea, he has undertaken a greater work; therefore I will make him as flaming fire and a ministering angel; he shall minister for those who shall be heirs of salvation who dwell on the earth.

7 And I will make thee to minster for him and for thy brother James; and unto you three I will give this power and the keys of this ministry until I come.

8 Verily I say unto you, ye shall both have according to your desires, for ye both joy in that which ye have desired.

Matt. 28	Mark 16	B of M	D & C

198. A Mountain In Galilee-- Another Appearance to the Apostles

16 ¶ Then the eleven disciples went away into Galilee, into a mountain where Jesus had appointed them.

17 And when they saw him, they worshipped him: but some doubted.

18 And Jesus came and spake unto them, saying, All power is given unto me in heaven and in earth.

19 ¶ Go ye therefore, and teach all nations, baptizing them in the name of the Father, and of the Son, and of the Holy Ghost:

20 Teaching them to observe all things whatsoever I have commanded you:

and, lo, I am with you alway, even unto the end of the world. Amen.

(JST changes "alway" to "always" and deletes "even.")

---

15 And he said unto them, Go ye into all the world, and preach the gospel to every creature.

16 He that believeth and is baptized shall be saved; but he that believeth not shall be damned.

17 And these signs shall follow them that believe; In my name shall they cast out devils; they shall speak with new tongues;

18 They shall take up serpents; and if they drink any deadly thing, it shall not hurt them: they shall lay hands on the sick, and they shall recover.

Mormon 9:22 For behold, thus said Jesus Christ, the Son of God, unto his disciples who should tarry, yea, and also to all his disciples, in the hearing of the multitude: Go ye into all the world, and preach the gospel to every creature;

23 And he that believeth and is baptized shall be saved, but he that believeth not shall be damned;

24 And these signs shall follow them that believe-- in my name shall they cast out devils; they shall speak with new tongues; they shall take up serpents; and if they drink any deadly thing it shall not hurt them; they shall lay hands on the sick and they shall recover; (See also 2 Ne. 9:23-24; 3 Ne. 11:33-34; Ether 4:18-19.)

68:8 Go ye into all the world, preach the gospel to every creature, acting in the authority which I have given you, baptizing in the name of the Father, and of the Son, and of the Holy Ghost.

9 And he that believeth and is baptized shall be saved, and he that believeth not shall be damned.

10 And he that believeth shall be blest with signs following, even as it is written. (See also D&C 35:8-9; 58:64; 84:68-74; 112:28-29.)

105:41 Therefore, be faithful; and behold, and lo, I am with you even unto the end. Even so. Amen.

TPJS-- Upon looking over the sacred pages of the Bible, searching into the prophets and sayings of the apostles, we find no subject so nearly connected with salvation, as that of baptism. In the first place, however, let us understand that the word baptize is derived from the Greek verb "baptiso," and means to immerse or overwhelm, and that sprinkle is from the Greek verb "rantiso," and means to scatter on by particles; then we can treat the subject as one inseparably connected with our eternal welfare; and always bear in mind that it is one of the only methods by which we can obtain a remission of sins in this world, and be prepared to enter into the joys of our Lord in the world to come.

As it is well known that various opinions govern a large portion of the sectarian world as to this important ordinance of the gospel, it may not be amiss to introduce the commissions and commands of Jesus Himself on the subject. (p. 262)

... and lo I am with you always to the end of the world -- that is -- by the other comforter which the world cannot receive -- for ye are the witnesses -- having the testimony of Jesus which is the spirit of prophecy. (p. 265)

Mark 16	Luke 24	JST Luke 24 B of M	John 20-21

199. Bethany—The Ascension

	49 ¶ And, behold, I send the promise of my Father upon you: but tarry ye in the city of Jerusalem, until ye be endued with power from on high.		
	50 ¶ And he led them out as far as to Bethany, and he lifted up his hands, and blessed them.		
19 ¶ So then after the Lord had spoken unto them, he was received up into heaven, and sat on the right hand of God.	51 And it came to pass, while he blessed them, he was **parted** from them, and carried up into heaven.	50 And it came to pass, while he blessed them, he was **taken** from them, and carried up into heaven.	
20 And they went forth, and preached every where, the Lord working with them, and confirming the word with signs following. Amen.	52 And they worshiped him, and returned to Jerusalem with great joy: 53 And were continually in the temple, praising and blessing God. Amen.		

200. John's Testimony

		Mormon 7:5 Know ye that ye must come to the knowledge of your fathers, and repent of all your sins and iniquities, and believe in Jesus Christ, that he is the Son of God, and that he was slain by the Jews, and by the power of the Father he hath risen again, whereby he hath gained the victory over the grave; and also in him is the sting of death swallowed up.	20:30 ¶ And many other signs truly did Jesus in the presence of his disciples, which are not written in this book: 31 But these are written, that ye might believe that Jesus is the Christ, the Son of God; and that believing ye might have life through his name.
			21:24 This is. the disciple which testifieth of these things, and wrote these things: and we know that his testimony is true.
			25 And there are also many other things which Jesus did, the which, if they should be written every one, I suppose that even the world itself could not contain the books that should be written. Amen.

Scriptural Index

ABOUT THE AUTHOR

Monte S. Nyman received his bachelor's and master's degrees in physical education from Utah State University and earned his doctorate in education administration from Brigham Young University.

He has served as the director of the Edmonton (Canada) Institute of Religion, director of Book of Mormon Studies in BYU's Religious Studies Center, acting chairman of the Ancient Scripture Department, and associate dean of Religious Education at Brigham Young University. He has taught in twelve BYU study abroad programs in Jerusalem and has conducted many BYU tours to Israel and Central America for BYU travel study.

Brother Nyman retired from BYU in 1996. However, his academic activities have continued since that time. He served as the president of Southern Virginia University from May 2003 to June 2004 after serving as that university's academic vice president. From 1999 to 2000, he served as the university's head baseball coach.

His church service includes a mission to the North Central States and callings as a high councilor, stake mission president, bishop, and member of several stake presidencies. He was chairman of the Church Instructional Development Committee for writing Gospel Doctrine manuals and served for eleven years on the Church Translation and Correlation Committees.

He is the author of four commentaries on Old Testament prophets as well as two books on the Book of Mormon: *An Ensign to All People* and *The Most Correct Book, The Book of Mormon*. He recently published a six-volume commentary on The Book of Mormon: *I, Nephi, Wrote This Record, Vol. 1*; *These Records Are True, Vol. 2*; *The Record of Alma, Vol. 3*; *The Record of Helaman, Vol. 4*; *Third Nephi: The First Gospel, Vol. 5*; and *I, Mormon, Make a Record, Vol. 6*. He has also been published in the *Ensign* and *The Improvement Era*.

Brother Nyman and his wife, Mary Ann Sullivan, are the parents of eight children. They have twenty-five grandchildren.